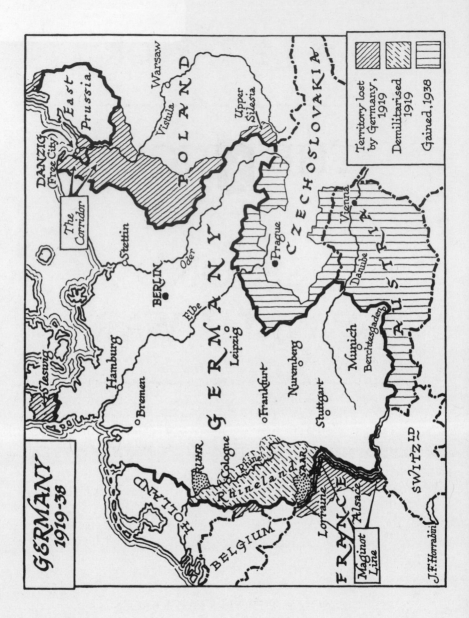

GERMANY 1919-38

Territory lost
by Germany,
1919

Demilitarised
1919

Gained, 1938

DANZIG
(Free City)

East
Prussia

The
Corridor

Warsaw

Vistula

POLAND

Upper
Silesia

Stassug

Stettin

Oder

BERLIN

Elbe

Hamburg

Bremen

Prague

CZECHOSLOVAKIA

Vienna

AUSTRIA

Danube

Leipzig

Frankfurt

Nuremberg

Munich
Berchtesgaden

Stuttgart

HOLLAND

Ruhr

Cologne

Rhine

Rhineland

Saar

BELGIUM

Lorraine

Alsace

FRANCE

Maginot
Line

SWITZ^LD

J.F.Horrabin

A. J. P. TAYLOR

THE ORIGINS OF THE SECOND WORLD WAR

WITH A PREFACE FOR THE AMERICAN READER
AND A NEW INTRODUCTION, *SECOND THOUGHTS*

SIMON & SCHUSTER PAPERBACKS
New York   London   Toronto   Sydney

SIMON & SCHUSTER PAPERBACKS
Rockefeller Center
1230 Avenue of the Americas
New York, NY 10020

This Simon & Schuster paperback edition 2005

For information about special discounts for bulk purchases,
please contact Simon & Schuster Special Sales:
1-800-456-6798 or business@simonandschuster.com.

Manufactured in the United States of America

30 29 28 27 26

Library of Congress Cataloging-in-Publication Data
Taylor, A. J. P. (Alan Jon Percivale), 1906–
    The origins of the Second World War.
    Bibliography : p
    Includes index.
    1. World War, 1939–1945—Causes.   I. Title.
D741.T34   1983940.53'11   83-6360

ISBN-13: 978-0-684-82947-0
ISBN-10:   0-684-82947-9

PREFACE FOR THE AMERICAN READER

M ost wars begin raggedly. In the minds of Englishmen 4 August 1914 is unshakably fixed as the date when the first World war began; yet by then France and Germany had been at war for twenty-four hours, Russia and Germany for three days, Serbia and Austria-Hungary for almost a week. The second World war was vaguer still in its opening; the Russians date it from 22 June 1941, the Chinese from November 1937, the Abyssinians, I suppose, from October 1935, and the Americans from 7 December 1941. The American date is the most sensible. The war became truly world-wide—much more so than the first World war—only after Pearl Harbor. However, that is not how it seems to English people. We date the second World war from 3 September 1939, the day when Great Britain and France declared war on Germany (not, incidentally, from 1 September, the day when Germany attacked Poland); and among non-Americans, only professional historians can remember the date of Pearl Harbor. The point is of no great importance as long as the reader knows exactly what he is in for and does not feel that he has been sold a book under false pretences. This book seeks to explain the war which began on 3 September 1939. It does not attempt to answer the questions: why did Hitler invade Soviet Russia? why did Japan attack Pearl Harbor? or why did Hitler and Mussolini then declare war on the United States? It is directed solely to the question: why did Great Britain and France declare war on Germany?

This may also meet another possible complaint from American readers: that there is very little about American policy. This has a simple explanation: American policy had very little to do with the British and French declaration of war on Germany. Perhaps it would be truer to say that what it had to do with their declarations of war was of a negative kind, like the significant episode of the dog in the night, to which Sherlock Holmes once drew attention. When Watson objected: "But the dog did nothing in the night," Holmes answered: "That was the significant episode." Even so, the United States could not avoid playing a great, maybe a decisive, part in European affairs. The German problem, as it existed between the wars, was largely the creation of American policy. The first World war would obviously have

rent end if it had not been for American intervention:
, to put it bluntly, would not have won. Equally, the
ver Germany would have had a different character if
ed States had been an Allied, not an Associated, Power.
Everyone knows how the detachment of the United States from
the European Allies was asserted when the Senate refused to
ratify the treaty of Versailles and, with it, American membership in the League of Nations; but this detachment existed even
in the days of closest co-operation, and ratification of the treaty
would not have made all that much difference. Woodrow Wilson
regarded the Allies with almost as much distrust as he regarded
Germany, or perhaps with more; and American membership in
the League, as he envisaged it, would have been far from an
asset to the Allied side.

Nor did the action of the Senate imply a retreat into isolation.
American policy was never more active and never more effective
in regard to Europe than in the nineteen-twenties. Reparations
were settled; stable finances were restored; Europe was pacified:
all mainly due to the United States. This policy of recovery
followed the doctrine of Keynes (and of other economists) that
Europe could be made prosperous only by making Germany
prosperous. The recovery of Germany was America's doing. It
was welcomed by most people in Great Britain and even by a
certain number in France. It would have happened, to a lesser
extent, in any case. Nevertheless, American policy was a powerful obstacle against any attempt to retard the recovery of Germany and a considerable assistance to those who promoted it.
What indeed—a thought which occurred to many Englishmen
also—can you do with Germany except make her the strongest
Power in Europe? Still, the process might have taken longer if
Americans had not been so insistent that Germany was the main
pillar of European peace and civilisation. The treaty of Locarno
and the admission of Germany to the League won American
approval; this was in fact a strong motive for them. The same
applied to disarmament. Every step towards treating Germany
as an equal and towards dismantling the special securities which
France obtained at the end of the first World war received
American backing, tempered only by impatience that the steps
were slow and halting.

Until 1931 or thereabouts, the policy of the Western Powers,

Great Britain and France, met broadly with American approval.
Then things changed. This was partly because of events in the
Far East. When Japan acted in Manchuria, the United States
wished to enlist the League of Nations against her; while Great
Britain and France thought that the League had enough to do
in Europe without attempting to extend its principles to the
Far East. The divergence went deeper. Americans attached
great value to "non-recognition"; with a fine old-fashioned
loyalty to nineteenth-century liberalism, they believed that
moral disapproval would be effective in itself. The belief had
already been proved false. The United States had refused to
recognize the Soviet Union ever since 1917 without the slightest
effect on anyone. The British particularly thought that the
same result, or lack of result, would follow if they applied the
principle of non-recognition to Japan. In their opinion, it was
more important to restore peace in the Far East than to preserve
their moral virtue. They succeeded, but at the price of permanently offending liberal sentiment in the United States. All
this was dead stuff when Republican rule was brought to an end
and Franklin D. Roosevelt became President. His victory was,
among other things, a victory for isolationism in American
foreign policy; and there is no evidence that he disapproved of
the isolationist legislation which the Democratic majority pushed
through Congress. The British and French were told, in effect,
by those who had been their closest friends in the United States
that they must face the German problem unaided. More than
that, American policy cut across their efforts. President Roosevelt's first act in foreign affairs was to wreck the World Economic
Conference, by means of which the British government had
hoped to make Nazi autarchy unnecessary.

American isolationism reinforced isolationism elsewhere.
British students learnt from American historians that the first
World war was a blunder and that Germany was a justly aggrieved Power. British liberals learnt from progressive American
politicians that wars were caused by armament manufacturers.
Americans, having repudiated the treaty of Versailles themselves,
were now eager that others should repudiate it also. The effect
of American isolationism was felt in more practical ways. It
supplied a strong argument for those who hesitated to make
collective security a reality. When it was proposed to cut off

Italy's supply of oil during the Abyssinian crisis, the objection
was at once raised that American oil would supply the deficiency;
and no assurance to the contrary came, or could come, from the
American government. Again, when the British government
were urged to close the Suez canal against Italy, in breach of the
Constantinople convention of 1889, the same answer was given:
the United States would not allow it. No doubt these obstacles
could have been overcome if British and French statesmen had
been sufficiently resolute; but where men hesitated, American
abstention helped to tip the scale. In much the same way, the
American attitude was invoked to justify non-intervention in
the Spanish civil war; any attempt to interfere with Franco's
supply of arms would, it was argued, meet with resistance from
the United States as well as from Germany and Italy. Yet, at
the same time, Great Britain and France earned censure in the
United States for failing to do things which American isolationism prevented them from doing. In particular, they were condemned for refusing to prolong a barren "non-recognition" once
Italy had conquered Abyssinia.

In the autumn of 1937 American policy began to change. This
was mainly due to the outbreak of war between Japan and China
in the Far East, where Americans would have liked to see action
by the European Powers, though they could promise none themselves. More than this, President Roosevelt set out to educate
American opinion. As always, he proceeded with great caution,
anxious not to outrun his people. His famous "quarantine"
speech against aggressors hinted at something more than non-
recognition. But how much more? Would the United States even
now have supported sanctions against Germany if any such had
been imposed? In any case, the "quarantine" speech was ill-
received in the United States. Roosevelt retreated, explaining
that he had meant nothing in particular. Soon afterwards he
renewed his attempt at education. His proposal for a world
conference to consider the grievances of the dissatisfied Powers
was made in the hope of demonstrating to Americans the mounting dangers throughout the world; but it contained no prospect
that the United States would actively support the Powers who
were trying to maintain some sort of peaceful order in the world.
Roosevelt seems to have hoped, so far as one can follow the de-
vious workings of his mind, that events would educate Americans

where he had failed to do so. He wanted public opinion to push him into supporting the Western Powers. When, instead, these Powers tried to push him, he had to react into isolationism for the sake of the very public opinion which he was seeking to educate. Thus, at the height of the Munich crisis, he repudiated sharply the attempt by Bullitt, American ambassador in Paris, to commit the United States on the French side; it was, he said, "one hundred per cent wrong"—yet he secretly wished it was right.

American policy was not altogether negative in the last year of peace. It was made clear to Great Britain and France that they would be able to buy supplies in the United States if they resolved on war; at the same time, since there was no prospect of active American support, they were left to make their own decisions—just as Sir Edward Grey had hesitated to encourage France and Russia before 1914. Unofficial American observers were busy exposing German and Italian designs, perhaps even in exaggerating them. They sounded the alarm in order to rouse American public opinion. In practice they succeeded more in alarming people in Great Britain and France, but not in the way they intended. They made British and French policy more fearful of war, instead of more resolved on it. No one is likely to underrate the effect which Lindbergh had with his inflated picture of the German air force. Like most people, he was taken in by Hitler's propaganda. The general moral of this book, so far as it has one, is that Great Britain and France dithered between resistance and appeasement, and so helped to make war more likely. American policy did much the same. A resolute continuance of isolationism might well have choked Great Britain and France off from war altogether; a resolute backing of them, based on rearmament launched long before, might well have choked off Hitler. Hesitation between the two helped war on. No one is to blame for this. It is very hard for a democracy to make up its mind; and when it does so, often makes it up wrong.

I would add one general word. Some English critics of this book complained that I had "apologized" for Hitler or for the appeasers. Nothing could be further from my thoughts. I have a clean record here. I was addressing public meetings against appeasement—and very uphill work it was—when my critics were confining their activities to the seclusion of Oxford common rooms. But I do not believe that a historian should either excuse or condemn. His duty is to explain. I have tried to explain how Hitler succeeded as much as he did and why the British and French governments finally declared war on Germany. If it be objected that Great Britain and France should have counted more firmly on American backing, it is worth bearing in mind that the United States were not drawn into the war either by the fall of France or even by Hitler's attack on Russia, and that we had to wait for the unlikely event of Hitler's declaring war on the United States before they came in.

SECOND THOUGHTS

I WROTE this book in order to satisfy my historical curiosity; in the words of a more successful historian, "to understand what happened, and why it happened". Historians often dislike what happened or wish that it had happened differently. There is nothing they can do about it. They have to state the truth as they see it without worrying whether this shocks or confirms existing prejudices. Maybe I assumed this too innocently. I ought perhaps to have warned the reader that I do not come to history as a judge; and that when I speak of morality I refer to the moral feelings at the time I am writing about. I make no moral judgement of my own. Thus when I write (p. 28) that "the peace of Versailles lacked moral validity from the start", I mean only that the Germans did not regard it as a "fair" settlement and that many people in Allied countries, soon I think most people, agreed with them. Who am I to say that it was "moral" or "immoral" in the abstract? From what point of view—that of the Germans, of the Allies, of neutrals, of the Bolsheviks? Some of its makers thought that it was moral; some thought it necessary; some thought it both immoral and unnecessary. This last class included Smuts, Lloyd George, the British Labour party, and many Americans. These moral doubts helped towards the overthrow of the peace settlement later on. Again, I wrote of the Munich agreement (p. 189): "It was a triumph for all that was best and most enlightened in British life; a triumph for those who had preached equal justice between peoples; a triumph for those who had courageously denounced the harshness and short-sightedness of Versailles". I ought perhaps to have added "(goak here)" in the manner of Artemus Ward. It was not however altogether a joke. For years past the best-informed and most conscientious students of international affairs had argued that there would be no peace in Europe until the Germans received the self-determination which had been granted to others. Munich was in part the outcome of their writings, however unwelcome its form; and its making would have been much more difficult if it had not been felt that there was some justice in Hitler's claim. Even during the second World war a Fellow of All Souls[1] asked President Benes whether he did not think that Czechoslovakia would have been stronger if it had included, say, a million and a half Germans fewer. So long did the spirit of "appeasement" linger. As a matter of fact, there was no half way house: either three and a half million Germans in Czechoslovakia or none. The Czechs themselves recognised this by expelling the Germans after the second World war. It was not for me to endorse, or to condemn, Hitler's claim; only to explain why it was so widely endorsed.

I am sorry if this disappoints simple-minded Germans who imagined that my book had somehow "vindicated" Hitler. I have however no sympathy with those in this country who complained that my book had been welcomed, mistakenly or not, by former supporters of Hitler. This seems to me a disgraceful argument to be used against a work of history. A historian must not hesitate even if his books lend aid and comfort to the Queen's enemies (though mine did not), or even to the common enemies of mankind. For my part, I would even record facts which told in favour of the British government if I found any to record (goak again). It is not my fault that, according to the record, the Austrian crisis was launched by Schuschnigg, not by Hitler; not my fault that the British government, according to the record, not Hitler, took the lead in dismembering Czechoslovakia; not my fault that the British government in 1939 gave Hitler the impression that they were more concerned to impose concessions on the Poles than to resist Germany. If these things tell in favour of Hitler, it is the fault of previous legends which have been repeated by historians without examination. These legends have a long life. I suspect I have repeated some. For instance I went on believing until the last moment that Hitler summoned Hacha to Berlin; only when the book was in proof, did I look at the records again and discover that Hacha asked to come to Berlin, not the other way round. No doubt other legends have slipped through.

Destroying these legends is not a vindication of Hitler. It is a service to historical truth, and my book should be challenged only on this basis, not for the political morals which people choose to draw from it. This book is not a contribution to "revisionism" except in the lesser sense of suggesting that Hitler

[1] Mr. A. L. Rowse, as recounted in his book, *All Souls and Appeasement*.

used different methods from those usually attributed to him.
I have never seen any sense in the question of war guilt or war
innocence. In a world of sovereign states, each does the best it
can for its own interests; and can be criticised at most for
mistakes, not for crimes. Bismarck, as usual, was right when he
said of the Austro-Prussian war in 1866: "Austria was no more
in the wrong in opposing our claims than we were in making
them". As a private citizen, I think that all this striving after
greatness and domination is idiotic; and I should like my country
not to take part in it. As a historian, I recognise that Powers will
be Powers. My book has really little to do with Hitler. The vital
question, it seems to me, concerns Great Britain and France.
They were the victors of the first World war. They had the
decision in their hands. It was perfectly obvious that Germany
would seek to become a Great Power again; obvious after 1988
that her domination would be of a peculiarly barbaric sort. Why
did the victors not resist her? There are various answers:
timidity; blindness; moral doubts; desire perhaps to turn German
strength against Soviet Russia. But whatever the answers, this
seems to me the important question, and my book revolves
round it, though also of course round the other question: why
did they resist in the end?

Still, some critics made a great fuss about Hitler, attributing
to him sole responsibility for the war or something near it. I will
therefore discuss Hitler's part a little more, though not in a
polemical spirit. I have no desire to win, only to get things right.
The current versions of Hitler are, I think, two. In one view, he
wanted a great war for its own sake. No doubt he also thought
vaguely of the results: Germany the greatest Power in the world,
and himself a world conqueror on the pattern of Alexander the
Great or Napoleon. But mainly he wanted war for the general
destruction of men and societies which it would cause. He was a
maniac, a nihilist, a second Attila. The other view makes him
more rational and, in a sense, more constructive. In this view,
Hitler had a coherent, longterm plan of an original nature which
he pursued with unwavering persistence. For the sake of this
plan he sought power; and it shaped all his foreign policy. He
intended to give Germany a great colonial empire in eastern
Europe by defeating Soviet Russia, exterminating all the
inhabitants, and then planting the vacant territory with Germans.

This Reich of a hundred or two hundred million Germans would last a thousand years. I am surprised, incidentally, that the advocates of this view did not applaud my book. For surely, if Hitler were planning a great war against Soviet Russia, his war against the western Powers was a mistake. There is evidently some point here which I have not understood.

Now, of course Hitler speculated a good deal about what he was doing, much as academic observers try to put coherence into the acts of contemporary statesmen. Maybe the world would have been saved a lot of trouble if Hitler could have been given a job in some German equivalent of Chatham House, where he could have speculated harmlessly for the rest of his life. As it was, he became involved in the world of action; and here, I think, he exploited events far more than he followed precise coherent plans. The story of how he came to power in Germany seems to me relevant to his later behaviour in international affairs. He announced persistently that he intended to seize power and would then do great things. Many people believed him. The elaborate plot by which Hitler seized power was the first legend to be established about him and has been the first also to be destroyed. There was no long-term plot; there was no seizure of power. Hitler had no idea how he would come to power; only a conviction that he would get there. Papen and a few other conservatives put Hitler into power by intrigue, in the belief that they had taken him prisoner. He exploited their intrigue, again with no idea how he would escape from their control, only with the conviction that somehow he would. This "revision" does not "vindicate" Hitler, though it discredits Papen and his associates. It is merely revision for its own sake, or rather for the sake of historical truth.

Hitler in power had once more no idea how he would pull Germany out of the Depression, only a determination to do it. Much of the recovery was natural, due to the general upturn in world conditions which was already beginning before Hitler gained power. Hitler himself contributed two things. One was anti-semitism. This, to my mind, was the one thing in which he persistently and genuinely believed from his beginning in Munich until his last days in the bunker. His advocacy of it would have deprived him of support, let alone power, in a civilised country. Economically, it was irrelevant, indeed harmful. His other contribution was to encourage public spending on roads and buildings. According to the only book which has looked at what happened instead of repeating what Hitler and others said was happening[1], German recovery was caused by the return of private consumption and nonwar types of investment to the prosperity levels of 1928 and 1929. Rearmament had little to do with it. Until the spring of 1936, "rearmament was largely a myth".[2] Hitler in fact did not apply any prepared economic plans. He did the nearest thing that came to hand.

The same point is illustrated in the story of the Reichstag fire. Everyone knows the legend. The Nazis wanted an excuse for introducing Exceptional Laws of political dictatorship; and themselves set fire to the Reichstag in order to provide this excuse. Perhaps Goebbels arranged the fire, perhaps Goering; perhaps Hitler himself did not know about the plan beforehand. At any rate somehow, the Nazis did it. This legend has now been shot to pieces by Fritz Tobias, in my opinion decisively.[3] The Nazis had nothing to do with the burning of the Reichstag. The young Dutchman, van der Lubbe, did it all alone, exactly as he claimed. Hitler and the other Nazis were taken by surprise. They genuinely believed that the Communists had started the fire; and they introduced the Exceptional Laws because they genuinely believed that they were threatened with a Communist rising. Certainly there was a prepared list of those who should be arrested. But not prepared by the Nazis. It had been prepared by Goering's predecessor: the Social Democrat, Severing. Here again there is no "vindication" of Hitler, only a revision of his methods. He expected an opportunity to turn up; and one did. Of course the Communists, too, had nothing to do with the burning of the Reichstag. But Hitler thought they had. He was able to exploit the Communist danger so effectively largely because he believed in it himself. This, too, provides a parallel with Hitler's attitude later in international affairs. When other countries thought that he was preparing aggressive war against them, Hitler was equally convinced that these others intended to prevent the restoration of Germany as an independent Great Power. His belief was not altogether unfounded. At any rate, the British and French

---

[1] Burton H. Klein, *Germany's Economic Preparations for War* (1959.) Mr. Klein is an economist with the RAND Corporation.

[2] Klein, p. 16–17.   [3] Fritz Tobias, *Reichstagbrand* (1962).

governments have often been condemned for not undertaking a preventive war in good time.

Here, it seems to me, is the key to the problem whether Hitler deliberately aimed at war. He did not so much aim at war as expect it to happen, unless he could evade it by some ingenious trick, as he had evaded civil war at home. Those who have evil motives easily attribute them to others; and Hitler expected others to do what he would have done in their place. England and France were "hate-inspired antagonists"; Soviet Russia was plotting the overthrow of European civilisation, an empty boast which indeed the Bolsheviks had often made; Roosevelt was out to ruin Europe. Hitler certainly directed his generals to prepare for war. But so did the British, and for that matter every other, government. It is the job of general staffs to prepare for war. The directives which they receive from their governments indicate the possible war for which they are to prepare, and are no proof that the government concerned have resolved on it. All the British directives from 1935 onwards were pointed solely against Germany; Hitler's were concerned only with making Germany stronger. If therefore we were (wrongly) to judge political intentions from military plans, the British government would appear set on war with Germany, not the other way round. But of course we apply to the behaviour of our own governments a generosity of interpretation which we do not extend to others. People regard Hitler as wicked; and then find proofs of his wickedness in evidence which they would not use against others. Why do they apply this double standard? Only because they assume Hitler's wickedness in the first place.

It is dangerous to deduce political intentions from military plans. Some historians, for instance, have deduced from the Anglo-French military conversations before 1914 that the British government were set on war with Germany. Other, and in my opinion wiser, historians have denied that this deduction can be drawn. The plans they argue, were precautions, not "blueprints for aggression". Yet Hitler's directives are often interpreted in this latter way. I will give one remarkable example. On 30 November 1938 Keitel sent to Ribbentrop a draft for Italo-German military talks which he had prepared on Hitler's instruction. Clause 3 read: "Military-political basis for the Negotiation. War by Germany and Italy against France and Britain, with the object first of knocking out France"[1]. A responsible critic has claimed that this provides clear proof of Hitler's intentions and so destroys my entire thesis. Yet what could German and Italian generals talk about when they met, except war against France and Britain? This was the only war in which Italy was likely to be involved. British and French generals were discussing war against Germany and Italy at this very time. Yet this is not counted against them, still less against their governments. The subsequent history of Keitel's draft is instructive. The Italians, not the Germans, had been pressing for military talks. After the draft had been prepared, nothing happened. When Hitler occupied Prague on 15 March 1939, the talks had still not been held. The Italians grew impatient. On 22 March Hitler ordered: "The military-political bases. . . . are to be *deferred* for the present"[2]. Talks were held at last on 4 April. Keitel recorded: "The conversations were started somewhat suddenly in consequence of Italian pressure"[3]. It turned out that the Italians, far from wanting war, wished to insist that they could not be ready for war until 1942 at the earliest; and the German representatives agreed with them. Thus, this marvellous directive merely proves (if it proves anything) that Hitler was not interested at this time in war against France and Great Britain; and that Italy was not interested in war at all. Or maybe it shows that historians should be careful not to seize on an isolated clause in a document without reading further.

Of course, in British eyes, their government only wanted to keep things quiet, while Hitler wanted to stir them up. To the Germans, the *status quo* was not peace, but a slave treaty. It all depends on the point of view. The victor Powers wanted to keep the fruits of victory with some modifications, though they did it ineffectively. The vanquished Power wanted to undo its defeat. This latter ambition, whether "aggressive" or not, was not peculiar to Hitler. It was shared by all German politicians, by the Social Democrats who ended the war in 1918 as much as by Stresemann. No one defined precisely what undoing the defeat of the first World war meant; and this applies also to

[1] Keitel to Ribbentrop, 30 Nov. 1938. *German Foreign Policy*, Series D, iv. No. 411.

[2] Keitel directive. 22 March, 1939. *Ibid.* vi. Appendix I.

[3] Keitel report. 4 April, 1939. *Ibid.* Appendix III.

Hitler. It involved recovering the territory lost then; restoring the German predominance over central Europe which had previously been given by the alliance with Austria-Hungary; ending of course all restrictions on German armaments. The concrete terms did not matter. All Germans, including Hitler, assumed that Germany would become the dominant Power in Europe once she had undone her defeat, whether this happened by war or otherwise; and this assumption was generally shared in other countries. The two ideas of "liberation" and "domination" merged into one. There was no separating them. They were merely two different words for the same thing; and only use of the particular word decides whether Hitler was a champion of national justice or a potential conqueror of Europe.

A German writer[1] has recently criticised Hitler for wanting to restore Germany as a Great Power at all. The first World war, this writer argues, had shown that Germany could not be an independent Power on a world scale; and Hitler was foolish to try. This is not much more than a platitude. The first World war shattered all the Great Powers involved, with the exception of the United States, who took virtually no part in it; maybe they were all foolish to go on trying to be Great Powers afterwards. Total war is probably beyond the strength of any Great Power. Now even preparations for such a war threaten to ruin the Great Powers who attempt them. Nor is this new. In the eighteenth century Frederick the Great led Prussia to the point of collapse in the effort to be a Great Power. The Napoleonic wars brought France down from her high estate in Europe, and she never recovered her former greatness. This is an odd, inescapable dilemma. Though the object of being a Great Power is to be able to fight a great war, the only way of remaining a Great Power is not to fight one, or to fight it on a limited scale. This was the secret of Great Britain's greatness so long as she stuck to naval warfare and did not try to become a military power on the continental pattern. Hitler did not need instruction from a historian in order to appreciate this. The inability of Germany to fight a long war was a constant theme of his; and so was the danger which threatened Germany if the other Great Powers combined against her. In talking like this, Hitler was more sensible than the German generals who imagined that all would

[1] Wolfgang Sauer in *die nationalsozialistische Machtergreifung* (1960).

be well if they got Germany back to the position she occupied
before Ludendorff's offensive in March 1918. Hitler did not
however draw the moral that it was silly for Germany to be a
Great Power. Instead he proposed to dodge the problem by
ingenuity, much as the British had once done. Where they relied
on sea power, he relied on guile. Far from wanting war, a general
war was the last thing he wanted. He wanted the fruits of total
victory without total war; and thanks to the stupidity of others
he nearly got them. Other Powers thought that they were faced
with the choice between total war and surrender. At first they
chose surrender; then they chose total war, to Hitler's ultimate
ruin.

This is not guesswork. It is demonstrated beyond peradventure
by the record of German armament before the second World war
or even during it. It would have been obvious long ago if men
had not been blinded by two mistakes. Before the war they
listened to what Hitler said instead of looking at what he did.
After the war they wanted to pin on him the guilt for everything
which happened, regardless of the evidence. This is illustrated,
for example, by the almost universal belief that Hitler started
the indiscriminate bombing of civilians, whereas it was started
by the directors of British strategy, as some of the more honest
among them have boasted. However, the record is there for
anyone who wishes to use it, dispassionately analysed by Mr.
Burton Klein. I have already quoted his conclusion for Hitler's
first three years: until the spring of 1936 German rearmament
was largely a myth. This does not mean merely that the preliminary stages of rearmament were not producing increased
strength, as always happens. Even the preliminary stages were
not being undertaken at all seriously. Hitler cheated foreign
powers and the German people in exactly the opposite sense
from that which is usually supposed. He, or rather Goering,
announced: "Guns before butter". In fact, he put butter before
guns. I take some figures at random from Mr. Klein's book. In
1936, according to Churchill, two independent estimates placed
German rearmament expenditure at an annual rate of 12
thousand million marks.[1] The actual figure was under 5 thousand
million. Hitler himself asserted that the Nazi government had
spent 90 thousand million marks on armaments before the out-

[1] Churchill, *The Second World War*, i. 226.

break of war. In fact total German government expenditure, war and nonwar, did not amount to much more than this between 1933 and 1938. Rearmament cost about 40 thousand million marks in the six fiscal years ending 31 March 1939, and about 50 thousand millions up to the outbreak of war.[1]

Mr. Klein discusses why German rearmament was on such a limited scale. For one thing, Hitler was anxious not to weaken his popularity by reducing the standard of civilian life in Germany. The most rearmament did was to prevent its rising faster than it otherwise would have done. Even so the Germans were better off than they had ever been before. Then the Nazi system was inefficient, corrupt, and muddled. More important, Hitler would not increase taxes and yet was terrified of inflation. Even the overthrow of Schacht did not really shake the financial limitations, though it was supposed to do so. Most important of all, Hitler did not make large war preparations simply because his "concept of warfare did not require them". "Rather he planned to solve Germany's living-space problem in piecemeal fashion—by a series of small wars".[2] This is the conclusion at which I also arrived independently from study of the political record, though I suspect that Hitler hoped to get by without war at all. I agree that there was no clear dividing line in his mind between political ingenuity and small wars, such as the attack on Poland. The one thing he did not plan was the great war, often attributed to him.

Pretending to prepare for a great war and not in fact doing it was an essential part of Hitler's political strategy; and those who sounded the alarm against him, such as Churchill, unwittingly did his work for him. The device was new and took everyone in. Previously governments spent more on armaments than they admitted, as most do to the present day. This was sometimes to deceive their own people; sometimes to deceive a potential enemy. In 1909, for instance, the German government were accused by many British people of secretly accelerating naval building without the approval of the Reichstag. The accusation was probably untrue. But it left a permanent legacy of suspicion that the Germans would do it again; and this suspicion was strengthened by the evasions of the disarmament imposed by the treaty of Versailles, which successive German governments

[1] Klein, 17.   [2] Klein, 26.

practised, though to little advantage, after 1919. Hitler encouraged this suspicion and exploited it. There is a very good illustration. On 28 November 1934 Baldwin denied Churchill's statement that German air strength was equal to that of Great Britain's. Baldwin's figures were right; Churchill's, supplied by Professor Lindemann, were wrong. On 24 March 1935 Sir John Simon and Anthony Eden visited Hitler. He told them that the German air force was already equal to that of Great Britain, if not indeed superior. He was at once believed, and has been believed ever since. Baldwin was discredited. Panic was created. How was it possible that a statesmen could exaggerate his armaments instead of concealing them ? Yet this was what Hitler had done. German rearmament was largely a myth until the spring of 1936. Then Hitler put some reality into it. His motive was principally fear of the Red Army; and of course Great Britain and France had begun to rearm also. Hitler in fact raced along with others, and not much faster. In October 1936 he told Goering to prepare the German army and German economy for war within four years, though he did not lay down any detailed requirements. In 1938–39, the last peacetime year, Germany spent on armament about 15% of her gross national product. The British proportion was almost exactly the same. German expenditure on armaments was actually cut down after Munich and remained at this lower level, so that British production of aeroplanes, for example, was way ahead of German by 1940. When war broke out in 1939, Germany had 1450 modern fighter planes and 800 bombers; Great Britain and France had 950 fighters and 1300 bombers. The Germans had 3500 tanks; Great Britain and France had 3850.[1] In each case Allied intelligence estimated German strength at more than twice the true figure. As usual, Hitler was thought to have planned and prepared for a great war. In fact, he had not.

It may be objected that these figures are irrelevant. Whatever the deficiencies of German armament on paper, Hitler won a war against two European Great Powers when the test came. This is to go against Maitland's advice and to judge by what happened, not by what was expected to happen. Though Hitler won, he won by mistake—a mistake which he shared. Of course the Germans were confident that they could defeat Poland if they were left undisturbed in the west. Here Hitler's political judge-

[1] Klein, 17.

ment that the French would do nothing proved more accurate than the apprehensions of the German generals. But he had no idea that he would knock France out of the war when he invaded Belgium and Holland on 10 May 1940. This was a defensive move: to secure the Ruhr from Allied invasion. The conquest of France was an unforeseen bonus. Even after this Hitler did not prepare for a great war. He imagined that he could defeat Soviet Russia without serious effort as he had defeated France. German production of armaments was not reduced merely during the winter of 1940-41; it was reduced still more in the autumn of 1941 when the war against Russia had already begun. No serious change took place after the initial setback in Russia nor even after the catastrophe at Stalingrad. Germany remained with "a peacelike war economy". Only the British bombing attacks on German cities stimulated Hitler and the Germans to take war seriously. German war production reached its height just when Allied bombing did: in July 1944. Even in March 1945 Germany was producing substantially more military material than when she attacked Russia in 1941. From first to last, ingenuity, not military strength, was Hitler's secret of success. He was done for when military strength became decisive, as he had always known he would be.

Thus I feel justified in regarding political calculations as more important than mere strength in the period before the war. There was some change of emphasis in the summer of 1936. Then all the Powers, not merely Hitler, began to take war and preparations for war seriously into account. I erred in not stressing this change of 1936 more clearly, and perhaps in finding too much change in the autumn of 1937. This shows how difficult it is to shake off legends even when trying to do so. I was taken in by the Hossbach Memorandum. Though I doubted whether it was as important as most writers made out, I still thought that it must have some importance for every writer to make so much of it. I was wrong; and the critics were right who pointed back to 1936, though they did not apparently realise that, by doing this, they were discrediting the Hossbach memorandum. I had better discredit this "official record", as one historian has called it, a little further. The points are technical and may seem trivial to the general reader. Nevertheless scholars usually and rightly attach importance to such technicalities. In modern practice, an official record demands three things. First, a secretary must attend to take notes which he writes up afterwards in orderly form. Then his draft must be submitted to the participants for correction and approval. Finally, the record must be placed in the official files. None of this took place in regard to the meeting on 5 November 1937, except that Hossbach attended. He took no notes. Five days later he wrote an account of the meeting from memory in longhand. He twice offered to show the manuscript to Hitler, who replied that he was too busy to read it. This was curiously casual treatment for what is supposed to be his "last will and testament". Blomberg may have looked at the manuscript. The others did not know it existed. The only certificate of authenticity attached to it was the signature of Hossbach himself. One other man saw the manuscript: Beck, chief of the general staff, the most sceptical among German generals of Hitler's ideas. He wrote an answer to Hitler's arguments on 12 November 1937; and this answer was later presented as the beginning of the German "resistance". It has even been suggested that Hossbach wrote the memorandum in order to provoke the answer.

These are speculations. At the time, no one attached importance to the meeting. Hossbach left the staff soon afterwards. His manuscript was put in a file with other miscellaneous papers, and forgotten. In 1943 a German officer, Count Kirchbach, looked through the file, and copied the manuscript for the department of military history. After the war, the Americans found Kirchbach's copy, and copied it in their turn for the prosecution at Nuremberg. Both Hossbach and Kirchbach thought that this copy was shorter than the original. In particular, according to Kirchbach, the original contained criticisms by Neurath, Blomberg, and Fritsch of Hitler's argument—criticisms which have now fallen out. Maybe the Americans "edited" the document; maybe Kirchbach, like other Germans, was trying to shift all the blame on to Hitler. There are no means of knowing. Hossbach's original and Kirchbach's copy have both disappeared. All that survives is a copy, perhaps shortened, perhaps "edited", of a copy of an unauthenticated draft. It contains themes which Hitler also used in his public speeches: the need for *Lebensraum*, and his conviction that other countries would oppose the restoration of Germany as an independent Great Power. It contains no directives for action beyond a wish for increased armaments. Even at

Nuremberg the Hossbach memorandum was not produced in order to prove Hitler's war guilt. That was taken for granted. What it "proved", in its final concocted form, was that those accused at Nuremberg—Goering, Raeder, and Neurath—had sat by and approved of Hitler's aggressive plans. It had to be assumed that the plans were aggressive in order to prove the guilt of the accused. Those who believe the evidence in political trials may go on quoting the Hossbach memorandum. They should also warn their readers (as the editors of the *Documents on German Foreign Policy* for example do not) that the memorandum, far from being an "official record", is a very hot potato.[1]

The Hossbach memorandum is not the only alleged blueprint of Hitler's intentions. Indeed, to judge from what some historians say, Hitler produced such blueprints continually—influenced no doubt by his ambition to be an architect (yet another goal). These historians even underrate Hitler's productivity. They jump straight from *Mein Kampf* to the Hossbach memorandum, and then to the *Table Talk* during the Russian war.[2] In fact Hitler produced a blueprint nearly every time he made a speech; this was the way his mind worked. Obviously there was nothing secret about these blueprints either in *Mein Kampf* which sold by the million after Hitler came to power, or in speeches delivered to large audiences. No one therefore need pride himself on his perspicacity in divining Hitler's intentions. It is equally obvious that *Lebensraum* always appeared as one

---

[1] Hossbach's account: affidavit in *International Military Tribunal*, xlii, 228, and, with variants, in Hossbach, *Von der militärischen Verantwortlichkeit in der Zeit vor dem zweiten Weltkreig* (1948), 28. Kirchbach's copy and subsequent doubts: G. Meinck, *Hitler und die deutsche Aufrustung 1933–37*, (1956), 236. Beck's counter-memorandum in: W. Foerster, *Ein General kampft gegen den Krieg* (1949), 62. Beginning of the Resistance: Hans Rothfels, *Die deutsche Opposition gegen Hitler* (1951), 71. At Nuremberg, Blomberg, Goering, and Neurath testified against the authenticity of the memorandum. Their testimony is generally held to be worthless; or rather of worth only so far as it tells against Hitler.

[2] Now they can halt also at Hitler's second or, as it is called in the English edition, his secret book, which he wrote in 1928 and which remained unpublished until recently. Of course there is nothing secret about it. It is a rehash of the speeches which he was making at the time; and it was unpublished merely because it was not worth publishing. The "secret" is typical of the romantic fancies with which everything to do with Hitler is treated.

element in these blueprints. This was not an original idea of
Hitler's. It was a commonplace of the time. *Volk ohne Raum*,
for instance, by Hans Grimm sold much better than *Mein
Kampf* when it was published in 1928. For that matter, plans for
acquiring new territory were much aired in Germany during the
first World war. It used to be thought that these were the plans
of a few crack-pot theorisers or of extremist organisations. Now
we know better. In 1961 a German professor reported the result
of his investigations into German war aims[1]. These were indeed
"a blue print for aggression" or, as the professor called them, "a
grasp at world power": Belgium under German control; the
French iron-fields annexed to Germany; the Ukraine to become
German; and, what is more, Poland and the Ukraine to be cleared
of their inhabitants and to be resettled with Germans. These
plans were not merely the work of the German general staff.
They were endorsed by the German foreign office and by "the
good German", Bethmann Hollweg. Hitler, far from transcend-
ing his respectable predecessors, was actually being more moderate than they when he sought only *Lebensraum* in the east and
repudiated, in *Mein Kampf*, gains in the west. Hitler merely
repeated the ordinary chatter of Rightwing circles. Like all
demagogues, Hitler appealed to the masses. Unlike other demagogues, who sought power to carry out Left policies, Hitler
dominated the masses by Leftwing methods in order to deliver
them to the Right. This is why the Right let him in.

But was *Lebensraum* Hitler's sole idea or indeed the one which
dominated his mind? To judge from *Mein Kampf*, he was
obsessed by anti-semitism, [which occupies most of the book.]
Lebensraum gets only seven of the seven hundred pages. Then
and thereafter, it was thrown in as a final rationalisation, a sort
of "pie in the sky" to justify what Hitler was supposed to be up
to. Perhaps the difference between me and the believers in
Hitler's constant plan for *Lebensraum* is over words. By "plan"
I understand something which is prepared and worked out in
detail. They seem to take "plan" as a pious, or in this case
impious, wish. In my sense Hitler never had a plan for *Lebensraum*. There was no study of the resources in the territories
that were to be conquered; no definition even of what these
territories were to be. There was no recruitment of a staff to

1 Fritz Fischer, *Griff nach der Weltmacht* (1961).

carry out these "plans", no survey of Germans who could be moved, let alone any enrolment. When large parts of Soviet Russia were conquered, the administrators of the conquered territories found themselves running round in circles, unable to get any directive whether they were to exterminate the existing populations or to exploit them, whether to treat them as friends or enemies.

[Hitler certainly thought that Germany was most likely to make gains in eastern Europe when she became again a Great Power.] This was partly because of his belief in *Lebensraum*. There were more practical considerations. For a long time he thought, whether mistakenly or not, that it would be easier to defeat Soviet Russia than the Western Powers. Indeed, he half believed that Bolshevism might break down without a war, a belief shared by many western statesman. Then he could collect his gains with no effort at all. Moreover *Lebensraum* could easily be presented as an anti-Bolshevik crusade; and thus helped to win the hearts of those in western countries who regarded Hitler as the champion of Western civilisation. However he was not dogmatic about this. He did not refuse other gains when they came along. After the defeat of France, he annexed Alsace and Lorraine despite his previous declarations that he would not do so; and he carried off the industrial regions of Belgium and north-eastern France for good measure, just as Bethmann had intended to do before him. The rather vague terms which he projected for peace with Great Britain in the summer of 1940 included a guarantee for the British Empire, but he also intended to claim Irak, and perhaps Egypt, as a German sphere. Thus, whatever his theories, he did not adhere in practice to the logical pattern of *status quo* in the west and gains in the east. The abstract speculator turned out to be also a statesman on the make who did not consider beforehand what he would make or how. He got as far as he did because others did not know what to do with him. Here again I want to understand the "appeasers", not to vindicate or to condemn them. Historians do a bad day's work when they write the appeasers off as stupid or as cowards. They were men confronted with real problems, doing their best in the circumstances of their time. They recognised that an independent and powerful Germany had somehow to be fitted into Europe. Later experience suggests that they were right. At

any rate, we are still going round and round the German problem. Can any sane man suppose, for instance, that other countries
could have intervened by armed force in 1933 to overthrow
Hitler when he had come to power by constitutional means and
was apparently supported by a large majority of the German
people? Could anything have been designed to make him more
popular in Germany, unless perhaps it was intervening to turn
him out of the Rhineland in 1936? The Germans put Hitler into
power; they were the only ones who could turn him out. Again
the "appeasers" feared that the defeat of Germany would be
followed by a Russian domination over much of Europe. Later
experience suggests that they were right here also. Only those
who wanted Soviet Russia to take the place of Germany are
entitled to condemn the "appeasers"; and I cannot understand
how most of those who condemn them are now equally indignant at the inevitable result of their failure.

Nor is it true that the "appeasers" were a narrow circle,
widely opposed at the time. To judge by what is said now, one
would suppose that practically all Conservatives were for strenuous resistance to Germany in alliance with Soviet Russia and
that all the Labour party were clamouring for great armaments.
On the contrary, few causes have been more popular. Every
newspaper in the country applauded the Munich settlement
with the exception of *Reynolds' News.* Yet so powerful are the
legends that even when I write this sentence down I can hardly
believe it. Of course the "appeasers" thought firstly of their
own countries as most statesmen do and are usually praised for
doing. But they thought of others also. They doubted whether
the peoples of eastern Europe would be best served by war. The
British stand in September 1939 was no doubt heroic; but it
was heroism mainly at the expense of others. The British people
suffered comparatively little during six years of war. The Poles
suffered catastrophe during the war, and did not regain their
independence after it. In 1938 Czechoslovakia was betrayed.
In 1939 Poland was saved. Less than one hundred thousand
Czechs died during the war. Six and a half million Poles were
killed. Which was better—to be a betrayed Czech or a saved
Pole? I am glad Germany was defeated and Hitler destroyed. I
also appreciate that others paid the price for this, and I recognise
the honesty of those who thought the price too high.

These are controversies which should now be discussed in historical terms. It would be easy to draw up an indictment of the appeasers. Maybe I lost interest from having often done so already at a time when, to the best of my recollection, those who now display indignation against me were not active on the public platform. I am more interested to discover why the things I wanted did not work out than in repeating the old denunciations; and if I am to condemn any mistakes, I prefer to condemn my own. However it is no part of a historian's duty to say what ought to have been done. His sole duty is to find out what was done and why. Little can be discovered so long as we go on attributing everything that happened to Hitler. He supplied a powerful dynamic element, but it was fuel to an existing engine. He was in part the creation of Versailles, in part the creation of ideas that were common in contemporary Europe. Most of all, he was the creation of German history and of the German present. He would have counted for nothing without the support and co-operation of the German people. It seems to be believed nowadays that Hitler did everything himself, even driving the trains and filling the gas chambers unaided. This was not so. Hitler was a sounding board for the German nation. Thousands, many hundred thousand, Germans carried out his evil orders without qualm or question. As supreme ruler of Germany, Hitler bears the greatest responsibility for acts of immeasurable evil: for the destruction of German democracy: for the concentration camps; and, worst of all, for the extermination of peoples during the second World war. He gave orders, which Germans executed, of a wickedness without parallel in civilised history. His foreign policy was a different matter. He aimed to make Germany the dominant Power in Europe and maybe, more remotely, in the world. Other Powers have pursued similar aims, and still do. Other Powers treat smaller countries as their satellites. Other Powers seek to defend their vital interests by force of arms. In international affairs there was nothing wrong with Hitler except that he was a German.

CONTENTS

		PAGE
	Preface for the American Reader	v
	Second Thoughts	xi
I	FORGOTTEN PROBLEM	7
II	THE LEGACY OF THE FIRST WORLD WAR	18
III	THE POST-WAR DECADE	40
IV	THE END OF VERSAILLES	61
V	THE ABYSSINIAN AFFAIR AND THE END OF LOCARNO	87
VI	THE HALF-ARMED PEACE, 1936-38	102
VII	ANSCHLUSS: THE END OF AUSTRIA	131
VIII	THE CRISIS OVER CZECHOSLOVAKIA	151
IX	PEACE FOR SIX MONTHS	187
X	THE WAR OF NERVES	215
XI	WAR FOR DANZIG	248
	Bibliography	279
	Index	285

Maps

GERMANY BETWEEN THE WARS

EUROPE BETWEEN THE WARS

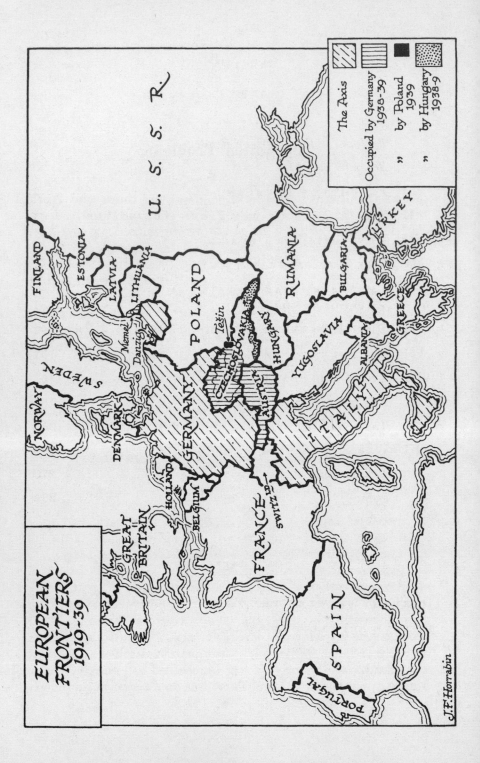

EUROPEAN
FRONTIERS
1919-39

The Axis

Occupied by Germany 1938-39

" by Poland 1939

" by Hungary 1938-9

U. S. S. R.

NORWAY
SWEDEN
FINLAND
ESTONIA
LATVIA
LITHUANIA
GREAT BRITAIN
DENMARK
Memel
Danzig
POLAND
HOLLAND
BELGIUM
GERMANY
Těšín
CZECHOSLOVAKIA
AUSTRIA
HUNGARY
RUMANIA
FRANCE
SWITZ.
YUGOSLAVIA
BULGARIA
TURKEY
ITALY
ALBANIA
GREECE
SPAIN
PORTUGAL

J.F.Horrabin.

CHAPTER ONE

Forgotten Problem

MORE than twenty years have gone by since the second World war began, fifteen since it ended. Those who lived through it still feel it as part of their immediate experience. One day they suddenly realise that the second World war, like its predecessor, has passed into history. This moment comes for a university teacher when he has to remind himself that his students were not born when the war started and cannot remember even its end. The second World war is as remote to them as the Boer war was to him; they may have heard anecdotes of it from their parents, but more likely, they have to learn of it from books if they learn at all. The great figures have left the scene. Hitler, Mussolini, Stalin, and Roosevelt are dead; Churchill has withdrawn from leadership; only de Gaulle is having a second innings. The second World war has ceased to be "today" and has become "yesterday". This makes new demands on historians. Contemporary history, in the strict sense, records events while they are still hot, judging them from the moment and assuming a ready sympathy in the reader. No one will depreciate such works with the great example of Sir Winston Churchill before him. But there comes a time when the historian can stand back and review events that were once contemporary with the detachment that he would show if he were writing of the Investiture conflict or the English civil war. At least, he can try.

Historians attempted this after the first World war, but with a different emphasis. There was relatively little interest in the war itself. The dispute over grand strategy between Westerners and Easterners was regarded as a private war between Lloyd George and the generals, which the academic historian passed by. The official British military history—itself a polemical contribution to this private war—proceeded so leisurely that it was only completed in 1948. There was no attempt at an official

civil history, except for the Ministry of Munitions. Hardly anyone examined the attempts at a negotiated peace. No one studied
the development of war aims. We have had to wait almost until
the present day for detailed study of such a decisive topic as
the policy of Woodrow Wilson. The great subject which eclipsed
all else and monopolised the interest of historians was how the
war began. Every government of a Great Power, except the
Italian, made copious revelations from its diplomatic archives.
The conscientious historian saw his shelves filling with books in
every major language and regretted that he could not read
others. Periodicals in French, German, and Russian were
devoted exclusively to the subject. Historians established their
reputation as authorities on the origins of the first World war—
Gooch in England, Fay and Schmitt in the United States,
Renouvin and Camille Bloch in France, Thimme, Brandenburg,
and von Wegerer in Germany, Pribram in Austria, Pokrovsky in
Russia, to name but a few.

Some of these writers concentrated on the events of July 1914;
others ranged back to the Moroccan crisis of 1905 or to the
diplomacy of Bismarck. But all agreed that here was the field
of consuming interest for the recent historian. University courses
stopped abruptly at August 1914, as some still do. The students
approved. They wanted to hear about William II and Poincaré,
about Grey and Izvolski. The Kruger telegram seemed more
important to them than Passchendaele, the treaty of Björkö
more important than the agreement of St. Jean de Maurienne.
The great event which had shaped the present was the outbreak
of war. What happened afterwards was merely a muddled work-
ing-out of inevitable consequences, without lessons or significance
for the present. If we understood why the war began, we should
know how we got where we were—and of course how not to get
there again.

With the second World war it has been almost the exact
opposite. The great subject of interest, for reader and writer
alike, has been the war itself. Not merely the campaigns, though
these have been described again and again. The politics of the
war have also been examined, particularly the relations of the
Great allies. It would be difficult to count the books on the
French armistice of 1940, or on the meetings of the Big Three at
Teheran and Yalta. The "Polish question" in relation to the

second World war means the disputes between Soviet Russia and the Western Powers with which the war ended, not the German demands on Poland with which it began. The origins of the war excite comparatively little interest. It is generally felt that, while new details may emerge, there is nothing of general significance to find out. We already know the answers, and do not need to ask further questions. The leading authors to whom we turn for accounts of the origins of the second World war— Namier, Wheeler-Bennett, Wiskemann in English, Baumont in French—all published their books soon after the war ended; and all expressed views which they had held while the war was on, or even before it began. Twenty years after the outbreak of the first World war, very few people would have accepted without modification the explanations for it given in August 1914. Twenty years and more after the outbreak of the second World war nearly everyone accepts the explanations which were given in September 1989.

It is of course possible that there really is nothing to find out. Maybe the second World war, unlike almost any other great event in history, had a simple and final explanation which was obvious to everyone at the time and which will never be changed by later information or research. But it seems unlikely that historians a hundred years hence will look at these events exactly as men did in 1939; and the present-day historian should seek to anticipate the judgements of the future rather than repeat those of the past. There are indeed practical reasons why historians have neglected this theme. Every historian tries to be a detached and impartial scholar, choosing his subject and making his judgements without thought of his surroundings. Yet, as a human being living in a community, he responds even if unconsciously to the needs of his time. The great Professor Tout, for example, whose work transformed the study of mediaeval history in this country, no doubt changed his emphasis from politics to administration purely for reasons of abstract learning. All the same, it was not irrelevant to the change that the twentieth century historian is training potential civil servants, whereas the nineteenth century historian trained statesmen. So, too, the writers on the two World wars were bound to consider what still raised problems, or provided answers for the present. No one is going to write a book that will not interest some others; least of all to write a book that does not interest himself.

The first World war seemed to present few problems on the military side. Most people, particularly in Allied countries, regarded the war as a slogging-match, much like a nineteenth-century prize-fight, which went on until one combatant fell down from exhaustion. Only when men's minds were sharpened by experience of the second World war did they begin to debate seriously whether the first war could have been ended earlier by a superior strategy or a superior policy. Besides, it was generally assumed after the first World war that there would never be another; therefore study of the last war seemed to provide no lessons for the present. On the other hand, the great problem which had caused the war still lay at the centre of international affairs when the war ended. This great problem was Germany. The Allies might claim that the war had been brought about by German aggression; the Germans might answer that it had been caused by their refusal to grant Germany her rightful place as a Great Power. In either case, it was the place of Germany which was in dispute. There remained other problems than Germany in the world from Soviet Russia to the Far East. But it was reasonable to assume that these would be manageable and that there would be a peaceful world if only the German people were reconciled to their former enemies. Hence the study of war-origins had an urgent and practical importance. If the peoples of Allied countries could be convinced of the falsity of German "war-guilt", they would relax the punitive clauses in the treaty of Versailles, and accept the German people as victims, like themselves, of a natural cataclysm. Alternatively, if the Germans were persuaded of their war-guilt, they would presumably accept the treaty as just. In practice, "revisionism" took only the first course. British and American historians, to some extent French historians also, laboured to show that the allied governments were a good deal guiltier and the German government more innocent than the peace-makers of 1919 supposed. Few German historians attempted the contrary demonstration. This was natural enough. Even the most aloof historian feels the tug of patriotism when his country has been defeated in war and humiliated after it. On the other side, foreign policy had been the subject of controversy in every Allied country before the outbreak of war. The critics of Grey in England, of Poincaré in France, of Woodrow Wilson in the United States—to say nothing of the Bolsheviks in Russia who had attacked the government of the Tsar—now stepped forward as the scholarly champions of a "revisionist" outlook. The rights and wrongs of these controversies, international and domestic, no longer matter. It is enough that they stoked the fires of interest which led men to study the origins of the first World war.

This fuel has been lacking for the origins of the second World war. On the international side, Germany, as a Great Power, ceased to be the central problem in world affairs almost before the war was over. Soviet Russia took her place. Men wanted to know about the mistakes that had been made in dealing with Soviet Russia during the war, not about those made in dealing with Germany before it started. Moreover, as both the Western powers and Russia were proposing to enlist different sections of Germany as their ally, the less said about the war the better. The Germans seconded this neglect. After the first World war, they insisted that they must still be treated as a Great Power. After the second, they were the first to suggest that Europe had ceased to determine world events—with the unspoken implication that Germany could never again provoke a great war, and could therefore be left to go her own way without interference or control. It was much the same on the domestic side. There had been fierce controversy within Allied countries before the war— indeed far fiercer than anything known before 1914. But the contestants made up their quarrel during the war and were anxious, for the most part, to forget it afterwards. The former advocates of "appeasement" could renew their old policy with more justification; the former advocates of resistance gave up their old alarms in regard to Germany with the need to resist Soviet Russia.

The origins of the second World war had little attraction when men were already studying the origins of the third. There might still have been some kick in the subject if there had remained great areas of doubt and question. But an explanation existed which satisfied everybody and seemed to exhaust all dispute. This explanation was: Hitler. He planned the second World war. His will alone caused it. This explanation obviously satisfied the "resisters" from Churchill to Namier. They had given it all along, were already giving it before the war broke out. They could say: "We told you so. There was no alternative to resisting Hitler from the first hour." The explanation also satisfied the "appeasers". They could claim that appeasement was a wise, and would have been a successful, policy if it had not been for the unpredictable fact that Germany was in the grip of a madman. Most of all, this explanation satisfied the Germans, except for a few unrepentant Nazis. After the first World war, the Germans tried to shift the guilt from themselves to the Allies, or to make out that no one was guilty. It was a simpler operation to shift the guilt from the Germans to Hitler. He was safely dead. Hitler may have done a great deal of harm to Germany while he was alive. But he made up for it by his final sacrifice in the Bunker. No amount of posthumous guilt could injure him. The blame for everything—the second World war, the concentration camps, the gas-chambers—could be loaded on to his uncomplaining shoulders. With Hitler guilty, every other German could claim innocence; and the Germans, previously the most strenuous opponents of war-guilt, now became its firmest advocates. Some Germans managed to give Hitler's wickedness a peculiarly effective twist. Since he was obviously a monster of wickedness, he ought to have been resolutely resisted. Hence any guilt left over after Hitler had been condemned could be passed on to the French for failing to expel him from the Rhineland in 1936 or on to Chamberlain for flinching in September 1938.

Everyone was happily agreed on the cause of the second World war. What need then of "revisionism"? A few neutrals raised a peep of doubt, particularly from Ireland. But usually participation in the cold war against Soviet Russia silenced even those who had been neutral in the war against Germany; and a similar consideration the other way round worked with Soviet historians also. A school of persistent revisionists remains in the United States—survivors of the campaigners after the first World war, who still regard their own government as more wicked than any other. Their works are not impressive from a scholarly point of view. Moreover this revisionism is mainly concerned with the war against Japan, and for a good reason. Hitler declared war on the United States, not the other way round; and it is difficult to see how Roosevelt could ever have got his country into the European war, if Hitler had not gratuitously done it for him. There is not much room for controversy even in regard to Japan. The fight has gone out of the issue. Once there was a practical question at stake: whether the United States should co-operate with Japan or with China? The question has now been answered by events, much to the disarray of American policy. It is universally agreed that Japan is America's only reliable friend in the Far East; and the war against her therefore appears as a mistake on somebody's part—though perhaps of course on the part of the Japanese.

These considerations of present-day politics help to explain why the origins of the second World war are not a subject of strong controversy. All the same, they are not enough to explain the almost universal agreement among historians. Even the most "engaged" scholar is affected by academic standards; and many scholars are not heavily engaged. If the evidence had been sufficiently conflicting, scholars would soon have been found to dispute the popular verdict, however generally accepted. This has not happened; and for two apparently contradictory reasons—there is at once too much evidence and too little. The evidence of which there is too much is that collected for the trials of war-criminals in Nuremberg. Though these documents look imposing in their endless volumes, they are dangerous material for a historian to use. They were collected, hastily and almost at random, as a basis for lawyers' briefs. This is not how historians would proceed. The lawyer aims to make a case; the historian wishes to understand a situation. The evidence which convinces lawyers often fails to satisfy us; our methods seem singularly imprecise to them. But even lawyers must now have qualms about the evidence at Nuremberg. The documents were chosen not only to demonstrate the war-guilt of the men on trial, but to conceal that of the prosecuting Powers. If any of the four Powers who set up the Nuremberg tribunal had been running the affair alone, it would have thrown the mud more widely. The Western Powers would have brought in the Nazi-Soviet Pact; the Soviet Union would have retaliated with the Munich conference and more obscure transactions. Given the four-Power tribunal, the only possible course was to assume the sole guilt of Germany in advance. The verdict preceded the tribunal; and the documents were brought in to sustain a conclusion which had already been settled. Of course the documents are genuine. But they are "loaded"; and anyone who relies on them finds it almost impossible to escape from the load with which they are charged.

If we seek instead for evidence assembled in a more detached and scholarly way, we discover how much worse off we are than our predecessors who studied the origins of the first World war. A generation or so after the first war every Great Power except Italy had made an almost complete revelation from its diplomatic records for the immediate pre-war crisis. In addition, there were vast series of published documents ranging far back with more or less intensity—Austro-Hungarian documents going back to 1908, British to 1898, German and French to 1871; the Russian publications, though more spasmodic, were also voluminous. There were some obvious gaps. We could complain about the lack of Italian documents, which is now being remedied; we could complain, as we still do, about the lack of Serbian documents. In the published collections there may have been some deliberate omissions; and no conscientious historian would be content until he has seen the archives for himself. Still, broadly speaking, it was possible to follow the diplomacy of five out of the six Great Powers in unparalleled detail and range. The evidence has not yet been fully digested. As we go over it, we find new topics to explore, new interpretations to make.

The contrast with the material available for studying the years before 1939 is lamentable indeed. Austria-Hungary had disappeared from the ranks of the European Great Powers. Of the remaining five, three had produced until recently no line or sentence of evidence from their archives. The Italians have begun to repair this omission: they have published their documents from 22 May 1939 until the outbreak of war, and they will in time outdo everyone by carrying their publication back to 1861. French and Russian policy remains totally without illumination from their archives. The French have some excuse. Most of their records for the years between 1933 and 1939 were burnt on 16 May 1940, at the alarm of a German breakthrough at Sedan. Duplicates are now being laboriously reassembled from the French posts abroad. The reasons for Soviet silence are, like everything else in Soviet policy, a matter of conjecture. Have the Soviet government something peculiarly disgraceful to hide? Do they shrink from submitting their conduct, however remote, to general scrutiny? Are there perhaps no records—the commissariat of foreign affairs having been too incompetent to make any? Or have the Soviet government learnt the lesson of many past disputes over historical topics—that the only watertight way of sustaining a case is never to submit evidence in its support? Whatever the varied reasons for this silence on the part of three Great Powers, the result is that we can turn only to German and British documents for a continuous record of diplomatic transactions between the wars. Hence, the perhaps misleading impression that international relations between the wars were an Anglo German duologue.

Even here the material is less adequate than it was for the period before 1914. The Allies captured the German archives in 1945; and originally intended to publish a complete series from 1918 to 1945. Later this was cut down on grounds of expense to the years since Hitler's accession to power in 1933. Even this plan is not complete: there is still a yawning gap between 1985 and 1987. The archives have now been restored to the German government at Bonn; and this may well lead to further delays. Moreover the Allied editors, conscientious as they were, shared the Nuremberg outlook on war-guilt at one remove. As an additional complication, the German foreign ministry, whose records these are, often claimed to be working against Hitler, not on his behalf; and we can never be sure whether a particular document represents a serious transaction or whether it was composed in order to provide evidence for the innocence of its author. The British publication will ultimately cover the entire period from the signing of the peace of Versailles until the outbreak of war in 1939. But it is a slow process. At the moment, we have virtually nothing on the nineteen-twenties, and another gap between the middle of 1934 and March 1938. The volumes are restricted to British policy in action. They do not reveal its motives, as the volumes relating to the period before the first World war tried to do. There are few minutes to show the process of debate within the foreign office, and no records of ministerial deliberations, though it is notorious that the prime minister and the cabinet counted for more, the foreign office for less, than in the earlier period.

We are also much worse off in regard to less official records. Most of those who made the first World war survived to write at length afterwards in apology or justification. In the second World war, some leaders died while the war was on; some were killed at the end, with or without trial; others were too proud, or too cautious to write. It makes a startling contrast to set down the substantial volumes produced after each World war by those who were in the decisive positions when it started. Here is the list for the first World war:

Great Britain: prime minister.
foreign secretary.
France: president.
prime minister who was also foreign minister.
Russia: foreign minister.
Italy: prime minister.
Germany: chancellor.
foreign minister.

The list for the second World war reads thus:

France: foreign minister.

The Italian foreign minister, who was shot, left diaries. The German foreign minister wrote a fragmentary defence while waiting to be hanged. There are a few scraps of correspondence by the British prime minister; a few pages of autobiography by the British foreign secretary. From the three dictators—Hitler, Mussolini, and Stalin—and from the Russian foreign minister, not a line, not a word. We have to make do with gossip from secondary figures—interpreters, foreign office clerks, journalists; men who often knew little more than the general public.

However, historians never have enough evidence to satisfy them. I doubt whether much will be gained by waiting another ten or fifteen years; and much might be lost. The few survivors of civilisation may have given up reading books by then, let alone writing them. I have therefore attempted to tell the story as it may appear to some future historian, working from the records. The result may be to demonstrate how much historians miss or misunderstand. We must go on writing history all the same. Like my imaginary successor, I have often had to confess ignorance. I have also found that the record, considered in detachment, often pushed me towards interpretations different from those

which men (including myself) gave at the time. This has not
weighed with me one way or the other. I am concerned to understand what happened, not to vindicate or to condemn. I was an
anti-appeaser from the day that Hitler came to power; and no
doubt should be again under similar circumstances. But the
point has no relevance in the writing of history. In retrospect,
though many were guilty, none was innocent. The purpose of
political activity is to provide peace and prosperity; and in this
every statesman failed, for whatever reason. This is a story
without heroes; and perhaps even without villains.

CHAPTER TWO

The Legacy of the First World War

THE second World war was, in large part, a repeat performance
of the first. There were obvious differences. Italy fought on the
opposite side, though she changed back again before the end.
The war which began in September 1939, was fought in Europe
and North Africa; it overlapped in time, though not in space,
with the Far Eastern war, which began in December 1941. The
two wars remained distinct, though the Far Eastern war created
great embarrassments for Great Britain and the United States.
Germany and Japan never linked forces; the only real overlap
was when the Japanese attack on Pearl Harbour provoked
Hitler, very mistakenly, to declare war on the United States.
Otherwise the European war and its origin can be treated as a
story in itself, the Far East providing occasional distractions
off-stage. In the second World war approximately the same
European allies fought approximately the same adversaries as in
the first. Though the tide of battle swung more violently to and
fro, the war ended in much the same way—with the defeat of
Germany. The link between the two wars went deeper. Germany
fought specifically in the second war to reverse the verdict of the
first and to destroy the settlement which followed it. Her
opponents fought, though less consciously, to defend that
settlement; and this they achieved—to their own surprise. There
was much Utopian projecting while the second war was on; but
at the end virtually every frontier in Europe and the Near East
was restored unchanged, with the exception—admittedly a large
exception—of Poland and the Baltic. Leaving out this area of
north-eastern Europe, the only serious change on the map
between the English Channel and the Indian Ocean was the
transference of Istria from Italy to Yugoslavia. The first war
destroyed old Empires and brought new states into existence.
The second war created no new states and destroyed only

Esthonia, Latvia, and Lithuania. If one asks the rather crude question, "what was the war about?", the answer for the first is: "to decide how Europe should be remade", but for the second merely: "to decide whether this remade Europe should continue". The first war explains the second and, in fact, caused it, in so far as one event causes another.

Though the outcome of the first World war was the remaking of Europe, this was far from being its original cause or even its conscious purpose. The war had certain immediate causes on which men are now more or less agreed. The assassination of the Archduke Franz Ferdinand provoked Austria-Hungary to declare war on Serbia; the Russian mobilisation in support of Serbia provoked Germany to declare war on Russia and on France, Russia's ally; the German refusal to respect the neutrality of Belgium provoked Great Britain to declare war on Germany. Behind these lay deeper causes about which historians still differ. Some point to the conflict between Teuton and Slav in Eastern Europe; others call it "the war of the Turkish succession". Some blame Imperialist rivalry outside Europe; others the breakdown of the Balance of Power on the European continent. More precise topics of dispute have been stressed: the German challenge to British naval supremacy; the French desire to recover Alsace-Lorraine; Russia's ambition to control Constantinople and the Straits. This very opulence of explanations suggests that none alone is the right one. The first war was fought for all these reasons—and for none of them. At any rate, this is what all the contesting Powers discovered once they were in. Whatever plans, projects, or ambitions they might have had before the war, the Powers fought simply for victory, to decide Humpty Dumpty's question: "who's to be master?" The combatants sought to "impose their will on the enemy"—in the military phrase of the day—without any clear idea what that will would be. Both sides found it difficult to define their war aims. When the Germans put forward peace terms, as they did in 1917 to Russia and, less specifically, to the Western Powers, their only concern was to improve their strategical position for the next war; though in reality a second war would not be necessary if the Germans won the first. The Allies had, in some ways, an easier time of it: they could simply demand that the Germans should surrender the fruits of their early victories. Beyond this the Allies gradually formulated a series of idealistic war-aims, with American assistance or under American prompting. These certainly did not represent the objects with which the Allies had started the war; they did not even represent the objects for which, for the most part, they were now fighting it. The idealistic programme sprang rather from the conviction that a war, fought on such a scale and with such sacrifices, ought to have a great, ennobling outcome. The ideals were a by-product, a gloss on the basic struggle, though they were not without influence on later events. Essentially, victory remained the war-aim. Victory would provide the subsequent policy. Failing this, victory would, at any rate, provide the result. And so it did. The second World war grew out of the victories in the first, and out of the way in which these victories were used.

There were two decisive victories in the first World war, although at the time one was obscured by the other. In November 1918 Germany was decisively defeated by the Western Powers on the Western front; but before that Germany had decisively defeated Russia in the East, and this had a profound effect on the pattern of the inter-war years. Before 1914 there had been a Balance, in which the Franco-Russian alliance was set off against the Central Powers. Though Great Britain was loosely associated with France and Russia in the Triple Entente, few supposed that her weight was essential to turn the scale. The war, when it started, was a continental war, fought on two fronts: each continental Power put into the field millions of men, the British a mere hundred thousand. For the French in particular, Russian co-operation seemed the vital necessity, and British support an agreeable extra. All this changed as the war proceeded. The British also built up a mass army and put their millions on the Western front. These were seconded by the prospect of more millions when the United States entered the war in 1917. This strengthening of the Western front came too late to save Russia. The two revolutions of 1917, combined with military catastrophe, drove her out of the war. In March 1918 the new Bolshevik rulers made a peace of surrender at Brest-Litovsk. Subsequent defeat in the West compelled Germany to abandon the gains which she then made. The larger result could not be undone. Russia fell out of Europe and ceased to exist, for the time being, as a Great Power. The constellation of Europe was profoundly changed—and to Germany's advantage. Where there had formerly been a Great Power on her Eastern frontier, there was now a No Man's land of small states and beyond it an obscurity of ignorance. No one could tell, for long years after 1918, whether Russia had any power and, if so, what use she would make of it.

At the close of 1918 this did not seem much to matter. The significant thing then was that Germany had been defeated without Russia's assistance, and defeated predominantly—if not exclusively—on the Western front. Victory in this narrow, congested area determined the fate of all Europe, if not of all the world. This unexpected outcome gave Europe a different character from what it had before 1914. Then the Great Powers were France, Germany, Italy, Austria-Hungary, and Russia, with Great Britain only half-involved. The centre of Europe was Berlin. Now the Great Powers were France, Germany, and Great Britain—Italy included by courtesy, and the United States occupying the former British position on the circumference. The centre of this new Europe lay on the Rhine or, one might even say, at Geneva. Russia had ceased to count as a Great Power; the Habsburg Monarchy had ceased to exist. "Europe" as a political conception moved bodily westwards. In 1918, and for many years afterwards—indeed until the spring of 1939—men assumed that the shaping of the world lay in the hands of those who had formerly been "the Western Powers".

Though both Russia and Germany were defeated in 1918, the results of the two defeats were very different. Russia disappeared from view—her revolutionary government, her very existence, ignored by the victorious Powers. Germany however remained united, acknowledged by the victors. The decision which ultimately led to the second World war was taken, from the highest and most sensible motives, a few days before the first war ended. This was the decision to grant an armistice to the German government. The decision was taken primarily on military grounds. The German army had been beaten in the field. It was in retreat. But it had not been routed or destroyed. The British and French armies, although victorious, were also near exhaustion. It was difficult to gauge from outside the extent of Germany's collapse. Only Pershing, the American commander-in-chief, had no fears of a fresh campaign. His forces were fresh, almost unblooded. He would have liked to push on to Berlin. It was an additional attraction for him that by 1919 the Americans would be carrying the brunt of the war and could then dictate to the Allies almost as much as to the Germans, in a way that they could not do in 1918. For the European Powers, however, this was a reason for ending the war quickly if it were at all possible to do so. The Americans had no concrete war aims, no precise territorial demands. This, too, made them, paradoxically, less eager for an armistice. They wanted only the "unconditional surrender" of Germany, and were ready to go on until this was achieved. The Allies also wanted the defeat of Germany; but they had urgent practical desires as well. Both Great Britain and France wanted the liberation of Belgium; the French wanted the liberation of north-eastern France; the British wanted the elimination of the German fleet. All these could be secured by an armistice. How then could the two governments justify further bloodshed to their war-weary peoples? Even apart from this, an armistice, as sought by the German government, would satisfy the more general aims of the Allies. They had always insisted that they did not desire the destruction of Germany; they were fighting to prove to the Germans that aggressive war could not succeed. This proof would now be given. It was obvious to the Allies and to the German military leaders that Germany had been defeated; only later did it appear that this was less obvious to the German people. In November 1918 it seemed rather that the German people, too, had made their contribution to ending the war. The Allies had generally claimed, though not with unbroken unanimity, that they were fighting the German emperor and his military advisers, not the German people. Now Germany had become a constitutional monarchy, and became a republic before the armistice was signed. The German government was democratic; it acknowledged defeat; it was ready to surrender all Germany's conquests; and it accepted, as basis for a future peace, the idealistic principles laid down by President Wilson in the Fourteen Points—principles which the Allies also accepted, however grudgingly, with two reservations. Thus everything argued in favour of an armistice; and little against it.

The armistice was more than a cessation of fighting. Its terms were carefully framed to ensure that Germany could not renew the war. The Germans had to surrender large stocks of war-material; to withdraw their forces behind the Rhine; and to hand over their fleet for internment. The Allies occupied the left bank of the Rhine and the bridgeheads beyond it. These terms succeeded in their purpose: in June 1919, when the Germans were debating whether to sign the peace treaty, their High Command had to confess, however reluctantly, that renewal of the war was impossible. But the armistice had another side. It tied the Germans in the immediate present; it tied the Allies for the future. They were anxious to ensure that the German nation acknowledged defeat; and therefore the armistice was concluded with representatives of the German government, not with a military delegation. The Germans duly acknowledged defeat; in return—and almost without realising it—the Allies acknowledged the German government. Enterprising Frenchmen might try later to smuggle in "separatism" by the backdoor; highflying historians might lament that the work of Bismarck had not been undone. It was in vain. The armistice settled the question of German unity so far as the first World war was concerned. The Habsburg Monarchy and the Ottoman Empire vanished. The German Reich remained in existence. More than this, the Allies not only recognised the German Reich; its continued existence now became essential to them if the armistice were to be maintained. The Allies were transformed, without conscious intent, into allies of the Reich against anything which threatened to destroy it—against popular discontent, against separatism, against Bolshevism.

This was carried further by the peace treaty, again without deliberation. The treaty contained many harsh provisions—or so it appeared to most Germans. The German consent to it was given grudgingly and unwillingly, after long debate whether it would not be better to refuse to sign. Consent was given because of the weakness of the German army, the exhaustion of the German people, the pressure of the Allied blockade, and not from any conviction that the terms were just or even tolerable. Nevertheless, the German government accepted the treaty; and, by doing so, acquired a valuable asset. The treaty was designed to provide security against a new German aggression, yet it could work only with the co-operation of the German government. Germany was to be disarmed; but the German government would arrange this—the Allies only provided a Control commission to see that the disarmament had been carried out. Germany *control?*

pay reparations; again, the German government would the money and pay it over—the Allies merely received it. Even the military occupation of the Rhineland depended on German co-operation. The civil administration remained in German hands; and a German refusal to co-operate would produce a state of confusion for which the peace treaty made no provision. In the immediate situation of 1919 the peace treaty seemed crushing and vindictive; a *Diktat* or a slave-treaty as the Germans called it. In a longer perspective, the most important thing in the treaty is that it was concluded with a united Germany. Germany had only to secure a modification of the treaty, or to shake it off altogether; and she would emerge as strong, or almost as strong, as she had been in 1914.

This was the decisive, fateful, outcome of the armistice and the peace treaty. The first World war left "the German problem" unsolved, indeed made it ultimately more acute. This problem was not German aggressiveness or militarism, or the wickedness of her rulers. These, even if they existed, merely aggravated the problem; or perhaps actually made it less menacing by provoking moral resistance in other countries. The essential problem was political, not moral. However democratic and pacific Germany might become, she remained by far the greatest Power on the continent of Europe; with the disappearance of Russia, more so than before. She was greatest in population—65 million against 40 million in France, the only other substantial Power. Her preponderance was greater still in the economic resources of coal and steel which in modern times together made up power. At the moment in 1919, Germany was down-and-out. The immediate problem was German weakness; but given a few years of "normal" life, it would again become the problem of German strength. More than this, the old balance of power, which formerly did something to restrain Germany, had broken down. Russia had withdrawn; Austria-Hungary had vanished. Only France and Italy remained, both inferior in man-power and still more in economic resources, both exhausted by the war. If events followed their course in the old "free" way, nothing could prevent the Germans from overshadowing Europe, even if they did not plan to do so.

Men by no means ignored "the German problem" in 1919. A few, it is true, denied its existence. These were the men—a tiny

minority in every country—who had opposed the war as
unnecessary, men who had always regarded the German danger
as imaginary. Even some of those who had supported the war
and conducted it with vigour were now inclined to think that
Germany was weakened for a long time. A British statesman
might be forgiven for supposing that his troubles were over,
when the German navy sank beneath the waves. Germany was
threatened with revolution, racked by social discontent; and it
was generally held, except by revolutionaries, that such experiences destroyed a country's strength. Moreover men, reared in
the stable economic world of the later nineteenth century,
assumed that a country could not flourish without a balanced
budget and a gold currency. On such a test Germany had a long
way to go; and it seemed more important, for everyone's sake, to
raise her up than to hold her down. Even the most alarmist
Frenchmen did not claim that they were threatened with a new
German invasion there and then. The danger lay in a hypothetical future; and who could tell what the future would hold?
Every great war had been followed by the murmur that it was
but a truce and that the defeated Power would strike again. It
rarely did so, or with half-hearted effect. France, for instance,
waited over forty years before acting against the settlement of
1815; and then with no terrible result. Men who thought like this
guessed wrong; but they had history on their side. Germany's
recovery, though delayed, was unprecedented in its speed and
strength.

There was an alternative way of denying the German problem.
German power could be admitted; but it could be added that this
did not matter. Germany would again grow strong, would again
rank among the Great Powers. But the Germans had learnt not
to promote their aims by war. If they came to dominate the lesser
states of Europe by economic power and political prestige, this—
far from being dangerous—was to be welcomed. The Great War
had produced independent national states throughout Europe;
strangely enough, this was now deplored by many idealists who
had once been champions of nationalism. The national states
were regarded as reactionary, militaristic, economically backward.
The sooner Germany pulled them together, the better for
everyone concerned. This view was early propounded by the
enlightened Cambridge economist J. M. Keynes; and Lloyd

George himself was not altogether hostile to it. The important
thing was not to prevent German recovery, but to ensure that it
would take a peaceful form. Precautions should be taken against
German grievances, not against German aggression.

In 1919 this view still lay beneath the surface. The peace
treaty was in large part shaped by the desire to provide security
against Germany. This was least true of the territorial provisions.
These were determined by principles of natural justice, as then
interpreted. Germany only lost land to which she was not
entitled on national grounds. Even the Germans did not complain
about the loss of Alsace and Lorraine or north Sleswig—or at
least did not complain openly. They complained about the loss of
land to Poland; but this loss followed inevitably once the
existence of Poland was recognised, and, though Poland was
treated generously, this sprang from an exaggeration of her
national claims, not from considerations of strategy. On one
point Lloyd George carried the day in favour of Germany against
his own Allies. The French and the Americans proposed that
Danzig, a city inhabited by Germans though economically
essential to Poland, should be incorporated in Poland. Lloyd
George insisted that it become a Free City under a High Commissioner appointed by the League of Nations. In this odd way
the German grievance which ostensibly produced the second
World war was actually set up for Germany's benefit. One
territorial provision of a negative nature went against the
national principle for reasons of security. German-speaking
Austria, the rump of the Habsburg monarchy, was forbidden to
unite with Germany without the permission of the League of
Nations. This was a grievance for most Austrians, including the
German corporal Hitler, who was at this time still an Austrian
citizen. It was not a grievance for most Germans of the Reich.
They had grown up in Bismarckian Germany, and regarded
Austria as a foreign country. They had no wish now to add
her troubles to their own. This was still more the case with
the German-speaking peoples elsewhere—in Czechoslovakia,
Hungary, and Rumania. They might be aggrieved at becoming
citizens of alien national states. The Germans of the Reich knew
little about them, and cared less.

One other territorial provision was strictly of a strategical
nature in origin. This was the occupation of the Rhineland by

Allied forces. The British and Americans proposed it as a temporary measure of security, and laid down that it should last only for fifteen years. The French wanted it to be permanent; and, since they failed to get this by the peace treaty, hoped to achieve the same result by tying evacuation to a satisfactory payment of reparations by the Germans. Reparations became the dominant problem of the next few years; and the more intractable from being two problems—soon indeed three. Ostensibly, reparations sprang from the sensible demand that the Germans should pay for the damage they had caused. The French, however, retarded any settlement in the hope of remaining on the Rhine. War debts between the Allies added a further cause of confusion. When the British were called upon to repay their debt to the United States, they declared in 1922 that they would claim from their Allies only enough to meet the American obligation. The Allies in their turn proposed to pay their debt to Great Britain with what they received from Germany as reparations. The final decision had thus passed, unperceived, to the Germans. They had signed the treaty; they had admitted an obligation; they alone could discharge it. They could agree to pay reparations, and in this way a peaceful world would be achieved; the Rhineland would be evacuated, the question of war-debts would lose its sting. Alternatively, they could refuse to pay, or plead their inability to do so. Then the Allies were presented with the question: what security did they possess other than the signature of the German government?

The same question was raised by German disarmament. This aimed at security and nothing else, despite the rider that it was instituted to make possible the disarmament of others. German disarmament worked if the Germans chose to make it work. And if not? Once more the Allies were faced with the problem of enforcement. The Germans had this measureless advantage that they could undermine the system of security against them merely by doing nothing; by not paying reparations and by not disarming. They could behave as an independent country normally behaves. The Allies had to use conscious effort, "artificial" expedients, if the system of security were to be maintained. This ran against the common sense of mankind. The war had been fought to settle things. What was the good of it if now there had to be new alliances, more armaments, greater international complexities than before the war started? The question had no easy answer; failure to answer it cleared the way for the second World war.

The peace of Versailles lacked moral validity from the start. It had to be enforced; it did not, as it were, enforce itself. This was obviously true in regard to the Germans. No German accepted the treaty as a fair settlement between equals "without victors or vanquished". All Germans meant to shake off at any rate some part of the peace treaty as soon as it was convenient to do so. They differed as to timing—some wanting to repudiate at once, others (perhaps the majority) wishing to leave this to a future generation. But the German signature in itself carried no weight or obligation. There was little respect for the treaty in other countries. Men in 1919 were constantly aspiring to do better than the peacemakers at Vienna a century before; and the gravest charge against the Congress of Vienna was its attempt to rivet a "system" on the future. The great liberal victories of the nineteenth century had been won against this "treaty system"; how could liberally-minded men defend a new treaty system, a new rigidity? Some liberals now advocated a "system", but one very different from the security of the peace treaty. Having previously advocated national independence for all, they swung round to belief in an overriding international order, the order of the League of Nations. There was no room in this order for discrimination between former enemies and former Allies; all were to join in a system for ensuring and enforcing peace. President Wilson himself, who contributed as much as any man to the drafting of the peace treaty, acquiesced in the clauses directed against Germany solely from the belief that the League of Nations would get rid of them—or make them unnecessary—once it was established.

Enforcing the peace treaty ran against practical difficulties quite apart from these moral objections. The Allies could threaten; but each threat was less effective and less weighted than the one before. It had been easier to threaten to continue the war in November 1918 than to threaten its renewal in June 1919. It was easier to threaten renewal in June 1919 than in June 1920; easier then than in 1923; and finally virtually impossible to threaten renewal at all. Men became increasingly reluctant to leave their homes in order to fight a war which they were told they had already won; taxpayers were increasingly reluctant to pay for a new war when they were already groaning under the cost of the last one. Besides, every threat broke on the question: if it had not been worth while continuing the war to secure "unconditional surrender", how could it make sense to renew it for some lesser object? "Positive pledges" could be taken; the Ruhr or other industrial regions of Germany occupied. But what would be achieved? Only a new signature by the German government, which could be honoured or dishonoured as before. Sooner or later, the occupying forces would have to come away. Then the former situation would be restored: the decision would rest in German hands.

There were other measures of coercion than the renewal of the war and occupation of German territory. These measures were economic—some form of the blockade which was believed to have contributed decisively to Germany's defeat. The blockade helped to push the German government into accepting the peace treaty in June 1919. Once removed, it could not be restored in its wartime rigour, if only for fear of its being too effective. For if Germany were reduced to economic chaos and her government collapsed, who then would operate the terms of the treaty? The negotiations between Germany and the Allies became a competition in blackmail, sensational episodes in a gangster film. The Allies, or some of them, threatened to choke Germany to death; the Germans threatened to die. Neither side dared carry its threat to extremity. Increasingly, threats dwindled; and inducements took their place. The Allies offered to restore Germany to her rightful place in the world if their demands were fulfilled; the Germans answered that there would not be a peaceful world until these demands were reduced. It was an almost universal belief, except in Bolshevik circles, that the only secure future for mankind lay in a return to the liberal economic system of a free world-market which had been abandoned—temporarily, it was supposed—during the war. The Allies had a valuable bargaining weapon in offering to readmit Germany to this world-market. But the Germans had it too, for a stable world could not be restored without them. The Allies were thus led, by their own policy, into treating Germany as an equal; and with this they were back at the old, intractable problem. If Germany were put on an equal footing with others, she would be the strongest

Power in Europe; if special precautions were taken against her, she would not receive equal treatment.

What the Allies really wanted was a treaty system directed against Germany which the Germans would voluntarily accept. It is strange that anyone ever thought this possible; but this was a moment of history when abstractions pulled hard in international relations. The old monarchies had valued treaties in so far as these conferred rights; they had never troubled much about treaties which involved obligations. The new attitude corresponded to the "sanctity of contract" which is the fundamental element in bourgeois civilisation. Kings and aristocrats do not pay their debts, and rarely keep their word. The capitalist system would collapse unless its practitioners honoured, without question, their most casual nod; and the Germans were now expected to observe the same ethic. There were more practical reasons for the reliance on treaties; the most practical being the lack of anything else. Here lay the great contrast between the period after the first World war and previous epochs of a similar nature. The problem of one great Power in Europe being markedly stronger than the rest was by no means new. On the contrary, it had occurred again and again during the past four hundred years. Men had not relied on treaty provisions or on promises by the stronger not to use his strength. The weaker, more pacific Powers, had gravitated together, almost unconsciously. They had formed alliances and associations which had defeated or deterred the aggressor. So it had been against Spain in the sixteenth century; against Bourbon France in the seventeenth century; and against Napoleon in the nineteenth. So it had been, for that matter, in the first World war.

This old, tried system failed to work after 1919. The great coalition dissolved. There was a reason of high principle for this. Though the victors had acted according to the doctrine of the Balance of Power, they were ashamed to have done so. Many men believed that the Balance of Power had caused the war, and that adherence to it would cause another. On a more practical level, the Balance of Power seemed unnecessary. The Allies had had a great fright; but they had also achieved a great victory. They slipped easily into the assumption that it would be final. Those who have won one war find it difficult to conceive that they can lose the next. Each of the victorious Powers felt free to pursue its own policy, to follow its own inclinations; and these did not happen to coincide. There was no deliberate rejection of the wartime partnership. Events pulled the Allies apart; and none of them strove hard enough to avert the process.

The united front among the Allies did not long survive the peace conference, nor indeed continue without challenge during the conference itself. The French pressed for security; the Americans and, to some extent, the British were inclined to think that they had done their work. The victors managed to agree on a peace treaty, but President Wilson failed to secure its confirmation by the American Senate. Though this was a blow against the new order, it was not such a decisive blow as was later made out. America's relations with Europe were determined more by geography than by policy. Whatever the treaty arrangements, the United States were far away from Europe across the Atlantic Ocean. American troops would have been withdrawn from Europe even if the Senate had endorsed the treaty of Versailles. As it was, some remained on the Rhine. It would no doubt have increased the prestige of the League of Nations if the United States had been a member; but British policy at Geneva suggests that membership of a second Anglo-Saxon Power would not necessarily have transformed the League into the effective instrument of security which the French desired. Much was made both in 1919 and later of the American failure to implement the treaty of guarantee with which Wilson and Lloyd George persuaded Clemenceau to renounce annexation of the Rhineland. This abortive treaty, too, offered only a paper security. No American troops were to remain in France, nor British troops either; and, with both British and American forces reduced to the peacetime level, there would have been no troops to send in case of danger. Briand pointed this out in 1922 when Lloyd George revived the proposal, though without American participation. The Germans, he said, will have plenty of time to reach Paris and Bordeaux before British troops arrive to stop them; and this is exactly what happened, despite a British alliance, in 1940. The Anglo-American guarantee, even if had been implemented, was no more than a promise to liberate France if she were conquered by the Germans—a promise fulfilled in 1944 even without a treaty. The United States were debarred both by geography and by political outlook from belonging to a European system of security; the most that could be expected from them was that they would intervene belatedly if this system of security failed.

The American withdrawal was not absolute. Though the United States failed to confirm the treaty of Versailles, Americans wanted a peaceful Europe and a stable economic order. American diplomacy was ceaselessly active in European questions. The two schemes for the payment of German reparations, the Dawes plan and the Young plan, were both devised under American guidance; each bore the name of an American chairman. American loans restored German economy—for good or ill; American insistence on the payment of allied war debts complicated the problem of reparations. American representatives attended the prolonged discussions on disarmament. Americans indeed constituted the "world opinion" for whose benefit these discussions, economic and political, were largely conducted; and American historians made the campaign against Germany's "war guilt" more effective than if it had been left solely in German hands. The United States could not dissociate themselves from Europe merely by rejecting the treaty of Versailles. America's participation in the war had largely determined the defeat of Germany; equally American policy after the war largely determined her recovery. Americans were misled by their own strength. They started from the correct assumption that Germany, after defeat, was no danger to themselves; they went on from this to the mistaken assumption that she could not be a danger to the countries of Europe.

American policy would have mattered less if the European Great Powers had been of one mind. France, Italy, and Great Britain were a formidable coalition, despite the depreciatory remarks made about them later. They had held their own against Germany, though they had not managed to defeat her. Italy was the weakest of the three, both in economic resources and political coherence. She was also estranged from her allies by resentment that she had not received her due share of war-prizes. She missed her cut of the Ottoman empire; and was fobbed off, after much complaint, with worthless colonial land. On the other hand, she enjoyed an illusory security, a detachment from Europe which almost turned her into an island. Her enemy had been Austria-Hungary, not Germany; and when the Habsburg

Monarchy fell to pieces, she acquired a screen of small neighbours. The "German problem" seemed remote from her. Italian statesmen even welcomed the embarrassment which this problem caused to France. Sometimes they exploited the embarrassment; sometimes they posed as impartial arbiters between France and Germany. Italy had in any case little to contribute to a system of security; and that little she did not contribute.

Italian abstention too would have mattered less if Great Britain and France had seen eye to eye. Here was the final and decisive crumbling of the wartime coalition. The two countries remained closely associated. The occasional talk in England that France was aiming at a new Napoleonic domination of Europe, or had even achieved it, was no more than a temporary aberration. Broadly speaking, the two continued to act together as "the Western democracies", trustees for Europe and joint-victors in the Great War. The association was, if anything, too close; for each managed to retard the policy of the other. The British had denounced Germany fiercely enough while the war was on; they had insisted without illusion that this was a struggle for existence. It seemed to them now that the struggle had been won. The German navy had vanished; the German colonial challenge was over; and, in economic matters, the British were more concerned to restore Germany than to hold her down. The heads of the fighting services were early instructed that they need not anticipate a major war for at least ten years; and this instruction was annually renewed until 1932. Much was made later of British "disarmament by example". If by this be meant disarmament beyond the limit of national safety as then envisaged, there was none. There was British disarmament from economy; there was disarmament from negligence and mistaken judgement; there was no disarmament from principle. On the contrary, the British assumed that they were more secure than they had been. The British dissolved their mass army after the Great War in the belief that they would never have to fight another; and when later they failed to build up armoured forces, this was on the advice of the most respected military authorities who held that tanks were of less use than horses. British naval predominance was greater than ever before in European waters, certainly much greater than before 1914. All other navies had vanished except the French; and it was inconceivable that

Great Britain and France would ever go to war despite occasional hotheaded talk.

If "security" meant simply freedom from invasion, then the British Isles seemed more secure than at any time in their history. British sentiment swung back towards isolation as it had often done after a great war. It doubted whether the war had been worth while; became resentful of former allies, and friendly towards the former enemy. British statesmen did not go as far as this. They still wished to co-operate with France; and they recognised that a peaceful, stable Europe was itself a British interest. But this did not make them ready to underwrite every French claim against Germany. They tended to regard talk of the German danger as historical romanticism, which indeed it was in the immediate present. The French obsession with security seemed not so much exaggerated as mistaken; and even those British statesmen who sought to lull this obsession with a form of words did not suppose that they would ever have to translate their words into action. More than this, British promises of support to France were not offered as a supplement to the other measures of security; they were designed as an alternative, with the intention that the French would let the other measures go. Englishmen reflected deeply on their mistakes of policy in the pre-war years. Some, of course, held that Great Britain ought not to have become involved in continental affairs at all. But many of those who held that the war had to be fought when it came, also held that it could have been avoided if Great Britain had made a formal defensive alliance with France. This would have warned the Germans that Great Britain would fight; it would also have warned the French, and still more the Russians, that she would not fight in an "eastern quarrel". Now, after the war, alliance with France expressed a modified form of isolation. Great Britain, by pledging herself to defend France's frontier, would also show that she had no commitment beyond it.

Hence British policy, even at its most co-operative, did not work against German recovery; it only offered security of a sort against the consequences of that recovery. The price of British support was that France should renounce all interest east of the Rhine, and hence all standing as a European Great Power. The same promptings had come from London before 1914; but then the French had two irons in the fire. The association with Great

Britain had offered some limited help if France were actually invaded, and ultimately provided much greater help than had been expected, after the invasion took place. But this association was secondary in French politics right up to the outbreak of war. What gave France independence as a Great Power was the alliance with Russia, which automatically halved German strength. Even in 1914 the French military leaders rightly attached much greater importance to the Russian forces rolling into East Prussia than to the tiny British Expeditionary Force on the French left flank. The Russian alliance continued to give France independence and an illusory greatness until 1917. Then Russia was defeated and fell out of the war. France's European policy collapsed. The war was won solely in the west—the east being liberated as a consequence of this, not in association with it; and France found herself the junior partner of the Western democracies.

Some French statesmen welcomed this development. Clemenceau, in particular, had always disliked the alliance with Russia, as alien to French democracy and as involving her in remote Balkan quarrels. He had tried to prevent the alliance being made; he was delighted when it collapsed; and his fierce hostility to Bolshevism sprang not merely from resentment against Russia's desertion—it was also an insurance that the alliance would not be renewed. Clemenceau knew England and the United States better than most Frenchmen; and he believed passionately that the future both of France and of humanity lay with the Western Powers. He told the Chamber on 29 December 1918: "For this Entente, I shall make every sacrifice." And so he did. It was only because Clemenceau was of all French statesmen the most favourable to Great Britain and the United States that the treaty of Versailles was agreed at all. Other French leaders were less single-minded. Only a few ranters on the extreme Right kept up the old hatred of England; virtually none disliked America. But many distrusted the constancy of the two Anglo-Saxon Powers; some, intoxicated by victory, dreamt of restoring France to the position of European predominance which she had enjoyed under Louis XIV or even before the time of Bismarck; the more modest recognised that Eastern allies would redress Germany's superiority in manpower and restore France's former position as a Great Power.

That Eastern ally could not be Russia. The ostensible reason for this was Bolshevism. The Western Powers had entangled themselves in wars of intervention against Bolshevik rule even while the war against Germany was still on; then they encouraged the *cordon sanitaire* of states on Russia's western border; finally they resigned themselves to a policy of non-recognition, morally sustained even when the door was grudgingly opened to some Russian trade. The Soviet leaders, on their side, ostentatiously broke with the corrupt world of capitalism when they seized power in November 1917, and staked all on international revolution. The Third International continued to be more important in their eyes than the Soviet Foreign Ministry even when this revolution failed to come off. In theory the relations between Soviet Russia and the European Powers remained those of suspended war. Some historians even regard this concealed war as the key to the inter-war period. Soviet historians claim that Great Britain and France wished to win over Germany for a European crusade—a new war of intervention against Soviet Russia; and some western historians allege that the Soviet leaders constantly stirred up trouble in international affairs in the hope of fomenting revolution. This is what each side ought to have done if it had taken its principles and beliefs seriously. Neither did so. The Bolsheviks implicitly confessed their sense of security and their indifference to the rest of the world when they went over to "Socialism in a single country". Western statesmen never took the Bolshevik danger seriously enough to plan new wars of intervention against it. Communism continued to haunt Europe as a spectre—a name men gave to their own fears and blunders. But the crusade against Communism was even more imaginary than the spectre of Communism.

There were other, cruder reasons why no attempt was made to draw Russia back into European affairs. Defeat during the war destroyed her reputation as a Great Power; revolution after it was supposed, not altogether wrongly, to have condemned her to weakness for a generation. After all, Germany was being pulled down by a political revolution of the mildest character; how much more devastating must the results be in Russia of a basic social upheaval. As well, many Western statesmen were somewhat relieved at Russia's disappearance. Though she had been a useful counterweight against Germany, she had also been a difficult and exacting ally. Throughout the twenty years of the Franco-Russian alliance, the French had held out against Russian demands on Constantinople. They had yielded, most reluctantly, in 1915, and were delighted to be able to repudiate their wartime promise. The British cared less about Constantinople, but they, too, had had their troubles with Russia in the Near and Middle East. The post-war Communist propaganda in India, for instance, was nothing like so menacing as the old Russian activity in Persia. Quite apart from such specific questions, international affairs always run more easily without Russian participation, as everyone knows nowadays. The most practical reason for Russia's exclusion was, however, a simple matter of geography. The *cordon sanitaire* did its work. This had been foreseen by Balfour, and apparently by Balfour alone. He told the Imperial War Cabinet on 21 March 1917: "If you make an absolutely independent Poland, . . . you cut off Russia altogether from the West. Russia ceases to be a factor in Western politics, or almost ceases." And so it proved. Russia could not play a part in European affairs even if she would. But why should she? The *cordon sanitaire* worked also the other way round, though this was less perceived for some years. It excluded Russia from Europe; but it also excluded Europe from Russia. In a perverse way, the barrier designed against Russia became Russia's protection.

The new national states which made up the *cordon sanitaire* had another, more important function in French eyes. They were providential substitutes for the vanished Russian ally: less erratic and independent, more reliable and respectable. Clemenceau told the Council of Four: "Our firmest guarantee against German aggression is that behind Germany, in an excellent strategic position, stand Czechoslovakia and Poland." If even Clemenceau believed this, it is not surprising that other Frenchmen made alliance with the Succession states the dominant theme of French foreign policy. Few of them realised its paradoxical character. The new states were satellites and clients: inspired by national enthusiasm, but carried to independence by Allied victory and helped thereafter by French money and French military advisers. The French treaties of alliance with them made sense as treaties of protection, like those which Great Britain made with the new states in the Middle East. Frenchmen

saw things the other way round. They regarded their Eastern
alliances as assets, not liabilities; bringing protection to France,
not commitment. They recognised that the new states needed
French money. So had Russia, and a great deal more money at
that. The need would be temporary. In every other way, the new
states were a great improvement. Unlike Russia, they would not
be distracted by irrelevant ambitions in Persia or the Far East.
Unlike Russia, they could never be on close terms with Germany.
Democratic and national on the French model, they would be
more stable in peacetime and steadier in war. They would never
question their historic role: to distract and divide German forces
for France's benefit.

This was a surprising exaggeration of Czech and Polish
strength. The French were misled by the experience of the recent
war. Despite their somewhat belated use of tanks, they continued
to regard infantry as, in Pétain's phrase, "queen of the battle-
field"; and they counted rifle strength as the decisive factor.
France, with a population of 40 million, was obviously inferior to
Germany, with 65 millions. But add the 30 millions in Poland,
and France became equal or, with the 12 million Czechoslovaks,
superior. Moreover, men see the past when they peer into the
future; and the French found it impossible to imagine a future
war which did not begin with a German attack on themselves.
Therefore they always asked—how can our Eastern allies help
us; and never—how can we help them? Their own military
preparations after 1919 were increasingly defensive. The army
was equipped for trench warfare; the frontier was lined with
fortifications. French diplomacy and French strategy ran in clear
contradiction. There was contradiction even within the diplomatic system itself. The Anglo-French entente and the Eastern
alliances did not supplement each other; they cancelled out.
France could act offensively, to aid Poland or Czechoslovakia,
only with British support; but this support would be given only
if she acted defensively, to protect herself, not distant countries
in Eastern Europe. This deadlock was not created by changed
conditions in the nineteen-thirties. It existed implicitly from the
first moment, and no one, either British or French, ever found a
way round it.

These difficulties are clear to us. They were less obvious to men
at the time. Despite the disappearance of Russia and the

withdrawal of the United States, Great Britain and France still composed the Supreme Council, laying down the law to all Europe. As well, alliances and future wars were alike dwarfed by the new institution which came out of the peace-conference: the League of Nations. It is true that there was a deep, underlying divergence between England and France as to the nature of the League. The French wanted the League to develop into a system of security directed against Germany; the British regarded it as a system of conciliation which would include Germany. The French believed that the last war had been caused by German aggression; the British came more and more to hold that it had happened by mistake. The two countries never argued this difference out to a conclusion. Instead, each pretended to compromise with the other, though with the unspoken reservation that it was not convinced. Each waited for events to prove the other wrong; and each was in time duly satisfied, though not to any good purpose. In practice, the British interpretation carried the day. For one thing, the Covenant of the League was couched in general terms. It was directed against aggression, not against Germany; and indeed it was difficult to use the League against Germany unless she were already a member with equal rights. Again, a negative policy is always stronger than a positive: abstention is easier than action. Most of all, the British view followed inevitably from the decision of November 1918: the decision to make an armistice, and then peace, with the German government. Once it had been decided not to destroy Germany, then sooner or later she must return to the comity of nations. The British and French governments were both too distracted by difficulties, domestic and foreign, to have a clear and consistent policy. But so far as there was a coherent pattern in the post-war years, it was the story of efforts to conciliate Germany and of their failure.

CHAPTER THREE

The Post-War Decade

THE history of Europe between the wars revolved round "the German problem". If this were settled, everything would be settled; if it remained unsolved, Europe would not know peace. All other problems lost their sting or were trivial in comparison. The Bolshevik peril, for example—never as acute as people thought—ended abruptly when the Red armies were thrown back from Warsaw in August 1920; from that moment there was not the slightest prospect, during the next twenty years, that Communism would triumph anywhere in Europe beyond the Russian frontiers. Again, Hungarian "revisionism" made much noise during the nineteen-twenties—more noise indeed than German revisionism from a territorial point of view. It did not raise more than a shadow even of local war, never a shadow of general upheaval. Italy, too, bickered with Yugoslavia over Adriatic questions; and later claimed to be an unsatisfied "have-not" nation. The most Italy could do was to hit the headlines, not raise an alarm. The German problem stood alone. This was new. The problem of German strength had existed before 1914, though not fully recognised; but there had been other problems—Russia's desire for Constantinople; French desire for Alsace-Lorraine; Italian irredentism; the South Slav problem within Austria-Hungary; the endless troubles in the Balkans. Now there was nothing of any moment except the position of Germany.

There was a second difference of great significance. Before 1914 the relations of the Great European Powers had often been shaped by questions outside Europe—Persia, Egypt, Morocco, tropical Africa, Turkey-in-Asia, and the Far East. Some good judges believed, though wrongly, that European questions had lost their vitality. H. N. Brailsford, an intelligent and well-informed observer, wrote early in 1914: "The dangers which forced our ancestors into European coalitions and Continental wars have gone never to return. . . . It is as certain as anything in politics can be, that the frontiers of our modern national states are finally drawn."[1] The exact opposite proved to be the case. Europe was turned upside down and then continued to harass statesmen. Not a single one of the problems outside Europe which had raised difficulties before 1914 caused a serious crisis among the European powers between the wars. No one could really suppose, for example, that Great Britain and France would go to war over Syria, as they might once have done over Egypt. The only exception was the Abyssinian affair of 1985, but this concerned European politics in the shape of the League of Nations; it was not a conflict over Africa. There was another apparent exception: the Far East. This caused grave difficulties in international affairs, but Great Britain was the only European power on whom it had practical impact.

This, too, was new. Great Britain was now the only world power in Europe. Before 1914, too, she had been a world power of the first rank. But Russia, Germany, and France also counted for much in "the age of imperialism". Now Russia was outside Europe and in alliance with the anti-European revolt of the colonial peoples. Germany had lost her colonies and had relinquished her Imperial ambitions at any rate for the time being. France, though still a colonial power, was obsessed with European difficulties and let her Empire take second place in disputes with others, including of course the British. The Far East showed how things had changed. Before 1914 there had been a balance there, quite as complicated as the balance in Europe. Japan had had to reckon with Russia, Germany, and France as well as with Great Britain; and the British could safely go sometimes with Japan, sometimes against her. The United States had an active policy in the Far East for a few years after the war, but it was short indeed. By the time of the Manchurian crisis of 1931, Great Britain faced Japan in the Far East virtually alone. It is easy to understand why the British felt distinct from the Powers of Europe and why they often wanted to withdraw from European politics.

It is also easy to understand why the German problem seemed exclusively a European affair. The United States and Japan did

[1] II. N. Brailsford, *The War of Steel and Gold* (1914), 35

not feel themselves threatened by a Power which had no fleet and, apparently, no colonial interests. Great Britain and France were acutely conscious that they must settle the German question alone. Immediately after 1919 they assumed that it would be settled fairly quickly—at any rate in the sense that the peace treaty would be fully applied. Nor were they altogether mistaken. The frontiers of Germany were all defined by 1921, when a plebiscite, somewhat artificially interpreted, divided Upper Silesia between Germany and Poland. German disarmament proceeded more slowly than laid down in the treaty and with some evasion; but it proceeded. The German army ceased to exist as a major fighting-force, and no one had to worry about actual war with Germany for many years to come. The occasional evasions were made much of at a later date; and people then talked as though the disarmament clauses of the treaty had either never been observed or were of no value. In fact they achieved their purpose so long as they remained in force. As late as 1984 Germany could not contemplate war against Poland, let alone against France. Of the other treaty-provisions, the trials of war-criminals were dropped after a few unsatisfactory attempts. This was partly a surrender to German outcry and obstruction. It sprang more from the feeling that it was absurd to proceed against lesser criminals when the chief offender, William II, was safe in Holland.

By 1921 much of the peace-treaty was being enforced. It was reasonable to assume that it would gradually lose its contentious character. Men cannot go on wrangling over a settled question year after year, however embittered they may feel at first. The French forgot Waterloo; they even tended to forget Alsace and Lorraine, despite repeated resolves not to do so. The Germans, too, might have been expected to forget, or at any rate to acquiesce, after a time. The problem of German power would remain; but it would not be aggravated by an acute determination to destroy the settlement of 1919 at the first opportunity. The reverse happened: resentment against the treaty increased with every year. For one part of the treaty remained unsettled; and the disputes over this put the rest of the treaty in constant question. The unsettled issue was the payment of reparations— a striking example of good intentions, or to be correct, good ingenuity, gone wrong. In 1919 the French wished to lay down uncompromisingly the principle that Germany must pay the full bill for war damage—an indeterminate liability that would swell in the future with every step of German economic recovery. The Americans, more sensibly, proposed to state a fixed sum. Lloyd George appreciated that, in the heated atmosphere of 1919, this sum, too, would be far beyond German capacity. He hoped that in time men (himself included) would come to their senses: the Allies would make a reasonable demand, the Germans would make a reasonable offer, and the two figures would more or less coincide. He therefore swung round behind the French, though for exactly the opposite reason: they wanted to make the bill fantastically large, he wanted to scale it down. The Americans gave way. The peace treaty merely stated the principle of reparations; their amount was to be settled at some time in the future.

Lloyd George had meant to make reconciliation with Germany easier; he made it almost impossible. For the divergence between British and French views which had been covered over in 1919 rose again to the surface as soon as they tried to fix a figure: the French still trying to push it up, the British impatiently scaling it down. Nor did the Germans show any willingness to co-operate. Far from attempting to estimate their capacity to pay, they deliberately kept their economic affairs in confusion, well knowing that, if they once got things straight, the bill for reparations would follow. In 1920 there were angry meetings between the Allies, and then conference with the Germans; more conferences in 1921; still more in 1922. In 1928 the French tried to enforce payment by occupying the Ruhr. The Germans first answered with passive resistance; then surrendered at discretion, under the catastrophe of inflation. The French, almost as exhausted as the Germans, agreed to a compromise: the Dawes plan, drafted—largely at British prompting—under an American chairman. Though this temporary settlement was resented by both French and Germans, reparations were in fact paid for the next five years. Then there was another conference—more wrangling, more accusations, more demands, and more evasions. The Young plan, again under an American chairman, emerged. It had hardly begun to operate before the great depression struck Europe. The Germans claimed that they could not go on paying. In 1981 the Hoover moratorium suspended reparations for twelve months. In 1932 a last conference at Lausanne wiped the slate clean. Agreement was at last reached; but it had taken thirteen years, years of mounting suspicion and grievance on all sides. At the end the French felt swindled; and the Germans felt robbed. Reparations had kept the passions of war alive.

Reparations would, no doubt, have been a grievance in any case. It was the uncertainty and argument over them which made the grievance chronic. In 1919 many people believed that the payment of reparations would reduce Germany to a state of Asiatic poverty. J. M. Keynes held this view, as did all Germans; and probably many Frenchmen did also, though without regretting the consequence. During the second World war an ingenious young Frenchman, Étienne Mantoux, demonstrated that the Germans could have paid reparations, without impoverishment, if they had wanted to do so; and Hitler gave a practical demonstration of this when he extracted vast sums from the Vichy government of France. The question has only an academic interest. No doubt the apprehensions of Keynes and the Germans were grotesquely exaggerated. No doubt the impoverishment of Germany was caused by war, not by reparations. No doubt the Germans could have paid reparations, if they had regarded them as an obligation of honour, honestly incurred. In actual fact, as everyone now knows, Germany was a net gainer by the financial transactions of the nineteen-twenties: she borrowed far more from private American investors (and failed to pay back) than she paid in reparations. This was of course little consolation to the German taxpayer, who was not at all the same person as the German borrower. For that matter, reparations gave little consolation to the taxpayers of allied countries, who immediately saw the proceeds transferred to the United States in repayment of war debts. Setting one thing against another, the only economic effect of reparations was to give employment to a large number of bookkeepers. But the economic facts about reparations were of little importance. Reparations counted as a symbol. They created resentment, suspicion, and international hostility. More than anything else, they cleared the way for the second World war.

Reparations fixed the French in an attitude of sullen, but rather hopeless, resistance. They had, after all, a not unjustified claim. North-east France had been devastated during the war;

and, whatever the rights and wrongs of war guilt, it was reasonable that the Germans should help to restore the damage. But the French soon cheated over reparations, as everyone else did. Some Frenchmen wanted to ruin Germany for ever. Others hoped that reparations would not be paid, so that the armies of occupation should stay in the Rhineland. French taxpayers had been told that Germany would pay for the war; and were indignant against the Germans when their own taxes went up. In the end, the French were cheated in their turn: they got virtually nothing except the moral blame for having demanded reparations at all. As the French saw it, they had made a series of concessions over reparations in order to please the Germans. Finally they had abandoned all claim to reparations. The Germans emerged more dissatisfied than ever. The French concluded from this experience that concessions in other fields— over disarmament or frontiers—would be equally futile. They also concluded, though less consciously, that the concessions would be made. The French were distinguished, in the years before the second World war, by lack of faith in their leaders and in themselves. This despairing cynicism had a long and complicated origin which has often been dissected by historians. But the record of reparations was its immediate, practical cause. Here the French had certainly lost; and their leaders had as certainly displayed a singular incapacity, or at least a singular failure, to fulfil their promises. Reparations did almost as much damage to democracy in France as in Germany itself.

Reparations had also a critical influence on the relations between France and Great Britain. In the last days of the war, the British—both politicians and public—had shared the French enthusiasm for reparations. It was a British statesman of high competence, not a Frenchman, who proposed to squeeze the German orange till the pips squeaked; and even Lloyd George had been more clamorous for reparations than he subsequently liked to imagine. Soon however the British changed round. They began to denounce the folly of reparations once they had themselves carried off the German merchant navy. Perhaps they were influenced by the writings of Keynes. Their more practical motive was to restore the economic life of Europe so as to promote the recovery of their own export industries. They listened readily to the German stories of the endless woes which would follow the payment of reparations; and, once they had condemned reparations, they soon condemned other clauses of the peace treaty. Reparations were wicked. Therefore the disarmament of Germany was wicked; the frontier with Poland was wicked; the new national states were wicked. And not only wicked: they were a justified German grievance, and the Germans would be neither content nor prosperous until they were undone. The British grew indignant at French logic, at French anxiety about German recovery, and particularly indignant at French insistence that treaties should be honoured once they had been signed. French claims to reparations were pernicious and dangerous nonsense; therefore their claim for security was pernicious and dangerous nonsense also. The British had some plausible ground for complaint. In 1931 they were forced off the gold-standard. The French, who had claimed to be ruined by the war, had a stable currency and the largest gold-reserve in Europe. It was a bad beginning for the years of danger. The disagreements over reparations in the years after the first World war made it almost impossible for the British and French to agree over security in the years before the second.

The most catastrophic effect of reparations was on the Germans themselves. Of course they would have been aggrieved in any case. They had not only lost the war. They had lost territory; they had been compelled to disarm; they had been saddled with a war-guilt which they did not feel. But these were intellectual grievances: things to grumble over in the evenings, not the cause of sufferings in everyday life. Reparations hit every German, or seemed to, at each moment of his existence. It would be useless to discuss now whether reparations in fact impoverished Germany; and it was equally useless to argue the point in 1919. No German was likely to accept the proposition which Norman Angell had advanced in *The Great Illusion* that the payment of an indemnity by the French in 1871 benefited France and injured Germany. The common sense of mankind says that a man is the poorer for paying out money; and what is true for an individual appears true for a nation. Germany was paying reparations; and was therefore the poorer for it. By an easy transition reparations became the sole cause of German poverty. The business-man in difficulties; the underpaid schoolteacher; the unemployed worker all blamed their troubles on reparations. The cry of a hungry child was a cry against reparations. Old men stumbled into the grave because of reparations. The great inflation of 1923 was attributed to reparations; so was the great depression of 1929. These views were not held merely by the German man-in-the-street. They were held just as strongly by the most distinguished financial and political experts. The campaign against "the slave-treaty" hardly needed the prompting of extremist agitators. Every touch of economic hardship stirred the Germans to shake off "the shackles of Versailles".

Once men reject a treaty, they cannot be expected to remember precisely which clause they reject. The Germans began with the more or less rational belief that they were being ruined by reparations. They soon proceeded to the less rational belief that they were being ruined by the peace treaty as a whole. Finally, retracing their steps, they concluded that they were being ruined by clauses of the treaty which had nothing to do with reparations. German disarmament, for instance, may have been humiliating; it may have exposed Germany to invasion by Poland or France. But economically it was to the good so far as it had any effect at all.[1] This is not what the ordinary German felt. He assumed that, since reparations made him poorer, disarmament did also. It was the same with the territorial clauses of the treaty. There were defects, of course, in the settlement. The eastern frontier put too many Germans in Poland—though it also put too many Poles in Germany. It could have been improved by some redrawing and by an exchange of populations—an expedient not contemplated in those civilised days. But an impartial judge, if such existed, would have found little fault with the territorial settlement once the principle of national states was accepted. The so-called Polish corridor was inhabited predominantly by Poles; and the arrangements for free railway-communication with East Prussia were adequate. Danzig would actually have been better off economically if it had been included in Poland. As to the former German colonies—also a fertile cause of grievance—they had always been an expense, not a source of profit.

All this was lost sight of, thanks to the link between reparations

---

[1] With remarkable, though not unique, ingenuity the German generals managed to make disarmament more expensive than armament had been. It cost the German taxpayer less to maintain the great army and navy of 1914 than to maintain a small army and no navy after 1919.

and the rest of the treaty. The German believed that he was ill-dressed, hungry, or out-of-work, because Danzig was a Free City; because the corridor cut off East Prussia from the Reich; or because Germany had no colonies. Even the highly intelligent banker Schacht attributed Germany's financial difficulties to the loss of her colonies—a view which he continued to hold, sincerely no doubt, even after the second World war. The Germans were not being self-centred or uniquely stupid in holding such views. This outlook was shared by enlightened liberal Englishmen such as Keynes; by nearly all the leaders of the British Labour party; and by all Americans who thought about European affairs. Yet it is difficult to see why the loss of colonies and land in Europe should have crippled Germany economically. After the second World war Germany had much greater territorial losses, yet became more prosperous than at any time in her history. There could be no clearer demonstration that the economic difficulties of Germany between the wars were due to defects in her domestic policy, not to unjust frontiers. The demonstration has been in vain; every textbook continues to attribute Germany's difficulties to the treaty of Versailles. The myth went further, and still does. First, the economic problems of Germany were blamed on the treaty. Then it was observed that these problems continued. From this it was held to follow that nothing was done to conciliate Germany or to modify the system set up in 1919. "Appeasement" was supposed to have been attempted only in 1938; and by then it was too late.

This is far from the truth. Even reparations were constantly revised, and always downwards; though no doubt the revision dragged out tiresomely long. In other ways appeasement was attempted sooner, and with success. Lloyd George made the first attempt. Emerging with difficulty from the morass of reparations, he resolved to summon a new, and more genuine, peace conference, which should be attended by everyone, by the United States, by Germany, by Soviet Russia, as well as by the Allies. A fresh start should be made on creating a better world. Lloyd George's initiative was seconded by Briand, then French premier—another political wizard, who could conjure problems out of existence. The partnership had an abrupt end. In January 1922 Briand was defeated in the French Chamber—ostensibly for having taken a lesson in golf from Lloyd George, actually because he was "weakening" over the peace treaty. Poincaré, his successor, was unmoved by a British offer to guarantee France's eastern frontier; and a French representative attended the conference, which met at Genoa in April 1922, only to insist on the payment of reparations. The Americans refused to attend.

The Russians and Germans attended, but with the not unjustified suspicion that they were to be played off one against the other. The Germans were to be invited to join in exploiting Russia; the Russians were to be urged to claim reparations from Germany. Instead the representatives of the two countries met secretly at Rapallo and agreed not to work against each other. The treaty of Rapallo wrecked the Genoa conference, and acquired great notoriety in the world. At the time, the Bolsheviks were regarded as outcasts, and it was therefore counted great wickedness in the Germans to conclude a treaty with them. Later on, when the Germans became the cause of offence, the moral obliquity of Rapallo was chalked up against the Russians.

In fact the treaty of Rapallo was a modest, negative affair. It is true that it prevented a European coalition for a new war of intervention against Russia; it is also true that it prevented any revival of the old Triple Entente. Neither of these was a practical proposition in any case; and the treaty did no more than record the fact. But there was equally little chance of active co-operation between the two signatories. Neither was in a position to challenge the peace-settlement; both asked no more than to be left alone. The Germans thereafter provided Soviet Russia with a certain amount of economic assistance, though—absurdly enough—the Americans, who did not recognise Soviet Russia at all, provided more. The Russians enabled the Germans to evade the restrictions of the treaty of Versailles (to which after all the Russians were not a party) by setting up gas schools and flying schools on Soviet territory. These were trivialities. There was no sincerity in German-Soviet friendship; and both sides knew it. The German generals and conservatives, who promoted the friendship, despised the Bolsheviks; and they in their turn were friendly with Germany only according to the Leninist maxim of taking a man by the hand, preparatory to taking him by the throat. Rapallo gave a warning that it was easy for Russia and Germany to be friendly on negative terms, whereas the Allies would have to pay a high price for the friendship of either. But it was a warning which took effect in a comparatively distant future.

The conference of Genoa was Lloyd George's last creative effort. His position as the sporadically enlightened leader of an obscurantist coalition made it impossible for him to achieve any striking result. In the autumn of 1922 he fell from power. The Conservative government under Bonar Law which succeeded him was impatiently sceptical of European affairs. The way was clear for Poincaré, then French premier, to attempt the enforcement of reparations by occupying the Ruhr. This was the one break in the record of appeasement; and it was a break of a limited kind. Whatever secret hopes some Frenchmen might have that Germany would disintegrate, the sole purpose of the occupation was to get an offer of reparations from the Germans; and it had to be ended as soon as an offer was made. The occupation had a terrible effect on the French franc. Poincaré may have thought at the outset that France could act independently. By the end of 1923 he was as convinced as Clemenceau had been that the prime necessity for France was to be on close terms with England and America. The French voter passed his own verdict on the affair in 1924 by returning a Left coalition hostile to Poincaré. The occupation of the Ruhr provided, in the long run, the strongest argument in favour of appeasement. For how did it end? In fresh negotiations with Germany. It gave a renewed, and more powerful, demonstration that the treaty of Versailles could be carried out only with the co-operation of the German government; in that case more was to be gained by conciliation than by threats. The argument was not only effective in the present; it went on being effective in the future. When Germany began to disregard the conditions of the treaty on a more massive scale, men—particularly Frenchmen—looked back to the occupation of the Ruhr, and asked: what would be gained by the use of force? Only new German promises to fulfil the promises which they are now breaking. The cost would be ruinous; the result negligible. Security could be regained only by winning the Germans over, not by threatening them.

It would be wrong to suggest that the occupation of the Ruhr was without effect on Germany. Though it taught the French the folly of coercion, it also taught the Germans the folly of resistance. The occupation ended with a surrender by Germany, not by

France. Stresemann came to power with the avowed policy of fulfilling the treaty. Of course this did not mean that he accepted the French interpretation of the treaty or that he would acquiesce in the French demands. It meant only that he would defend German interests by negotiations, not by resistance. Stresemann was as determined as the most extreme nationalist to get rid of the whole treaty lock, stock, and barrel: reparations, German disarmament, the occupation of the Rhineland, and the frontier with Poland. But he intended to do this by the persistent pressure of events, not by threats, still less by war. Where other Germans insisted that revision of the treaty was necessary for the revival of German power, Stresemann believed that the revival of German power would inevitably lead to revision of the treaty. There was a great outcry in allied countries against Stresemann after his death when the publication of his papers revealed clearly his intention to destroy the existing treaty-settlement. The outcry was grotesquely unjustified. Given a great Germany— and the Allies had themselves given it by their actions at the end of the war—it was inconceivable that any German could accept the treaty of Versailles as a permanent settlement. The only question was whether the settlement would be revised, and Germany become again the greatest Power in Europe, peacefully or by war. Stresemann wanted to do it peacefully. He thought this the safer, the more certain, and the more lasting way to German predominance. He had been a bellicose nationalist during the war; and even now was no more inclined to peace from moral principle than Bismarck had been. But, like Bismarck, he believed that peace was in Germany's interest; and this belief entitles him to rank with Bismarck as a great German, even as a great European, statesman. Maybe even as a greater. His task was certainly more difficult. For Bismarck had only to maintain an existing settlement; Stresemann had to work towards a new one. It is the measure of his success that, while he lived, Europe moved towards peace and treaty revision at the same time.

This achievement was not due to Stresemann alone. Allied statesmen also contributed their part, foremost among them Ramsay MacDonald, who came to power in 1924; and thereafter, whether in or out of office, set his mark on British foreign policy for the next fifteen years. The MacDonald policy seemed to end in catastrophic failure with the outbreak of the second World

war in 1989. His name is now despised; his very existence
ignored. Yet MacDonald should be the patron-saint of every
contemporary Western politician who favours co-operation with
Germany. More than any other British statesman, MacDonald
faced "the German problem" and attempted to solve it. Coercion
was futile, as the occupation of the Ruhr had just shown. The
alternative of bringing Russia back into Europe as a Great Power
was ruled out on both sides during the nineteen-twenties, for
good or ill. Only conciliation of Germany remained; and if
conciliation were to be practised at all, it should be practised
wholeheartedly. MacDonald did not ignore French anxieties. He
met them more generously than any other British statesman had
done or was to do. He assured Herriot in July 1924 that violation of the Treaty "would lead to the collapse of the permanent
foundations on which rests the peace so painfully achieved"; and
he promoted at the League of Nations the abortive Geneva
Protocol, by which Great Britain, along with the other members
of the League, guaranteed every frontier in Europe. But he was
thus generous with the French because he thought that their
anxieties had no real foundation. Even in August 1914 he had
not believed that Germany was a dangerous and aggressive
power, bent on the domination of Europe. He certainly did not
believe it in 1924. Therefore the promises of the Protocol, which
looked "Black . . . and big on paper", were in fact "a harmless
drug to soothe nerves". Every problem could be solved by "the
strenuous action of good-will". The important thing was to
launch negotiations. If the French could be lured into negotiating
only by promises of security, then the promises should be given,
much as a small child is lured into the sea by assurances that the
water is warm. The child discovers that the assurances are false;
but he gets used to the cold, and soon learns to swim. So it would
be in international affairs. Once the French began to conciliate
Germany, they would find the process less alarming than they
imagined. British policy should urge the French to concede much,
and the Germans to ask little. As MacDonald put it some years
later: "Let them especially put their demands in such a way that
Great Britain could say that she supported both sides."[1]

MacDonald came just at the right time. The French were ready

---

[1] Minutes of Five Power Meeting, 6 Dec. 1932. *Documents on British
Foreign Policy*, second series, iv. No. 211.

to disentangle themselves from the Ruhr by moderating their demand for reparations; the Germans were ready to make a serious offer on the other side. The temporary settlement of reparations by the Dawes plan, and the wider relaxation of temper between France and Germany which accompanied it, were essentially MacDonald's doing. The general election of November 1924 ended the Labour government; but, though MacDonald ceased to direct British foreign policy, he continued to shape it indirectly. The path of conciliation was, from the British point of view, too attractive to be abandoned by any British government. Austen Chamberlain, MacDonald's Conservative successor, specialised in loyalty (if only to atone for his father's activities in the other direction); and in his puzzled way would have liked to renew the offer of a direct alliance with France. British opinion—not Labour only, but Conservative also—was now resolutely against this. Stresemann suggested a way out: a pact of peace between France and Germany, guaranteed by Great Britain and Italy. This was wonderfully attractive to the British. A guarantee against an unnamed "aggressor" offered exactly the even-handed justice to which Grey had aspired before the war and which MacDonald preached now; yet the friends of France like Austen Chamberlain could console themselves that the only conceivable aggressor would be Germany—hence the Anglo-French alliance would be smuggled in unperceived. The proposal was also wonderfully attractive to the Italians who had been treated as poor relations ever since the war and now found themselves elevated to the British level as arbiters between France and Germany. The idea was less attractive to the French. Even though the Rhineland was to remain demilitarised, it would cease to provide France with an open door through which to threaten Germany, once it was placed under an Anglo-Italian guarantee.

But the French too had found the right statesman for the moment. In 1925 Briand returned as French foreign minister. He was a match for Stresemann in diplomatic skill, the equal of MacDonald in high-minded aspiration, and master of all in romantic utterance. Other French statesmen talked "hard" without meaning it. Briand talked "soft", and did not mean that either. The outcome of the Ruhr occupation had shown the futility of the hard way. Briand now had another chance to find security for France in a cloud of words. He deflated Stresemann's moral lead by proposing that Germany should promise to respect all her frontiers, east as well as west. This was an impossible condition for the German government. Most Germans had acquiesced in the loss of Alsace and Lorraine; few of them even raised the question until after the defeat of France in 1940. The frontier with Poland was felt as a grievance by all Germans. It might be tolerated; it could not be confirmed. Stresemann stretched conciliation a long way, in German eyes, when he agreed to conclude treaties of arbitration with Poland and Czechoslovakia. Even so, he added that Germany intended to "revise" her frontiers with these two countries at some time in the future, though of course she would do it peacefully—a favourite phrase of statesmen who are not yet ready to go to war though perhaps, in Stresemann's case, sincere.

Here was a gaping hole in the system of security—an open repudiation by Stresemann of Germany's eastern frontiers. The British would not fill the gap. Austen Chamberlain spoke complacently of the Polish Corridor "for which no British Government ever will or ever can risk the bones of a British grenadier". Briand provided an alternative solution. France reaffirmed her existing alliances with Czechoslovakia and Poland; and the signatories of Locarno agreed that French action under these alliances would not constitute aggression against Germany. In theory France thus remained free to go to the assistance of her Eastern allies across the demilitarised Rhineland without forfeiting British friendship. Her two contradictory systems of diplomacy were reconciled, at any rate on paper. Locarno enshrined the Western alliance with Great Britain, yet preserved the Eastern alliance with the two satellite-states at the same time.

Such was the treaty of Locarno, signed on 1 December 1925. It was the turning-point of the years between the wars. Its signature ended the first World war; its repudiation eleven years later marked the prelude to the second. If the object of an international agreement be to satisfy everyone, Locarno was a very good treaty indeed. It satisfied the two guarantor Powers. They had reconciled France and Germany and brought peace to Europe without incurring, as they supposed, anything beyond a moral obligation, a mere form of words. Neither Great Britain nor Italy ever made any preparations to fulfil their guarantee.

How could they when the "aggressor" would not be known until the moment for decision arrived? The practical result of the treaty, odd and unforeseen, was to prevent any military co-operation between Great Britain and France so long as it remained in force. Yet Locarno also satisfied the French. Germany accepted the loss of Alsace and Lorraine; she agreed to keep the Rhineland demilitarised; Great Britain and Italy underwrote the German promise. Any French statesman of 1914 would have been bewildered with delight at such an achievement. At the same time the French were still free to operate their eastern alliances and to play a great part in Europe if they wished to do so. The Germans could be satisfied too. They were firmly protected against a new occupation of the Ruhr; they were treated as equals, not as the defeated enemy; and they kept the door open for a revision of their eastern frontier. A German statesman of 1919, or even of 1923, would have found no cause for complaint. Locarno was the greatest triumph of "appeasement". Lord Balfour called it rightly "the symbol and the cause of a great amelioration in the public feeling of Europe".

Locarno gave to Europe a period of peace and hope. Germany was admitted to the League of Nations, though after more delay than had been expected. Stresemann, Chamberlain, and Briand appeared regularly at the League Council. Geneva seemed to be the centre of a revived Europe: the Concert really in tune at last, and international affairs regulated by discussion instead of by the jangling of arms. No one in these years lamented the absence of Russia and the United States—affairs ran more smoothly without them. On the other hand, no one seriously proposed to turn the Europe of Geneva into either an anti-American or an anti-Soviet *bloc*. Far from wishing to be independent of the United States, the European countries were all busy borrowing American money. A few wild projectors talked of a European crusade against Communism; but there was nothing in it. Europeans had no desire to go on a crusade against anyone. Apart from this, the Germans wanted to keep friendship with Russia as a card in reserve, a form of reinsurance treaty which might some day be used against France's eastern alliances. Immediately after signing the treaty of Locarno, Stresemann renewed with the Russians the agreement made at Rapallo in 1922; and when Germany joined the League, Stresemann declared that she could not, in her disarmed state, participate in sanctions—a veiled assertion of neutrality towards Soviet Russia.

A graver flaw in the Locarno-Geneva system than the absence of the United States and Soviet Russia was the presence of Italy. She had been brought into the Locarno arrangement solely in order to reinforce the British appearance of impartiality. No one supposed at this time that Italy could really hold the balance between Germany and France. This did not matter while Locarno, like the League, rested on calculation and good-will, not on direct force. Later, when circumstances grew harsher, the memory of Locarno helped to foster the delusion that Italy had real weight to throw into the scales; the Italian leaders themselves were the victims of this delusion. In the Locarno era Italy had a worse defect than lack of strength: she lacked moral standing. The Locarno Powers claimed to represent the great principles for which the war had been fought; and the League claimed to be an association of free peoples. No doubt there was something fraudulent in these claims. No country is ever as free or as high-principled as it makes out to be. But there was something genuine in the claims as well. The Great Britain of Baldwin and MacDonald; the Weimar republic in Germany; the Third republic in France were truly democratic countries, with freedom of expression, the rule of law, and good intentions towards others. They were entitled to claim that, grouped in the League, they offered the best hope for mankind; and that, broadly speaking, they offered a superior political and social order to that offered by Soviet Russia.

All this became a tawdry pretence when it was extended to the Italy of Mussolini. Fascism never possessed the ruthless drive, let alone the material strength, of National Socialism. Morally it was just as corrupting—or perhaps more so from its very dishonesty, Everything about Fascism was a fraud. The social peril from which it saved Italy was a fraud; the revolution by which it seized power was a fraud; the ability and policy of Mussolini were fraudulent. Fascist rule was corrupt, incompetent, empty; Mussolini himself a vain, blundering boaster without either ideas or aims. Fascist Italy lived in a state of illegality; and Fascist foreign policy repudiated from the outset the principles of Geneva. Yet Ramsay MacDonald wrote cordial letters to Mussolini—at the very moment of Matteoti's murder;

Austen Chamberlain and Mussolini exchanged photographs; Winston Churchill extolled Mussolini as the saviour of his country and a great European statesman. How could anyone believe in the sincerity of Western leaders when they flattered Mussolini in this way and accepted him as one of themselves? It is not surprising that the Russian Communists regarded the League and all its works as a capitalist conspiracy—though also not surprising that Soviet Russia and Fascist Italy early established and always maintained cordial international relations. Of course there is always some gap between theory and practice. It is disastrous for both rulers and ruled when the gap becomes too wide. The presence of Fascist Italy at Geneva, the actual presence of Mussolini at Locarno, were the extreme symbols of unreality in the democratic Europe of the League of Nations. The statesmen no longer believed their own phrases; and the peoples followed their example.

Though Stresemann and Briand were both in their different ways sincere, they did not carry their peoples with them; and each justified Locarno in his own country by contradictory arguments which were bound to end in disillusionment. Briand told the French that Locarno was a final settlement, barring the way against further concessions. Stresemann assured the Germans that the purpose of Locarno was to bring further concessions at an ever faster rate. Briand, the great rhetorician, hoped that a cloud of benevolent phrases would make the Germans forget their grievances. Stresemann, in his patient way, believed that the habit of concession would grow on the French with practice. Both men were disappointed; both were in sight of failure by the time they died. Further concessions were made, but always with ill-will. The Control Commission on German disarmament was withdrawn in 1927. Reparations were revised downwards by the Young plan in 1929, and external control of German finances was abandoned; the occupying forces left the Rhineland in 1980—five years ahead of time. Appeasement was not achieved. On the contrary German resentment was greater at the end than at the beginning. In 1924 German Nationalists sat in the Cabinet and helped to carry the Dawes plan; in 1929 the Young plan was carried only against fierce Nationalist opposition. Stresemann, who had put Germany back among the Great Powers, was harried into the grave.

The German resentment was partly a matter of calculation: the obvious way to obtain more concessions was to condemn each gain as not enough. The Germans had a plausible case. Locarno treated them as equals, freely negotiating an agreed treaty. What justification then could there be for preserving reparations or one-sided German disarmament? The French could think of no logical answer to this argument, yet knew that, if they accepted it, German predominance in Europe must follow. Most contemporaries blamed the French. Englishmen, particularly, agreed more and more with MacDonald that appeasement, once started, should be continued fast and whole-heartedly. Later on, men blamed the Germans for not accepting the defeat of 1918 as final. It is futile to suppose that more concessions, or fewer, would have made much difference. The conflict between France and Germany was bound to go on as long as the illusion persisted that Europe was still the centre of the world. France would seek to preserve the artificial securities of 1919; Germany would strive to restore the natural order of things. Rival states can be frightened into friendship only by the shadow of some greater danger; neither Soviet Russia nor the United States cast this shadow over the Europe of Stresemann and Briand.

This is far from saying that the shadow of war hung over the Europe of 1929. Even the Soviet leaders no longer shook at the turnip-ghost of a new capitalist war of intervention. Turning their backs on the outer world more firmly than ever, they translated "Socialism in a single country" into the practical terms of the Five Year plan. Indeed the only war which prophets of war could foresee was that most nonsensical of anticipations: a war between Great Britain and the United States. In fact the two Powers had already agreed to equality of battleships in 1921; and were to carry agreement further at the London Naval conference of 1930. There was still Nationalist agitation in Germany; but most people drew from this the not unreasonable conclusion that the process of conciliation had been too slow. In any case, the Nationalists were a minority of Germans. The majority, though also opposed to Versailles, still accepted Stresemann's view that its system could be spirited away by peaceful means. Hindenburg, President since 1925, was the symbol of this; a Field-Marshal and a Nationalist, but the conscientious head of a democratic Republic, loyally working the foreign policy of Locarno and presiding, without complaint, over an army restricted to impotence by the peace-treaty. The most popular cry in Germany was "No More War", not "Down with the slave treaty"; and the Nationalists were heavily defeated when they organised a referendum against the Young plan. 1929 saw the publication in Germany of the most famous of all anti-war books, Remarque's *All Quiet on the Western Front*; and books of a similar character filled the shelves in England and France. It looked as though treaty-revision would go on gradually, almost imperceptibly, and that a new European system would emerge without anyone noticing the exact moment when the watershed was crossed.

The one possible danger seemed to be a renewal of aggressive action by "militarist" France, the only country with a great army and, despite Italian assertions, the only Great Power on the European continent. But this, too, was an apprehension without substance. There were more solid grounds than Briand's rhetoric for supposing that France had already acquiesced in failure. In theory, France still kept the door open for action against Germany. The Rhineland was still demilitarised; the alliances with Poland and Czechoslovakia were still in force. In fact France had already taken the decisive step which made action against Germany impossible. Germany was far stronger in man-power and industrial resources. Therefore the only hope for France was to strike an overwhelming blow before Germany could begin to mobilise. France needed "an active, independent, and mobile army, always ready to penetrate into enemy terri-tory". France never possessed such an army. The victorious army of 1918 had been trained only for trench warfare; and had no time to change its character during the brief period of rapid advance. Nor were reforms introduced after 1918. The French army found it difficult to carry through the occupation of the Ruhr even though there was no German force opposing them. Domestic politics pushed the same way. There was incessant demand for one-year service; and it was duly instituted in 1928. Henceforward the French armies, even when fully mobilised, would only be strong enough to defend "the national territory". The soldiers were given purely defensive training and equipment. The Maginot line provided the eastern frontier with the most gigantic system of fortifications ever known. The divorce between

French policy and French strategy was complete. French politicians still talked of acting against Germany; the means of action did not exist. Lenin said in 1917 that the Russians soldiers had voted for peace with their feet by running away. So the French, without realising it, had voted by their military preparations against the system of Versailles. They had renounced the fruits of victory before the dispute over these fruits began.

CHAPTER FOUR

The End of Versailles

IN 1929 the system of security against Germany, devised in the treaty of Versailles, was still complete. Germany was disarmed; the Rhineland was demilitarised; the victors were ostensibly united; and the system was reinforced by the authority of the League of Nations. Seven years later all this had gone without a blow being struck. International stability was first shaken by the collapse of economic stability in the great Depression which began in October 1929. The Depression had little to do with the preceding war, though men did not think so at the time. It had nothing to do with the surviving provisions of the peace-treaty. The Depression was started by the collapse of a speculative boom in the United States; and the unemployment which followed was swelled by the failure of purchasing power to keep pace with the increased resources of production. Everyone understands this now; just as they know that the way out of a depression is to increase government spending. In 1929 hardly anyone knew it; and the few who did had no influence on policy. It was generally believed that deflation was the only cure. There must be sound money, balanced budgets, cuts in government expenditure, and reductions in wages. Then, presumably, prices would somehow become low enough for people to start buying again.

This policy caused hardship and discontent in every country where it was applied. There was no reason why it should cause international tension. In most countries the Depression led to a turning-away from international affairs. In Great Britain the lowest arms-estimates between the wars were introduced by Neville Chamberlain, chancellor of the exchequer in the National government, in 1932. The French became even less assertive than they had been before. American policy under F. D. Roosevelt became in 1933 markedly more isolationist than it had been under his Republican predecessor. Germany was a special case.

The Germans had experienced the terrible evils of inflation in 1923, and now went equally far in the opposite direction. Most Germans regarded this as inevitable; but the results were highly unpopular. Everyone applauded the measures when applied to others, yet resented them when applied to himself. The Reichstag failed to provide a majority for a deflationist government, though such a government was what it wanted. As a result Brüning governed Germany for more than two years without a majority, imposing deflation by presidential decree. High-minded and sincere, he would not win popularity by mitigating the rigours of deflation; but his government sought popularity by success in foreign affairs. Curtius, his foreign minister, tried to carry economic union with Austria in 1931—a project which offered no economic advantage; and Treviranus, another member of his government, started an agitation against the Polish frontier. In 1932 Papen, Brüning's successor, demanded equality of armaments for Germany. All these things were irrelevant to the economic difficulties, but the ordinary German could not be expected to understand this. He had been told for years that all his troubles were due to the treaty of Versailles; and now that he was in trouble he believed what he had been told. Moreover the Depression removed the strongest argument for doing nothing: prosperity. Men who are well off forget their grievances; in adversity they have nothing else to think about.

There were other reasons for the increase in international difficulties. In 1931 the League of Nations faced its first serious challenge. On 18 September Japanese forces occupied Manchuria, which was theoretically part of China. China appealed to the League for redress. It was not an easy problem. The Japanese had a good case. The authority of the Chinese central government—nowhere strong—did not run in Manchuria, which had been for years in a state of lawless confusion. Japanese trading interests had suffered greatly. There were many precedents in China for independent action—the last being a British landing at Shanghai in 1927. Besides, the League had no means of action. No country, at the height of the economic crisis, welcomed the idea of cutting off its remaining fragment of international trade with Japan. The only Power with any stake in the Far East was Great Britain; and action was to be least expected from the British at the exact moment when they were being forced off the gold standard and facing a contentious general election. In any case even Great Britain, though a Far Eastern Power, had no means of action. The Washington naval treaty gave Japan a local supremacy in the Far East; and successive British governments confirmed this supremacy when they deliberately postponed the building up of their base at Singapore. What would be gained if the League of Nations condemned Japan? Merely a display of moral rectitude which, in so far as it had any effect, would set Japan against British trading interests. There was one argument in favour of this moral condemnation. The United States, though not a member of the League, were very much a Far Eastern Power; and they propounded "non-recognition" of any territorial change carried through by force. This was consoling to the doctrinaires of Geneva. But, as the Americans did not propose to curtail their trade with Japan, it was less consoling to the Chinese and to the practical sense of the British.

Rightly or wrongly, the British government attached more importance to the restoration of peace than to a display of moral rectitude. Nor was this view confined to the hardened cynics who staffed the foreign office or to the supposedly reactionary politicians—headed by MacDonald—who composed the National government. It was shared by the Labour party who at this time condemned not "aggression" but "war". Any British action against Japan in 1932, if such had been possible, would have met with unanimous opposition from the Left as a wicked defence of Imperialist interests. What the Labour party wanted—and in this it represented a general British feeling—was that Great Britain should not profit from war. Labour proposed a ban on supplying arms to either side, both China and Japan; and this proposal was accepted by the National government. The government went further. The British had always regarded the League as an instrument of conciliation, not a machine of security. They now operated this instrument. The League set up the Lytton commission, actually on Japanese initiative, to discover the facts about Manchuria and to propound a solution. The Commission did not reach a simple verdict. It found that most of the Japanese grievances were justified. Japan was not condemned as an aggressor, though she was condemned for resorting to force before all peaceful means of redress were exhausted. The Japanese withdrew in protest from the League of Nations. But in fact British policy succeeded. The Chinese reconciled themselves to the loss of a province which they had not controlled for some years; and in 1933 peace was restored between China and Japan. In later years the Manchurian affair assumed a mythical importance. It was treated as a milestone on the road to war, the first decisive "betrayal" of the League, especially by the British government. In reality, the League, under British leadership, had done what the British thought it was designed to do: it had limited a conflict and brought it, however unsatisfactorily, to an end. Moreover, the Manchurian affair, far from weakening the coercive powers of the League, actually brought them into existence. It was thanks to this affair that the League—again on British prompting—set up machinery, hitherto lacking, to organise economic sanctions. This machinery, to everyone's misfortune, made possible the League action over Abyssinia in 1935.

The Manchurian affair had a contemporary importance, though not that subsequently attributed to it. It diverted attention from Europe just at the moment when European questions became acute; and in particular it made the British government exceptionally impatient with European troubles. It reinforced, with unanswerable arguments, the British preference for conciliation as against security. It set the pattern for the arguments which were now unrolled by the meeting of the Disarmament conference early in 1932. The time of this meeting was peculiarly inappropriate. The victorious Powers had been committed to some such act ever since 1919, when the peace treaty had imposed disarmament on Germany as the first step towards "a general limitation of the armaments of all nations". This was far from a promise that the victors would disarm down to the German level; but it was a promise that they would do something. The promise was steadily evaded throughout the nineteen-twenties. This evasion played into German hands. The Germans increasingly insisted that the victors should either fulfil their promise or release Germany from hers. The British Labour government which took office in 1929 seconded this German prompting. Most Englishmen held that great armaments were themselves a cause of war; or—to put it another way—that great armaments allowed muddle and misunderstanding to turn into war (as happened in August 1914) before the "cooling-off period" could operate. Ramsay MacDonald, the prime minister, was eager to resume the initiative which he had taken in 1924 and to complete the work of appeasement. He was mainly responsible for the success of the London naval conference in 1930, which extended to wider classes of vessels the mutual limitation of battleships, agreed by Great Britain, the United States, and Japan in 1921. Even the London conference contained a sinister warning for the future, disregarded at the time. The discussions here first provoked Italy into demanding naval equality with France—a demand which the French were determined to resist; and thus began the estrangement between the two countries which finally carried Italy on to the German side.

In the second Labour government MacDonald grudgingly yielded the Foreign Office to Arthur Henderson. The two men did not see precisely eye to eye. Henderson, unlike MacDonald, had been a Cabinet minister during the World war and could hardly regard that war as an unnecessary folly. Where Mac-Donald dismissed French anxieties as a fantasy, Henderson wished to reconcile disarmament and security. He proposed to use disarmament as a lever for increasing British commitments to France, rather as Austen Chamberlain before him had hoped to do with Locarno; though of course the commitments would not be onerous when armaments had been everywhere reduced. Henderson held out to the French the prospect that, if they co-operated in disarmament, they would get increased backing from Great Britain in return. This was a good bargain from the French point of view. Though few Frenchmen—or perhaps none—fully realised the ineffectiveness of their army as an offensive weapon, even fewer welcomed the prospect of holding Germany in check for ever, solely by French strength. Security would assume a different aspect when the British, instead of relying on Locarno, had to think in practical military terms. Perhaps they would recognise at last the need for a great French army; alternatively they would increase their own. The French, too, therefore pressed for a Disarmament conference; and with Henderson as president. This was not simply a tribute to his gifts as a conciliator, great as these were. It was also a matter of calculation: Great Britain could hardly escape the increased obligations which would follow from general disarmament when the British foreign secretary was actually in the chair at the Disarmament conference.

Circumstances had gravely changed by the time that the Disarmament conference met in the early days of 1932. The Labour government had fallen. Henderson was no longer foreign secretary; as president of the conference, he could no longer commit Great Britain, but could only push ineffectively a government to which he was politically hostile. MacDonald was no longer pulled along by Henderson; he was, if anything, pulled back by the new foreign secretary, Sir John Simon, a Liberal who almost resigned at the outbreak of war in 1914 and actually resigned in protest against conscription eighteen months later. Simon, like MacDonald, regarded French anxieties as imaginary. Moreover the National government were hard set for economy: far from being willing to increase British commitments, they were eager to reduce still further those that existed. The French found to their dismay that they were being pressed to disarm without receiving any compensation. MacDonald told them again and again: "French demands always created the difficulty that they required of Great Britain that she should assume further obligations, and this at the moment could not be contemplated."[1] The only false note in this statement was the hint that the British attitude might change.

The British had their own device for twisting disarmament in favour of security. Where the French hoped to involve the British, they in their turn hoped to draw in the United States— a party to the Disarmament conference, though not in the League of Nations. This plan had perhaps some sense while the Republicans were in power. It misfired in November 1932 with the election of the Democrat, F. D. Roosevelt, as president. For though the Democrats had been committed to the League of Nations by Wilson in 1919 and though Roosevelt was to embed the United States in world policy later, the vote of November 1932 was a victory for isolationism. The Democrats were now disillusioned Wilsonians. Some believed that Wilson had deceived the American people; others that the European statesmen had deceived Wilson. Nearly all of them believed that the European Powers, especially the former Allies, were incorrigibly wicked and that the less America had to do with Europe the better. The idealism which had once made Americans eager

[1] MacDonald, conversation with Paul-Boncour, 2 Dec. 1932. *British Foreign Policy*, second series, iv. No. 204.

to save the world now made them turn their backs on it. The Democratic majority in Congress carried a series of measures which made it impossible for the United States to play any part in world affairs; and President Roosevelt accepted these measures without any sign of disagreement. Their effect was reinforced by the intensely nationalist economics which accompanied the New Deal. It was a minor sign of the same trend when the Roosevelt régime at last "recognised" Soviet Russia and welcomed Litvinov, the foreign commissar, in Washington. Russia's exclusion from Europe now counted for righteousness in American eyes. No European commitment could be expected from America; and the British themselves were pulled out of Europe by American influence—so far as it counted.

It was a further misfortune for the Disarmament conference that reparations reached a final settlement in the summer of 1932. For, while it would have been admirable if they had been disposed of before, this was the worst moment to do it. The German government, now transferred from Brüning to Papen, was weaker and more unpopular than ever, hence still more anxious for popularity in foreign affairs. Reparations no longer provided a grievance; and the one-sided disarmament of Germany had to take their place. Any real negotiations were impossible; the German government needed a sensational success. The Germans left the Disarmament conference in dramatic protest; and were then tempted back by a promise of "equality of status within a system of security". This promise was meaningless. If the French got security, there would be no equality of status; if they did not get security, there was to be no equality. The promise did not impress the German electors. Nor would they have been impressed even by a real concession. What weighed with them was poverty and mass unemployment; and they treated the wrangling over disarmament as a gigantic red-herring, which indeed it was. The Allied statesmen did their best to help Papen by juggling with words. It did not yet occur to them that there was any serious German danger. In 1932 men feared, and rightly feared, the collapse of Germany, not German strength. How could any competent observer suppose that a country with seven million unemployed, no gold reserves, and an ever-shrinking foreign trade, would suddenly become a great military power? All modern experience taught that power

went with wealth; and in 1932 Germany seemed very poor
indeed.

These calculations were turned upside down on 30 January
1933, when Hitler became Chancellor, an event now as encrusted
with legend as the arrival in Kent of Hengist and Horsa. It was
not a "seizure of power" despite National Socialist boasting.
Hitler was appointed Chancellor by President Hindenburg in a
strictly constitutional way and for solidly democratic reasons.
Whatever ingenious speculators, liberal or Marxist, might say,
Hitler was not made Chancellor because he would help the
German capitalists to destroy the trade unions, nor because he
would give the German generals a great army, still less a great
war. He was appointed because he and his Nationalist allies
could provide a majority in the Reichstag, and thus end the
anomalous four years of government by presidential decree. He
was not expected to carry through revolutionary changes in
either home or foreign affairs. On the contrary the conservative
politicians led by Papen, who recommended him to Hindenburg,
kept the key posts for themselves and expected Hitler to be a
tame figurehead. These expectations turned out to be wrong.
Hitler broke the artificial bonds which had been designed to tie
him and gradually became an all-powerful dictator—though
more gradually than the legend makes out. He changed most
things in Germany. He destroyed political freedom and the rule
of law; he transformed German economics and finance; he
quarrelled with the Churches; he abolished the separate states
and made Germany for the first time a united country. In one
sphere alone he changed nothing. His foreign policy was that of
his predecessors, of the professional diplomats at the foreign
ministry, and indeed of virtually all Germans. Hitler, too, wanted
to free Germany from the restrictions of the peace treaty; to
restore a great German army; and then to make Germany the
greatest power in Europe from her natural weight. There were
occasional differences in emphasis. Perhaps Hitler would have
concentrated less on Austria and Czechoslovakia if he had not
been born a subject of the Habsburg Monarchy; perhaps his
Austrian origin made him less hostile originally to the Poles. But
the general pattern was unchanged.

This is not the accepted view. Writers of great authority have
seen in Hitler a system-maker, deliberately preparing from the

first a great war which would destroy existing civilisation and make him master of the world. In my opinion, statesmen are too absorbed by events to follow a preconceived plan. They take one step, and the next follows from it. The systems are created by historians, as happened with Napoleon; and the systems attributed to Hitler are really those of Hugh Trevor-Roper, Elizabeth Wiskemann, and Alan Bullock. There is some ground for these speculations. Hitler was himself an amateur historian, or rather a generaliser on history; and he created systems in his spare time. These systems were day-dreams. Chaplin grasped this, with an artist's genius, when he showed the Great Dictator transforming the world into a toy balloon and kicking it to the ceiling with the point of his toe. Hitler always saw himself, in these day-dreams, as master of the world. But the world which he dreamt to master and the way he would do it changed with changing circumstances. *Mein Kampf* was written in 1925, under the impact of the French occupation of the Ruhr. Hitler dreamt then of destroying French supremacy in Europe; and the method was to be alliance with Italy and Great Britain. His *Table Talk* was delivered far in occupied territory, during the campaign against Soviet Russia; and then Hitler dreamt of some fantastic Empire which would rationalise his career of conquest. His final legacy was delivered from the Bunker, when he was on the point of suicide; it is not surprising that he transformed this into a doctrine of universal destruction. Academic ingenuity has discovered in these pronouncements the disciple of Nietzsche, the geopolitician, or the emulator of Attila. I hear in them only the generalisations of a powerful, but uninstructed, intellect; dogmas which echo the conversation of any Austrian café or German beer-house.

There was one element of system in Hitler's foreign policy, though it was not new. His outlook was "continental", as Stresemann's had been before him. Hitler did not attempt to revive the "World Policy" which Germany had pursued before 1914; he made no plans for a great battle-fleet; he did not parade a grievance over the lost colonies, except as a device for embarrassing the British; he was not even interested in the Middle East—hence his blindness to the great opportunity in 1940 after the defeat of France. One could attribute this outlook to Hitler's Austrian origin, far from the ocean: or believe that he learnt it from some geopolitician in Munich. But essentially it reflected the circumstances of the time. Germany had been defeated by the Western Powers in November 1918; and had herself defeated Russia the preceding year. Hitler, like Stresemann, did not challenge the Western settlement. He did not wish to destroy the British Empire, nor even to deprive the French of Alsace and Lorraine. In return, he wanted the Allies to accept the verdict of March 1918; to abandon the artificial undoing of this verdict after November 1918; and to acknowledge that Germany had been victorious in the East. This was not a preposterous programme. Many Englishmen, to say nothing of Milner and Smuts, agreed with it even in 1918; many more did so later; and most Frenchmen were coming round to the same outlook. The national states of Eastern Europe enjoyed little popularity; Soviet Russia still less. When Hitler aspired to restore the settlement of Brest-Litovsk, he could pose also as the champion of European civilisation against Bolshevism and the Red peril. Maybe his ambitions were genuinely limited to the East; maybe conquest there would have been only the preliminary to conquest in Western Europe or on a World scale. No one can tell. Only events could have given the answer; and by a strange twist of circumstances they never did. Against all expectations, Hitler found himself at war with the Western Powers before he had conquered the East. Nevertheless, Eastern expansion was the primary purpose of his policy, if not the only one.

There was nothing original in this policy. The unique quality in Hitler was the gift of translating commonplace thoughts into action. He took seriously what was to others mere talk. The driving force in him was a terrifying literalism. Writers had been running down democracy for half a century. It took Hitler to create a totalitarian dictatorship. Nearly everyone in Germany thought that "something" should be done about unemployment. Hitler was the first to insist on "action". He disregarded the conventional rules; and so stumbled on the economics of full employment, exactly as F. D. Roosevelt did in the United States. Again, there was nothing new in anti-semitism. It had been "the Socialism of fools" for many years. Little had followed from it. Seipel, Austrian Chancellor in the nineteen-twenties, said of the anti-semitism which his party preached but did not practice: "Das is für die Gasse".[1] Hitler was "die Gasse". Many Germans had qualms as one act of persecution succeeded another, culminating in the unspeakable wickedness of the gas-chambers. But few knew how to protest. Everything which Hitler did against the Jews followed logically from the racial doctrines in which most Germans vaguely believed. It was the same with foreign policy. Not many Germans really cared passionately and persistently whether Germany again dominated Europe. But they talked as if they did. Hitler took them at their word. He made the Germans live up to their professions, or down to them—much to their regret.

In principle and doctrine, Hitler was no more wicked and unscrupulous than many other contemporary statesmen. In wicked acts he outdid them all. The policy of Western statesmen also rested ultimately on force—French policy on the army, British policy on sea-power. But these statesmen hoped that it would not be necessary to use this force. Hitler intended to use his force, or would at any rate threaten to use it. If Western morality seemed superior, this was largely because it was the morality of the *status quo*; Hitler's was the immorality of revision. There was a curious, though only superficial, contradiction in Hitler between aims and methods. His aim was change, the overthrow of the existing European order; his method was patience. Despite his bluster and violent talk, he was a master in the game of waiting. He never made a frontal attack on a prepared position—at least never until his judgement had been corrupted by easy victories. Like Joshua before the walls of Jericho, he preferred to wait until the forces opposing him had been sapped by their own confusions and themselves forced success upon him. He had already applied this method to gain power in Germany. He did not "seize" power. He waited for it to be thrust upon him by the men who had previously tried to keep him out. In January 1933 Papen and Hindenburg were imploring him to become Chancellor; and he graciously consented. So it was to be in foreign affairs. Hitler did not make precise demands. He announced that he was dissatisfied; and then waited for the concessions to pour into his lap, merely holding out his hand for more. Hitler did not know any foreign countries at first hand. He rarely listened to his foreign minister, and

[1] That is for the street—or perhaps the gutter.

never read the reports of his ambassadors. He judged foreign statesmen by intuition. He was convinced that he had taken the measure of all *bourgeois* politicians, German and foreign alike, and that their nerve would crumble before his did. This conviction was near enough to the truth to bring Europe within sight of disaster.

Perhaps this waiting was not at first conscious or deliberate. The greatest masters of statecraft are those who do not know what they are doing. In his first years of power, Hitler did not concern himself much with foreign affairs. He spent most of his time at Berchtesgaden, remote from events, dreaming in his old feckless way. When he turned to practical life, his greatest concern was to keep his own absolute control over the National Socialist party. He watched, and himself promoted, the rivalry between the principal Nazi leaders. Then came the maintenance of Nazi control over the German state and the German people; after that, rearmament and economic expansion. Hitler loved details of machinery—tanks, aeroplanes, guns. He was fascinated by road building, and even more by architectural schemes. Foreign affairs came at the bottom of the list. In any case, there was little he could do until Germany was rearmed. Events imposed upon him the waiting which he preferred. He could safely leave foreign policy to the old professionals of the foreign office. After all, their aims were the same as his; they, too, were concerned to sap the settlement of Versailles. They needed only an occasional spur to action, the sporadic and daring initiative which suddenly brought things to a head.

This pattern was soon shown in the discussions over disarmament. Allied statesmen were under no illusions as to Hitler's intentions. They were given precise and accurate information by their representatives at Berlin—information which Sir John Simon found "terrifying".[1] For that matter they could read the truth in any newspaper, despite the steady expulsion from Germany of British and American correspondents. There is no greater mistake than to suppose that Hitler did not give foreign statesmen plenty of warning. On the contrary he gave them only too much. Western statesmen saw the problem all too clearly. Germany had now a strong government; and this government

[1] Minute by Simon on Phipps to Simon, 31 Jan. 1934. *British Foreign Policy*, second series, vi. No. 240.

would again make Germany a great military power. But what were the Allied statesmen to do? They posed the question to themselves, and to each other, again and again. One obvious course was to intervene and to prevent German rearmament by force. This was suggested by the British military representative at the Disarmament conference[1]; it was constantly suggested by the French. The suggestion was repeatedly considered and always turned down. It was unworkable from every aspect. The United States would clearly not take part in intervention. On the contrary American opinion would be violently opposed to it; and this weighed much with Great Britain. British opinion was equally opposed; not only the opinion of the Left, but inside the government itself. Apart from any objections of principle, the government could not contemplate increased expenditure—and an intervention would be expensive—nor had they any armed force to spare. Mussolini also held aloof, already hoping to turn "revisionism" in Italy's favour. This left only France; and the French were resolute all along that they would not act alone. If they had been honest with themselves, they would have added that they too had no forces capable of intervention. Besides, what would intervention achieve? If Hitler fell, chaos would follow in Germany worse than that which followed the occupation of the Ruhr; if he did not fall, German rearmament would presumably be renewed as soon as the occupying forces were withdrawn.

The alternative on the other side was to do nothing: to abandon the Disarmament conference and let events take their course. Both British and French dismissed this as "inconceivable"; "unthinkable"; "a counsel of despair". What way out remained? Where was the ingenious twist, always just over the horizon, which would satisfy the Germans without endangering the French? The French went on insisting that they could agree to equality of arms with Germany only if they had a solid British guarantee, backed by staff talks and an enlarged British army. The British as firmly rejected this proposal and argued that since equality would satisfy the Germans, any guarantee would be unnecessary. If Hitler made an agreement, "he might even feel inclined to honour it. . . . His signature would bind all Germany

[1] Memorandum by A. C. Temperley, 10 May 1933. *British Foreign Policy*, second series, v. No. 127.

like no other German's in all her past."[1] If Germany did not keep the agreement, "the strength of world opposition to her cannot be exaggerated";[2] "the world will know what her real intentions are".[3] It is impossible to tell whether the British took their own arguments seriously. Probably they still believed that French intransigence was the main obstacle to a peaceful Europe, and were not over-scrupulous how this obstinacy was removed. The precedent of 1871 was much in their minds. Then Russia had repudiated the clauses of the treaty of Paris which imposed disarmament on her in the Black Sea; and the other Powers had acquiesced on condition that Russia sought approval from an international conference. The public law of Europe was maintained. One conference had made the treaty; therefore another could tear it up. So now the important thing was not to prevent German rearmament, but to ensure that it should take place within the framework of an international agreement. The British supposed, too, that Germany would be willing to pay a price "for legalising her illegalities".[4] The British always liked to be on the right side of the law themselves, and naturally assumed that the Germans felt the same. It was inconceivable to them that any Power should prefer a return to "international anarchy". And of course Hitler did not intend to return to international anarchy. He too wanted an international order; but it was to be "a new order", not a modified version of the system of 1919.

There was a further consideration which did most of all to determine the atmosphere of these years. Everyone, particularly the British and French, assumed that there was plenty of time. Germany was still virtually disarmed when Hitler came to power. She had no tanks, no aeroplanes, no heavy guns, no trained reservists. It would take her ten years, according to normal experience, to become a formidable military Power. This calculation was not altogether wrong. Hitler and Mussolini shared it. In their conversations they always assumed that 1948

---

[1] Phipps to Simon, 21 Nov. 1933. *British Foreign Policy*, second series, vi. No. 60.

[2] MacDonald, conversation with Daladier, 16 March 1933. *Ibid.* iv. No. 310.

[3] Foreign Office Memorandum, 25 Jan. 1934. *Ibid.* vi. No. 206.

[4] Minute by Eden on Tyrell to Simon, 8 March 1934. *Ibid.* vi. No. 337.

would be the year of destiny. Many of the early alarms about German rearmament were false alarms. Thus, when Churchill claimed in 1934 that the German air force was much greater than the British government alleged, and Baldwin contradicted him, Baldwin—as we now know from the German records themselves—was right, and Churchill was wrong. Even in 1939 the German army was not equipped for a prolonged war; and in 1940 the German land forces were inferior to the French in everything except leadership. The Western powers made two mistakes. They failed to allow for the fact that Hitler was a gambler who would play for high stakes with inadequate resources. They also failed to allow for the economic achievement of Schacht, who ensured that German resources were less inadequate than they would otherwise have been. Countries with the more or less free economy of the time operated to 75% of their efficiency. Schacht first worked the system of full employment and so used German economic power almost to capacity. This is all commonplace now. It seemed wizardry beyond imagination then.

The Disarmament conference itself did not long survive Hitler's coming. During the summer of 1933 the British and Italians pressed the French to grant Germany a theoretical "equality" of armaments. After all, there was plenty of time before this equality became real. These promptings were nearly successful. The French almost took the plunge. On 22 September British and French ministers met in Paris. The French implied that they would agree to equality or something near it. Then Daladier, the French premier, asked: "what guarantee would there be of the observance of the Convention?" The old difficulty was back again. Simon replied: "His Majesty's Government could not accept new responsibilities in the nature of sanctions. Public opinion in England would not support it." A more authoritative voice than Simon's was heard. Baldwin, leader of the Conservative party and unacknowledged head of the British government, had come from Aix to attend the meeting. He had been brooding during his holiday on the European situation. Now he supported Simon: there could be no new British commitment. He added: "If it could be proved that Germany was rearming, then a new situation would immediately arise, which Europe would have to face. . . . If that situation arose, His Majesty's Government would have to consider it very seriously, but that situation had not yet arisen."¹ The voice was the voice of Baldwin; the spirit still that of MacDonald. The French were being asked to give up a superiority which they imagined to be real; and were being offered only the prospect that something undefined might be done if the Germans misbehaved. This did not satisfy them. The French withdrew their tentative offer. When the conference resumed, they announced that they would agree to equality with Germany only if the Germans remained disarmed during a further "trial period" of four years.

This was Hitler's opportunity. He knew that France stood alone, that both Great Britain and Italy sympathised with the German position. On 14 October Germany withdrew from the Disarmament conference; a week later she left the League of Nations. Nothing happened. The German Ministers had been terrified by Hitler's initiative. Now he told them: "The situation has developed as expected. Threatening steps against Germany have neither materialised nor are they to be expected. . . . The critical moment has probably passed".² So it proved. Hitler had tried out his method in foreign affairs; and it had worked. He had waited until the opposition to Germany was inwardly demoralised and had then blown it away like thistledown. After all, the French could not very well march into Germany merely because the Germans had left the Disarmament conference. They could act only when Germany actually rearmed; and then it would be too late. The British went on sympathising with Germany's claims. As late as July 1934 *The Times* wrote: "In the years that are coming, there is more reason to fear for Germany than to fear Germany". The Labour party continued to demand general disarmament as the preliminary to security. MacDonald still set the course for both government and opposition. So confident was Hitler that he teased the French by offering to accept inequality— a German army limited to 300,000 men, and an air force half the size of the French. Hitler's confidence was justified: the French were now exasperated beyond endurance. On 17 April 1934, Barthou—right-wing foreign minister in the National government which followed the riots of 6 February—refused to legalise

¹ Anglo-French meeting, 22 Sept. 1933. *British Foreign Policy*, second series. v. No. 406.
² Conference of Ministers, 17 Oct. 1933. *Documents on German Foreign Policy*, series C. ii. No. 9.

any German rearmament, and declared: "France will henceforth assure her security by her own means". The Disarmament conference was dead, despite some posthumous attempts to revive it. The French had fired the starting-pistol for the arms race. Characteristically they then failed to run it. Their arms estimates had been cut down during the preparations for the Disarmament conference, and did not even return to the level of 1932 until 1936.

The end of the Disarmament conference did not necessarily mean war. There was a third course, despite British outcry to the contrary: a return to the traditional instruments of diplomacy. Everyone began shamefacedly to edge back to this course from the moment of Hitler's appearance. Mussolini was the first. He had never liked Geneva and all it stood for. As the senior Fascist in Europe, he was flattered at Hitler's imitation of him, and supposed that Germany would always be Italy's jackal, never the other way round. No doubt he supposed that Hitler's threats and boasts were as empty as his own. At any rate, far from fearing the revival of Germany, he welcomed it as a lever with which to extract concessions for himself from France and perhaps later from Great Britain as well—a point conveniently overlooked by the British. Mussolini proposed a Four Power Pact. The Four Great Powers—Germany, Great Britain, France, and Italy— were to set themselves up as a European directory, laying down the law to the smaller states and carrying through "peaceful revision". The British were delighted. They too wanted to extract concessions from the French—though primarily for Germany's benefit. The idea of Great Britain and Italy benignly mediating between France and Germany was an old one. It was enshrined in Locarno, though then Mussolini had played a subordinate role; it had been advocated by John Morley in 1914, when he had tried to keep Great Britain out of war; it had been supported by Simon and MacDonald in 1914 and was welcomed by them now, so that former Radicals were in the odd position of regarding Mussolini as the chief pillar of European peace. Hitler too was prepared to let Mussolini do the preliminary hunting for him. The French were indignant, imprisoned—as it were—between British and Italian warders. They first acquiesced, though insisting that revision could only be carried through by unanimous consent, including that of the interested parties. Then they used the excuse of Germany's withdrawal from the League of Nations to wreck the Pact altogether. It was never ratified. Nevertheless it remained the basis of Italian policy for some years, and of British policy almost until the outbreak of war. Even odder, the French came round to it before the end of the story.

The main importance of the Pact at the time was in eastern Europe. Both Soviet Russia and Poland took alarm, though with opposite results. Russia went over from the German side to the French; Poland, to some extent, from the French side to the German. An association of the four European Powers had always been the nightmare of Soviet statesmen: it would be the prelude, they believed, to a new war of intervention. They had guarded against it until the coming of Hitler by encouraging German resentment against France and by promoting the economic and military co-operation with Germany which had been initiated at Rapallo. Now they changed round. Unlike the statesmen of western Europe, they took Hitler's talk seriously. They believed that he meant to destroy Communism not only in Germany but in Russia as well; and they feared that most European statesmen would applaud him if he did. They were convinced that Hitler intended to seize the Ukraine. Their own interest was purely defensive. Their dreams of world revolution had long vanished. Their greatest fear was in the Far East, where—with Japan in Manchuria and at peace with China—they seemed in imminent danger of a Japanese attack. The best Soviet troops were in the Far East; and the Soviet leaders asked of Europe only to be left alone. Where once they had denounced "the slave treaty" of Versailles, they now preached respect for international law; loyally attended the Disarmament conference—formerly a "*bourgeois* sham"; and in 1934 even joined that other *bourgeois* sham, the League of Nations. Here was an associate ready-made for the French: a Great Power resolute against "revision", who would rescue them from the pressure of Great Britain and Italy. The association drifted into unacknowledged existence during 1933. It was an association of a limited kind. The Russians had swung over to the French system solely because they believed that it would offer them increased security; they did not foresee that it might involve increased obligations. They overrated French strength, both material and moral; and, like everyone except Hitler, they overrated the strength of paper commitments, despite their ostensible freedom from *bourgeois* morality. They, too, thought it an asset to have international law on their side. The French, on the other hand, did not intend to restore the Russian alliance on any serious scale. They had little faith in Russian strength, and less in Soviet sincerity. They knew that friendship with Soviet Russia was much disapproved of in London; and though they were sometimes irritated at British promptings towards appeasement, they were still more terrified at losing even the thin shreds of British support. The Franco-Soviet rapprochement was a reinsurance, no more.

Even so, it was enough to alarm the directors of German foreign policy. In their eyes, the friendship of Rapallo had been an essential element in German recovery. It had given security against Poland; it had helped to extract concessions from the Western powers; on the practical level, it had assisted some measure of illegal rearmament. Neurath, the foreign minister, said: "We cannot do without Russia's cover for our rear".[1] Bülow, his assistant, wrote: "good German-Soviet relations are of essential importance to Germany".[2] Hitler alone was unmoved. No doubt his anti-communism was genuine; no doubt, as an Austrian, he did not share the attachment to Russia common among Prussian conservatives; no doubt he saw that a breach between Germany and Soviet Russia would put up his stock as the defender of European civilisation against Communist revolution. His immediate motive, however, was one of practical calculation: Russia could do nothing against Germany. Not merely was she separated from Germany by Poland. The Soviet leaders did not want to do anything. On the contrary, they had gone over to the French side because they believed that this made fewer demands on them and entailed fewer risks than remaining friendly to Germany. They would vote against Germany at Geneva; they would not act. Hitler saw Rapallo dissolve without a twinge.

On the other hand, Poland could act against Germany and was talking of doing so; repeated, though empty, calls came from Warsaw for a preventive war. No German minister since 1918 had contemplated friendship with Poland, even of a temporary

[1] Conference of Ministers, 7 April 1933. *German Foreign Policy*, series C. i. No. 142.
[2] Bülow to Nadolny, 13 Nov. 1933. *Ibid.* ii. No. 66.

nature; the sore of Danzig and the corridor cut too deep. Hitler was as free from this prejudice as from any other. It was a measure of the mastery which Hitler had already attained over the German "governing-class" that he could disregard their most deep-seated grievance; a measure too of the indifference felt by the German people over their so-called grievances that this disregard passed without any popular murmur. Some Germans consoled themselves that the renunciation was temporary; and Hitler let them think so. His real intention was less fixed one way or the other. Fundamentally he was not interested merely in "revising" Germany's frontiers. He wanted to make Germany dominant in Europe; and for this he was more concerned to transform her neighbours into satellites than to clip off bits of their territory. He followed this policy with Italy, where he renounced what was for him a much deeper grievance than Danzig or the corridor—south Tyrol—in order to secure Italian friendship in exchange. He recognised that Poland, like Italy, was a "revisionist" Power, even though she owed her independence to the Allied victory of 1918; hence he believed that Poland, like Italy and Hungary, would be won to his side. For such a gain, Danzig and the corridor were a price worth paying. Hitler never annexed territory for its own sake. As his later policy showed, he had no objection to preserving other countries so long as they acted as Germany's jackals.

But in this Polish affair, as in most others, Hitler did not take the initiative. He let others do his work for him. Pilsudski and his associates who ruled Poland aspired to play the part of a Great Power. They were indignant at the Four Power Pact which seemed to be directed principally against Poland; and they were alarmed when France and Soviet Russia drew together. The Poles could never forget that, while Danzig and the corridor roused German resentment on their western frontier, they held ten times as much non-Polish territory in the east; and though they feared Germany much, the Polish colonels of Pilsudski's system feared Soviet Russia more. Apart from this, the Poles had been flattered to be France's chief friend in eastern Europe; it was a different matter to act merely as advance guard for a Franco-Soviet alliance. Beck, the foreign minister, always possessed complete self-confidence, though not much else. He was sure that he could treat Hitler as an equal, or even tame the tiger. He offered better relations with Germany; and Hitler responded. The result was the Non-Aggression Pact of January 1934 between Germany and Poland, another peg removed from the crumbling system of security. Hitler was freed from any threat of Polish support for France; in return, without renouncing Germany's grievances, he promised not to redress them by force—a high-sounding formula much used also by the West German government after the second World war. The agreement was Hitler's first great achievement in foreign affairs; and it brought him much subsequent success. There was in it a deep equivocation as one might expect in an agreement between two such men as Hitler and Beck. Hitler assumed that Poland had been detached from the French system, which indeed she had. He further assumed that "the colonels" would accept the logical consequence of this. Poland would become a loyal satellite, accommodating herself to German plans and German wishes. Beck had proposed the agreement not to become anybody's satellite, but to make Poland more independent than before. So long as she had only the alliance with France, Poland had to follow French policy and, in the new circumstances, might even find herself put under Soviet orders. The agreement with Germany enabled Poland to disregard French promptings; yet at the same time she still had the French alliance to fall back on if Germany became troublesome. The agreement was not a choice in favour of Germany even as between Germany and Russia; it was meant as a device by which Poland could balance the two more securely.

These divergences were for the future. In 1934 the agreement greatly improved Hitler's freedom of manoeuvre. He was not yet ready to take advantage of this. German rearmament had only just begun; and he had domestic worries to keep him busy—opposition both from his old conservative backers and from his own revolutionary followers. This domestic crisis was not overcome until 30 June, when those who had been making trouble were murdered on Hitler's orders. A month later Hindenburg died. Hitler succeeded him as President—another step on the road to supreme power. This was not the moment for an adventurous foreign policy, or indeed for any foreign policy at all. For once the drift of events, on which Hitler relied, turned against him. It was Austria, his own birthplace, which caused the set-back. This rump-state, last fragment of the Habsburg empire, had had independence artificially imposed upon it by the peacemakers in 1919. Independent Austria was the prime guarantee of Italy's security, the harmless buffer interposed between her and Europe. Italy would lose all aloofness from Europe if Austria were absorbed into Germany or fell under German control. Besides, there were three hundred thousand German-speaking people in what had been South Tyrol and was now Alto Adige: former Austrians, present Italians, always German in national sentiment. Here would be another cause of danger for Italy if German nationalism triumphed in Austria.

Hitler knew well that improved relations with Italy would bring even greater advantage than good relations with Poland. Already in *Mein Kampf* he had pointed to Italy as the pre-destined ally against France. Now, in 1934, anyone could see that friendship between the two dictators would be of immense value to Germany during the "danger period". Yet it was harder for Hitler to renounce Austria for Italy's sake than it had been for him to postpone controversy over Danzig and the corridor for the sake of Poland. Not harder for him as leader of the German people: they cared little for this supposedly German cause, while many of them felt strongly about Danzig and the corridor. It was harder for him as a man, as one who had been a German nationalist in Austria long before he became the leader of nationalism in Germany. Besides, the Austrian question thrust itself forward even against the needs of high policy. Independent Austria was in poor shape. She had never found self-confidence since the peace treaties, though she had not done badly from an economic point of view. Austrian Clericals and Austrian Socialists remained incurably hostile one to the other; nor were they drawn together even by the threat from Nazi Germany. Instead Dollfuss, the clerical Chancellor, put himself under Italy's guidance; and, prompted by Mussolini, destroyed both the Austrian Socialist movement and the democratic republic in February 1934.

This civil war stirred up in turn the Austrian Nazis. The Clericalist dictatorship was unpopular; the Nazis hoped to capture much of the old Socialist following. They received money and equipment from Germany; they were encouraged by Munich radio. Yet they were not, as foreign powers often thought, mere

German agents to be turned on and off at will. It was easy for Hitler to turn them on; difficult however for him to turn them off, particularly when he reflected that he would be an Austrian Nazi agitator himself if he had not become leader of Germany. The most that could be expected of him was that he should not actively push the Austrian question. He said in the Council of Ministers: "I am ready to write off Austria for years to come, but I cannot say so to Mussolini".[1] The German diplomatists—themselves unable to check Hitler—hoped that he might be pushed into concession if he met Mussolini face to face; and they therefore arranged a meeting of the two dictators at Venice on 14 June. For the first time, though by no means the last, Mussolini was to perform the task that was too difficult for anyone else: he was to "moderate" Hitler.

The meeting did not come up to expectations. The two men agreed in their dislike of France and Soviet Russia; and, in their pleasure at this, forgot to agree about Austria. Hitler renounced, truthfully enough, any desire to annex Austria. "A personage of independent outlook" should become Austrian Chancellor; then there should be free elections, and afterwards the Nazis would join the Government. This was a simple solution; Hitler would get what he wanted without the trouble of fighting for it. Mussolini replied that the Nazis should drop their terroristic campaign, and then Dollfuss would treat them more sympathetically—as he well might once they became harmless.[2] Hitler, of course, did nothing to fulfil Mussolini's demand. He did not attempt to check the Austrian Nazis; and they, excited by the events of 30 June in Germany, were eager to stage their own blood-bath. On 25 July the Nazis of Vienna occupied the Chancellery; murdered Dollfuss; and attempted to seize power. Hitler, though delighted by Dollfuss's death, could do nothing to help his Austrian adherents. Italian troops were demonstratively moved to the Austrian frontier; and Hitler had to stand helplessly by while Schuschnigg, successor to Dollfuss, restored order under Mussolini's protection.

The Austrian revolt landed Hitler in a gratuitous humiliation.

[1] Memorandum by Bülow, 30 Apr. 1934. *German Foreign Policy*, series C. ii. No. 393.

[2] Memorandum by Neurath, 15 June 1934; Hassell to Neurath, 21 June 1934. *Ibid.* iii. No. 5 and 26.

It also upset the nice balance from which Mussolini had expected to reap much profit. He had assumed that German policy would develop along its old lines, demanding concessions from France and next from Poland, but leaving Austria alone. He would balance happily between France and Germany, receiving rewards from both, committing himself to neither. Suddenly he found the position reversed: with Austria threatened, he needed backing from France instead of the other way round. Mussolini had to become the upholder of treaties and the champion of collective security, where he had previously been the advocate of revision—at the expense of others. His conversion was welcomed by the British. They consistently exaggerated Italian strength—it is impossible to explain why. They never looked at the hard facts of Italy's economic weakness: at her lack of coal and her comparative lack of heavy industry. Italy was to them simply a "Great Power"; and of course millions even of half-armed men looked formidable when compared to their own limited forces. Also they were taken in by Mussolini's boasting. He called himself a strong man, a warrior-chief, a great statesman; they believed him.

The French were at first less forthcoming. Barthou, the foreign minister, hoped to thwart Germany without paying Mussolini's price. His solution was an Eastern Locarno: France and Russia jointly guaranteeing the existing settlement to the east of Germany, as Great Britain and Italy guaranteed it on the west. This scheme was unwelcome to Germany and Poland, the two Powers most concerned. Germany did not want any extension of French influence in eastern Europe; the Poles were determined that Russia should not be allowed to re-enter European affairs. Hitler, with his usual gift for waiting, sat back and let the Poles wreck the eastern Locarno for him. Barthou was left only with a vague understanding that France and Soviet Russia would act together in the unlikely chance that they were ever asked to do so. In any case, his days were numbered. In October 1934 King Alexander of Yugoslavia visited France to consolidate his alliance with her. At Marseilles he was murdered by a Croat terrorist who had been trained in Italy. Barthou at his side, also wounded by the assassin's bullet, was left to bleed to death on the pavement. Pierre Laval, his successor, was a man of a more modern mould, the cleverest and perhaps the most unscrupulous of French statesmen. He had started as an extreme Socialist; he had been on the anti-war side during the first World war. Like many lapsed Socialists, Ramsay MacDonald for example, Laval had a poor opinion of Soviet Russia and a high opinion of Fascist Italy. Though he allowed Barthou's policy to drift as far as a Franco-Soviet pact in May 1935, the pact was empty: never reinforced as the old alliance had been by military conversations, never taken seriously by any French government, maybe not by the Soviet government either. All the French got out of it was Stalin's instruction to the French Communist party that they should no longer impede the work of national defence— an instruction almost enough of itself to transform French patriots in their turn into defeatists.

Laval placed all his hopes on Italy. He visited Rome, flattered himself that Mussolini was now cured by the Austrian affair of any revisionist longings. Hitler on his side seemed deliberately bent on consolidating the united front against Germany. He chipped away the remaining restrictions on German armament with increasing contempt; and finally announced the restoration of conscription in March 1935. For once the former victors showed signs of resistance. In April 1935 there was a great gathering at Stresa: MacDonald and Simon, Flandin—French prime minister—and Laval, Mussolini a host in himself. There had been nothing like this since the meetings of the Supreme Council in the days of Lloyd George. It was a last display of Allied solidarity, a mocking echo from the days of victory; all the odder in that the three Powers who had "made the world safe for liberal democracy" were now represented by renegade Socialists, two of whom—MacDonald and Laval—had opposed the war, while the third, Mussolini, had destroyed democracy in his own country. Italy, France and Great Britain solemnly resolved to maintain the existing treaty settlement of Europe and to resist any attempt to change this settlement by force. This was an impressive display of words, though rather late in the day when so much had been changed already. Did any of the three mean what they said? The Italians promised to send troops for the defence of Belfort; the French promised to send troops to Tyrol. But in truth each of the three Powers hoped to receive help from the others without providing any in return; and each rejoiced to see the others in difficulty.

Hitler, on his side, had just received a powerful reinforcement of sentiment. In January 1935, the Saar—detached from Germany in 1919—held a plebiscite on its future destiny. The inhabitants were mostly industrial workers—Social Democrats or Roman Catholics. They knew what awaited them in Germany: dictatorship, destruction of trade unions, persecution of the Christian churches. Yet, in an unquestionably free election, 90% voted for return to Germany. Here was proof that the appeal of German nationalism would be irresistible—in Austria, in Czechoslovakia, in Poland. With this force behind him, Hitler did not worry about old-fashioned diplomatic demonstrations. Less than a month after the meeting at Stresa, he repudiated the remaining disarmament clauses of the treaty of Versailles, "given that the other Powers had not fulfilled the obligation to disarm, incumbent upon them". At the same time he promised to respect the territorial settlement of Versailles and the provisions of Locarno. The "artificial" system of security was dead—striking proof that a system cannot be a substitute for action, but can only provide opportunities for it. Hitler had shaken off the restrictions on German armament in just over two years; and there had never been a moment when he had had to face real danger. The experience of these two years confirmed what he had already learnt from German politics. He believed that strong nerves would always win; his "bluff", if it were bluff, would never be called. Henceforth he would advance with "the certainty of a sleep-walker". The events of the next twelve months only strengthened this certainty.

CHAPTER FIVE

The Abyssinian Affair and the End of Locarno

VERSAILLES was dead. Everyone except the French rejoiced; for what took its place was the system of Locarno, a system which the Germans had voluntarily accepted and which Hitler had just voluntarily reaffirmed. The British showed what they thought of "the Stresa front" by immediately concluding with Hitler a private deal which limited the German navy (still almost non-existent) to a third of their own. This could be justified as a sensible attempt to save the system of naval restrictions after the wreck of the Disarmament conference; it was however hardly compatible with that respect for treaties which the Stresa powers had just proclaimed. The French made a great grievance of the Anglo-German naval agreement, alleging that Hitler had been on the point of capitulation when his nerve was restored by the British deserting the common front. This view, though still held by French historians, is not supported by evidence from the German side; and it seems likely that Hitler was content to wait for the Stresa front to break up.

He was again correct. The Stresa meeting had been designed to establish a firm alliance against aggression. Instead it opened the door to events which not only dissolved this alliance, but destroyed also the League of Nations and, with it, the entire system of collective security. These events centred on Abyssinia. Their outward course is clear; their background and significance still somewhat of a mystery. Abyssinia was an old object of Italian ambition, and the scene of her catastrophic defeat at Adowa in 1896. Revenge for Adowa was implicit in Fascist boasting; but no more urgent in 1935 than at any time since Mussolini came to power in 1922. Conditions in Italy did not demand a war. Fascism was not politically threatened; and economic circumstances in Italy favoured peace, not the inflation of war. Nor does Italy's diplomatic position in regard to

Abyssinia seem to have been endangered. Though Abyssinia had been admitted to the League of Nations in 1925, this had been done on Italian initiative—to check supposed British encroachments there; and it was the British who had protested that Abyssinia was too barbarous to join the civilised community at Geneva. Both Great Britain and France recognised Abyssinia as Italy's "sphere of interest"; and the unity of Stresa made this recognition even firmer. Perhaps the Italians were alarmed by the presence of American speculators in Abyssinia, and by the welcome they received from Haile Selassie, the Emperor. But this is conjecture. Mussolini himself alleged that he wanted to take advantage of the favourable circumstance that Italy was heavily armed—at any rate in theory—while the rearmament of the other Powers had hardly begun. He pointed especially to the German threat to Austria, which would obviously be renewed. The Italian army, he made out, had to conquer Abyssinia at once, so as to be back on the Brenner for the defence of Austria when Germany had rearmed. This seems a nonsensical explanation. If Austria were endangered, Mussolini should surely have concentrated on her defence without becoming distracted by Abyssinia. Perhaps he sensed that he would lose Austria sooner or later and therefore seized Abyssinia as a consolation. More probably, he was merely intoxicated out of his senses by the militaristic blustering which he had started and in which Hitler was now outbidding him.

At any rate, for reasons which are still difficult to grasp, Mussolini decided in 1934 to conquer Abyssinia. He received encouragement when Laval visited Rome in January 1935. Laval was anxious to win Mussolini for the anti-German front, and was, no doubt, generous with soft words. According to one account, he spoke favourably of Italian ambitions on condition that her control over Abyssinia was established peacefully as, allegedly, French control had been over Morocco. According to another version, Laval promised to ensure that the League of Nations, if it became involved, would not harm Italy and, in particular, that there should be no interference with Italy's supply of oil. This sounds like a story made up later when sanctions were actually imposed; in January 1935 Laval could not foresee that this would happen. Probably Laval merely encouraged Mussolini in a general way, so as to keep him in a good temper. The Stresa meeting gave Mussolini a chance to sound the British. It is impossible to say whether he did so or what he learnt from them. One story has it that Mussolini ran over the various topics of European policy with MacDonald and Simon, and then asked whether there was anything else which the British wished to discuss. MacDonald and Simon shook their heads; and Mussolini concluded that they had no objection to his Abyssinian adventure. On the other hand, the African expert at the foreign office accompanied the British ministers to Stresa; and it is difficult to believe that he found nothing to say to his Italian colleagues. However that may be, the British could not ignore the increase in Italian armaments in the Red Sea. A foreign office committee was set up to consider the implications; and it reported that an Italian conquest of Abyssinia would not affect Great Britain's imperial interests.

There was one awkward point: Abyssinia was a member of the League of Nations, and the British government did not want to see a repetition of the difficulties which had been caused by Japan's action in Manchuria. For one thing, they genuinely wished to maintain the League as an instrument for coercion—and for conciliation—against Germany. For another, they were increasingly hampered by their own public opinion. Propaganda for the League of Nations and for collective security was at its height. The two phrases solved many a moral dilemma. Supporting the League of Nations provided an altruistic cover for all those who would have turned with horror from defending the treaty-settlement of Versailles. Collective security, which was supposed to assemble the forces of fifty-two nations, presented a way of resisting aggression without an increase in British armaments. In the autumn of 1934 the miscalled Peace Ballot showed that ten million people in Great Britain favoured economic sanctions, and six millions favoured even military sanctions, against an aggressor condemned by the League of Nations—expression of opinion very far from pacifist. It would be unfair to suggest that the British government merely exploited this sentiment. British ministers usually share the principles and prejudices of their contemporaries; and to some extent they did so now. Still, it was not irrelevant to their calculations that a general election was approaching. Collective security offered a wonderful opportunity for splitting the Labour Opposition, where one section, the majority indeed, favoured the League of Nations, while another, the more vocal, still opposed any support for this "capitalist" institution or any co-operation with a British "imperialist" government.

These are all conjectures. No one knows why the British government took the line they did; probably they did not know themselves. They were committed to riding two horses: they wanted to conciliate Mussolini and yet to sustain the authority of the League of Nations. In June 1935 Eden, at that time a junior minister in charge of League of Nations affairs, went to Rome in the hope of sorting the tangle out. He brought a solid offer: Great Britain would give Abyssinia access to the sea through British Somaliland, and Abyssinia in return would surrender some of her outlying territory to Italy. He also brought a warning: there must be no flagrant challenge to the Covenant of the League of Nations. The professionals at the Italian foreign ministry wished to accept the British offer. Mussolini was unmoved. He wanted the glory of a victorious war, not a mere adjustment of territory. There was a stormy meeting between Mussolini and Eden—Mussolini denouncing British hypocrisy as shown in the Anglo-German naval treaty, Eden reiterating his high principles. Eden came home bitterly anti-Italian, as he ever afterwards remained. The British foreign office was less dismayed. It still hoped to settle the conflict between Italy and Abyssinia by means of a compromise; it was confident that the Abyssinians would put up a substantial resistance. Mussolini would learn moderation when he ran into difficulties; and then the British government would arrange a settlement which would restore both the Stresa front and the prestige of the League of Nations.

Just at this moment British foreign policy received a more vigorous leadership. In June 1935 Baldwin succeeded MacDonald as prime minister. The opportunity was taken for a general reshuffle. Sir John Simon had been discredited, whether deservedly or not, by his part in the Manchurian affair; he was regarded by public opinion as too conciliatory, too ingenious in finding excuses for the aggressor. He now left the foreign office; and was succeeded by Sir Samuel Hoare. Hoare was as able intellectually as any British foreign secretary of the twentieth century—perhaps not a very high standard. His weakness was impetuosity. He braved difficulties instead of evading them, as he showed at the end of his life by writing a defence of "appease-ment", where the other participants, more wisely, remained silent. Hoare understood the dangers of collective security—a system where the British shouldered the burdens and others did the talking. But he thought that these dangers might be over-come if British policy were resolute enough; there was some chance then that others would follow. In September 1935 Hoare delivered at Geneva the most ringing assertion in favour of collective security ever made by a British statesman. When Abyssinia was actually attacked in October, he took the lead in pressing for sanctions against Italy. The members of the League responded. The machinery for economic sanctions had been set up after the Manchurian affair; and this machinery was now operated by every country in the League except Italy's three client-states—Albania, Austria, and Hungary. This was not much of a loophole. Complaint was made of the graver breach in the system of sanctions provided by Germany and the United States, the two Great Powers outside the League. This, too, was not serious. Hitler was playing for British friendship after the Anglo-German naval treaty; he was also delighted to see a dispute springing up between Italy and France. It was therefore worth his while to appear to be co-operating, unofficially, with the League of Nations. On a more practical level the Germans, for solid economic reasons, did not wish to be saddled with worthless liras and cut down their trade with Italy. The United States, in the heyday of neutrality, could not take sides; but they forbade American trade with both combatants, and, as there was no American trade with Abyssinia, this was in fact a sanction against Italy.

The real weakness was within the League. Though the French could not afford to quarrel with Great Britain, Laval was dis-mayed by the crumbling of the Stresa front. The old British arguments in favour of conciliation and against the automatic working of collective security reappeared in French mouths. France applied sanctions; but Laval assured Mussolini now, if not earlier, that Italy's oil supplies would not be interfered with. There was divergence of views in Great Britain also. The division was not merely between the "idealists" who supported the League of Nations and the cynics who believed that collective security always involved risk and burdens for Great Britain,

without any compensating gain. The division was also one
between the generations. Younger men, represented by Eden,
were strenuously anti-Italian and were much more ready to
conciliate Germany. The traditionalists, particularly strong in
the foreign office, were concerned only with the German danger;
they regarded the League of Nations as a nuisance and wished to
win back Italy for the united front against Germany. Vansittart,
permanent under-secretary at the foreign office, took this view;
from first to last he was the unrepentant advocate of alliance
with Italy, which he seemed to treat as the solution for every
problem. Even Winston Churchill, who was already sounding the
alarm over Germany, remained out of the country during the
autumn of 1935 so as to avoid having to pronounce for or against
Italy. On the surface British policy was firm for collective
security. Behind the scenes influential figures waited to put
forward some version of the compromise which Mussolini had
rejected in the previous June. At that time, the Emperor of
Abyssinia, too, had been obstinate—confident that a martyr's
adherence to collective security would strengthen his tottering
throne, as indeed it did, though in a longer run than he expected.

The British advocates of compromise were not discouraged by
their initial check. Military experts, in Great Britain and elsewhere, were confident that the Italian conquest of Abyssinia,
though likely, would take a long time—at least two winter
campaigning seasons. Before then, economic difficulties would
tame Mussolini; and defeat would tame the Emperor of Abyssinia. The way to compromise would be open. Hence there was
no hurry. The government also received a report from their naval
advisers to the effect that the British navy in the Mediterranean,
though reinforced by the entire Home fleet, was no match for the
combined Italian navy and air force. Here was another argument
for caution and delay: far better that time should teach moderation to both sides than that Mussolini should be provoked by
sharper pressure into attacking—and presumably destroying—
the British navy. Both expert opinions were flagrantly wrong.
The military opinion was proved wrong within a few months
when the Italian army conquered all Abyssinia by May 1936; the
naval opinion was proved wrong in the darkest days of the second
World war, when the British navy in the Mediterranean went from
victory to victory over the Italian, despite far worse odds than

those of 1935. No doubt these were, in the main, honest errors. The experts got their calculations wrong. The generals underrated the Italian army; the admirals overrated the Italian navy.

But there was more to it. Every expert is a human being; and technical opinions reflect the political views of those who give them. Generals and admirals are confident of winning a war when they want to fight; they always find decisive arguments against a war which they regard as politically undesirable. The British generals and admirals at this time were mostly elderly; they were all Conservatives of an extreme cast. They admired Mussolini. They found in Fascism a display of all the military virtues. On the other hand, they detested the League of Nations and everything associated with it. To them, "Geneva" meant the Disarmament conference, the abandonment of national sovereignty, and the pursuit of impractical idealistic aims. Those who were clamouring for sanctions against Italy had spent earlier years denouncing British armaments and British military experts. It was hardly to be expected that these experts should now wish to fight a war as the agents of the League of Nations Union. For the admirals in particular, the temptation was irresistible to round on those who had harassed them, and to declare that, thanks to the agitation for disarmament, Great Britain was now too weak to run the risk of war. Hence the successors of Nelson put their names to a craven opinion which would have earned them instant dismissal from an earlier Board of Admiralty.

Cautious support for the League of Nations, though inadequate to restrain Mussolini, proved a triumphant manoeuvre in domestic politics. During the previous two years, the Labour Opposition had made all the running in foreign affairs. It caught the National government both ways round, denouncing at one moment the failure to assert collective security and at the next the alleged sabotage of the Disarmament conference. Thus Labour hoped to win the votes both of pacifists and of enthusiasts for the League. With casual adroitness, Baldwin turned the tables. "All sanctions short of war", which Hoare was supposed to be advocating at Geneva, presented Labour with a terrible dilemma. Should they demand stronger sanctions, with the risk of war, and thus lose the votes of the pacifists? Or should they denounce the League as a dangerous sham, and thus lose the votes of the enthusiasts for it? After fierce debate, Labour decided to do both; and the inevitable result followed. In November 1935 there was a general election. The government had done enough to satisfy the supporters of the League; not enough to alarm those who disliked the thought of war. Labour, with its demand for more sanctions, was branded as the war-party. The National government was returned with a majority of nearly two hundred and fifty. This seemed later a triumph of hypocrisy. Yet "all sanctions short of war" was the policy favoured by most Englishmen, including the supporters of the Labour party. They were in favour of the League, but not to the point of war. There was sense in this view. What was the good of an institution for preventing war, if war were the result of its activities? This was a new form of the problem which had confronted the victors ever since 1919. They had fought "a war to end war". How then could they fight another?

With the election out of the way, the British government had to face the consequences. There was a growing demand at Geneva for cutting off Italy's supplies of oil. This could be answered only by producing a compromise which would end the war. The way was clear to revive the scheme which Eden had taken to Rome in June, and which Mussolini had then rejected. Vansittart revised it, making it more generous to Italy. She would receive a mandate for the fertile plains which Abyssinia had conquered quite recently; the Emperor would retain his old kingdom in the mountains, and the British would give him access to the sea by means of a port in British Somaliland (this was the provision damned by *The Times* as "a corridor for camels"). Early in December Hoare took the plan to Paris. Laval welcomed it. Mussolini, warned by his equally erring experts that the war was going badly, was ready to accept it. The next step was to present it at Geneva; then, with the League's concurrence, to impose it on the Emperor of Abyssinia —a beautiful example, repeated at Munich, of using the machinery of peace against the victim of aggression. But something went wrong. Hardly had Hoare left Paris on his way to Geneva than the so-called Hoare-Laval plan appeared in the French press. No one knows how this happened. Perhaps Laval doubted whether the National government were solidly behind Hoare and therefore leaked the plan in order to commit Baldwin and the rest beyond redemption. Perhaps Herriot, or some other enemy of Laval's, revealed the plan in order to ruin it, believing that, if the League were effective against Mussolini, it could then be turned against Hitler. Maybe there was no design at all, merely the incorrigible zest of French journalists to exploit their contacts with the Quai d'Orsay.

At any rate, the revelation produced an explosion in British public opinion. The high-minded supporters of the League who had helped to return the National government felt cheated and indignant. Hoare himself was out of action, having broken his nose when he overrated his proficiency as a skating champion on the Swiss ice. Baldwin first admitted that the plan had been endorsed by the government; then repudiated both the plan and Sir Samuel Hoare. Eden took Hoare's place as foreign secretary. The Hoare-Laval plan disappeared. Otherwise nothing was changed. The British government were still resolved not to risk war. They enquired of Mussolini whether he would object to his oil being cut off; when told that he would, they successfully resisted oil sanctions at Geneva. Compromise was still in the air; another version of the Hoare-Laval plan waiting to be produced when the campaigning season was over. Mussolini was too quick for the British military experts—and his own. The Italian general staff had gloomily advocated withdrawal to the old frontier after the initial difficulties. Instead Mussolini sent out Badoglio, the chief of staff, with orders to finish the war quickly; and, for once, his orders were obeyed. It was said that the Abyssinian armies were demoralised by the use of gas. But these armies, like the Empire itself, were more pretence than reality. They soon crumbled into nothing. On 1 May the Emperor Haile Selassie left Abyssinia. A week later Mussolini proclaimed the foundation of a new Roman empire.

This was the deathblow to the League as well as to Abyssinia. Fifty-two nations had combined to resist aggression; all they accomplished was that Haile Selassie lost all his country instead of only half. Incorrigible in impracticality, the League further offended Italy by allowing Haile Selassie a hearing at the Assembly; and then expelled him for the crime of taking the Covenant seriously. Japan and Germany had already left the League; Italy followed in December 1937. The League continued in existence only by averting its eyes from what was happening around it. When foreign Powers intervened in the Spanish civil war, the Spanish government appealed to the League. The Council first "studied the question"; then expressed its "regrets", and agreed to house the pictures from the Prado at Geneva. In September 1938 the Assembly actually met at the height of the Czech crisis; it managed to get through the session without noting that a crisis was taking place. In September 1939 no one bothered to inform the League that war had broken out. In December 1939 the League expelled Soviet Russia for invading Finland—the Assembly loyally observing Swiss neutrality by not mentioning the war between Germany and the Western Powers. In 1945 the League had a last meeting to wind itself up and transfer its assets to the United Nations.

The real death of the League was in December 1935, not in 1939 or 1945. One day it was a powerful body imposing sanctions, seemingly more effective than ever before; the next day it was an empty sham, everyone scuttling from it as quickly as possible. What killed the League was the publication of the Hoare-Laval plan. Yet this was a perfectly sensible plan, in line with the League's previous acts of conciliation from Corfu to Manchuria. It would have ended the war; satisfied Italy; and left Abyssinia with a more workable, national territory. The common sense of the plan was, in the circumstances of the time, its vital defect. For the League action against Italy was not a common sense extension of practical policies; it was a demonstration of principle pure and simple. No concrete "interest" was at stake in Abyssinia—not even for Italy: Mussolini was concerned to show off Italy's strength, not to acquire the practical gains (if any such exist) of Empire. The League powers were concerned to assert the Covenant, not to defend interests of their own. The Hoare-Laval plan seemed to show that principle and practical policy could not be combined. The conclusion was false: every states-man of any merit combines the two, though in varying propor-tions. But everyone accepted it in 1935. From this moment until the outbreak of war, "realists" and "idealists" stood on opposing sides. Practical statesmen, particularly those in power, pursued policies of expediency without thought of principle; disillusioned idealists refused to believe that the men in power could ever be supported or even entrusted with arms. The few who tried to bridge the gap were in the worst case. Eden, for example, remained foreign secretary in order to save something from the wreck; in practice he became simply a cover for the cynical "elder statesmen", Simon, Hoare, and Neville Chamberlain. Even Winston Churchill who talked in high terms of collective security and resistance to aggression estranged the idealists by talking also of the need for greater British armaments; and so remained until the outbreak of war a solitary figure, distrusted by both sides. Of course there is always some cleavage between principle and expediency; but it was never so wide as in the four years after December 1935.

The Abyssinian affair had more immediate effects. Hitler watched the conflict with sharp eyes, fearful that a triumphant League might next be used against Germany, yet eager to drive a wedge between Italy and her two former partners in the Stresa front. Germany cut down her trade with Italy almost as much as if she had been a member of the League loyally operating sanctions; and in December Hitler, anxious to wreck the Hoare-Laval plan, even offered to return to the League—on conditions of course. When the plan failed and Italian arms began to succeed, Hitler resolved to exploit the breakdown of the Stresa front. At least this seems the most likely explanation for his decision to reoccupy the demilitarised Rhineland, though at present there is no solid evidence of what was in his mind. Hitler's excuse was the French ratification of the Franco-Soviet pact on 27 February 1936. This, he claimed, had destroyed the assumptions of Locarno; not much of an argument, but a useful appeal no doubt to anti-Bolshevik-feeling in Great Britain and France. The actual move on 7 March was a staggering example of Hitler's strong nerve. Germany had literally no forces available for war. The trained men of the old Reichswehr were now dispersed as instructors among the new mass army; and this new army was not yet ready. Hitler assured his protesting generals that he would withdraw his token force at the first sign of French action; but he was unshakably confident that no action would follow.

The reoccupation of the Rhineland did not take the French by surprise. They had been brooding on it apprehensively ever since the beginning of the Abyssinian affair. In January 1936 Laval left the foreign ministry—a victim, like Hoare, of the outcry against the Hoare-Laval plan. Flandin, his successor, claimed to be more pro-British. He at once went to London to discuss the

Rhineland problem. Baldwin asked: what has the French government decided to do? It had decided nothing; and Flandin returned to Paris to extract a decision from his colleagues. He failed; or rather he obtained only a declaration that "France would place all her forces at the disposal of the League of Nations to oppose a violation of the Treaties". Thus the decision was passed in advance from Paris to Geneva, where the League was already in full dissolution.

On 7 March the French ministry met in a state of high indignation. Four ministers, including Flandin and Sarraut, the prime minister, were for immediate action; but, as often happened with French ministers, these strong men had ascertained that they were in a minority before raising their voices. General Gamelin, the chief of staff, was called in and delivered the first of those oracular judgements with which he was to tantalise French statesmen, and British also, in the following years. Gamelin was a man of high intelligence, but without fighting spirit; fitted to be a politician rather than a soldier, he was determined that the politicians should not shift the decision from their shoulders to his own. As chief of the fighting services, he had to claim that they were ready for any task that they might be called upon to fulfil; on the other hand, he wished to impress upon the politicians that they must spend a great deal more money on the army if it were to be of any use. At bottom Gamelin's subtle equivocations were more than an expression of his personality. They reflected the contradiction between France's conscious determination to maintain her traditional position as a Great Power and her unconscious, but more genuine, resignation to a modest, defensive position. Gamelin might talk of taking the initiative against Germany; the defensive equipment of the French army and the psychology of the Maginot line made this impossible.

Gamelin began with brave words. Of course the French army could advance into the Rhineland and defeat the German forces there. Then he unfolded the difficulties. Germany, he claimed, had nearly a million men under arms, of whom 300,000 were already in the Rhineland. Some classes of French reservists would have to be called up; and, if there were any German resistance, there must be general mobilisation. Moreover, it would be a long war; and, in view of Germany's industrial superiority, France could not hope to win it if she fought alone. There must be the certainty of at least British and Belgian support. This was also necessary for political reasons. The Treaty of Locarno authorised France to act immediately and alone only in case of "flagrant aggression". But was a movement of German troops into the Rhineland "flagrant aggression"? It did not affect the "national territory" of France; given the Maginot line, it did not even threaten French security in a more remote future. If France acted alone, she might find herself condemned as the aggressor by the Locarno Powers and the Council of the League.

Here were riddles for the politicians to solve. With a general election approaching in France, none of the ministers could contemplate general mobilisation; only a minority supported the recall of reservists. All thought of action disappeared; diplomacy took its place. The French could shift the blame from themselves to their allies, just as Gamelin had shifted it from himself to the politicians. Italy, though a Locarno Power, would of course do nothing while sanctions were still being applied against her. Poland declared that she would fulfil her obligations under the Franco-Polish treaty of 1921; but this treaty was strictly defensive, and the Poles were only committing themselves to go to war if France were actually invaded—which they knew Hitler did not at the moment intend. The Poles offered to mobilise if France did so; on the other hand, the Polish representative abstained from voting against Germany when the question came before the Council of the League. Belgium was equally reticent. In 1919 the Belgians had given up their old neutrality and made an alliance with France in the hope that this would increase their security. Now that the alliance threatened to involve action, they jettisoned it abruptly.

Only the British remained. Flandin went over to London, ostensibly canvassing for support. Actually he was more concerned to take his responsibility across the Channel and to leave it there. Baldwin displayed his usual sympathy and goodwill. Tears stood in his eyes as he confessed that the British had no forces with which to support France. In any case, he added, British public opinion would not allow it. This was true: there was almost unanimous approval in Great Britain that the Germans had liberated their own territory. What Baldwin did not add was that he agreed with this public opinion. The German reoccupation of the Rhineland was, from the British point of

view, an improvement and a success for British policy. For years
past—ever since Locarno if not before—the British had been
urging France to adopt a strictly defensive policy and not to be
drawn into war for some remote "eastern" cause. As long as the
Rhineland remained demilitarised, the French could still
threaten Germany, or so it appeared. The British were haunted
by the fear that the situation of 1914 might be repeated—that
they might be dragged into war for the sake of Czechoslovakia or
Poland as, in 1914, they supposed they had been dragged into
war for the sake of Russia. The German reoccupation of the
Rhineland removed this fear. Henceforward France had a
defensive policy imposed upon her, whether she would or no; and
most Frenchmen made no great complaint.

Flandin accepted Baldwin's veto without much argument. He
never contemplated independent action by France. Any attempt
to emulate the French statesmen of 1914 would, he believed,
involve a breach with Great Britain; and Gamelin had laid
down that action was impossible in such conditions. The British
insisted on diplomacy. Therefore diplomacy there must be. The
Council of the League met in London. Only Litvinov, the Soviet
foreign commissar, proposed sanctions against Germany; and his
advocacy was in itself enough to damn the proposal. The Council
resolved, though not unanimously, that the treaties of Versailles
and Locarno had been broken. Hitler was invited to negotiate a
new arrangement of European security, to replace that which had
been destroyed. He responded to the invitation: he had "no
territorial claims in Europe", wanted peace, proposed a twenty-
five-year pact of non-aggression with the Western Powers. The
British in their turn sought further definition with a list of
precise questions. To this Hitler did not reply at all. Silence
followed. The last remnants of Versailles had gone, and Locarno
with them. It was the end of an epoch: the capital of "victory"
was exhausted.

7 March 1936 marked a turning-point of history, but more
in appearance than in reality. In theory Germany's reoccupation
of the Rhineland made it difficult, or even impossible, for France
to aid her eastern allies, Poland and Czechoslovakia; in fact, she
had abandoned any such idea years ago, if indeed she had ever
had it. The reoccupation of the Rhineland did not affect France
from the defensive point of view. If the Maginot line were all it

claimed to be, then her security was as great as before; if the Maginot line was no good, then France had never been secure in any case. Nor was the situation all loss for France. Germany, by reoccupying the Rhineland, used up the priceless asset which had brought her so many advantages: the asset of being disarmed. The purpose of armies is to defeat other armies. The defeat in itself has political consequences: it shakes the national will of the conquered people and so makes them ready to obey the conqueror. But what can an army do when there is not another army to defeat? It can invade the disarmed country; but the national will of the invaded is unshaken. That will can be broken only by terror—the secret police, the torture chamber, the concentration camp. This method is hard to apply in peace-time. The Germans found it difficult to apply, even in war-time, with countries such as Denmark which they had overrun without fighting. Democratic countries particularly cannot develop the machinery of terror, except to some extent in their colonies outside Europe. Hence France and her allies had been baffled what to do with Germany so long as she remained disarmed. Once she reoccupied the Rhineland and built up a great army, it was possible to envisage coercing her in the normal way—by war. The Western Powers did not prepare for this war with much competence; but before the reoccupation of the Rhineland they did not prepare for it at all. It was said at the time, and has often been said since, that 7 March 1936 was "the last chance", the last occasion when Germany could have been stopped without all the sacrifice and suffering of a great war. Technically, on paper, this was true: the French had a great army, and the Germans had none. Psychologically, it was the reverse of the truth. The Western peoples remained helpless before the question: what could they do? The French army could march into Germany; it could exact promises of good behaviour from the Germans; and then it would go away. The situation would remain the same as before, or, if anything worse—the Germans more resentful and restless than ever. There was in fact no sense in opposing Germany until there was something solid to oppose, until the settlement of Versailles was undone and Germany rearmed. Only a country which aims at victory can be threatened with defeat. 7 March was thus a double turning-point. It opened the door for Germany's success. It also opened the door for her ultimate failure.

CHAPTER SIX

The Half-armed Peace, 1936-38

THE German reoccupation of the Rhineland marked the end of the devices for security which had been set up after the first World war. The League of Nations was a shadow; Germany could rearm, free from all treaty restrictions; the guarantees of Locarno were no more. Wilsonian idealism and French realism had both failed. Europe returned to the system, or lack of system, which had existed before 1914. Every sovereign state, great or small, again had to rely on armed strength, diplomacy, and alliances for its security. The former victors had no advantage; the defeated, no handicap. "International anarchy" was restored. Many people, including some historians, believe that this in itself is enough to explain the second World war. And so, in a sense, it is. So long as states admit no restriction of their sovereignty, wars will occur between them—some wars by design, more by miscalculation. The defect of this explanation is that, since it explains everything, it also explains nothing. If "international anarchy" invariably caused war, then the states of Europe should never have known peace since the close of the middle ages. In fact there have also been long periods of peace; and before 1914 international anarchy gave Europe its longest peace since the end of the Roman empire.

Wars are much like road accidents. They have a general cause and particular causes at the same time. Every road accident is caused, in the last resort, by the invention of the internal combustion engine and by men's desire to get from one place to another. In this sense, the "cure" for road accidents is to forbid motor-cars. But a motorist, charged with dangerous driving, would be ill-advised if he pleaded the existence of motor-cars as his sole defence. The police and the courts do not weigh profound causes. They seek a specific cause for each accident—error on the part of the driver; excessive speed; drunkenness; faulty brakes;

102

bad road surface. So it is with wars. "International anarchy" makes war possible; it does not make war certain. After 1918 more than one writer made his name by demonstrating the profound causes of the first World war; and, though the demonstrations were often correct, they thus diverted attention from the question why that particular war happened at that particular time. Both enquiries make sense on different levels. They are complementary; they do not exclude each other. The second World war, too, had profound causes; but it also grew out of specific events, and these events are worth detailed examination.

Men talked more about the profound causes of war before 1989 than they had done previously; and in this way these causes counted for more. It became a commonplace after 1919 that future wars could be avoided only if the League of Nations succeeded. Now the League had failed; and men were quick to say that henceforth war was inevitable. Many even felt that it was wicked to try to prevent war by the old-style instruments of alliances and diplomacy. Men said also that Fascism "inevitably" produced war; and there was no denying this, if one believed the pronouncements of the two Fascist leaders themselves. Hitler and Mussolini glorified war and the warlike virtues. They used the threat of war to promote their aims. But this was not new. Statesmen had always done it. The rhetoric of the dictators was no worse than the "sabre-rattling" of the old monarchs; nor, for that matter, than what English public-schoolboys were taught in Victorian days. Yet there had been long periods of peace then despite the fiery talk. Even the Fascist dictators would not have gone to war unless they had seen a chance of winning; and the cause of war was therefore as much the blunders of others as the wickedness of the dictators themselves. Hitler probably intended a great war of conquest against Soviet Russia so far as he had any conscious design; it is unlikely that he intended the actual war against Great Britain and France which broke out in 1939. He was as much dismayed on 3 September 1989 as Bethmann had been on 4 August 1914. Mussolini, despite all his boasting, strove desperately to keep out of war, more desperately even than the despised last leaders of the third French republic; and he went to war only when he thought that it was already won. Germans and Italians applauded their leaders; but war was not popular among them, as it had been in 1914. Then cheering crowds everywhere greeted the outbreak of war. There was intense gloom in Germany during the Czech crisis of 1988; and only helpless resignation the following year when war broke out. The war of 1989, far from being welcome, was less wanted by nearly everybody than almost any war in history.

Another type of profound cause was much discussed before 1939. Economic circumstances, it was held, were inevitably leading to war. This was accepted Marxist doctrine at the time; and, by dint of repeated assertion, the doctrine won acceptance, too, from many people who did not call themselves Marxists. This was a new idea. Marx himself knew nothing of it. Before 1914 Marxists foretold that the great capitalist Powers would share out the world between themselves; and, so far as they foretold wars at all, expected these to be struggles for national emancipation by the colonial peoples outside Europe. Lenin was the first to discover that capitalism "inevitably" caused war; and he discovered this only when the first World war was already being fought. Of course he was right. Since every great state was capitalist in 1914, capitalism obviously "caused" the first World war; but just as obviously it had "caused" the previous generation of peace. Here was another general explanation which explained everything and nothing. Before 1939 the great capitalist states, England and America, were the most anxious to avoid war; and in every country, including Germany, capitalists were the class most opposed to war. Indeed, if one were to indict the capitalists of 1939, it would be for pacifism and timidity, not for seeking war.

However, capitalism could be found guilty in a more limited way. Though the successful imperialist Powers were perhaps sated and pacific, Fascism, it was claimed, represented the last aggressive stage of capitalism in decline, and its momentum could be sustained only by war. There was an element of truth in this, but not much. The full employment which Nazi Germany was the first European country to possess, depended in large part on the production of armaments; but it could have been provided equally well (and was to some extent) by other forms of public works from roads to great buildings. The Nazi secret was not armament production; it was freedom from the then orthodox principles of economics. Government spending provided all the happy effects of mild inflation; while political dictatorship, with its destruction of trade unions and rigorous exchange control, prevented such unfortunate consequences as a rise in wages, or in prices. The argument for war did not work even if the Nazi system had relied on armament production alone. Nazi Germany was not choking in a flood of arms. On the contrary, the German generals insisted unanimously in 1939 that they were not equipped for war and that many years must pass before "rearmament in depth" had been completed. Hence there was no need to worry about full employment. In Fascist Italy, the economic argument was altogether irrelevant. There was no Fascist system of economics—only a poor country ruled by a mixture of terror and glamour. Italy was quite unprepared for war, as Mussolini admitted by remaining "non-belligerent" in 1939. When he finally took the plunge in 1940, Italy was worse equipped for war, in every way, than she had been when she entered the first World war in 1915.

An economic explanation of a different sort was popular before 1939. Germany and Italy, it was argued, were "have-not"Powers, with inadequate access to foreign markets or to raw materials. The British government were being constantly urged by the Labour Opposition to redress these economic grievances instead of entering the race for rearmament. Maybe Germany and Italy were "have-not" Powers. But what did they want to have? Italy had conquered Abyssinia. Far from drawing profit from this, she found its pacification and development an almost impossible drain on her limited resources. Though some Italians settled there this work of colonisation was done for reasons of prestige; it would have been cheaper and more profitable to maintain them at home. Immediately before the outbreak of war, Mussolini repeatedly demanded Corsica, Nice, and Savoy. None of these, except possibly Nice, offered any economic advantage; even Nice could not help in solving Italy's real problem of a poor country and a dense population.

Hitler's claim to living space, *Lebensraum*, sounded more plausible—plausible enough to convince Hitler himself. But what did it amount to in practice? Germany was not short of markets. On the contrary, Schacht used bilateral agreements to give Germany practically a monopoly of trade with south-eastern Europe; and similar plans were being prepared for the economic conquest of South America when the outbreak of war interrupted them. Nor did Germany suffer from a shortage of raw materials. Scientific ingenuity provided substitutes for those which she could not readily buy; and Germany was never handicapped by any shortage of raw materials during the second World war, despite the British blockade, until her synthetic oil-plants were destroyed by Allied bombing in 1944. *Lebensraum*, in its crudest sense, meant a demand for empty space where Germans could settle. Germany was not over-populated in comparison with most European countries; and there was no empty space anywhere in Europe. When Hitler lamented: "If only we had a Ukraine . . . ," he seemed to suppose that there were no Ukrainians. Did he propose to exploit, or to exterminate, them? Apparently he never considered the question one way or the other. When Germany actually conquered the Ukraine in 1941, Hitler and his henchmen tried both methods—neither to any economic advantage. Empty space existed overseas; and the British government, taking Hitler's grievance at its face value, often held out colonial concessions to him. He never responded. He knew that colonies were an expense, not a source of profit, at any rate until they had been developed; in any case, possession of them would rob him of his grievance. *Lebensraum*, in short, did not drive Germany to war. Rather war, or a warlike policy, produced the demand for *Lebensraum*. Hitler and Mussolini were not driven on by economic motives. Like most statesmen, they had an appetite for success. They differed from others only in that their appetite was greater; and they fed it by more unscrupulous means.

The effect of Fascism was seen in public morality, not in economics. It permanently debased the spirit of international affairs. Hitler and Mussolini boasted of their freedom from accepted standards. They made promises without any intention of keeping them. Mussolini defied the Covenant of the League of Nations, to which Italy was committed. Hitler reaffirmed Locarno one year, only to repudiate it the next. During the Spanish civil war both men openly mocked the system of non-intervention to which they were pledged. Carrying the same method further, they grew indignant when anyone doubted their word or reminded them of their broken promises. The statesmen of other countries were baffled by this disregard of accepted standards, yet could think of no alternative. They went on seeking an agreement so attractive to the Fascist rulers that it would win them back to good faith. Chamberlain did this at Munich in 1938; Stalin with the Nazi-Soviet pact of 1939. Both were later to display a naïve indignation that Hitler should continue to behave as he had always behaved. Yet what else were they to do? Agreement of some sort seemed the only alternative to war; and there remained till the end an exasperated feeling that some impossible agreement was just round the corner. The non-Fascist statesmen did not escape the contamination of the time. Pretending to treat the Fascist dictators as "gentlemen", they ceased to be gentlemen themselves. British and French ministers, having once committed themselves to the non-existent good faith of the dictators, grew indignant in their turn when others continued to doubt. Hitler and Mussolini lied openly about non-intervention; Chamberlain and Eden, Blum and Delbos, did little better. The statesmen of western Europe moved in a moral and intellectual fog—sometimes deceived by the dictators, sometimes deceiving themselves, often deceiving their own public. They, too, came to believe that an unscrupulous policy was the only resource. It is difficult to believe that Sir Edward Grey or Delcassé would have set his name to the agreement of Munich; difficult to believe that Lenin and Trotsky, despite their contempt for *bourgeois* morality, would have set their names to the Nazi-Soviet Pact.

The historian must try to push through the cloud of phrases to the realities beneath. For there were still realities in international affairs: Great Powers attempting, however ineffectually, to maintain their interests and independence. The European pattern had been profoundly modified by the events of 1935 and 1936. The two Western Powers had followed the worst of all possible courses in the Abyssinian affair; they had straddled indecisively between two contradictory policies, and had failed in both. They would not sustain the League of Nations at the risk of war or even of ruining Mussolini in Italy; yet neither would they openly jettison the League for his sake. These contradictions continued even when the war in Abyssinia was over, and the Emperor an exile. Obviously nothing more could be done for the unfortunate victim of Western idealism. Sanctions were ended, Neville Chamberlain dismissing them as "the very midsummer of madness". But Italy still stood condemned as an aggressor; and the two Western

Powers could not bring themselves to recognise the King of Italy as Emperor of Abyssinia. The Stresa front was gone beyond recall, Mussolini forced on to the German side. This outcome was unwelcome to him. In attacking Abyssinia, Mussolini had intended to exploit the international tension on the Rhine, not to opt for Germany. Instead he had lost his freedom of choice.

Hitler found freedom just when Mussolini lost it. The ending of Locarno made Germany a fully independent Power, no longer hampered by artificial restrictions. Further initiatives in international affairs might have been expected to follow. Instead German policy remained quiet for almost two years. This "loaded pause", as Churchill called it, was in part due to the inescapable fact that armament plans take a long time to mature; and Hitler therefore had to wait until Germany was truly "rearmed"—a moment which he usually fixed as 1943. But he was also at a loss what to do next even if he had the power to do it. Whatever his long-term plans (and it is doubtful whether he had any), the mainspring of his immediate policy had been "the destruction of Versailles". This was the theme of *Mein Kampf* and of every speech which he made on foreign affairs. It was a policy which won the unanimous support of the German people. It had also the great advantage that, in practical terms, it virtually wrote itself: after each success, Hitler had only to look into the peace treaty, and there he found another clause ripe for destruction. He had assumed that the process would take many years and that he would encounter great difficulties. Triumph over these would provide a running stock of mounting prestige. Actually the destruction of Versailles and Locarno alike took only three years; and it raised so few alarms that we now wonder why Hitler did not do it more quickly. After March 1936 there was no more prestige to be squeezed out of attacking Versailles. When Hitler later denounced one of the few unequal clauses remaining—the internationalisation of German rivers—nobody noticed either at home or abroad. The days of easy success were over. It was one thing to destroy the legal provisions of a peace treaty; quite another to destroy the independence of other countries, even small ones. Besides, it was never Hitler's method to take the initiative. He liked others to do his work for him; and he waited for the inner weakening of the European system, just as he had waited for the peace settlement to crumble of itself. Things might have been different if Hitler had had an urgent, concrete grievance after the reoccupation of the Rhineland. But German grievances were, for the time being, in short supply. Many Germans felt strongly about Danzig and the Polish corridor; but the Non-Aggression Pact with Poland was scarcely two years old. It was Hitler's most original stroke in foreign policy; and he was reluctant to move against it. The Germans of Czechoslovakia were hardly aware as yet that they were an oppressed minority.

Only Austria remained. The blundering Nazi revolt of 25 July 1934 and the murder of Dollfuss which accompanied it had been a bad knock for Hitler—one of the few which he experienced. He pulled out of this setback with remarkable agility. Papen, the frivolous conservative who had helped to make Hitler chancellor, was sent as German ambassador to Vienna. The choice was peculiarly appropriate. Not only was Papen a devout Roman Catholic, loyally serving Hitler, and hence a model to the Austrian clericals; negotiator, too, of the Concordat with the Papacy. He had also been within an ace of being murdered during the purge of 30 June 1934, and was therefore uniquely qualified to persuade the Austrian rulers that Nazi murder attempts should not be taken seriously. Papen did his work well. The Austrian government were authoritarian in an inefficient way. They were ready to persecute the Socialists, though not the Roman Catholics or the Jews. They were even ready to use the phrases of German nationalism so long as Austria was allowed to remain in some sort of existence. This suited Hitler. Though he wanted an Austria dependent on Germany in international affairs, he was in no hurry to destroy Austria altogether. Probably the idea did not even enter his head. He was Austrian enough to find the complete disappearance of Austria inconceivable until it happened; even if conceivable, it was unwelcome to him that Vienna (to say nothing of Linz) should be eclipsed by Berlin.

It took Papen two years to win the confidence of the Austrian government. Mutual suspicion was relaxed, if not extinguished. On 11 July 1936 the two countries concluded a Gentleman's Agreement—first use, incidentally, of this absurd phrase. The phrase was a characteristic invention of Papen's; and he soon found imitators. Hitler recognised the "full sovereignty" of Austria. Schuschnigg acknowledged in return that Austria was "a German State", and agreed to admit members of "the so-

called National Opposition" to his government. Later events
made the agreement seem fraudulent on both sides. This was not
so, though of course each signatory heard in the agreement what
he wanted to hear. Hitler assumed that Austrian Nazis would
gradually penetrate the government there and would transform
Austria into a Nazi state. But he was content that this should
happen imperceptibly, without a dramatic crisis. The agreement
of July 1986 gave him almost exactly what he had proposed to
Mussolini at the Venice meeting two years previously, except that
Schuschnigg did not make way for "a personage of independent
outlook". Instead Schuschnigg became this neutral personage, or
so Hitler hoped. He was confident that the walls of Vienna would
fall of themselves. As late as February 1988 he told the Austrian
Nazi leaders: "The Austrian question can never be solved by a
revolution. . . . I want the evolutionary course to be taken, not a
solution by violent means, since the danger for us in the field of
foreign policy becomes less each year."[1]

Schuschnigg, on his side, was relieved to escape from dependence on Italy—a dependence which all Austrians disliked and
which most of them knew to be unreliable. There was no democracy to save in Austria, only a separate name. Schuschnigg
could stomach everything the Nazis wanted except his own disappearance; and he supposed that he was now secured from this.
The agreement of July 1986 gave Schuschnigg the shadow, and
Hitler the substance. With this both men were satisfied. Mussolini
was satisfied also. He could not defend the independence of
Austria except by a humiliating reconciliation with the Western
Powers, and perhaps not even then. He, too, was content with
the shadow—the preservation of Austria's name. Underneath
there was still conflict between German and Italian policy.
Mussolini wished to maintain his protectorate over Austria and
Hungary, and to extend Italian power in the Mediterranean,
principally at the expense of France. Hitler intended to make
Germany the leading Power in Europe, with Italy as, at best, a
junior partner. Neither was eager to promote the ambitions of the
other; each planned to exploit the other's challenge to the
Western Powers in order to extract concessions for himself. In
such circumstances, discussion of practical questions might

[1] Memorandum by Keppler, 28 Feb. 1988. *German Foreign Policy*, series
D. i. No. 338.

easily lead to a quarrel. Instead therefore they stressed their
"ideological" similarity—the modern and creative spirit of their
two states which allegedly made them superior to the decadent
democracies. This was the Rome-Berlin Axis, loudly announced
by Mussolini in November 1986, round which European politics
were henceforward expected to revolve.

Hitler was following the same policy at this time with Japan.
Here also the two Powers did not see eye to eye in practical
affairs. Hitler wanted to push Japan forward against Russia and
Great Britain, without himself sacrificing Germany's close con-
nexion with China, whose army was still being organised by
German generals; Japan would no more tolerate Germany in the
Far East than any other European Power. Each intended the
other to provide the conflict so that it could collect the reward.
Ribbentrop, Hitler's private adviser on foreign affairs, provided
the solution—his first success which carried him to the foreign
ministry little over a year later. This was the Anti-Comintern
Pact, a ringing declaration of principle which committed neither
side to action. Being directed solely against Communism, it was
not even an alliance against Russia; and, as things turned out,
the two countries were never allies in an anti-Russian war. But
the Pact looked as though it were an anti-Russian alliance. The
Soviet leaders were made fearful; and, if there be a key to their
policy, it is to be found here. They were convinced that they were
about to be attacked—perhaps by Germany, perhaps by Japan,
perhaps by the two combined. Their greatest, and most immediate, fear was of war in the Far East between themselves and
Japan. By a wild irony, such as history often produces, this was
the one war, foreseen at the time, which was never fought.

The Anti-Comintern Pact between Germany and Japan,
together with the vaguer anti-Communist Axis of Rome and
Berlin, did not only affect Soviet policy. It had a strong influence
in England and France also. Russia and the Western Powers
could draw together so long as international relations operated
on an abstract basis, detached from home politics. France made
the Franco-Soviet Pact; the Western Powers accepted Soviet
Russia, somewhat grudgingly, as a loyal member of the League
of Nations, and were themselves shamed into loyalty towards it
by Litvinov's praise of "collective security". When the Anti-
Comintern Pact pushed political ideas forward, men in the two

democratic countries also felt the call of anti-Communism. They inclined to be neutral in the struggle between Fascism and Communism, or perhaps even on the Fascist side. They feared Hitler as the ruler of a strong, aggressive Germany; they welcomed him—or many did—as the protector of European civilisation against Communism. There was a difference of attitude here between Englishmen and Frenchmen. Many Englishmen, particularly in the Conservative party, said: "Better Hitler than Stalin". It did not occur to any Englishman, except the Fascist leader, Sir Oswald Mosley, to say: "Better Hitler than Baldwin —or Chamberlain—or even Attlee". In France the general election of May 1936 produced a Left-wing majority of Radicals, Socialists, and Communists. When a government of the Popular Front followed, conservative, well-to-do Frenchmen said not merely: "Better Hitler than Stalin", but "Better Hitler than Léon Blum".

This was not the only reason why the relations between Soviet Russia and the West, which had seemed to be improving, now ran downhill. 1936 saw the beginning of the great purge in Russia: practically every old Bolshevik leader was executed or imprisoned, thousands—perhaps millions—of lesser Russians sent off to Siberia. In the following year the purge extended to the armed forces: Tukhachevsky the chief of staff, three out of five marshals, 18 out of 15 army commanders, and many others, were shot after a secret trial or none at all. No one knows the reason for this slaughter. Was Stalin mad with autocratic power? Had he grounds for supposing that the generals or his political rivals were planning to enlist German backing for an anti-Stalinist revolution? Or was he himself planning a reconciliation with Hitler and did he therefore remove possible critics? According to one story, President Benes of Czechoslovakia discovered that Tukhachevsky and others were negotiating with Hitler, and passed the evidence on to Stalin. According to another, the German secret service itself manufactured this evidence, and planted it on Benes. We do not know anything about it; and perhaps we never shall. But the effect was unmistakable. Nearly every Western observer was convinced that Soviet Russia was useless as an ally: her ruler a savage and unscrupulous dictator, her armies in chaos, her political system likely to collapse at the first strain. The American ambassador,

Joseph Davies, was the one exception. He always insisted that there had been a genuine plot, that the trials were fairly conducted, and that the Soviet power was stronger as a result. But he, too, was guessing. No one knew the truth then; and no one knows it now. The Soviet armies stood up well against the Germans in 1941, though only after terrible disasters at the outset. This may prove that they were also efficient armies in 1936 or 1938; on the other hand it may suggest that they were hardly ready for war even in 1941. All speculation on the subject is futile. The practical outcome was to drive the Western Powers firmly behind their defensive lines—an odd result when one reflects that the Franco-Soviet Pact was Hitler's excuse for the destruction of Locarno.

The two Western Powers did not stand still after the events of March 1936. They began to improve their defensive position, or so they thought: mainly from fear of Germany, though also to lessen their connexion with Soviet Russia. When Hitler moved into the Rhineland, the British government changed their two-sided guarantee under the treaty of Locarno into a straight promise of assistance if France were directly attacked. This was meant as a temporary affair until negotiations provided a substitute for Locarno. But these negotiations ran away to nothing; no substitute for Locarno was found. In this accidental way, Great Britain was committed—for the first time in her history— to peacetime alliance with a continental Great Power. This marked a change indeed, evidence perhaps of Great Britain's increased awareness of continental matters, perhaps only of increased weakness. But it was not really such a profound change. Partnership, in the sense of common interests with France, had existed for a long time. The formal alliance, though ostensibly a precise commitment, was not put forward as the preliminary to action; on the contrary it was offered in order to prevent any effective French reply to the occupation of the Rhineland. The practical test of an alliance is the military planning which goes with it. Staff conversations were held between Great Britain and France immediately after the German move into the Rhineland. They lasted five days, and then lapsed. No more were held until February 1939. France did not get increased security or strength from the alliance with Great Britain. Rather she got an ally who was ceaselessly holding her back for fear that the alliance might have to become effective—not that the French needed much restraining.

The German reoccupation of the Rhineland did not directly weaken the defensive position of France, however much it might impede her offensive plans, which were in any case non-existent. Indirectly, however, it had a grave consequence. Belgium had been in alliance with France since 1919, the two armies closely co-ordinated. Now the Belgians had a rearmed Germany on their frontier. Were they still to rely on their French ally who had proved so ineffective? Or should they step aside, hoping to avoid the coming storm? They chose the second alternative. In the autumn of 1936 they withdrew from the French alliance; early in 1987 they reverted to the neutral position which they had held before 1914. This created a terrible strategical problem for the French. The Maginot line, a most formidable defence, extended only from the Swiss frontier to the Belgian. Hitherto the French had assumed—though without much justification—that the Belgians would provide some similar fortification on the short frontier between Belgium and Germany. What were they to do now? They could not insist on Belgian defences, or even enquire about them, without infringing her neutrality. The frontier between France and Belgium was enormously long. The cost of fortifying it was prohibitive. Besides, the French could not attempt it without implicitly admitting both that they had renounced the defence of Belgium and that they regarded her as a possible enemy. They therefore did what men often do when faced with an insoluble problem: they closed their eyes to it and pretended that it did not exist. No attempt was made to protect the French frontier with Belgium. This neglect continued even after the outbreak of war. British forces were stationed on the Belgian frontier during the winter of 1989–1940, and many officers reported on its defenceless state. Their complaints reached Hore-Belisha, the secretary of state for war. When he raised the question in high quarters, he was dismissed from office. A few weeks later, the Germans duly invaded Belgium, and—assisted by the strategical blunders of Gamelin, the Allied supreme commander—achieved there the decisive victory which had eluded them in 1914.

Our knowledge of these later events makes it difficult to see the pre-war arguments over British and French policy in perspective.

We know that the Allied armies in France were routed by the Germans; therefore we easily conclude that they were inadequately prepared from a military point of view. This conclusion seems to be reinforced by the figures. In 1988, when Germany was devoting 16.6% of her total production to armaments, Great Britain and France were devoting only 7% of theirs. But, before we accept the explanation that the defeat of the Western Powers was due to their failure to rearm adequately, we should ask: "adequately for what?" Would increased expenditure, for instance, have overcome the strategic neglect of Belgium? It was commonly assumed, as it still is, that the ideal aim should be equality of armaments with a possible opponent, or group of opponents. This is, in fact, the most pointless of aims: too much if a country wishes only to defend itself, too little if it hopes to impose its will on the other side. The British admiralty was never content with equality. It aimed at a decisive superiority over Germany and Italy and, from 1987 onwards, over Japan as well. This Three Power standard was not attained; but from lack of time, not from lack of money.

Military armaments were, however, decisive so far as Europe was concerned; and here the objective of equality was peculiarly misleading. In the first World war defence had been immensely more powerful than attack: the attacker needed a superiority of three, if not five, to one. The campaign of 1940 in France seemed to disprove this experience: the Germans won a decisive victory without great superiority in either man-power or equipment. As a matter of fact the French campaign proved nothing except that even armies adequately prepared for defence can be destroyed if they are led badly enough. Later on, the great coalition of Great Britain, Soviet Russia, and the United States had to wait for a superiority of five to one before defeating Germany. If therefore Great Britain and France merely hoped to defend themselves, quite a small increase in their land armaments would enable them to do so; and this increase was more than provided between 1986 and 1939. On the other hand, if they wished to defeat Germany and to recover the position of triumphant dominance which they had enjoyed in 1919, they would have to multiply their armaments not by two, but by six or even by ten—an impossible proposition. No one appreciated this. Men clung to the misleading concept of equality, believing that this would somehow give them not merely security, but power. Ministers talked of "defence", yet implied that a successful defence was the same thing as victory; and their critics assumed that a successful defence was either impossible or no better than defeat. There is therefore no simple answer to the question: "were British and French armaments adequate before 1989?" They were adequate to defend the two countries, if properly used; they were inadequate to prevent the extension of German power in eastern Europe.

In one aspect of armaments the normal calculation of three to one did not seem to apply. It was the universal belief that there was no defence against attack from the air. Baldwin expressed this when he said: "The bomber will always get through". It was expected that every great city would be levelled to the ground immediately on the outbreak of war; and the British government, acting on this assumption, made preparations for more casualties in London alone during the first week of war than in fact the entire British people suffered during five long years. The only answer was supposed to be "the deterrent"—a bomber-force as large as the enemy's. Neither Great Britain nor France claimed to possess such a force in 1986 or even in 1989; hence, in large part, the timidity of their statesmen. All these calculations turned out to be wrong. The Germans had never planned for independent bombing. Their bomber-force was an auxiliary for the army on the ground, and they had to improvise the air-attack on Great Britain in the summer of 1940. The Germans were answered and defeated not by British bombing, but by fighter-command, which had been despised and comparatively neglected before the war. When the British, in their turn, went over to the bombing of Germany, this did more harm to themselves than to the Germans—that is, it used up more British men and materials than it destroyed German. No one could grasp this before the event, as many indeed failed to grasp it afterwards. The pre-war years ran their course under the shadow of hideous misapprehension.

Wars, when they come, are always different from the war that is expected. Victory goes to the side that has made fewest mistakes, not to the one that has guessed right. In this sense, Great Britain and France did not prepare adequately. The military experts gave the wrong advice and pursued the wrong strategy;

ministers did not understand what they were told by their
experts; politicians and the public did not grasp what they were
told by ministers. The critics were not much nearer the correct
course. Winston Churchill, for instance, was "right" only in
demanding more of everything. He did not demand arms or
strategy of a different kind; and on many subjects—such as the
power of the French army and the efficacy of bombing—he was
peculiarly obstinate in error. Technical misjudgements were the
main cause of Anglo-French failure. Political difficulties played
some part as well, though less than is often claimed. In France
the government of the Popular Front, which took office in June
1986, might have been expected to be specially resolute against
the Fascist Powers; but it was also concerned to introduce social
reforms which were long overdue. These modest reforms caused
bitter resentment among the propertied classes; and French
armaments paid the penalty. When the French military leaders,
themselves conservatives, demanded more expenditure on the
armed forces, they voiced no doubt genuine needs; but they also
hoped that this increased expenditure would ruin the programme
of social reform. The supporters of the Popular Front—that is,
the majority of French people—replied in kind: recognising that
some of the arms expenditure was demanded in order to prevent
social reform, they refused to believe that any increase was
necessary.

British armament was retarded for a different reason. The
government, it is true, sometimes claimed that they were held
back by the unpatriotic pacifism of the Labour opposition; and
this excuse was greatly exaggerated later, when events revealed
the government's shortcomings. In fact, the British government
deliberately chose to limit expenditure on armaments to a
modest figure. It had an enormous majority in the House of
Commons—250 in all; and Labour would have been helpless to
resist government proposals, quite apart from the fact that many
Labour men actually wanted increased arms. The government
proceeded slowly for reasons of policy and economic outlook, far
more than from fear of Labour opposition. The initial attacks by
Churchill delayed government action. Once having denied his
charges, it was difficult for ministers to confess that he had been
right. Even when they set out to increase armaments, they did so
with excessive caution—the exact opposite of Hitler who often

boasted of armaments which he did not possess. He wanted to shake the nerve of his opponents; they wanted to conciliate him and win him back to peaceful negotiations. Hence the British government tried, for Hitler's sake, to make their measures seem harmless and ineffective, at the very time when they were assuring the British public, and even themselves, that Great Britain would soon be secure. Baldwin held out firmly against setting up a Ministry of Supply; and, when finally driven to concede the empty post of Minister for the Co-ordination of Defence, chose not Churchill or even Austen Chamberlain, but Sir Thomas Inskip—an appointment rightly described as the most extraordinary since Caligula made his horse a consul. But indeed there were enough British appointments of this kind to compose a regiment of Caligula cavalry.

The British government feared to offend economic principle even more than to offend Hitler. The secret of Pandora's box which Schacht had opened in Germany and which the American New Deal had also revealed, was still unknown to them. Wedded to stable prices and a stable pound, they regarded increased public spending as a great evil, excusable only in the event of actual war, and even then lamentable. They had no inkling that public spending on anything, even on armaments, brought with it increased prosperity. Like nearly all contemporary economists except of course J. M. Keynes, they still treated public finance as though it were the finance of a private individual. When an individual spends money on wasteful objects, he has less to spend elsewhere, and there is less "demand". When the state spends money, this creates an increased "demand", and therefore increased prosperity, throughout the community. This is obvious to us now. Few knew it then. Before we condemn Baldwin and Neville Chamberlain too contemptuously, we should reflect that even in 1959 an economist was elevated to the House of Lords for preaching the very doctrine of public miserliness which stultified British policy before 1939. Perhaps we are not more enlightened; merely more fearful of the popular explosion which would be caused if the economists got their way, and there was a return to mass unemployment. Before 1939 this unemployment was regarded as a law of nature; and the government could claim, in all sincerity, that there were no unused resources in the country when nearly two million men remained unemployed.

Here again, Hitler had a great advantage over the democratic countries. His principal achievement was the conquest of unemployment; and most Germans did not mind what heretical methods he used, so long as he did it. Moreover, even if German bankers objected, they had no effective means of saying so. When Schacht himself grew anxious, he could only resign; and few Germans cared. A dictatorship like Hitler's could escape the usual consequences of inflation. Since there were no trade unions, wages could be kept stable, and prices too; while a rigorous exchange control—backed by the weapons of terror and the secret police—prevented any depreciation of the mark. The British government still lived in the psychological atmosphere of 1931: more terrified of a flight from the pound than of defeat in war. Its measures of rearmament were therefore determined less by strategic need, even if that had been known, than by what the taxpayer would stand; and he, constantly assured that the government had already made Great Britain strong, would not stand much. Limitation of income-tax, and the confidence of the City of London, came first; armaments came second. Under such circumstances, it is not necessary to invoke the opposition of the Labour party in order to understand why British preparations for war before 1939 lagged behind those of Germany. The wonder is rather that, when war came, Great Britain was as well prepared as she was—a triumph of scientific and technical ingenuity over the economists.

It would however be too simple an explanation for all that happened between 1936 and 1939 merely to say that Great Britain and France were less equipped for war than Germany and Italy. Of course governments ought to weigh their strength and resources before deciding on action—or inaction; they rarely do so. In real life governments which want to do nothing are unshakably convinced of their country's weakness; and they become equally confident of its strength the moment they wish to act. Germany, for instance, was little more prepared for a great war between 1933 and 1936 than she had been before Hitler came to power. The difference was that he had strong nerves and his predecessors had not. At the other end of the story, the British government in March 1939 had little reason for believing that Great Britain could face the risk of war better than before—rather the contrary, from a technical point of view. The change was psychological—an access of obstinacy as unreasoning as the timidity which had preceded it. There is little evidence that the rulers of the democratic countries (or of the dictatorial ones for that matter) ever consulted their military experts in a detached way before deciding on policy. They decided policy first; and then asked the experts for technical arguments with which this policy could be justified. So it had been over the British and French hesitation to support the League of Nations uncompromisingly in the autumn of 1935; so it was over their reluctance to take a firm stand against the dictators in 1936. British ministers wanted peace for the sake of the taxpayer; French ministers, in order to carry out their programme of social reform. Both governments were composed of well-meaning, elderly men who rightly shrank from a great war, if it could possibly be avoided; and it was against their nature to reject in foreign affairs the policy of compromise and concession which they applied at home.

Their response might have been different if Hitler had followed the reoccupation of the Rhineland with a further, more direct, challenge to the existing territorial settlement of Europe; or if Mussolini had sought further fields of conquest immediately after overrunning Abyssinia. But Hitler remained quiet; Italian strength was exhausted. The great happening of 1936 was elsewhere—a conflict of ideologies, or so it seemed, instead of a direct clash of power. This was the Spanish civil war. In 1931 Spain had become a republic. In 1936 a general election gave power there, as in France, to a coalition of Radicals, Socialists, and Communists—another Popular Front. Its programme was more anti-clerical and democratic than socialist. Even this was enough to provoke the old vested interests—monarchist, military, and fascist. Plans for an anti-democratic revolt had been laid as early as 1934; and had received a rather vague blessing from Mussolini. In July 1936 these plans exploded as a full-scale military rebellion. It was universally believed at the time that this rebellion was the next stage in a deliberate Fascist strategy of conquest—Abyssinia the first step; reoccupation of the Rhineland the next; and now Spain. The Spanish rebels were supposed to be puppets of the two Fascist dictators. Knowledge of Spanish history and Spanish character should have taught that this view was wrong. Spaniards, even Fascist Spaniards, were too proudly independent to be anyone's puppets; and the revolt was prepared without serious consultation in either Rome or Berlin. Mussolini provided aeroplanes in general resentment against democracy. Some German agents sympathised with the rebels; but Hitler knew no more than anyone else of the actual rebellion beforehand.

The rebels expected quick victory; and most others expected it for them. Instead, the republic rallied the workers of Madrid; beat off the military conspirators in the capital; and asserted its hold over most of Spain. A long civil war was in the offing. Mussolini increased his help to the rebels, first with material, then with men; Hitler sent help in the air on a more modest scale. On the other side, ten days after the rebellion broke out, Soviet Russia began sending military equipment to the republic. It is easy to understand why the two dictators aided the rebels. Mussolini wanted to discredit democracy; and hoped, mistakenly, to acquire the use of Spanish naval bases from which to challenge France in the Mediterranean. He wanted the Spanish Fascists to win, and to win quickly, with as little strain as possible on Italy's meagre resources. Hitler, too, was glad to discredit the democracies; but he did not take the Spanish civil war very seriously. His main interest was to encourage dissension between Italy and France, not to secure the victory of Spanish Fascism. The German air force used Spain as a testing-ground for their machines and pilots. Otherwise Hitler supported the Spanish rebels mainly with words. It was widely believed at the time that Germany and Italy would themselves fight on the rebel side, if their intervention were challenged. Strangely enough, this was not true. One of the few well-documented facts of this time is that both Hitler and Mussolini were determined not to risk war over Spain. If challenged, they would have withdrawn. Their attitude was exactly the same as that of Great Britain and France over Abyssinia: action to the verge of war, but not beyond it. In 1935 Mussolini called the bluff of the two democratic Powers; they, when their turn came in 1936, failed to call the bluff of the dictators.

British and French policy, or lack of it, not the policy of Hitler and Mussolini, decided the outcome of the Spanish civil war. The republic had greater resources, greater popular backing. It could win if it received the correct treatment to which it was entitled by international law: foreign arms for the legitimate government, none for the rebels. It could even win if both sides received foreign aid, or if both were denied it. The rebels had a chance only if they received foreign aid, while the republic received none or very little; and this extraordinary arrangement was provided, though not deliberately, by London and Paris. The first impulse of the French government, itself based on a Popular Front, was to allow the export of arms to the Spanish republic. Then doubt began. The French Radicals, though co-operating with Socialists in the government, objected to aiding an allegedly Communist cause abroad; the French Socialists feared being involved in war with the Fascist Powers. Léon Blum, the premier, went over to London for advice; and here he was restrained even more firmly. The British government made a seemingly attractive proposal: if France refrained from helping the Spanish republic, then Italy and Germany could be urged not to help the rebels. The Spanish people could decide their own destiny; and in all probability, if non-intervention really worked, the republic would win. We do not know why the British government made this proposal. It was against the tradition of British policy. A century or so before, when there had also been civil war in Spain, Great Britain had actively supported the cause of constitutional monarchy with arms, and had rejected the principle of non-intervention, advocated by the Holy Alliance. Now, in 1936, the British government claimed to be acting solely in the interests of general peace. If all the Great Powers kept clear of Spain, the civil war could burn itself out beyond the pale of civilisation, as Metternich had hoped would happen with the Greek revolt in the eighteen-twenties. Left-wing critics alleged that the government had Fascist sympathies and wanted the rebels to win. The British financiers, with interests in Spain, were not enthusiastic for the republic; and the government may have been influenced by them. The service chiefs did not look kindly on a Popular Front. Maybe the British government would have been less insistent on non-intervention if the situation had been reversed, and there had been a Communist, or even a radical, rebellion in Spain against an established Fascist régime. We have no means of knowing. Probably timidity—the desire to avoid a new topic of conflict in Europe—counted most; and Fascist sympathies, if they existed, ranked second.

At any rate, the British government got their way. Blum accepted the policy of non-intervention. More than this, he persuaded the leaders of the Labour party to support this policy also, so as not to make his position difficult in France. Thus, the

National government first imposed non-intervention on Blum; he imposed it on the Labour leaders; and they imposed it on their followers—all in the name of European peace. A non-intervention committee was set up in London. All the European Great Powers were represented, and solemnly devised schemes to prevent the import of arms into Spain. Germany and Italy made no pretence of keeping their promises: arms went continuously from both countries, and from Italy military formations as well. The Spanish republic seemed doomed to early destruction. Then Soviet Russia upset this neat expectation. The Russians announced that they would keep their promise of non-intervention only to the extent that Germany and Italy kept theirs. Soviet arms went to Spain, though never on the Fascist scale; and these arms enabled the republic to keep going for more than two years.

It is unlikely that Soviet Russia intervened in Spain on grounds of principle. Soviet policy had not been remarkable, under Stalin's guidance, for its backing of Communism, let alone of democracy. It had allowed Chiang Kai Shek to butcher the Chinese Communists without a murmur; and it would have continued friendly relations with Nazi Germany, if Hitler had been willing. Schulenburg, the German ambassador in Moscow, thought that Soviet Russia aided the Spanish republic in order to restore its prestige with the Communists of Western Europe after the shock of the great purge.[1] Probably there were more solid reasons. Conflict in Spain was more welcome to the Russians than conflict near their own border. They hoped, too, that this conflict would cause estrangement between the two Western democracies and the Fascist Powers. But of course the Russians did not intend to run any risk of being involved in the war themselves. Their interest was to keep the Spanish civil war going, not that the republic should win—exactly the same attitude as Hitler took up towards Spanish Fascism.

The Spanish civil war became the dominating topic of international affairs and, in Great Britain and France, the theme of passionate domestic controversy as well. The great issue of the age between democracy and Fascism seemed to be at stake in Spain. This appearance was misleading. The Spanish republic had never been securely democratic and, as the war went on, naturally fell

[1] Schulenburg to Foreign Ministry, 12 Oct. 1936. *German Foreign Policy*, series D. iii. No. 97.

increasingly under the direction of the Communists who controlled the supply of arms. On the other side, the rebels were
certainly enemies of democracy, but they were concerned with
Spain, not with the "Fascist International", and Franco, their
leader, had no intention of tying Spain to any foreign power or
foreign cause. Though he paid Hitler and Mussolini with high-
sounding declarations of ideological solidarity, he was a hard
bargainer when it came to economic concessions and, in strategical matters, made no concessions at all. The rebels won the
civil war; and, to everyone's surprise, their victory did not affect
the general balance in Europe. The French did not need to move
forces to the Pyrenees, despite the talk of their being weakened
by a third hostile frontier. The British never needed to be
anxious about Gibraltar. Franco proclaimed his neutrality during
the Czech crisis of 1988—to Hitler's annoyance. Spain duly
remained neutral during the second World war, except in regard
to Russia; and even here the Spanish Blue Division was never
more than a moral (or immoral) gesture.[1]

This strange outcome was foreseen by few; and the Spanish
civil war had great international effect while it was being fought.
It did much to prevent national unity in Great Britain and
France. Perhaps the bitterness, caused by the electoral victory
of the Popular Front, made French unity impossible in any case;
but there had been serious efforts towards a true National
government in Great Britain after Hitler's reoccupation of the
Rhineland. The controversy over non-intervention ended these
efforts. Liberals and Labour accused the government of betraying
the democratic cause; and ministers in their turn, excusing the
pretences of the non-intervention committee, grew exasperated
when its dishonesty was exposed. The Spanish civil war distracted
attention from the graver problems, raised by the revival of
German power. Men felt that all would be well if Franco were
defeated; they ceased to consider how Hitler should be checked.

[1] Ingenious speculators have even argued that Hitler would have gone
straight on to invade Spain after his conquest of France if the Republic had
won and that therefore Franco's victory brought gain to the Allies. These
"Ifs" of history are unrewarding. One might as well argue that a Republican
victory would so have shaken Fascism that there would have been no war.
Hitler stopped at the Spanish frontier partly from lack of resources, partly
because he was not interested in the western Mediterranean. The character
of the Spanish régime did not much affect him.

In the early days of 1986 Winston Churchill had seemed the rallying-point for patriotic and democratic opinion. He was neutral in the Spanish civil war or even perhaps slightly sympathetic towards Franco. His prestige ran downhill and was not restored on the Left until the autumn of 1938.

The civil war also drove a further wedge between Soviet Russia and the Western Powers—or rather between Soviet Russia and Great Britain, on whom western policy mainly turned. The British government did not care how the war ended, only that it should end quickly. The Italian government, too, wanted a quick end to the war, but on condition that Franco won. British statesmen easily slipped into the position of agreeing with Italy. Franco's victory would end the war; it would make no difference, except to the Spaniards; the price was therefore well worth paying. Hitler also would be content with Franco's victory, even though German policy was glad to see the war dragging on. All the British resentment was turned against Soviet Russia. Maisky, the Soviet representative on the non-intervention committee, exposed its shams, and talked in high terms of democracy; Soviet supplies sustained the republic. What, British statesmen felt, did Soviet Russia care about democracy? Why did she gratuitously intervene in Spain, so far from her own borders? It was purely to cause mischief or, even worse, to promote international Communism. A detached observer might suppose that it was Italian, and then German, intervention which had turned the Spanish civil war into an international problem; British ministers, worried by the prospect of further crisis and badgered by their own Opposition, saw only that the civil war would soon be over, were it not for Soviet aid to the republic. On the other side, far away in Moscow, the Soviet leaders built up similar suspicions of their own. They concluded that British statesmen were as indifferent towards democracy as they were themselves towards international Communism, indifferent even to national interests. British policy made sense in Moscow only on the assumption that it desired the triumph of Fascism. The British had allowed Hitler to rearm and to destroy the system of security; they were helping Franco to win in Spain. Soon, surely, they would stand approvingly by while Hitler attacked Soviet Russia; or maybe even co-operate in the enterprise.

These mutual suspicions were to make a deep mark on the

future. The immediate effect of the Spanish civil war was to send British statesmen hurrying after the favour of Mussolini. He seemed to hold the key to peace. Some Englishmen, such as Vansittart, hoped that he could be won back for the Stresa front and full-scale opposition to Hitler; others, more modest, accepted the Axis and hoped only that Mussolini would moderate Hitler. Mussolini was ready to hold out promise, though not performance. He knew that Italy had made gains in the past by balancing between the two sides, not by committing herself to either; and he imagined that he himself was still free. But he expected from the British more than they were in a position to offer. They thought that he would be content with the prestige of victory in Spain; he wanted to be won over by concessions from France, which would make Italy dominant in the Mediterranean. As an added flaw in the project, the Spanish republicans, somewhat stiffened with Soviet arms, denied him the victory which the British were trying to arrange, and instead routed Italian troops on the Guadalajara. However, the British went on trying. In January 1987, there was a "gentleman's agreement" between Great Britain and Italy, each solemnly assuring the other that it did not intend to change the *status quo* in the Mediterranean. In May there was a change of government in Great Britain. Baldwin, adept at overthrowing Kings though less successful with dictators, resigned; and Neville Chamberlain took his place as prime minister. Chamberlain was a harder, more practical man, impatient with drift in foreign affairs and confident that he could stop it. Agreement with Mussolini seemed to him the urgent need. On 27 July he wrote personally to Mussolini, regretting that Anglo-Italian relations were unsatisfactory and proposing conversations to improve them. Mussolini replied graciously in his own hand—quite as in old times to Austen Chamberlain or Ramsay MacDonald.

An unfortunate setback followed. "Unknown" submarines took to torpedoing the Soviet ships, which supplied the Spanish republic; some torpedoes hit British ships as well. For once, the British Admiralty stirred in its sleep. Eden, the foreign secretary, stirred too. He had not hitherto been a "strong man". Though carried to office by general indignation against the Hoare-Laval plan, he had urged the League to abandon Abyssinia; he had acquiesced in Hitler's reoccupation of the Rhineland without

serious protest; he had sponsored the pretences of the non-
intervention committee. Perhaps he was weak while Baldwin left
the responsibility to him; resentful and even resolute when
Chamberlain took it over. Or maybe he had lost faith in Mussolini's promises. At any rate, Great Britain and France summoned
a conference at Nyon; and there set up a naval patrol of the
Mediterranean which ended the ravages of the mysterious
submarines. Here was a demonstration, never repeated, that
Mussolini would respect a show of strength. Yet this show could
by itself settle nothing. The political reasons for tolerating
German and Italian intervention in Spain still remained. The
Nyon conference only provided that this intervention must not
take the form of conflict between the Great Powers.

The Far East now provided additional reason why the British
shrank from further naval action in the Mediterranean. In July
1987 the cool relations between China and Japan turned into
open war. Within eighteen months the Japanese established their
control over all the coast of China, cutting her off from most
outside assistance and threatening also British interests at
Shanghai and Hong Kong. Once more the Chinese appealed to
the League of Nations; this moribund institution could only refer
the appeal to a conference of Powers at Brussels. On the previous
occasion of the Manchurian affair, the British had received the
full blast of a moral disapproval which was largely undeserved:
they had seemed to be opposing the American doctrine of non-
recognition instead of showing that it provided no help for China.
At Brussels, the British got their blow in first: they offered to
second any aid to China which the Americans would propose. As
before the Americans would do nothing. They wanted the moral
satisfaction of non-recognition and also the material satisfaction
of their profitable trade with Japan. Non-recognition was an
American device, unconscious no doubt, for pushing others—and
particularly the British—forward against the Japanese. The
Americans would express the indignation; the British would
provide the opposition. This was not an attractive offer. The
Brussels conference did nothing to help China; it did not even
interfere with the supply of arms to Japan. The British allowed
some supplies to reach China over the Burma road; but their
main concern was to strengthen their own position in the Far
East against future difficulties. The interaction between the

problems of Europe and the Far East is hard to trace in detail:
each department of the Foreign Office went its separate way.
But the connexion was there. Great Britain alone was attempting
to be both a European and a World Power. The attempt was
beyond her strength; and difficulties in the one sphere held her
back whenever she tried to act in the other.

The Brussels conference had also a decisive effect on relations
between Great Britain and the United States. British policy had
long had a fixed point: not to quarrel with the Americans. It
never departed from this point. In the nineteen-twenties it had
gone further: it had sought to draw the United States into
European affairs and had welcomed American participation, for
instance, in regard to reparations and disarmament. This participation had ended with the "isolationism" which accompanied the
victory of F. D. Roosevelt and the Democrats. The Americans
had been too busy with the New Deal to have time for Europe or
even for the Far East. All they had to offer was moral disapproval; and this was turned less against the dictators than
against the Powers who failed to resist them. Great Britain and
France were condemned for their failure to save Abyssinia; for
their timidity over the Spanish Civil War; for their general
cravenness towards Hitler. Yet in none of these cases had the
United States done anything at all, except to maintain an even-
handed neutrality which usually benefited the aggressor. The
Brussels conference showed that it would be the same in the Far
East. The Powers were invited to commit themselves to non-
recognition for the sake of the United States. But there was no
chance of American assistance if they resisted Japan. On the
contrary, Japan would overcome them with American equipment.

American isolationism completed the isolation of Europe.
Academic commentators observed, rightly, that the problem of
the two dictators would be "solved", if the two World Powers,
Soviet Russia and the United States, were drawn into European
affairs. This observation was a desire, not a policy. Western
statesmen would have grasped eagerly at material backing from
across the Atlantic. This was not on offer. The United States were
unarmed except in the Pacific; and neutrality legislation made it
impossible for them to act even as a base of supply. President
Roosevelt could provide only moral exhortation; and this was the
very thing which Western statesmen feared. It would tie their

hands in dealing with Hitler and Mussolini; it would work against the concessions which they were ready to make. Great Britain and France had already too much moral capital; what they lacked was material strength. None was forthcoming from the United States.

Co-operation with the Soviet Union raised different problems. Soviet statesmen were eager to play a part in Europe, or so it appeared. They supported the League of Nations; preached collective security; and championed the cause of democracy in Spain. Their real intentions were a riddle. Were they really enthusiastic for collective security? Or did they advocate it merely to lead the Western Powers into trouble? Had Soviet Russia any effective strength? Even if she had, would it ever be used? The Soviet Government took an impeccable line at the non-intervention committee. Things looked different in Spain, where Soviet supplies were used to establish a Communist dictatorship over the democratic forces. It seemed obvious to Western statesmen that the Spanish civil war would soon be over, if only Soviet Russia abandoned the cause of the republic. Hence it was the Russians, not the Fascist dictators, who appeared in practical terms as the disturbers of the peace. Eden defined the object of Western policy as "peace at almost any price". The presence of Soviet Russia and the United States made it difficult to pay that price. They could afford moral indignation; the Western Powers had to live with the dictators. Western statesmen wanted Europe to settle its own affairs, free from reminders about democracy, collective security, and the sanctity of peace-settlements.

Perhaps, too, there was a common European jealousy of interference from outside; a half-formulated desire to show that the states of Europe were still the Great Powers. The experiment of calling in the New World to redress the balance of the Old had already been tried in the first World war. American intervention had been decisive; it had enabled the Allies to win the war. Twenty years afterwards, the result did not seem so happy. Victory had not solved the German question; rather Great Britain and France had it still on their hands, more insoluble than before. In retrospect, would it not have been better if they had been forced to a compromise peace with the more or less moderate Germany of 1917? Should they not, in any case, strive for such a compromise now? Even if the United States were again persuaded to intervene, they would again withdraw afterwards; and the Western Powers would once more have to settle with Germany on their own. As to Soviet intervention, which was the more dreaded—its success or its failure? Germany would be intolerably strengthened if she defeated Russia. Yet the alternative of Soviet victory was even worse. It would mean Communism all over Europe, or so men thought. Western statesmen wanted the *status quo* as near as possible; they could not get this with American or Soviet backing.

Here was the great decision in the two years of the half-armed peace. Probably nothing could have brought Soviet Russia and the United States into Europe in time. For reasons which then seemed convincing, Western statesmen strove to keep them out. The rulers of Europe behaved as though they were living in the days of Metternich or Bismarck, when Europe was still the centre of the world. European destinies were resolved in a closed circle. Negotiations for peace were confined, almost entirely, to the strictly European Powers. War, when it came, was to be a European war.

CHAPTER SEVEN

Anschluss : the End of Austria

THE watershed between the two World wars extended over precisely two years. Post-war ended when Germany reoccupied the Rhineland on 7 March 1936; pre-war began when she annexed Austria on 13 March 1938. From that moment, change and upheaval went on almost without interruption until the representatives of the Powers, victorious in the second World war, met at Potsdam in July 1945. Who first raised the storm and launched the march of events? The accepted answer is clear: it was Hitler. The moment of his doing so is also accepted: it was on 5 November 1937. We have a record of the statements which he made that day. It is called "the Hossbach memorandum", after the man who made it. This record is supposed to reveal Hitler's plans. Much play was made with it at Nuremberg; and the editors of the *Documents on German Foreign Policy* say that "it provides a summary of German foreign policy in 1937-38".[1] It is therefore worth looking at in detail. Perhaps we shall find in it the explanation of the second World war; or perhaps we shall find only the source of a legend.

That afternoon Hitler called a conference at the Chancellery. It was attended by Blomberg, the minister of war; Neurath, the foreign minister; Fritsch, commander-in-chief of the army; Raeder, commander-in-chief of the navy; and Goering, commander-in-chief of the air force. Hitler did most of the talking. He began with a general disquisition on Germany's need for *Lebensraum*. He did not specify where this was to be found— probably in Europe, though he also discussed colonial gains. But gains there must be. "Germany had to reckon with two hate-inspired antagonists, Britain and France. . . . Germany's problem could only be solved by means of force and this was never without attendant risk." When and how was there to be this resort to force? Hitler discussed three "cases". The first "case" was

[1] *Documents on German Foreign Policy*, series D. i., footnote on p. 29.

"period 1943-1945". After that the situation could only change for the worse; 1943 must be the moment for action. Case 2 was civil war in France; if that happened, "the time for action against the Czechs had come". Case 3 was war between France and Italy. This might well occur in 1938; then "our objective must be to overthrow Czechoslovakia and Austria simultaneously". None of these "cases" came true; clearly therefore they do not provide the blueprint for German policy. Nor did Hitler dwell on them. He went on to demonstrate that Germany would gain her aims without a great war; "force" apparently meant to him the threat of war, not necessarily war itself. The Western Powers would be too hampered and too timid to intervene. "Britain almost certainly, and probably France as well, had written off the Czechs and were reconciled to the fact that this question of Germany would be cleared up in due course". No other Power would intervene. "Poland—with Russia in her rear—will have little inclination to engage in war against a victorious Germany." Russia would be held in check by Japan.

Hitler's exposition was in large part day-dreaming, unrelated to what followed in real life. Even if seriously meant, it was not a call to action, at any rate not to the action of a great war; it was a demonstration that a great war would not be necessary. Despite the preliminary talk about 1943-1945, its solid core was the examination of the chances for peaceful triumphs in 1938, when France would be preoccupied elsewhere. Hitler's listeners remained doubtful. The generals insisted that the French army would be superior to the German even if engaged against Italy as well. Neurath doubted whether a Mediterranean conflict between France and Italy were imminent. Hitler waved these doubts aside: "he was convinced of Britain's non-participation, and therefore he did not believe in the probability of belligerent action by France against Germany". There is only one safe conclusion to be drawn from this rambling disquisition: Hitler was gambling on some twist of fortune which would present him with success in foreign affairs, just as a miracle had made him Chancellor in 1933. There was here no concrete plan, no directive for German policy in 1937 and 1938. Or if there were a directive, it was to wait upon events.[1]   *ARROGANCE ?*

[1] Memorandum by Hossbach, 10 Nov. 1937. *German Foreign Policy*, series D. i. No. 19.

Why then did Hitler hold this conference? This question was not asked at Nuremberg; it has not been asked by historians. Yet surely it is an elementary part of historical discipline to ask of a document not only what is in it, but why it came into existence. The conference of 5 November 1937 was a curious gathering. Only Goering was a Nazi. The others were old-style Conservatives who had remained in office to keep Hitler under control; all of them except Raeder were to be dismissed from their posts within three months. Hitler knew that all except Goering were his opponents; and he did not trust Goering much. Why did he reveal his inmost thoughts to men whom he distrusted and whom he was shortly to discharge? This question has an easy answer: he did not reveal his inmost thoughts. There was no crisis in foreign policy to provoke a broad discussion or sweeping decisions. The conference was a manoeuvre in domestic affairs. Here a storm was brewing. The financial genius of Schacht had made rearmament and full employment possible; but now Schacht was jibbing at further expansion of the armament programme. Hitler feared Schacht and could not answer his financial arguments. He knew only that they were wrong: the Nazi régime could not relax its momentum. Hitler aimed to isolate Schacht from the other Conservatives; and he had therefore to win them for a programme of increased armaments. His geopolitical exposition had no other purpose. The Hossbach memorandum itself provides evidence of this. Its last paragraph reads: "The second part of the conference was concerned with questions of armament". This, no doubt, was why it had been called.

The participants themselves drew this conclusion. After Hitler had left, Raeder complained that the German navy would be in no strength to face war for years ahead. Blomberg and Goering pulled him into a corner, where they explained that the sole object of the conference was to prod Fritsch into demanding a larger arms programme. Neurath made no comment at the time. He is said to have grasped the full import of Hitler's wickedness some days later, and then to have suffered "several severe heart-attacks". These attacks were first revealed in 1945 when Neurath was being tried as a war criminal; he showed no sign of ill-health in 1937 or for years afterwards. Fritsch prepared a memorandum, insisting that the German army must not be exposed to the risk of war against France, and took this to Hitler on 9 November. Hitler replied that there was no real risk and that, in any case, Fritsch would do better to speed up rearmament instead of dabbling in political questions. Despite this rebuke, Hitler's manoeuvre had succeeded: henceforward Fritsch, Blomberg, and Raeder had no sympathy with Schacht's financial scruples. Otherwise, none of the men who attended the meeting on 5 November gave it another thought until Goering found the record produced against him at Nuremberg as evidence of his war guilt. From that moment it has haunted the corridors of historical research. It is the basis for the view that there is nothing to be discovered about the origins of the second World war. Hitler, it is claimed, decided on war, and planned it in detail on 5 November 1937. Yet the Hossbach memorandum contains no plans of the kind, and would never have been supposed to do so, unless it had been displayed at Nuremberg. The memorandum tells us, what we knew already, that Hitler (like every other German statesman) intended Germany to become the dominant Power in Europe. It also tells us that he speculated how this might happen. His speculations were mistaken. They bear hardly any relation to the actual outbreak of war in 1939. A racing tipster who only reached Hitler's level of accuracy would not do well for his clients.

The speculations were irrelevant as well as mistaken. Hitler did not make plans—for world conquest or for anything else. He assumed that others would provide opportunities, and that he would seize them. The opportunities which he envisaged on 5 November 1937 were not provided. Others were. We must therefore look elsewhere for the man who provided an opportunity which Hitler could take and who thus gave the first push towards war. Neville Chamberlain is an obvious candidate for this position. From the moment that he became prime minister in May 1937, he was determined to start something. Of course he resolved on action in order to prevent war, not to bring it on; but he did not believe that war could be prevented by doing nothing. He detested Baldwin's sceptical, easy-going policy of drift. He had no faith in the hesitant idealism associated with the League of Nations which Eden half-heartedly put forward. Chamberlain took the lead in pressing for increases in British armaments. At the same time, he resented the waste of money involved, and believed it to be unnecessary. The arms race, he was convinced, sprang from misunderstandings between the Powers, not from deep-seated rivalries or from the sinister design of one Power to dominate the world. He believed, too, that the dissatisfied Powers—and Germany in particular—had legitimate grievances and that these grievances should be met. He accepted, to some extent, the Marxist view, held by many people who were not Marxists, that German discontent had economic causes, such as lack of access to foreign markets. He accepted more fully the "liberal" opinion that Germans were the victims of national injustice; and he had no difficulty in recognising where this injustice lay. There were six million Germans in Austria, to whom national reunification was still forbidden by the peace treaties of 1919; three million Germans in Czechoslovakia, whose wishes had never been consulted; three hundred and fifty thousand people in Danzig who were notoriously German. It was the universal experience of recent times that national discontent could not be challenged or silenced—Chamberlain himself had had to acknowledge this unwillingly in regard to Ireland and India. It was the general belief, though less sustained by experience, that nations became contented and pacific, once their claims were met.

Here was a programme for the pacification of Europe. It was devised by Chamberlain, not thrust upon him by Hitler. These ideas were in the air, shared by almost every Englishman who thought about international affairs. Only two groups dissented. One very small group rejected the validity of national claims. They held that policy should be determined by questions of Power, not of morality; and that nationalism should be subordinated to security. Churchill had recently fought a lone campaign against concessions to India; his opposition to concessions in regard to Germany was the logical sequel to this. Vansittart and some other senior members of the foreign service took much the same view. It was a view which shocked most Englishmen and which, by its apparent cynicism, deprived its holders of influence on policy. Power, it was held, had been tried during the first World war and afterwards. It had failed; morality should take its place. A larger group, predominant in the Liberal and Labour parties, accepted the rightfulness of German claims, but believed that these claims should not be met so long as Hitler remained in power. What they disliked in Hitler was his tyranny at home, and especially his persecution of the Jews; but they went on from this to assert that his foreign policy aimed at conquest, not at equal justice for Germany. It could be answered that non-interference in other countries was a long-standing tradition of British foreign policy, advocated by John Bright and by Chamberlain's father in his Radical days; and that Chamberlain was adopting towards Nazi Germany precisely the attitude which the Labour movement had always demanded should be adopted towards Soviet Russia. It could also be answered that Hitlerism was the product of "Versailles" and would lose its evil qualities as "Versailles" disappeared. These were powerful, though not conclusive, arguments. There remained many who wished to resist Hitler; but it was a weakness of their position all along that they admitted the justice of his supposed claims and denied only that he was entitled to make them. They tried to distinguish between Germany and Hitler and insisted that, while Germany was right, Hitler was wrong. Unfortunately this was not a distinction which the Germans were willing to make.

Chamberlain, at any rate, was confident that his programme would work. His motive throughout was the general pacification of Europe. He was driven on by hope, not fear. It did not occur to him that Great Britain and France were unable to oppose German demands; rather he assumed that Germany, and Hitler in particular, would be grateful for concessions willingly made—concessions which, if Hitler failed to respond with equal goodwill, could also be withheld. Chamberlain shared with Hitler a taste for doing things himself. He took as his principal adviser on foreign affairs Sir Horace Wilson, a professional conciliator who had made his name in industrial disputes; and he attached little weight to the opinions of the Foreign Office. When he first approached Hitler he did so through Lord Halifax, then Lord President, not through Eden, the foreign secretary. Halifax had a unique gift: he was always at the centre of events, yet managed somehow to leave the impression that he was not connected with them. Chamberlain and everyone else associated with British policy before the war were irremediably discredited when the crash came in 1940. Halifax, whose responsibility as foreign secretary for most of the time was second only to Chamberlain's, emerged unspotted; and could be seriously put forward by George VI and many others—including the leaders of the Labour party—as appropriate head for a government of national salvation. It is impossible to explain how this could happen.

On 19 November 1937 Halifax met Hitler at Berchtesgaden. It was a characteristically off-hand visit: officially Halifax was in Germany to see a hunting exhibition at Berlin. Halifax said all that Hitler expected to hear. He praised Nazi Germany "as the bulwark of Europe against Bolshevism"; he sympathised with past German grievances. In particular he pointed to certain questions where "possible alterations might be destined to come about with the passage of time". They were: Danzig, Austria, and Czechoslovakia. "England was interested to see that any alterations should come through the course of peaceful evolution and that methods should be avoided which might cause far-reaching disturbances".[1] Hitler listened and occasionally rambled. He remained passive according to his usual method: accepting offers from others, not making demands himself. Here, in Halifax's own words, was confirmation of what Hitler had told the generals a fortnight before: England would not seek to maintain the existing settlement in central Europe. There was a condition attached: the changes must come without a general war ("far-reaching disturbances"). This was exactly what Hitler wanted himself. Halifax's remarks, if they had any practical sense, were an invitation to Hitler to promote German nationalist agitation in Danzig, Czechoslovakia, and Austria; an assurance also that this agitation would not be opposed from without. Nor did these promptings come from Halifax alone. In London, Eden told Ribbentrop: "People in England recognised that a closer connexion between Germany and Austria would have to come about sometime".[2] The same news came from France. Papen, on a visit to Paris, "was amazed to note" that Chautemps, the premier, and Bonnet, then finance minister, "considered a reorientation of French policy in Central Europe as entirely open to discussion. . . ." They had "no objection to a marked extension of German influence in Austria obtained through evolutionary

[1] Memorandum, 19 Nov.; foreign ministry circular, 22 Nov. 1937. *German Foreign Policy*, series D. i. No. 31 and 33.
[2] Ribbentrop to Neurath, 2 Dec. 1937. *Ibid.* No. 50.

means"; nor in Czechoslovakia "on the basis of a reorganisation
into a nation of nationalities".[1]

All these remarks strengthened Hitler's conviction that he
would meet little opposition from Great Britain and France.
They did not provide a solution for the practical problem of
strategy: how to make the extension of German power appear to
be the result, in Halifax's words, of "reasonable agreements
reasonably reached". It might be possible for Germany to
conquer Czechoslovakia and Austria; it was more difficult to
arrange that these two countries should commit suicide, which is
what British and French statesmen wanted. There was a further
drawback in the promptings from London and Paris. They put
most emphasis on Austria. Hitler, when he thought in practical
terms, planned to deal first with Czechoslovakia—an order of
priorities which appears even in the Hossbach memorandum.
The Czechs had a strong army and some political sense; therefore
they might go to the aid of Austria. The Austrians had neither;
and so were unlikely to help Czechoslovakia. Besides—a more
important point—Mussolini was indifferent towards Czechoslovakia. He was still formally committed to the independence of
Austria; and maybe the British and French did not altogether
forget this when they pushed the question of Austria into the
forefront. Hitler did not mean to oblige them: he returned it
firmly to the background. In the autumn of 1937 he encouraged
German agitation in Czechoslovakia. He discouraged it in
Austria; and laid down firmly that "we should continue to seek
an evolutionary solution".[2] Far from taking the initiative over
Austria, Hitler did not want to begin there. Nor did the initiative
come from British or French statesmen. Halifax and others
advanced an academic proposition in their various conciliatory
statements, just as Hitler had done in his conference on 5
November—the proposition that it would be agreeable if Germany
extended her hegemony peacefully over her two neighbours.
Neither they nor he hit on a method by which this could be done.
It was all talk and no action.

Still, the initiative must have come from someone. Perhaps we
should look on the Austrian side. Schuschnigg was still chancellor

[1] Papen, report to the Führer, 8 Nov.; to Weizsäcker, 4 Dec. 1937.
German Foreign Policy, series D. i. No. 22 and 63.
[2] Memorandum by Keppler, 1 Oct. 1937. *Ibid.* No. 256.

of a nominally independent Austria. He had had a sad time of it since making the "gentleman's agreement" of 11 July 1986 with Germany. In an innocent, high-minded way, Schuschnigg had assumed that the agreement would end his troubles. Austria would announce her German character; respectable representatives of "the national opposition" would enter the Austrian government; imprisoned Nazis would be released. Then there would be an end of agitation and conspiracies: no more secret arming or illegal propaganda. Schuschnigg was soon disappointed. Nazi agitation went on as before; not even Hitler's orders could stop it. Schuschnigg's close colleagues themselves intrigued with Berlin against him. He complained to his old patron and protector, Mussolini. He received cold comfort. Mussolini liked to picture himself in a flattering posture as guarantor of Austria's existence—a Metternich in reverse, revenging Italian humiliations of a century before. He listened to the warnings of leading Fascists—from his son-in-law Ciano, the foreign minister, downwards—that Hitler was a dangerous associate who would destroy Italy after eating up the others first. He seemed to pay attention; but when it came to the point he never responded to their promptings. At heart Mussolini was the only realist in the Fascist crew, the only one who appreciated that Italy had little strength of her own and could simulate greatness only as Hitler's jackal. He might talk of an independent policy or of asserting Italian interest in central Europe. He knew that he would have to give way to Hitler if events reached a crisis. He was therefore impatient with Schuschnigg, the man who had to take Mussolini's pretences seriously. Mussolini, despite his brave talk, was in exactly the same position as the statesmen of Western Europe; he wanted to sell out on Austria so long as it could be done peacefully and in a decent way. Schuschnigg received no solid backing; only the repeated advice to behave reasonably and to keep things quiet.

Schuschnigg was however a victim, the last of them, of a peculiarly Austrian illusion—the belief that the conscience of Europe could be stirred into action if nationalist intrigue and agitation were clearly exposed. Austrian statesmen had this illusion about Italian nationalism in the middle of the nineteenth century; they had it about South Slav nationalism in the early years of the twentieth. It seemed to them axiomatic in 1859 that

Cavour would be deserted by Napoleon III and denounced by the
other Great Powers, once clear evidence was produced of his
complicity in nationalist agitation. It seemed equally axiomatic
to them in July 1914 that Serbia would be abandoned by all the
Great Powers if the assassination of Franz Ferdinand at Sarajevo
were brought home to her agents. In each case they found evidence which they regarded as convincing; in each case this
encouraged them along the road of decisive action to their own
undoing—to defeat in the Austro-French war of 1859, to defeat
and disaster in the first World war. The same spirit still lived in
Schuschnigg. He, too, supposed that the Austrian Nazis would be
universally condemned if decisive evidence were produced
against them—condemned by the Western Powers and by
Mussolini, condemned even by Hitler, who was after all the legal
head of an ostensibly law-abiding state. Schuschnigg, too, found
his evidence. In January 1938 the Austrian police raided Nazi
headquarters, and discovered detailed plans for an armed rising.
Hitler knew nothing of these plans, which had been prepared
despite his orders. To this extent Schuschnigg was right: the
Austrian Nazis were acting without authority. It was a different
question whether Hitler would apologise for his over-zealous
followers.

At any rate Schuschnigg had his evidence. The problem was
how to use it. Schuschnigg carried his evidence and his problem
to Papen, the German ambassador. After all, Papen was a
gentleman, wealthy and aristocratic, an impeccable conservative
and a more or less impeccable Roman Catholic. Surely he would
be shaken by this record of Nazi intrigue. Schuschnigg's complaints were music in Papen's ears. He resented the work of the
Nazi underground in Austria, which cast doubt on his own good
faith and impeded his efforts towards "an evolutionary solution".
His expostulations had gone unregarded in Berlin. Now
Schuschnigg would reinforce them. Papen at once suggested
that Schuschnigg should carry his complaints to Hitler. It is
impossible to tell what was in Papen's mind. Perhaps he hoped
that Hitler would rebuke the Nazi extremists; perhaps he foresaw that Schuschnigg would be driven to make further concessions to the German national cause in Austria. Probably there
would be a little of both. Either way Papen would gain. In the
one case, he would discredit his unruly rivals: in the other, he

would win prestige by advancing the German cause. He would manoeuvre a peaceful success in Austria just as he had peacefully manoeuvred Hitler into power in Germany. At precisely this moment, on 4 February, the telephone rang in the German embassy at Vienna; and Papen was abruptly informed by Berlin that he had been dismissed from his post.

Papen's dismissal had nothing to do with events in Austria. It was the accidental by-product of Hitler's conflict with Schacht. On 8 December 1937 Schacht resigned as Minister of Economics. Hitler shrank from revealing the breach; and Schacht's resignation was kept secret. A way out presented itself unexpectedly. On 12 January 1938 Blomberg, the Minister of War, married. Hitler and Goering were the principal witnesses. Immediately afterwards, Himmler, head of the secret police, produced evidence that Frau Blomberg was a woman of disreputable character—a former prostitute with a police record. We shall never know whether this was a stroke of luck for Hitler or a prepared intrigue. Nor does it matter; the effect was the same in either case. Hitler was indignant at having been involved in the marriage. The German generals were indignant at Blomberg's behaviour. They insisted that he must go; they also proposed that Fritsch, the commander-in-chief of the army, should succeed him. But Fritsch was a more resolute anti-Nazi than Blomberg. He must be kept out. Himmler obligingly furnished evidence of homosexuality against him. This evidence was altogether false. In the general moral turmoil it was believed for the moment. Hitler made a clean sweep. Blomberg went—to be succeeded by Hitler himself. Fritsch went. Not only this, all the conservatives who had held office to restrain Hitler were cleared out as well. Neurath was out; his place was taken by Ribbentrop. Papen and Hassell, ambassador to Italy, were dismissed. Most important of all, the resignation of Schacht could now be smuggled quietly in among the other changes. This was of course the object of the whole operation; yet in the stir of the time it passed almost unnoticed.

In Berlin the dismissed men left office without protest. Neurath later became "Protector" of Bohemia; the others vanished from public life. Papen alone was undismayed. He had often been in a tight corner before—on 30 June 1934 within an ace of assassination; he had always escaped triumphantly, and he meant to

escape again. On 5 February he went to see Hitler at Berchtesgaden, ostensibly to say farewell. He displayed his own successes
in Austria; described the difficulties awaiting a new German
ambassador; and casually slipped in the information that
Schuschnigg had been anxious to meet Hitler. This had been a
splendid opening, now—no doubt—lost. The effect was all that
Papen had expected. Hitler had been brooding gloomily how he
was to present the resignation of Schacht at a meeting of the
Reichstag which he had summoned for 20 February. Here was a
splendid diversion: Schuschnigg's visit would provide him with
some sort of success with which to cloak the awkward subject of
Schacht's financial protests. Hitler lit up: "An excellent idea.
Please go back to Vienna immediately, and arrange for us to
meet within the next few days".[1] Papen shammed reluctance: he
was no longer ambassador. Hitler was insistent; and Papen
agreed. On 7 February he was back in Vienna with the invitation.
Schuschnigg did not hesitate. After all, the idea of a meeting
with Hitler had been his in the first place, or so he now imagined;
Papen was the guarantor that all would be well. On 12 February
Schuschnigg, too, arrived in Berchtesgaden, whither Papen had
preceded him. The Austrian affair was under weigh. It had not
been launched by Hitler. It was sprung on him by surprise, and
he took a chance as always. There was here no planned aggression, only hasty improvisation. Papen, not Hitler, started the
ball rolling; and he did so for casual motives of personal prestige.
No doubt chance provided that he should give the decisive push;
yet it was strangely appropriate that the man who had frivolously
brought Hitler to power in Germany should also be the one who,
with equal frivolity, started Germany's advance towards
European domination.

Schuschnigg had intended to appear at Berchtesgaden as the
aggrieved party, unfolding his complaints and offering concessions
to the respectable nationalists only in exchange for a repudiation
of the Nazi extremists. His plan miscarried. Hitler always
believed that attack was the best form of defence; and he got his
blow in first. Schuschnigg, on arrival, was at once overwhelmed
with accusations that he had failed to honour the "gentleman's
agreement" of 11 July 1936. It was Hitler who laid down terms
for future co-operation. Schuschnigg was to make Seyss-Inquart,

[1] Papen, *Memoirs*, 408.

a supposedly respectable nationalist, Minister of the Interior and to give him control of the police. Austria was to coordinate her economic and foreign policy with that of Germany. Schuschnigg raised constitutional objections: he could not make binding promises without the consent of the Austrian government and President. He was bullied by Hitler; German generals, waiting outside, were ostentatiously called in. Yet, though these methods were abominable, Schuschnigg got most of what he wanted. His constitutional scruples were respected: in the final draft he merely "held out the prospect of the following measures". Seyss-Inquart was no worse than other German nationalists already in the Cabinet; and was indeed a boyhood friend of Schuschnigg— not that this prevented his becoming a Nazi later. Schuschnigg had long acknowledged that Austria was "a German state"; and this had implied a coordination of policy. He received what he believed to be the vital concession: the illegal activities of the Austrian Nazis were repudiated, and it was agreed that any unwanted Austrian Nazis should "transfer their residence to the Reich".

The agreement of 12 February was not the end of Austria; it was a further step in the "evolutionary solution" which Hitler had laid down. Schuschnigg made no attempt to disavow it when he had escaped from Hitler's presence. On the contrary he duly secured its confirmation by the Austrian government. Hitler, on his side, assumed that the crisis was over. On 12 February he told the attendant generals to keep up "military pressure shamming action" until 15 February. After this not even a show of action was maintained. On 20 February Hitler addressed the Reichstag. His main concern was to explain away the dismissal of the conservative ministers; but the agreement over Austria of 12 February enabled him to ride off on a more attractive subject. There was no attack on Schuschnigg, as there would surely have been if Hitler were already projecting aggression against Austria. Quite the reverse, Hitler announced in gentle tones: "Friendly co-operation between the two countries in every field has been assured"; and he concluded: "I would like to thank the Austrian Chancellor in my own name, and in that of the German people, for his understanding and kindness". The following day Hitler kept his part of the bargain. Leopold, the leader of the Nazi underground in Austria, was summoned before Hitler; told that his activities had been "insane"; and ordered to leave Austria along with his principal associates. A few days later Hitler saw these Nazis again, gave them another rating, and insisted that "the evolutionary course be taken, whether or not the possibility of success could today be foreseen. The Protocol signed by Schuschnigg was so far-reaching that if completely carried out the Austrian problem would be automatically solved".[1]

Hitler was satisfied. He made no preparations for action, but waited impassively for the automatic solution to mature. Others were less resigned to the inevitable—or perhaps merely sought to reap advantage from it. In Italy, Mussolini was always inclined to acquiesce in Hitler's success, despite bursts of irritation; Ciano, his foreign minister, more reluctant to be dragged along. His dream of an independent foreign policy was never realised; and maybe it was no more than a dream. At any rate Ciano tried to exploit the situation. On 16 February he wrote to Grandi, Italian ambassador in London, that this was the last moment for a reconciliation with Great Britain: "should the Anschluss be an accomplished fact, . . . it would become increasingly difficult for us to reach an agreement or even talk with the English".[2] Grandi welcomed this opening: he had always wanted to put Italian policy back on its traditional course, so far as any Fascist could favour a traditional line. Chamberlain welcomed it too. Eden at last revolted. He was already angry that Chamberlain, without consulting him, had turned down a proposal from President Roosevelt for a great international conference to discuss every imaginable grievance. Eden supposed, perhaps sincerely, that such a meeting would draw the United States on to the side of the Western Powers. Chamberlain feared, with more justification, that it would be a repetition of the Brussels conference over the Far East—the United States would propound moral principles; Great Britain and France would be expected to provide the force with which to sustain them. It was the Italian approach however which brought the dispute between the two men to a head. Eden had not forgotten his humiliation over Abyssinia; he was exasperated by the endless dishonesty of the

[1] Memorandum (by Keppler), 21 and 26 Feb. 1938. *German Foreign Policy*, series D. i. No. 318 and 328.

[2] Ciano to Grandi, 16 Feb. 1938. *Ciano's Diplomatic Papers*, 161.

non-intervention committee. He insisted that there could be no new conversations until the Italians fulfilled their existing promises by withdrawing the so-called volunteers from Spain. Chamberlain was prepared to tolerate a Fascist victory in Spain if he could win Italian support for moderating Hitler.

The argument between Eden and Chamberlain was fought out on 18 February, actually in Grandi's presence. Eden stood firm on the question of the Italian volunteers in Spain. Chamberlain brushed his objections aside, with Grandi's approval and support. Two days later Eden resigned; and Halifax became foreign secretary to carry out Chamberlain's policy. The Italian price was paid: conversations were to start at once, and it was agreed in advance that the Italian terms would be met—their empire in Abyssinia would be recognised, they would be promised equal partnership in the Mediterranean. Nothing was said about Austria; and Grandi recorded that the British attitude there would continue to be one of "indignant resignation".[1] This was true. Chamberlain did not intend to do anything about Austria. But he hoped that the simple fact of Anglo-Italian conversations would make Hitler hesitate, and perhaps even inspire Mussolini to resistance. Hitler was not deceived so easily. The Italians kept him informed of the discussions and assured him that the question of Austria would not be raised: "they would not tolerate any attempt to impair German-Italian relations".[2] This was the only course Italy could follow. The Italians had no means of stopping Hitler. As Ciano wrote on 23 February: "What in fact could we do? Start a war with Germany? At the first shot we fired every Austrian, without exception, would fall in behind the Germans against us".[3] Chamberlain maybe did not offer the Italians a very high price; but no price could have brought them to fight for the crumbling cause of Austrian independence.

These events in London increased Hitler's self-confidence. His opponents were falling by the wayside. The Axis was increasingly shaping European affairs; and he determined the policy of the Axis. Nevertheless he still did nothing. He continued to assume that events were doing his work for him. Once more, and for the

---

[1] Grandi to Ciano, 19 Feb. 1938. *Ciano's Diplomatic Papers*, 183.

[2] Memorandum by Ribbentrop, 23 Feb. 1938. *German Foreign Policy* series D. i. No. 123.

[3] *Ciano's Diary 1937-1938*, 79.

last time, the initiative came from Schuschnigg. In a puzzled, hesitant way, he built up resentment against the treatment he had received at Berchtesgaden and against the consequences of his own weakness. He resolved to arrest the inevitable slide into a National Socialist Austria by a dramatic challenge. Perhaps he was prompted by assurances from the Austrian minister in Paris that the French would take action if Austria were openly threatened. Perhaps the idea sprang only from his own brooding. We have no means of knowing. At any rate he determined to use Hitler's own method of a plebiscite, and to ask the Austrian people whether they wished to remain independent. On 7 March he consulted Mussolini, who replied abruptly: "It is a mistake". Schuschnigg ignored this feeble warning. On March 8 he told the Austrian ministers of his plan; on 9 March he announced it to the world. The plebiscite was to be held three days later on 12 March. Schuschnigg had made no preparations for the plebiscite; he had not considered how it was to be conducted. His only thought was to rush it through before Hitler could react in any way. Whatever the terms of the plebiscite, all the world knew that it was an open defiance of Hitler. The moment of conflict between German nationalism and independent Austria had arrived. Schuschnigg might have reflected on the words which Andrássy once addressed to another Austrian prime minister who embarked on a daring policy: "Are you prepared to carry through this policy with cannon? If not, do not embark upon it".

Hitler responded as though someone had trodden on a painful corn. He had received no warning, and had made no preparations. It was clear to him that "the evolutionary solution" was dead. He must either act or be humiliated; and he could not accept humiliation when the breach with the conservative ministers was just behind him. The military leaders were hastily summoned to Berlin. The German army was not yet equipped for any kind of serious campaign; but orders were issued that such forces as were stationed near Austria should be ready to cross the frontier on 12 March. A letter to Mussolini was drafted, reciting Hitler's attempts to reach agreement with Schuschnigg and ending with the assurance: "I have drawn a definite boundary . . . . between Italy and us. It is the Brenner".[1] The Prince of Hesse took the

[1] Hitler to Mussolini, 11 March 1938. *German Foreign Policy*, series D. i. No. 352.

letter to Mussolini. Ribbentrop was absent in London on a farewell visit; and Neurath was recalled to run the routine duties of the foreign ministry. The general conduct of affairs fell into the hands of Goering, who was to remain in Berlin when Hitler joined the invading forces.

Schuschnigg had lit the time-fuse of a considerable bomb. It was his turn to be taken by surprise when it exploded. On 11 March he learnt that the frontier between Germany and Austria had been closed. The Nationalist ministers in his government insisted, on Goering's instructions, that the plebiscite be cancelled. Schuschnigg turned disconsolately to the Powers who had once protected Austrian independence. He received cold comfort. Mussolini refused to answer the telephone. In London, Halifax told Ribbentrop that the threat of force was an *intolerable* method. The effect of this expostulation was weakened when Chamberlain said that they could begin working in earnest towards a German-British understanding "once we had all got past this unpleasant affair".[1] It was further weakened in Berlin when Nevile Henderson agreed with Goering that "Dr. Schuschnigg had acted with precipitate folly".[2] The only reply the British Government gave to Vienna was that they could not take the responsibility of giving advice which might land Austria in trouble.[3] The French government had fallen over a domestic issue three days before. The ministers, still in half-existence, decided to take "military measures"—meaning the recall of some reservists—if the British approved. No approval came from London; no French reservists were recalled.

Schuschnigg was abandoned and alone. In the early afternoon of 11 March he agreed to postpone the plebiscite. This was no longer enough. Goering told Seyss-Inquart over the telephone that the Germans had lost confidence in Schuschnigg: he must resign, and Seyss-Inquart take his place. This was a unique episode in history—an international crisis conducted from start to finish by telephonic threats. Schuschnigg duly resigned. Miklas, the President, however refused to appoint Seyss-

[1] Memoranda by Ribbentrop. 11 March. 1938. *German Foreign Policy*, series D. i. No. 150 and 151.

[2] Henderson to Halifax, 12 March 1938. *British Foreign Policy*, third series. i. No. 46.

[3] Halifax to Palairet, 11 March 1938. *Ibid.* No. 25.

Inquart—a last, despairing gesture of Austrian independence. Goering again came on the telephone to say that the German troops would stop at the frontier only if Seyss-Inquart was made Chancellor by 7.30 p.m. Since Miklas still held out, Seyss-Inquart appointed himself Chancellor at 8 p.m. It was too late. Seyss-Inquart was told to ask for German help in order to restore law and order. He did so in a telegram sent off at 9.10 p.m. Hitler had not waited for his appeal: the order to invade Austria was issued at 8.45 p.m. Yet the Germans had hesitated till the last moment. The plans for invading Austria had been called off earlier in the afternoon when the news of Schuschnigg's resignation arrived. Though British expostulations carried little weight, the Germans feared Czech intervention till the last moment. Goering told the Czech minister: "I give you my word of honour that Czechoslovakia has not the least reason to feel any anxiety". The Czechs at once replied that they would not mobilise. They hardly believed Goering's assurance, yet felt—like everyone else—that there was nothing they could do. Mussolini was the last to declare himself. At 10.25 p.m. Hesse telephoned to Hitler from Rome: Mussolini sent his best greetings—"Austria did not interest him at all". The anxieties which lay concealed beneath Hitler's resoluteness bubbled to the surface in emotional relief: "Tell Mussolini I will never forget this. . . . Never, never, never, whatever happens. . . . I will never forget, whatever may happen. . . . If he should ever need any help or be in any danger, he can be convinced that I shall stick to him, whatever may happen, even if the whole world be against him". This was one promise which Hitler kept.

The German army was invading Austria, or rather marching in to the general enthusiasm of the population. For what purpose? Seyss-Inquart was Chancellor. Goering had told Henderson that the troops would be withdrawn "as soon as the situation was stable" and that thereafter "completely free elections would be held without any intimidation whatever".[1] This had been the original Nazi plan, as botched up on 11 March. Seyss-Inquart thought that everything was successfully concluded with his own appointment, and at 2.30 a.m. on 12 March asked that the invasion should be stopped. He was told that this was impossible;

[1] Henderson to Halifax, 12 March 1938. *British Foreign Policy*, third series. i. No. 46 and 48.

and the German troops rolled on, though with some difficulty. The forces were not prepared for action; and 70% of their vehicles broke down on the road from the frontier to Vienna. Hitler, too, entered Austria on the morning of 12 March. At Linz, where he had gone to school, he addressed the excited crowds. He succumbed to this excitement himself. As he went on to the balcony of Linz Town Hall, he made a sudden, unexpected decision: instead of setting up a tame government in Vienna, he would incorporate Austria in the *Reich*. Seyss-Inquart, Chancellor for a day, was told to issue a law, ordering himself and Austria out of existence. He did so on 13 March. The Anschluss was submitted for approval to the people of Greater Germany. On 10 April 99.08% voted in its favour, a genuine reflection of German feeling.

Hitler had won. He had achieved the first object of his ambition. Yet not in the way that he had intended. He had planned to absorb Austria imperceptibly, so that no one could tell when it ceased to be independent; he would use democratic methods to destroy Austrian independence as he had done to destroy German democracy. Instead he had been driven to call in the German army. For the first time, he lost the asset of aggrieved morality and appeared as a conqueror, relying on force. The belief soon became established that Hitler's seizure of Austria was a deliberate plot, devised long in advance, and the first step towards the domination of Europe. This belief was a myth. The crisis of March 1938 was provoked by Schuschnigg, not by Hitler. There had been no German preparations, military or diplomatic. Everything was improvised in a couple of days—policy, promises, armed force. Though Hitler certainly meant to establish control over Austria, the way in which this came about was for him a tiresome accident, an interruption of his long-term policy, not the maturing of carefully thought-out plans. But the effects could not be undone. There was the effect on Hitler himself. He had got away with murder—the murder of an independent state, even though its independence was largely sham. Hitler's self-confidence was increased, and with it his contempt for the statesmen of other countries. He became more impatient and careless, readier to speed up negotiations by threats of force. In return, statesmen elsewhere began to doubt Hitler's good faith. Even those who still hoped to appease him began to think also of resistance. The uneasy balance tilted, though only slightly, away from peace and towards war. Hitler's aims might still appear justifiable; his methods were condemned. By the Anschluss—or rather by the way in which it was accomplished— Hitler took the first step in the policy which was to brand him as the greatest of war criminals. Yet he took this step unintentionally. Indeed he did not know that he had taken it.

How does this affect Hitler's plan?

CHAPTER EIGHT

The Crisis over Czechoslovakia

AFTER partitioning the Ottoman empire in Europe in 1918, Pasich, the prime minister of Serbia, is reputed to have said: "The first round is won; now we must prepare the second against Austria". The second round duly came a year later, though it was not of his making. Everyone in Europe felt much the same in March 1938 after the *Anschluss*. The Austrian round was over; the Czechoslovak round was due to begin. It was not necessary to prepare this second round. Geography and politics automatically put Czechoslovakia on the agenda. As an ally of France and the only democratic state east of the Rhine, she was a perpetual reproach to Hitler, thrust far into German territory. Nor was it easy to sustain her. The Italians, if they wished, had direct access to Austria. Czechoslovakia was cut off on every side. Germany divided her from France; Poland and Rumania from Soviet Russia. Her immediate neighbours were hostile: Hungary bitterly "revisionist"; Poland, though an ally of France, also revisionist because of Tešin, which the Czechs had acquired after the first World war, and blindly confident in her own non-aggression pact with Germany. There could be no question of "aiding" Czechoslovakia. It was full-scale European war or nothing.

The question of Czechoslovakia would have been less immediate if geography alone had been in play. Even her democracy and her alliances might not of themselves have provoked the crisis. But Czechoslovakia had a canker at her heart. Despite appearances, she was a state of nationalities, not a national state. Only the Czechs were genuine Czechoslovaks; and even they interpreted this to mean a centralised state of Czech character. The others— Slovaks, Hungarians, Ruthenes, and above all Germans—were national minorities: sometimes quiescent, sometimes discontented, but never convinced adherents of the existing order. The three million Germans (loosely, though wrongly, called Sudetens) were closely linked to the Austrians by history and blood. The

151

Anschluss stirred them to ungovernable excitement. Maybe they would have been wiser to remain contented with their lot—free, though not equal, citizens in a democratic community. But men are not wise when they hear the call of nationalism. The great German state—powerful, united, nationalist—lay just across their borders. Their Austrian cousins had just joined it. They wished to join it too. No doubt, in a muddled way, they also wished to remain in Czechoslovakia; and never considered how the two wishes could be reconciled. But the German national movement in Czechoslovakia, however confused, was a fact; and those who wanted to "stand by Czechoslovakia" never explained how they would deal with this fact. Hitler did not create this movement. It was waiting for him, ready—indeed eager—to be used. Even more than in the case of Austria, Hitler did not need to act. Others would do his work for him. The crisis over Czechoslovakia was provided for Hitler. He merely took advantage of it.

Hitler undoubtedly wished to "liberate" the Germans of Czechoslovakia. He was also concerned, in more practical terms, to remove the obstacle which a well-armed Czechoslovakia, allied to France and Soviet Russia, raised against German hegemony. He was by no means clear how this could be done. Like everyone else in Europe, he overrated French strength and French resolution. A direct German attack on Czechoslovakia would, he thought, provoke a French intervention. His initial solution, as he had revealed at the conference of 5 November 1937, was to hope for a conflict in the Mediterranean between France and Italy. Then, as he put it some time in April 1938, "we return with Czechoslovakia in the bag"; but, if Italy failed to move, "return with bag empty".[1] This plan, too, rested on a miscalculation: it overrated Italy's capacity for aggression. But, whether the Mediterranean war came off or not, it was worth while preparing the situation in Czechoslovakia by encouraging the Sudeten movement. It is as certain as anything can be that Hitler did not intend to overthrow the French system in Europe by a frontal assault. "Munich" still dominated his mind; and at this time Munich meant for him not the triumphant conference of September 1938, but the disastrous Nazi rising of November 1923. He meant to succeed by intrigue and the threat of violence,

[1] Note by Schmundt, April 1938. *German Foreign Policy*, series D. ii. No. 182.

not by violence itself. On 28 March he received the Sudeten representatives and appointed Henlein, their leader, his "viceroy". They were to negotiate with the Czechoslovak government; and, in Henlein's words, "we must always demand so much that we can never be satisfied". The movement was to remain legal and orderly; the Czechs must be given no excuse to crush it by force.[1] Perhaps the Czechs would put themselves in the wrong; perhaps the French would be preoccupied or would lose their nerve. In the spring of 1938 Hitler did not see his way clearly. He screwed up the tension in the hope that something would give somewhere.

Hitler's antagonist, President Benes of Czechoslovakia, had a similar aim. He, too, wished to screw up the tension, though in hope of exactly the opposite result. Faced with a crisis, the French, and the British also, would, he hoped, come to their senses; they would stand by Czechoslovakia; Hitler would draw back, and this humiliation would not only arrest his march to the domination of Europe—it might even bring down the Nazi régime in Germany itself. Benes had behind him twenty years of diplomatic experience and diplomatic success. He was the Metternich of democracy, with the same self-confidence; the same ingenuity of method and argument; with the same exaggerated reliance also on treaties and international rights. He handled the Sudeten problem much as Metternich handled the Italian problem a century earlier: insoluble at home, it could only be settled on the international field. Benes was as ready to negotiate with the Sudetens as they were to negotiate with him, and with equally little hope of a successful outcome. Perhaps even with less; for concessions to the Germans in Czechoslovakia would bring demands from the other national minorities, to the ruin of the existing state. Benes and the Sudetens alike negotiated solely with their ear cocked on British and French opinion. The Sudeten leaders tried to give the impression that they were merely asking for equal treatment within Czechoslovakia. Benes tried to force them into an open demand for her dissolution. Then, he believed, the Western Powers would assert themselves. He judged these Powers from his years in France during the first World war, and from his later experiences when they dominated the League of Nations at Geneva. Like most people, including

[1] Report by Henlein, 28 March 1938. *German Foreign Policy*, series D. ii. No. 107.

Hitler, he failed to recognise their present weakness, both moral and material—that of France in particular.

Benes had limitations of his own. Czechoslovakia's alliances looked formidable on paper. There was the alliance for mutual defence with France made in 1925; the alliance with Soviet Russia of 1935, which however only operated if France acted first; and the Little Entente with Rumania and Yugoslavia, directed against Hungary. Benes did not make the most of this position. He deliberately neglected the alliance with Soviet Russia. To his mind, it was a supplement to the French alliance, not a substitute for it. Others might speculate, usually with some scepticism, whether Soviet Russia would aid Czechoslovakia even if France remained neutral. Benes did not raise the question. He was a westerner, the heir of Masaryk, who had won Czechoslovakia's independence with Western, not with Russian, assistance. He told Newton, the British minister: "Czechoslovakia's relations with Russia had always been and would remain a secondary consideration. . . . His country would always follow and be bound to Western Europe".[1] The Spanish civil war gave additional warning against defending "democracy" with Russian backing. But Benes did not need this warning: his mind was made up long before. Even if he were tempted, there were strong restraining forces within Czechoslovakia. The Czech Agrarians, the largest party in the government coalition, dreaded any association with Communism. They, too, were inclined to say: "Better Hitler than Stalin". Moreover, Benes was a man of peace. The Czechoslovak army was a formidable force, its well-equipped 34 divisions probably a match in themselves for the half-trained German army of 1938. Benes never intended to use it, except in the unlikely event of a general war. The Czechs were a small people. It had taken them nearly three hundred years to recover from the disaster of the White Mountain in 1620. Benes was determined that they should not suffer another such catastrophe. He was ready to play against Hitler for high stakes; he would not risk the highest stake of all. In the last resort, he would bow his head to the storm and hope that the Czechs would survive it—as indeed they did.

Hitler and Benes both wished to increase the tension and to bring on a crisis. The British and the French, making the same

[1] Newton to Halifax, 18 May 1938. *British Foreign Policy*, third series. No. 229.

calculation, had exactly the opposite aim: they wished to avert a crisis so as to avoid the terrible choice between war and humiliation. The British were the more urgent of the two. The French seemed the more exposed: they had the precise obligation of alliance with Czechoslovakia, whereas the British were uncommitted except as members of the moribund League of Nations. But the French could transfer their dilemma to the British. They could talk of resisting Hitler; and when the British refused to back them, it was the British who would take the blame. This had a curious result. Hitler, Benes, and even the French, could wait for the crisis to mature, confident that this would force a decision from the British. For this very reason, the British had to act. They were most remote from the Czechoslovak question, yet the most insistent on raising it. Their motives were of the highest. They wished to prevent a European war; they wished also to achieve a settlement more in accordance with the great principle of self-determination than that made in 1919. The outcome was the precise opposite of their intention. They imagined that there was a "solution" of the Sudeten German problem and that negotiations would produce it. In fact the problem was insoluble in terms of compromise, and every step in negotiations only made this clearer. By seeking to avert a crisis, the British brought it on. The Czechoslovak problem was not of British making; the Czech crisis of 1938 was.

The British were alert to the problem from the very moment of the *Anschluss*—long before Hitler had formulated his intentions. On 12 March, when the French ambassador called to discuss the Austrian question, Halifax replied by asking: "What would be the French conception of rendering assistance to Czechoslovakia?" The ambassador "had no short answer".[1] Ten days later the British provided their own answer, or lack of it. In a memorandum for the French government, they stressed their commitments under Locarno. "Those commitments are, in their view, no mean contribution to the maintenance of peace in Europe, and, though they have no intention of withdrawing from them, they cannot see their way to add to them." There was "little hope" that military operations by France and the Soviet Union could prevent the occupation of Czechoslovakia by

[1] Halifax to Phipps, 12 March 1938. *British Foreign Policy*, third series, i. No. 62.

Germany; the British, even if they entered the war, could offer no more than the "economic pressure" of blockade. Hence the Czechoslovak government should be pushed into finding "such a solution of German minority questions as would be compatible with ensuring the integrity of the Czechoslovak State".[1] Privately Halifax added other arguments. "Quite frankly, the moment is unfavourable, and our plans, both for offence and defence, are not sufficiently advanced."[2] He said also to the French ambassador: "The French were disposed, perhaps, to rate more highly than ourselves the value of strong declarations".[3] The British had already rejected one such declaration. On 17 March the Soviet government proposed a discussion, "in the League of Nations or outside of it", of practical measures "for the collective saving of peace". Halifax did not think that this idea "had any great value"; and the Russians were told that a conference, "designed less to secure the settlement of outstanding problems than to organise concerted action against aggression . . . would not necessarily have a favourable effect upon the prospects of European peace".[4]

The French naturally disliked being prompted to make up their minds one way or the other. On 15 March the French Committee of National Defence discussed the question of aid to Czechoslovakia. Gamelin answered: the French could "tie down" some German troops; they could not break through the Siegfried line (which did not in fact exist at this time); hence the only effective way of attacking Germany was through Belgium, and, to secure permission for this, British diplomatic support was necessary.[5] It was his usual equivocation. The politicians asked a military question; and Gamelin, in reply, talked diplomacy. Paul-Boncour, the foreign minister, tried to take this strong line so far as diplomacy was concerned. He told Phipps, the British ambassador, on 24 March that "a definite warning to Germany by the two countries [Great Britain and France] . . . would be the best means of avoiding war . . . Time was not on our side, for Germany . . . was getting stronger and stronger, until she would

---

[1] Halifax to Phipps, 22 March 1938. *British Foreign Policy*, third series i. No. 106.

[2] Ditto, 23 March. *Ibid.* No. 107.   [3] Ditto, No. 109.

[4] Halifax to Maisky, 24 March 1938. *Ibid.* No. 116.

[5] Gamelin, *Servir*. ii. 324.

finally attain complete hegemony in Europe".[1] The British not reply to these remarks which they had often heard before. Nor did they need to. Paul-Boncour's days were numbered. On 10 April the government of Léon Blum, which had been in office less than a month, was itself overthrown. Daladier, the next prime minister, first thought of keeping Paul-Boncour; then took alarm at his talk of standing firm now, rather than fighting later in still more disastrous circumstances. Daladier telephoned to Paul-Boncour: "The policy you recommend is fine and worthy of France. But I do not believe that we are in a position to follow it. I am going to take Georges Bonnet".[2] Daladier survived as prime minister until April 1940; Bonnet as foreign minister until September 1939. These two men were to lead France into the second World war.

It was an uneasy partnership. Daladier was a Radical of the old tradition, anxious to preserve the honour of France and convinced that a firm policy could alone stop Hitler. But he was at a loss how to do it. He had served in the trenches during the first World war, and shrank with horror from a new holocaust. On every occasion he spoke decisively against appeasement, and then acquiesced in it. Bonnet, on the other hand, was appeasement personified, ready to pay almost any price in order to keep Hitler quiet. He believed that the pillars of French power had collapsed; and his main aim was to put the blame for the consequences on others—the British, the Czechs, the Poles, the Russians, he did not mind on whom, so long as his record, and France's, looked clean on paper. Never for one moment did either Daladier or Bonnet contemplate taking the lead in the hope that the British and others would follow. Rather they looked plaintively to London for some twist which would enable them to escape from their impossible situation.

In London, too, the partnership of Chamberlain and Halifax was by no means easy. Chamberlain had the strongest character of the four men who determined British and French policy. Timidity, or doubt of British strength, did not affect his calculations, though he had a natural dislike of war. He believed that Hitler could be won for peace; he believed also that Hitler had a good case so far as Czechoslovakia was concerned. Hence

---

[1] Phipps to Halifax, 24 March 1938. *British Foreign Policy*, third series i. No. 112. [2] Paul Boncour, *Entre Deux Guerres*. iii. 101.

he was determined to act on these two beliefs, whatever the opposition at home or abroad. He is often accused of ignorance in foreign affairs. But his opinions were shared by those supposedly most competent to judge. Nevile Henderson, the ambassador at Berlin, was equally confident that Hitler could be won for peace; and he had been chosen for the post by Vansittart as the best available British diplomatist.[1] Both Henderson at Berlin and Newton at Prague insisted that the Sudeten claims were well founded morally and that the Czechoslovak government were making no genuine attempt to meet them. Phipps at Paris stressed, and perhaps exaggerated, French weakness. Some members of the Foreign Office disliked Chamberlain's policy. But they were in much the same position as Daladier: though they disliked the policy, none of them could suggest an alternative. They regretted that Great Britain and France had not acted against the German reoccupation of the Rhineland; they thought that Hitler ought to be "hit on the head". But they had no idea how this operation could be performed. None of them placed any hope in the United States. None of them advocated alliance with Soviet Russia, Chilston the ambassador at Moscow least of all. He wrote, for instance, on 19 April: "The Red army, though no doubt equal to a defensive war within the frontiers of the Soviet Union, is not capable of carrying the war into the enemy's territory. . . . I personally consider it highly unlikely that the Soviet Government would declare war merely in order to fulfil their treaty obligations or even to forestall a blow to Soviet prestige or an indirect threat to Soviet security. . . . The Soviet Union must be counted out of European politics".[2] These views were fully accepted by the Foreign Office. Chamberlain had to devise policy where before there was none.

It is difficult to say whether Halifax agreed with this policy, still more difficult to discover one of his own. He was fertile in negations. He was contemptuous of French statesmen, particularly of Bonnet; he seems to have been sceptical about Soviet Russia and the United States. He had no sympathy with the

---

[1] Vansittart often told this himself with wry amusement. There is no foundation for the belief that Chamberlain chose Henderson as an instrument for appeasement.

[2] Chilston to Halifax, 19 April 1938. *British Foreign Policy*, third series. No. 148.

Czechs, and much impatience with Benes. Had he any greater faith in appeasement? Probably his visit to Berchtesgaden had given him a permanent distaste for Hitler; but Halifax passed much of his life among people whom he disliked. A Viceroy who could welcome Gandhi to his palace was not likely to be affected by personal feelings. The object of his policy, so far as he had one, was to buy time—though without any clear idea what use to make of it. His immediate object, like Bonnet's, was to keep his record clean. Unlike Bonnet, he succeeded. Halifax was steadily loyal to Chamberlain; this loyalty took the form of allowing Chamberlain to shoulder all responsibility, which he was eager to do. Yet now and then Halifax gave a tug in the opposite direction; and this tug sometimes had an effect at the decisive moment. Such were the four men who, between them, settled the destinies of Western civilisation.

The four took up this task unwillingly. They would have liked to turn their backs on central Europe if only they had known how to do it. Early in April Benes began to devise concessions which might be offered to the Sudeten Germans. His object was to win British support; if his concessions seemed reasonable to the British, he asked, would they not commend them to Berlin? The British backed away. They would make no commitment to Czechoslovakia. They even argued that, if they said nothing at Berlin, perhaps Hitler might not notice Czechoslovakia after all. Bonnet, too, was being urged to make up his mind. Noël, French ambassador at Warsaw and previously at Prague, visited Czechoslovakia, and came to Paris with his recommendations. He pointed out that neither the French alliance with Poland nor that with Czechoslovakia had been complemented by a military convention. They belonged to the paper guarantees of the League of Nations, and now could not be translated into reality. He said to Bonnet: "We are going towards war or capitulation". In his view Benes should be told that he had until the beginning of July to satisfy the Sudetens; after that time, he must not count on French help.[1] The decision was beyond Bonnet: he could not be resolute even for surrender. Instead he proposed to transfer the decision to the British: they should be asked to stand firmly and publicly behind Czechoslovakia. And if they refused? Bonnet had no answer.

[1] Noël, *L'agression allemande*, 198-202.

On 28 April Daladier and Bonnet came to London for a two-day conference with the British ministers. The patterns of policy were clearly revealed. The British stressed their commitment to France under the guarantee of March 1936, but more as the extreme limit of what they could do than as a serious promise. They would not even equip two divisions "specifically for a war on the Continent"; they would not agree to naval talks for fear of offending Italy. Chamberlain said that public opinion in Great Britain would not allow the government to run the risk of war, even if the chances against war were 100–1. He and Halifax recapitulated the arguments against war; and such arguments are always easy to find. England and France could not save Czechoslovakia, even if they could defend themselves—and this, too, was doubtful. Russia was useless; Poland "uncertain". Chamberlain said: "If Germany did decide to destroy Czechoslovakia, I do not see how this can be prevented". Then he struck a more hopeful note. Men usually believe what they want to believe; and Chamberlain was ready to believe that Hitler would be satisfied if the claims of the Sudeten Germans were met. Therefore, if the British and French pressed Benes to yield, all would be well.

Daladier liked none of this argument. "War could only be avoided if Great Britain and France made their determination quite clear to maintain the peace of Europe by respecting the liberties and the rights of independent peoples. . . . If we were once again to capitulate when faced by another threat, we should then have prepared the way for the very war we wished to avoid". Daladier, too, believed what he wanted to believe: "German policy was one of bluff. . . . We were at present still able to place obstacles in her path". The French were also ready to press concessions on Benes; but the British should agree to stand by Czechoslovakia if these failed to satisfy Hitler. The British refused. Deadlock followed. Lunch together was "pretty gloomy". Afterwards the French gave way. Daladier was not prepared to act on his belief: he would not give a lead to Great Britain and to Europe. Chamberlain was prepared to act on his: concessions from Czechoslovakia would avert a war—and no doubt he did not mind how great these concessions would be. No is always stronger than Yes; refusal to act will carry the day against half-hearted action. A compromise was devised which virtually accepted the British outlook. Both Great Britain and

France would urge concessions on the Czechs. The British would urge Hitler to be patient. If the concessions failed, then the British would warn the German government "of the dangers of which they were aware, namely, that France would be compelled to intervene . . . and that His Majesty's Government could not guarantee that they would not do the same".[1]

Thus, at the end of April 1938, the problem of the Germans within Czechoslovakia ceased to be a dispute between the Sudeten Germans and the Czechoslovak government; it even ceased to be, or rather never became, a dispute between Czechoslovakia and Germany. The British and French governments came forward as principals; and their object, however disguised, was to exact concessions from the Czechs, not to restrain Germany. Pressure came mainly from the British. The French— still theoretically allied to Czechoslovakia—dragged helplessly behind. This development upset the plans which Benes had made. Throughout April he had been making proposals to the Sudeten leaders, hoping to force them into intransigent refusal. He succeeded. On 24 April, Henlein, in a speech at Carlsbad, demanded the transformation of Czechoslovakia into a "state of nationalities", with full freedom for National Socialist propaganda, and—what was more—such a change of Czechoslovakia's foreign policy as would make her a German satellite. It was clear to Benes and, for that matter, to Newton also[2] that Czechoslovakia would cease to exist as an independent country if the Sudeten demands were met. Yet the demonstration apparently had no effect on the British and French governments: they continued to demand that Benes should commit suicide in order to secure their own peace of mind.

Not only did the British and French urge concessions on the Czechs. The British also urged Hitler to make demands. This took him by surprise; events were moving faster, and more favourably, than he had hoped, though not quite according to his expectations. The Mediterranean war between France and Italy showed no sign of coming off. The Anglo-Italian agreement which Chamberlain had insisted on over Eden's head was

---

[1] Anglo-French Conversations, 28 and 29 April 1938. *British Foreign Policy*, third series. i. No. 164.

[2] Newton to Halifax, 16 May 1938. *British Foreign Policy*, third series. i. No. 221.

actually signed on 16 April; it improved relations between the two countries and, by implication, between France and Italy as well. Hitler took it so seriously that he visited Rome early in May, as a demonstration that the Axis was still alive. While there, the news reached him that he hardly needed his Italian partner: the British were anxious to be enlisted on his side. The British assurances were emphatic. Henderson said: "France was acting for the Czechs and Germany for the Sudeten Germans. Britain was supporting Germany in this case".[1] Kirkpatrick, Henderson's second-in-command, told a German official at lunch: "If the German Government would advise the British Government confidentially what solution of the Sudeten German question they were striving after . . . the British Government would bring such pressure to bear in Prague that the Czechoslovak Government would be compelled to accede to the German wishes".[2] Halifax rebuked his representatives for going too fast. But he was no laggard. He told the German ambassador "with obvious emotion": "the best thing would be if the three kindred nations, Germany, Britain, and the United States, could unite in joint work for peace".[3] Hitler was not to be rushed. The more the question was delayed and tension mounted, the more the Western Powers would do his work for him; Czechoslovakia might even be broken without effort from the German side. Henlein was therefore sent to London where he paraded his conciliatory demeanour. He claimed to be acting without guidance from Berlin, and almost persuaded such critical observers as Churchill and Vansittart of his sincerity. There is even more striking, because secret, proof of Hitler's restraint. On 20 May the General Staff submitted, on his instructions, a draft-plan for operations against Czechoslovakia. It began with the limiting words: "It is not my intention to smash Czechoslovakia by military action in the immediate future without provocation"; and there followed the now antiquated speculations about war between Italy and the Western Powers.[4]

There was another Power concerned in the Czechoslovak

[1] Woermann to Ribbentrop, 7 May 1938. *German Foreign Policy*, series D. ii. No. 149.
[2] Memorandum by Bismarck, 10 May 1938. *Ibid*. No. 151.
[3] Kordt to Ribbentrop, 29 April 1938. *Ibid*. No. 139.
[4] Draft by Keitel, 20 May 1938. *Ibid*. No. 175.

question, though everyone, including the Czechs, tried to pretend that this was not the case. This Power was Soviet Russia: allied in a limited way to Czechoslovakia, and bound to be deeply affected if the European Balance of Power were changed. The British and French governments acknowledged Soviet Russia only to emphasise her military weakness; and this view, though it rested no doubt on their information, represented also their desire. They wanted Soviet Russia to be excluded from Europe; and therefore readily assumed that she was so by circumstances. Did their wishes go further? Did they plan to settle Europe not only without Soviet Russia, but also against her? Was it their intention that Nazi Germany should destroy the "Bolshevik menace"? This was the Soviet suspicion, both at the time and later. There is little evidence of it in the official record, or even outside it. British and French statesmen were far too distracted by the German problem to consider what would happen when Germany had become the dominant Power in Eastern Europe. Of course they preferred that Germany should march east, not west, if she marched at all. But their object was to prevent war, not to prepare one; and they sincerely believed—or at any rate Chamberlain believed—that Hitler would be content and pacific if his claims were met.

Soviet policy was a mystery to Western statesmen; is still so to us. The Soviet position was impregnable on paper. By the terms of their alliance with Czechoslovakia, they could firmly assert their readiness to act, if France did so first; and, since France never acted, their bluff—if it were bluff—was never called. Obviously it was in their interest to stiffen Czechoslovakia's resistance, whether they meant to support her or no. What they would have done if called upon is a hypothetical question which can never be answered. We must be content to record Soviet actions so far as these can be ascertained. In the spring of 1938 the Soviet government began to cut down their aid to the Spanish republic, and soon stopped it altogether. Ingenious commentators have suggested that this was a preliminary to getting on better terms with Hitler; but he wished the Spanish civil war to continue, and hence was unaffected by Soviet aid to the republic— rather he preferred that it should continue. A simpler explanation can be found in events in the Far East, where Japan was now engaged in a full-scale invasion of China; the Soviet government may have needed all their arms for their own defence. If they had any thought of Europe it was that ending Soviet intervention in Spain would make it easier to establish good relations with Great Britain and France. This hope was to be disappointed.

Soviet backing of Czechoslovakia was unequivocal on paper. On 23 April Stalin discussed the question with his principal colleagues. The Czechs were told: "If requested, the U.S.S.R. is prepared—in agreement with France and Czechoslovakia—to take all necessary measures relating to the security of Czechoslovakia. She disposes of all necessary means for doing so . . . Voroshilov [the Commander-in-Chief] is very optimistic".[1] On 12 May Litvinov, the Foreign Commissar, raised the Czech question with Bonnet during the meeting of the League of Nations at Geneva. Bonnet asked how Soviet Russia could aid Czechoslovakia in view of the Polish and Rumanian refusal to allow the passage of Soviet troops. Litvinov replied that France should obtain permission for this, since they were her allies. Again, this may have been a deliberate evasion. But it is more probable that Litvinov failed to appreciate the decline of French prestige and assumed that France could dictate to her allies as Soviet Russia would have dictated to hers, if she had had any. Bonnet however merely sighed. That, according to Litvinov, "terminated our talk".[2]

It was indeed no part of Bonnet's policy to make Soviet intervention possible. There is other proof of this. In the middle of May Coulondre, French ambassador at Moscow, came to Paris; he was one of the few resolute men in the French diplomatic service. Coulondre urged that military conversations should begin at once between the Soviet, Czech, and French General Staffs. Bonnet agreed in his usual weak way. But when Coulondre was back in Moscow, nothing happened; and no information concerning the talks ever reached him from Paris. In July he learnt from his Czech colleague that the talks were not to take place, for fear of offending British Conservative opinion. No enquiry had been made in London. Bonnet had turned down the talks on his own initiative. Thus, the Soviet government retained their moral integrity; and the Western Powers retained their material weakness.

[1] Fierlinger to Krofta, 23 April 1938. *New Documents on the History of Munich*, No. 7.

[2] Litvinov to Alexandrovsky, 25 May 1938. *New Documents*. No. 14.

Yet there were those who believed that Hitler would retreat before a show of strength; and this show was duly made. On 20 May Czechoslovak reservists were recalled; the frontier posts were manned; and the Czechoslovak government let it be known that Hitler had been on the point of launching a surprise attack, as he had allegedly done against Austria. The Germans denied this, with every display of offended honour; and an examination of their secret records, captured at the end of the war, confirms that their denial was correct. No German troops had been moved; no preparations for action had been made. What is the explanation of this mysterious episode? None has been found. It is possible that the Czechs were really misled by a false alarm. It is even possible that some Sudeten extremists were planning action in the Austrian manner despite their strict instructions to the contrary. Or maybe the Germans fed the Czechs with false rumours in order to provoke them into action. None of these explanations seems likely. It is more plausible that the Czech demonstration was undertaken to discredit appeasement and to show that Hitler would retreat before a show of force. Who thought of this? The Czechs themselves? Certainly not the Russians who were as surprised as everybody else. Some slight evidence suggests that the move was inspired by the "tough" members of the British Foreign Office, who disliked the existing course and who then refused to believe Henderson's denials, though they were correct.[1]

At any rate Hitler had been "hit on the head". To outward appearance the policy worked. The Germans protested their peaceful intentions; the morale of the Czechs was raised. The real effect was the other way round. Both the British and French governments were driven near to panic by the prospect of war. Halifax told the French ambassador that Great Britain would support France only in case of unprovoked aggression[2]; and Bonnet told not only Phipps, but the German ambassador, that "if Czechoslovakia were really unreasonable, the French Government might well declare that France considered herself released

---

[1] There is a tantalising footnote in the British Documents (third series. i. No. 450): "from the evidence at their disposition the Foreign Office did not agree with the views of Sir N. Henderson or the Military Attaché on this point"; no evidence is given.

[2] Halifax to Phipps, 22 May 1938. *Ibid.* No. 271.

from her bond".[1] Strang, of the Foreign Office, was sent to
Prague and Berlin to canvass the opinions of the British
representatives on the spot. He returned with precise recommendations. Czechoslovakia must renounce her existing alliances
and become a German satellite state; the Sudeten areas must
become autonomous or maybe even incorporated in Germany.
Since the Czechs were being obstinate, this policy must be forced
on them by the British government. It would be "the first serious
attempt made since the war to tackle one of the causes (rather
than merely one of the symptoms) of European unrest, and
to promote peaceful change in one of the danger spots of
Europe".[2] The Czech move pushed the British along the path
of action, but not at all in the direction which the Czechs had
intended.

The events of 21 May had also a dramatic effect on Hitler. He
was enraged at his apparent humiliation. Seizing the draft
directive of 20 May which Keitel had prepared for him, he struck
out the first sentence—which repudiated military action against
Czechoslovakia—and wrote instead: "It is my unalterable intention to smash Czechoslovakia by military action in the near
future".[3] Here seems the decisive proof that Hitler was resolved
to attack Czechoslovakia, whatever the circumstances. The proof
is less decisive than it seems. Even the document from which the
damning sentence is taken, goes on to assert, in Hitler's usual
way, that France would hesitate to intervene "as a result of
Italy's unequivocal attitude on our side". The sentence was in
fact a momentary display of temper. Hitler soon reverted to his
old line. A General Strategical Directive of 18 June stated: "I
shall only decide to take action against Czechoslovakia if, as in
the case of the occupation of the demilitarised zone and the entry
into Austria, I am firmly convinced that France will not march
and therefore Britain will not intervene either".[4] Of course
Hitler knew that his generals feared war with France, and may

[1] Phipps to Halifax, 23 May 1938. *British Foreign Policy*, third series.
i. No. 286. Welczeck to Ribbentrop, 26 May 1938, *German Foreign Policy*,
series D. ii. No. 210
[2] Notes by Strang, 26–7 May, 28–9 May 1938. *British Foreign Policy*,
third series. i. No. 349 and 350.
[3] Directive by Hitler, 30 May 1938. *German Foreign Policy*, series D.
ii. No. 221.
General Strategic Directive, 18 June 1938. *Ibid*. No. 282.

have planned to involve them in this war against their will. He played a game of bluff with everyone—with the Western Powers, with the generals, even with himself. There are solid grounds for believing that it was bluff. Few preparations were made for even a defensive war against France. A small section of the German air force was stationed in western Germany "to prevent France from obtaining complete freedom of action in the air".[1] Only two army divisions were placed on the Siegfried line; two more were added in September—as against a potential French strength of more than 80 divisions. Moreover, though Hitler fixed 1 October as his deadline with the General Staff, he did not make this public. He kept open his line of retreat, until it appeared that retreat was unnecessary.

The British government were convinced that Hitler had a deadline, though they did not know what it was. They talked themselves into believing that "he would not wait much longer" and that his patience was exhausted, though patience had been the outstanding feature of his career until this moment. They decided, on no grounds except intuition, that Hitler had fixed his deadline for 12 September, the last day of the Nazi party meeting at Nuremberg; and henceforward they were mesmerised by this date. The British had wanted to get ahead of Hitler; in settling for 12 September, instead of 1 October, they accidentally succeeded. Before that date, Benes—in the British view—must be driven to make the decisive concessions which would alone deter Hitler from war: Czechoslovakia must renounce her existing alliances with France and Soviet Russia, and the Sudeten Germans must receive whatever it was that they were demanding. But how was this to be done? Benes was obstinate—"pigheaded", in Henderson's phrase. The British shrank from the task of coercing him; they would have preferred to put the responsibility on others. This was not easy. Obviously, the Russians would not repudiate their alliance; on the contrary, they continually stressed it to everyone's embarrassment. Perhaps the French would prove more amenable. Here too the British were disappointed. First the French delayed; then they urged concessions on Benes, but principally with the argument that these would make British backing more likely. Halifax complained: "This memorandum does not

---

[1] Excerpt from a strategic Study of 1938, 2 June 1938. *German Foreign Policy*, series D. ii. No. 235.

contain any specific warning that France would have to reconsider her treaty position if the Czechoslovak Government were unreasonable on the Sudeten question".[1]

There was no escape. The French would not operate their alliance with Czechoslovakia; on the other hand they would not give it up. Weakness is infectious. The French were dragging the British down with them. Great Britain was the Power most remote from the Czech affair; yet she had to take the lead. The British could not directly attack Czechoslovakia's alliances; therefore they must undertake to "solve" the Sudeten question—how did not matter so long as war was averted. The French jumped at this idea; responsibility was safely removed from their shoulders. The Czechs were more reluctant. Benes aimed to present the question as a conflict between Czechoslovakia and Germany; the British proposal set it back as one between the Sudeten Germans and the Czechoslovak government. Once more the will o' the wisp of British support was brought out. Halifax wrote: "If the Czechoslovak government were to bring themselves to request our help in this matter, this would undoubtedly produce a favourable effect on public opinion here".[2] Once more Benes gave way. British backing was proving more difficult to win than he had hoped; but he still supposed that, with reasonableness and conciliation, it would be forthcoming in the end. On 26 July Chamberlain was able to announce in the House of Commons that Lord Runciman was going to Prague as mediator "in response to a request from the Government of Czechoslovakia". The "request" had been harder to extract than a tooth. Runciman was a former President of the Board of Trade, ostensibly chosen for his supposed skill in settling industrial disputes, but perhaps more from his ignorance of the issues at stake. Once an Asquithian Liberal fervent for Free Trade, and later a National Liberal who welcomed Protection, he could be counted on to produce a "soft" solution. He went to Prague as an individual, not as a representative of his government. In his own words to Halifax: "you are setting me adrift in a small boat in mid-Atlantic". The phrase revealed Runciman's origin as a shipowner: he was in fact going to a landlocked state in mid-Europe.

[1] Halifax to Bonnet, 7 July 1938. *British Foreign Policy*, third series No. 472.
[2] Halifax to Newton, 18 July 1938. *Ibid*. No. 508.

The Runciman mission has a melancholy interest for the historian. It was the last of the attempts, which had been going on for nearly a century, to devise a "solution" for the relations of Germans and Czechs in Bohemia—to discover, that is, some arrangement by which the two peoples could live more or less contentedly together in the same state. No such solution had been found, though many men superior in political ability and understanding than Runciman had sought it; none was found now. When Runciman went out, the British government—and he along with them—still supposed that there was a solution waiting to be discovered. The Czechoslovak government, by appearing to ask for Runciman, were committed to accepting his advice. He had therefore merely to find out what would satisfy the Sudeten Germans; and the Czechs would have to agree to it. This plan did not work. The Sudeten leaders, true to their instructions from Hitler, always kept a demand ahead, and tantalised Runciman as they had tantalised Benes. Worse was to follow. Benes was an incomparable negotiator, whatever his other defects; and the talent which had been a match for Lloyd George in 1919 soon took Runciman's measure in 1938. Runciman had been sent out to extract concessions from Benes, or alternatively to expose Czech obstinacy. If he succeeded in the first, the crisis would be averted; if in the second, Benes would be discredited, Czechoslovakia could be disavowed, and the honour of the Western Powers would be saved. Instead Runciman found that he was being manoeuvred into a position where he had to endorse the Czech offers as reasonable, and to condemn the obstinacy of the Sudetens, not of Benes. An appalling consequence loomed ever nearer: if Benes did all that Runciman asked of him and more, Great Britain would be saddled with the moral obligation to support Czechoslovakia in the ensuing crisis. To avert this consequence, Runciman, far from urging Benes on, had to preach delay. Benes did not allow him to escape. On 4 September Benes summoned the Sudeten leaders; told them to dictate their own terms; and, when they hesitated in dismay, wrote them down himself. The Sudetens were formally promised everything which they had demanded. Of course Benes only made this surrender when he knew that it would be rejected. But he had certainly won the diplomatic engagement. Runciman had to confess that there was no point in his proposing terms of agreement, when the Czechs had already agreed to everything which he might suggest. Even the Sudeten leaders were at a loss how to reject Benes's offer. President Benes enjoyed a last triumph of diplomatic skill.

This moral victory did not affect the clash of power. It was of decisive importance all the same. At the beginning of 1938, most English people sympathised with German grievances, however much they disliked Hitler's way of voicing them. The Sudeten Germans had a good case: they did not possess national equality, or anything like it. By September, thanks to Benes, the bottom had been knocked out of this case. Few people continued to believe that the Sudetens had genuine grievances; the Sudetens hardly believed it themselves. Hitler ceased to be an idealistic liberator of his fellow-nationals; he appeared instead as an unscrupulous conqueror, bent on war and domination. "Appeasement" had been in origin a high-minded attempt at the impartial redress of grievances. As the controversy between Benes and the Sudetens worked out, it came to be regarded as the craven, though perhaps inevitable, surrender to superior force. Englishmen had asked at first: "are the German claims justified?" They were now beginning to ask: "are we strong enough to resist Hitler?" Runciman, much against his intention, had helped to clear the way for world war. Having been outmanoeuvred by Benes, his only anxiety now was to scuttle his boat and go home. The Runciman mission drifted round Prague for a few more days; then returned to London without producing any scheme for "solving" the Sudeten question. Later, after Chamberlain's trip to Berchtesgaden, Runciman wrote a report at the dictation of the foreign office; this merely endorsed the plan for dismembering Czechoslovakia which had already been agreed between Chamberlain and Hitler. No one noticed it; no one supposed that it had any value. It was an echo from a past that was already dead.

British policy had failed to avert the crisis. 12 September was approaching. The issue was no longer between the Czechoslovak government and the Sudeten Germans; it had become a problem for the Great Powers. Their policy was still undefined. Hitler remained the master of delay, refusing to show his hand and probably, as on previous occasions, not knowing himself how he would emerge victorious. Preparations were pushed forward for attacking Czechoslovakia on 1 October. This was far from a decision for war. The German generals continued to insist that they could not face a general war; Hitler steadily replied that it would not be necessary. Some generals talked of overthrowing Hitler, and perhaps meant it. Later they were to claim that their plans had been thwarted by lack of encouragement from the Western Powers and particularly by Chamberlain's flight to Berchtesgaden. Actually, the generals were thwarted by Hitler. They would act only if he actually led Germany over the brink; and he never did so. He committed himself to war only when the other side had already surrendered. Until then he kept his hands free. During August he was still trying to find a back door. The war between Italy and France, on which he had counted, was obviously failing to come off. Quite the contrary, Mussolini, so full of bluster when war was far away, now became increasingly reluctant even to support Germany over Czechoslovakia. He asked to be told at least the time when Hitler intended to go to war. Hitler merely replied: "The Führer is unable to state any definite time because he does not know it himself"[1]—so much for his supposed time-table. An alternative opening seemed to offer itself when the Hungarians asked to share in the dismemberment of Czechoslovakia. This, too, proved disappointing. The Hungarians would follow Hitler; but, being still largely disarmed, they would not take the initiative. If Hitler wanted war, he must give the signal himself. A surprising result followed. The dreaded day of 12 September arrived. Hitler delivered an impassioned speech at Nuremberg. He recounted the Sudeten grievances; insisted that the Czechoslovak government must remedy them. And then? Nothing. No announcement of German mobilisation; no threat of war. Hitler's patience was not exhausted. He still waited for the nerves of others to crack.

He did not wait in vain. On 13 September, the day after Hitler's speech, the Sudeten leaders broke off negotiations with Benes, and gave the signal for revolt. The revolt was a failure. Within twenty-four hours order was restored. What was more, many Sudeten Germans who had hitherto remained silent or indifferent now insisted that they were not disloyal to Czechoslovakia nor wished to leave the existing state. Unlike rump-

[1] Philip of Hesse to Mussolini, Sept. 1938. *German Foreign Policy*, series D. ii. No. 415.

Austria, or the Habsburg Monarchy before it, Czechoslovakia did not disintegrate from within. The collapse came in Paris, not in Prague. The French government evaded decision till the last moment. Bonnet "was desperately anxious for a possible way out of this 'impasse' without being *obliged* to fight";[1] he was also, however, desperately anxious to put the blame on others. He tried again to shift it on to Soviet Russia. As before, Litvinov was too much for him, and returned a resolute answer. Appeal should be made to the League of Nations under Article XI of the Covenant, so that Soviet troops could go through Rumania; there should be staff talks between France, Czechoslovakia, and the Soviet Union; and in addition, a conference of France, Great Britain, and the Soviet Union to issue a ringing declaration against German aggression. In any case, Soviet Russia would fulfil "all her obligations" under the Soviet-Czechoslovak Pact; it only remained for France to make the first move.[2] Maybe Soviet resolution was fraudulent. This could have been tested by agreeing to staff talks, as Litvinov proposed. By evading these, Bonnet showed his fear that Soviet resolution was only too genuine.

Bonnet did better elsewhere. American isolationism was at its height. On 9 September President Roosevelt told his press conference that it was 100 per cent. incorrect to associate the United States with France and Great Britain in a front of resistance to Hitler. All that the Western Powers received from across the Atlantic was reproach from American intellectuals at being slightly less craven than the United States. The decisive answer, however, must come from the British. Here too old patterns were repeated, the French stressing the danger of surrendering to Hitler; Halifax refusing to sympathise with "an argument in favour of a certain war now, against the possibility of war, perhaps in more unfavourable conditions, later".[3] A final exchange displayed the elusive adroitness of each side. Bonnet asked: "what answer would His Majesty's Government give to a question from the French Government, in the event of a German

---

[1] Phipps to Halifax, 10 Sept. 1938. *British Foreign Policy*, third series. ii. No. 843, footnote.

[2] Litvinov to Alexandrovsky, 2 Sept.; Potyomkin, memoranda, 5 and 11 Sept. 1938. *New Documents*, No. 26, 27 and 30.

[3] Halifax to Phipps, 9 Sept. 1938. *British Foreign Policy*, third series. ii. No. 814.

attack on Czechoslovakia: 'we are going to march, will you march with us?' ''. Halifax answered: "The question itself, though plain in form, cannot be dissociated from the circumstances in which it might be posed, which are necessarily at this stage completely hypothetical". Bonnet "seemed genuinely pleased at the negative nature of the reply"[1]. This was not surprising. He was collecting negatives partly to protect himself, more to discourage his colleagues.

Daladier, too, repeated his old pattern—first full of fight, then irresolute, and finally capitulating. On 8 September he told Phipps: "if German troops cross the Czechoslovak frontier, the French will march to a man".[2] Then came 13 September: the Sudeten Germans on the point of revolt, and Hitler supposedly ready to assist them. The French Council of Ministers was torn asunder—6 for standing by Czechoslovakia, 4, including Bonnet, for surrender. Daladier gave no lead one way or the other. Bonnet went straight from the meeting to Phipps, and said: "Peace must be preserved at any price".[3] Phipps wanted confirmation of the French collapse; he asked to see Daladier. In the early evening, Daladier was still wavering. Faced by Phipps with a point-blank question, he replied "with evident lack of enthusiasm": "if Germans used force French would be obliged also". Phipps concluded his message to London: "I fear French have been bluffing".[4] At ten o'clock in the evening Phipps telephoned to London with a "very urgent message" from Daladier to Chamberlain. "Things are moving very rapidly and in such a grave manner that they risk getting quite out of control almost at once. . . Entry of German troops into Czechoslovakia must at all costs be prevented". Daladier urged that Runciman should publish his plan at once. If this were not enough, there should be a Three Power meeting—Germany for the Sudetens, France for the Czechs, and Great Britain for Lord Runciman.[5] Daladier had at last made up his mind: he had decided to surrender.

Here was Chamberlain's opportunity: the French decision

[1] Halifax to Phipps, 12 Sept. 1938, and footnotes, *British Foreign Policy*, third series. ii. No. 843.

[2] Phipps to Halifax, 8 Sept. 1938. *Ibid.* No. 807.

[3] Phipps to Halifax, 13 Sept. 1938. *Ibid.* No. 855.

[4] Phipps to Halifax, 13 Sept. 1938. *Ibid.* No. 857.

[5] Phipps to Halifax, 13 Sept. 1938. *Ibid.* No. 861.

between resistance and surrender which he had been pressing for since April—decision in favour of the latter course which Chamberlain had urged all along. He did not attempt to arrange a Three Power meeting. He knew from experience that Daladier, when challenged, could fall back into a sullen, hopeless determination. Instead Chamberlain flew to Munich on 15 September, alone except for Sir Horace Wilson, and saw Hitler at Berchtesgaden even without a British interpreter. Daladier "did not look very pleased" when told that he was being ignored; but again he acquiesced.[1] So far as we can tell from the records, Chamberlain took with him no brief, surveying the Czechoslovak question. He did not enquire whether a truncated Czechoslovakia could remain independent nor what the strategical consequences would be for the Western Powers; he did not consider how the national composition of Czechoslovakia could be ascertained. He went armed only with the prejudice of most Englishmen against "Versailles", and the firm conviction that Hitler would become pacific if German national grievances were met. Hitler, too, made no preparations for the meeting: as usual, he waited for gains to fall into his lap. His main concern was to keep the crisis going until Czechoslovakia disintegrated; and he pressed the claims of the Sudeten Germans in the belief that they would not be met, hence leaving him with the moral advantage. He had a further moral superiority. His military plans could not mature until 1 October, even if he meant to operate them; therefore he could offer to "hold his hand" without really conceding anything.

The meeting at Berchtesgaden was more friendly and successful than either man expected. Chamberlain was taken aback at the ranting with which Hitler always opened negotiations; but he remained faithful to his policy of appeasement. He said: "In principle I had nothing to say against the separation of the Sudeten Germans from the rest of Czechoslovakia, provided that the practical difficulties could be overcome". This was an offer which Hitler could not refuse, though it did not fulfil his real aim of destroying Czechoslovakia's independence in international affairs. Hitler, on his side, promised to make no military move while negotiations were proceeding—a promise which much impressed Chamberlain, though it meant nothing. Here was

[1] Phipps to Halifax, 14 Sept. 1938. *British Foreign Policy*, third series, ii. No. 883.

appeasement triumphant—a great dispute in sight of settlement without resort to war. Yet it had worked out all wrong. Chamberlain had intended to offer a concession on grounds of impartial justice. For this reason the most clear-sighted advocates of this policy, such as Nevile Henderson, always insisted that the Western Powers would win if it came to a war. But "our moral case must be copper-bottomed"; and over Czechoslovakia it was not.[1] Now, thanks to the French collapse, morality had been pushed aside; fear had taken its place. Hitler was not offered justice; he was asked how much he would take not to go to war. The Czechs had made things worse by successfully maintaining order despite the Sudeten call to revolt. Instead of being saved from disintegration, they were being asked to surrender territory which they firmly held so that France could escape war.

Chamberlain returned to London in order to win the consent of his colleagues and of the French. The British Cabinet agreed, though not, it is said, without some dispute. Runciman scrapped the report which he had been preparing and obediently wrote another which merely incorporated Hitler's demands—a report which was itself repeatedly amended in the next few days as Hitler's demands increased. On 18 September Daladier and Bonnet came to London for a meeting with the British ministers. Chamberlain gave an account of his discussions with Hitler and insisted that the question was whether to accept the partition of Czechoslovakia—or, as he called it, "the principle of self-determination". Daladier tried to shift the ground: "he feared that Germany's real aim was the disintegration of Czechoslovakia and the realisation of Pan-German aims through a march to the east". Halifax came in with the practical argument he had often used:

> Nothing was further from their thoughts than that the French Government should fail to honour their obligations to the Czechoslovak Government. . . . On the other hand we all knew—and he certainly thought their technical advisers would agree with them in this—that whatever action were taken by ourselves, by the French Government, or by the Soviet Government, at any given moment, it would be impossible to give any effective protection to the Czechoslovak

[1] Henderson to Halifax, 12 Aug. 1938. *British Foreign Policy*, third series. ii. No. 613.

State. We might fight a war against German aggression, but at the peace conference which followed such a war he did not think that the statesmen concerned would redraft the present boundaries of Czechoslovakia.

Chamberlain had an ingenious idea. The Czechs objected to surrendering territory after a plebiscite, for fear of the example to their Poles and Hungarians; then let it take place without a plebiscite. "It could be represented as the choice of the Czechoslovak Government themselves. . . . That would dispose of any idea that we were ourselves carving up Czechoslovak territory." Daladier gave way. But he posed an essential condition: Great Britain must join in guaranteeing the Czechoslovakia that remained. This was not for the sake of the Czechs—the British and French had already agreed that they could do nothing to help Czechoslovakia either now or thereafter. The British were being asked to underwrite Hitler's statement that he was seeking justice, not the domination of Europe. Daladier said:

> If he were certain that Herr Hitler were speaking the truth when he repeated the usual Nazi propaganda to the effect that nothing more was wanted than the Sudeten Germans and that German aims stopped there, then he would not insist upon a British guarantee. But he was convinced in his heart that Germany was aiming at something far greater. . . . A British guarantee for Czechoslovakia would therefore help France in the sense that it would help to stop the German march to the East.

The British were trapped. Chamberlain's policy rested on the dogma that Hitler was acting in good faith; he could not repudiate this dogma without accepting Daladier's arguments in favour of resistance. Therefore the guarantee had to be given. The British ministers withdrew for two hours. On their return Chamberlain said: "If the Czechoslovak Government accepted the proposals now being put to them and provided no military *coup* had taken place meanwhile, His Majesty's Government were prepared to join in the suggested guarantee". In this casual way, the British government, which had steadily refused to extend their commitments east of the Rhine and had professed themselves unable to help Czechoslovakia when she was strong, now underwrote Czechoslovakia when she was weak and, what was more, implicitly underwrote the existing territorial order throughout eastern Europe. The guarantee was given in the sure and certain hope that it would never be called upon—given simply to silence the last scrap of French reluctance. But Daladier had built better than he knew. He had committed Great Britain to opposing Hitler's advance in the east; and six months later the commitment came home to roost. At about 7.80 p.m. on the night of 18 September 1938 Daladier gave Great Britain the decisive, though delayed, push which landed her in the second World war.[1]

Chamberlain asked a final question: "what would be the position if Dr. Benes said 'No'?" Daladier answered: "the question would have to be discussed at the Council of Ministers". Events turned out differently. On 19 September the French ministers endorsed the Anglo-French proposals, but without reaching any decision as to what would happen if they were refused by the Czechs. Theoretically the Franco-Czech treaty was still in full existence. Moreover, on 19 September, Benes asked two questions of the Soviet Union: Will the U.S.S.R. render immediate effective assistance if France remains true and also renders assistance? Will the U.S.S.R. assist Czechoslovakia, as a member of the League of Nations, in accordance with Articles 16 and 17?[2] On 20 September the Soviet government replied to the first question: "Yes, instantly and effectively"; to the second: "Yes, in every respect".[3] Benes also tried to find out from Gottwald, the Czech Communist leader, whether the Soviet Union would act even if France did not. Gottwald refused to be drawn: "It was not his business to answer for the U.S.S.R., but nobody had any grounds to doubt that U.S.S.R. would meet its obligations. If it was a question of something over and above the obligations then Benes should formulate exactly what and put an enquiry to the Government of the U.S.S.R."[4] This Benes would not do. He had told Runciman at their farewell meeting: "Czechoslovakia had no special agreements with Russia even for

---

[1] Anglo-French Conversations, 18 Sept. 1938. *British Foreign Policy,* third series. ii. No. 928.

  [2] Alexandrovsky to Litvinov, 19 Sept. 1938. *New Documents,* No. 36.

  [3] Fierlinger to Krofta, 20 Sept. 1938. *Ibid.* No. 39.

  [4] Alexandrovsky to Litvinov, 20 Sept. 1938. *Ibid.* No. 37.

the event of war and she had not done, and would not do, anything without France".[1] Benes remained a "westerner" despite his disappointments; and even if he had been inclined to rely on Soviet Russia alone, the majority of the Czech cabinet—led by Hodza the prime minister—were strong enough to stop him. Benes did not yet despair. He was in constant touch with the more resolute groups in Paris, including some of the ministers; and he still believed that France could be swung back behind Czechoslovakia if his own acts were astute enough. All along Benes exaggerated the chance of changing French policy, and perhaps underrated that of changing British. At any rate his eyes were on Paris at this decisive moment. On 20 September the Czechoslovak government rejected the Anglo-French proposals, and appealed instead to the arbitration treaty with Germany. Half an hour later Hodza, so it seems, told the British and French representatives that, if the proposals were delivered "as a sort of ultimatum", Benes and the government would feel able to bow to *force majeure*.[2] Hodza, according to his own account, was merely trying to find out whether or no the French really intended to desert their ally; according to the French minister, Hodza positively implored an ultimatum, as "cover" for the Czech government which wished to surrender. This is a point on which the truth will never be known. Perhaps Hodza and his colleagues wished to surrender; undoubtedly Bonnet wanted them to do so. If Benes was associated with Hodza's manoeuvre, it was probably still in the hope of sparking off resistance among the "hards" in Paris. At any rate, Bonnet jumped at the chance, whether urged by Hodza or not. The ultimatum was duly drafted in Paris; authorised at midnight by Daladier and President Lebrun only; and delivered to Benes at 2 a.m. on 21 September. It was clear enough: if the Czechs refused the Anglo-French proposals, they would be responsible for the ensuing war; Anglo-French solidarity would be broken; and under such circumstances, France would not march, "as her assistance would not be effective".[3] When, on the following morning, some French ministers complained that

[1] Krofta to Masaryk and Osusky, 16 Sept. 1938. *New Documents*. No. 32.
[2] Newton to Halifax, 20 Sept. 1938. *British Foreign Policy*, third series. ii. No. 979.
[3] Bonnet, *de Washington à la quai d'Orsay*, 250. Krofta to Masaryk and Osusky, 21 Sept. 1938. *New Documents*, No. 42.

the Czechs had been abandoned without any decision by the Council of Ministers, Bonnet was able to reply that it had been done at Hodza's request; and once more the dissidents acquiesced. It was a shameful transaction; yet it only put in plain words what had been inevitable from the moment in April when the French decided that they could not go to war without British support and when the British decided, for their part, not to be involved in the defence of Czechoslovakia. No doubt it would have been kinder and more honourable to make this clear to Benes at the start. But countries that have long been Great Powers shrink from admitting that they are Great no longer. Both Great Britain and France in 1938 were for "peace at any price". Both feared war rather than defeat; hence the irrelevance of the calculations about German and allied strength, the debates whether Germany could have been defeated. Hitler could get his way by threatening war, without needing to count on victory.

The Czechs hesitated no longer. At midday on 21 September they accepted the Anglo-French proposals unconditionally. Yet Benes was still not defeated. He surmised that Hitler, presented with success, would put up his terms; and he hoped that British and French opinion would then at last revolt. He guessed correctly. On 22 September Chamberlain again met Hitler at Godesberg. Hitler declared that the Anglo-French proposals were no longer enough. Sudeten Germans were being massacred—a statement which was not true; and their territory must be occupied by German troops at once. Why did Hitler take this line, when he was to receive by negotiation all that he had demanded? Did he want war for its own sake? Most historians have accepted this explanation. But Hitler was still the successful conspirator, not yet "the greatest war leader of all time". There is a more plausible explanation. Others, inspired by the German example, were advancing claims to Czechoslovak territory. The Poles were demanding Tešin; the Hungarians were, at last, demanding Slovakia. There was a good chance that Czecho-slovakia would break to pieces, as in fact she did in March 1939. Germany would come in as a peace-maker, to create a new order, not to destroy an old one. Hitler himself "could have laughed in Chamberlain's face".[1] Hence, at Godesberg, Hitler was playing

[1] Conversation between Hitler and Csáky, 16 Jan. 1939. *German Foreign Policy*, series D. v. No. 272.

for time. Chamberlain's pleas and threats, even his hint that the new frontiers of Czechoslovakia could again be altered by negotiation, were irrelevant. Hitler was no longer interested in Czechoslovakia; he anticipated that, when the Polish and Hungarian mines exploded, she would cease to exist.

The Godesberg meeting therefore ended in failure. Chamberlain returned to London, faced with an apparent choice between war and abdication as a Great Power. He seems himself to have inclined towards the latter, if he could receive any crumb of acknowledgement. After all, nothing—in his view—could prevent the partition of Czechoslovakia. Why then go to war merely over the question of the exact time when this should take place? In London, however, Halifax had revolted—perhaps, as has been suggested, stirred by his conscience "in the watches of the night"; more likely, prompted by his permanent officials at the Foreign Office. On 23 September he had already told the Czechs, against Chamberlain's expressed opinion, that there could no longer be any objection against their mobilising; and they duly mobilised. Halifax also enquired of Litvinov, who was attending the meeting of the League at Geneva, "what action Soviet Government would take in event of Czechoslovakia being involved in war with Germany". This was the first British approach to Soviet Russia throughout the crisis. Litvinov gave his stock answer: "If French came to the assistance of the Czechs, Russia would take action". The Russians, it seems, saw their way more clearly, once Poland threatened to go against Czechoslovakia. There was now a road open for them into Europe; and, in case of war, they could recover the land lost to Poland in 1921, even if this did not much help the Czechs. On 23 September the Soviet government warned Poland that they would at once denounce the Soviet-Polish Non-Aggression Treaty, if the Poles invaded Czechoslovakia. On 24 September Gamelin also asked the Russians what they could do. They replied: Thirty infantry divisions were on the Western frontier (the French had at this moment only 15 in the Maginot line); aviation and tank forces were "in full readiness". As well, they urged the opening of immediate staff talks between the French, Czechs, and themselves. Gamelin agreed, allegedly with British approval.[1] No staff talks were, in fact, held.

[1] Fierlinger to Krofta, 29 Sept. 1938. *New Documents.* No. 55.

The French still hesitated. On 24 September Phipps wired from Paris: "All that is best in France is against war, *almost* at any price"; and he warned against "even appearing to encourage small, but noisy and corrupt war group".[1] In a later telegram he explained by this that he meant "the Communists who are paid by Moscow". The Foreign Office did not like this answer, and told Phipps to make wider enquiries. He did so, and replied two days later: "People are resigned but resolute. . . . The 'petit bourgeois' may feel disinclined to risk his life for Czechoslovakia, while most of the workmen are said to be in favour of France complying with her obligations".[2] The French Council of Ministers showed little of this resolute spirit. On 24 September the ministers failed to reach agreement on what France should do if Hitler invaded Czechoslovakia. Daladier and Bonnet were sent off to find an answer in London. On 25 September they met the British ministers. Daladier started, as usual, in fighting mood. Hitler should be asked to return to the Anglo-French proposals of 18 September. If he refused, "each of us would have to do his duty". Chamberlain answered: "One could not go into so great a conflict with one's eyes and ears closed. It was essential to know the conditions before making any decision. He would, therefore, like further information and would ask Sir John Simon to put certain points to M. Daladier". The great advocate then cross-examined the prime minister of France as though he were a hostile witness or a criminal. Would the French invade Germany? Would they use their air force? How could they aid Czechoslovakia? Daladier wriggled and dodged; evoked Soviet power; and kept returning to the question of principle. "There was one concession he would never make, and that was . . . the destruction of a country and Herr Hitler's domination of the world".[3] It was the old deadlock; fear of war on the one side; reluctance to surrender on the other. It was finally decided to ask Gamelin to come over and to meet again on the following day.

Gamelin's opinion was not helpful. The German air force was superior. "We shall suffer, particularly the civil population; but, if morale holds, this will not prevent a happy outcome for our

---

[1] Phipps to Halifax, 24 Sept. 1938. *British Foreign Policy*, third series. ii. No. 1076.

[2] Phipps to Halifax, 26 Sept. 1938. *Ibid.* No. 1119.

[3] Anglo-French conversations, 25 Sept. 1938. *Ibid.* No. 1093.

arms". Gamelin also thought that the Czechs, with 30 divisions against 40 German, could hold out, if they retreated to Moravia.[1] Later he told the British military experts that Soviet Russia was about to invade Poland—"a prospect which did not please our allies". The assembled ministers did not however consult Gamelin nor weigh his opinions. When they met, Chamberlain told them that he was sending Horace Wilson to Hitler with a personal message, appealing for peace. The French ministers accepted this solution and went home. Halifax was still restless. Winston Churchill called at the foreign office and urged him to stand firm. In the presence of the two men, an official, Rex Leeper, drafted a communiqué: "If German attack is made upon Czechoslovakia. . . . France will be bound to come to her assistance, and Great Britain and Russia will certainly stand by France". Though Halifax "authorised" the communiqué, he did not sign it. In this roundabout way, he secured his position both present and future: he retained Chamberlain's confidence, yet was later the only "man of Munich" who continued to stand high in favour with Churchill. At the time, the communiqué had little effect. In Paris, Bonnet denounced it as a forgery; and Chamberlain virtually disavowed it later in the evening by a statement of his own, again promising to fulfil all Hitler's demands.

Wilson saw Hitler on 26 September without effect. Quite the contrary, that evening Hitler delivered a speech, in which he announced, for the first time, his determination to occupy the Sudeten German territory by 1 October. Wilson was therefore instructed to deliver a special message, "more in sorrow than in anger":

> If Germany attacked Czechoslovakia France would feel that she must fulfil her treaty obligations. . . . If that meant that the forces of France became actively engaged in hostilities against Germany the British Government would feel obliged to support her.[2]

Hitler professed to be outraged by this alleged threat. It was not meant seriously. The British government were urging the French not to take the offensive even if Czechoslovakia were invaded,

[1] Gamelin, *Servir*, ii. 352.
[2] Conversation between Hitler and Wilson, 27 Sept. 1938. *British Foreign Policy*, third series. ii. No. 1129.

since this would "automatically start a world war without unhappily having any effect on saving Czechoslovakia".[1] Bonnet was in entire agreement; and Phipps reported: "France . . . will not fight with any heart in a hopeless offensive war against Germany, for which she is not prepared".[2] Appeals continued to flow in to Hitler: new appeals from Chamberlain; assurances from France that Germany could have at any rate three-quarters of the Sudeten territory by 1 October; finally, on 28 September, an appeal from Mussolini. To this last appeal, Hitler responded favourably: he would hold his hand for twenty-four hours, to allow of a Four Power conference at Munich. Why did Hitler pause at the last moment? Was he shaken by renewed warnings from his generals? Did he surmise that the German people were against war? Was he taken aback by Mussolini's hesitation? All these are possible explanations, on the assumption that he had intended to go to war. But the implications are all the other way. Hitler's judgements before the crisis, his skill in keeping the door open for compromise—or rather for peaceful victory—suggest that he never lost control of himself. He had waited for Czechoslovakia to disintegrate. But this did not happen. The Polish demand for Tešin, though ruthlessly pressed, was not enough. Only Hungarian action could shake Czechoslovakia; and the Hungarians, perhaps fearful of the Little Entente, perhaps reluctant to commit themselves fully to Hitler's side, failed to act. 28 September was the last moment when Hitler could call the war off. He could appear conciliatory and still collect his gains.

On 28 September Chamberlain spoke in the House of Commons. He had already appealed to Mussolini as mediator; and he had good grounds for believing that this mediation would be successful. British opinion had been hardening: the Czechs, not the Sudeten Germans, were now regarded by many as the oppressed people. Chamberlain wished to silence this opposition; and he therefore stressed the danger of war, not the justice of Germany's claims. The manoeuvre worked. When, towards the end of his speech, he announced—in a calculatedly dramatic way—that the Four Powers were to meet at Munich, the House broke into hysterical relief—at any rate on the Conservative side. "Thank God for the

[1] Halifax to Phipps, 27 Sept. 1938. *British Foreign Policy*, third series. ii. No. 1143.
[2] Phipps to Halifax, 28 Sept. 1938. *Ibid*. No. 1160.

Prime Minister". This was a triumph with bitter fruits. Appeasement had begun as an impartial consideration of rival claims and the remedying of past faults. Then it had been justified by the French fear of war. Now its motive seemed to be fear on the part of the British themselves. Chamberlain went to Munich not to seek justice for the Sudeten Germans nor even to save the French from war; he went, or so it appeared, to save the British themselves from air-attack. Appeasement had lost its moral strength. Before leaving, Chamberlain telegraphed to Prague: "Please assure Dr. Benes that I shall have the interests of Czechoslovakia fully in mind".[1] In fact, the Czechs were excluded from the meeting for fear that they might raise difficulties. The Russians were excluded also. Halifax tried to keep the future open by assuring Maisky, the Soviet ambassador, that this exclusion "in no way signified any weakening of a desire on our part, any more, no doubt, than on that of the French Government, to preserve our understandings and relations with the Soviet Government". Maisky's attitude seemed to Halifax, "as, indeed, it was likely to be, one of some suspicion".[2]

Chamberlain and Daladier did not meet beforehand to co-ordinate their policy. There was no need to co-ordinate surrender; or perhaps Chamberlain feared that Daladier would once more try ineffectually to co-ordinate resistance. Hitler met Mussolini, and alarmed him with plans for a lightning war against France, in which Italy was expected to take part. Just before the conference met, Mussolini received from Attolico, his ambassador at Berlin, terms drafted by the German foreign ministry— allegedly without Hitler's knowledge. Whether this were so or not, it was a convenient arrangement for Hitler. Mussolini produced the terms with the air of an impartial mediator; and Hitler was able to display conciliation by agreeing to them. The appearance of a *Diktat* was avoided. Right to the end, Hitler did not make demands; he graciously accepted what was offered by others. The terms agreed on were a compromise only in the sense that the Sudeten territory was to be occupied in stages, completed by 10 October, instead of at one bound on 1 October—a plan that was in any case technically impossible. No one queried the areas

[1] Halifax to Newton, 28 Sept. 1938. *British Foreign Policy*, third series ii. No. 1184.

[2] Halifax to Chilston, 29 Sept. 1938. *Ibid.* No. 1221.

to be surrendered. Chamberlain cavilled over the financial details. Mussolini raised the ethnic claims of the Hungarians, and was brushed aside by Hitler, who had no interest in the Hungarians once they had failed to destroy Czechoslovakia. The discussion rambled on till shortly after midnight, with a long break for dinner. Then the original terms, put forward by Mussolini, were adopted practically unchanged. When the four statesmen sat down to sign, they found that there was no ink in the ornate ink-well.

Czechoslovak representatives had been waiting in the ante-room, hoping to raise practical difficulties. They were denied a hearing. At 2 a.m. they were summoned to Chamberlain and Daladier, and shown the agreement. Daladier made it clear that "this was a sentence without right of appeal and without possibility of modification". Czechoslovakia must accept by 5 p.m., or take the consequences. Chamberlain yawned, and made no comment; he was "tired, but pleasantly tired". The following morning in Prague, Benes turned despairingly to the Soviet ambassador. "Czechoslovakia is confronted with the choice either of beginning war with Germany, having against her Britain and France, ... or capitulating to the aggressor". What would be the attitude of the U.S.S.R. to these two possibilities, "that is, of further struggle or capitulation"? Before the Soviet government could debate the question, another telegram informed them that no answer was necessary: "the Czechoslovak Government has already decided to accept all the conditions".[1] It is difficult to believe that the enquiry was made seriously. Benes remained true to his resolve that Czechoslovakia must not fight alone nor with Soviet Russia as sole ally. Years later, in 1944, he claimed that the Polish threat at Tešin had given him the final push into surrender; if so, it was only a push in the direction where he had determined to go. Benes still believed—rightly, as things turned out—that Hitler would over-reach himself; but the process took longer than he had hoped. Meanwhile, the Czechs were spared the horrors of war, not only in 1938 but throughout the second World war. Afterwards, surveying Prague from the President's palace, Benes could say: "Is it not beautiful? The only central European city not destroyed. And all my doing."

[1] Alexandrovsky to Litvinov, 30 Sept. 1938. *New Documents.* No. 57 and 58.

On 30 September Chamberlain and Hitler had another meeting. Chamberlain said: "I am very pleased at the results of yesterday's proceedings". Then, after a rambling discussion on disarmament and the Spanish question, he concluded: "it would be helpful to both countries and to the world in general if they could issue some statement which showed the agreement between them on the desirability of better Anglo-German relations, leading to a greater European stability"; and he produced a draft which he had brought with him. This statement presented "the agreement signed last night and the Anglo-German Naval Agreement as symbols of the desire of our two peoples never to go to war with one another again". It continued:

We are resolved that the method of consultation shall be the method adopted to deal with any other questions that may concern our two countries, and we are determined to continue our efforts to remove possible sources of difference and thus to contribute to assure the peace of Europe.[1]

The draft was translated to Hitler. He welcomed it enthusiastically. The two men signed. The statesmen departed for their respective countries. Daladier gloomily expected to be met by a hostile crowd. He was taken aback by the cheers that awaited him. Chamberlain had no such misgivings. As he stepped from the aeroplane, he waved the statement which he had signed with Hitler, and cried: "I've got it". On the way to London, Halifax urged him not to exploit the mood of the moment by holding a general election and to make a real National government of Liberal and Labour, along with Churchill and Eden. Chamberlain is reported to have shared Halifax's doubts; and to have said of the cheers: "All this will be over in three months". But that evening he appeared at the window of 10 Downing Street, and told the crowd: "This is the second time that there has come back from Germany to Downing Street peace with honour. I believe it is peace for our time".

[1] Conversation between Chamberlain and Hitler, 30 Sept. 1938. *British Foreign Policy*, third series. ii. No. 1228.

CHAPTER NINE

Peace for Six Months

THE conference at Munich was meant to mark the beginning of an epoch in European affairs. "Versailles"—the system of 1919—was not only dead, but buried. A new system, based on equality and mutual confidence between the four great European Powers, was to take its place. Chamberlain said: "I believe that it is peace for our time"; Hitler declared: "I have no more territorial demands to make in Europe". There were still great questions to be settled in international affairs. The Spanish civil war was not over. Germany had not recovered her colonies. More remotely, agreements would have to be reached over economic policy and over armaments, before stability was restored in Europe. None of these questions threatened to provoke a general war. The demonstration had been given that Germany could attain by peaceful negotiation the position in Europe to which her resources entitled her. The great hurdle had been successfully surmounted: the system, directed against Germany, had been dismantled by agreement, without a war. Yet, within six months, a new system was being constructed against Germany. Within a year, Great Britain, France, and Germany were at war. Was "Munich" a fraud from the start—for Germany merely a stage in the march towards world conquest, or, on the side of Great Britain and France, merely a device to buy time until their re-armament was more advanced? So it appeared in retrospect. When the policy of Munich failed, everyone announced that he had expected it to fail; and the participants not only accused the others of cheating, but boasted that they had been cheating themselves. In fact, no one was as clear-sighted as he later claimed to have been; and the four men of Munich were all in their different ways sincere, though each had reserves which he concealed from the others.

The French yielded most, and with least hope for the future. They surrendered the position of paramount European power which they had appeared to enjoy since 1919. But what they surrendered was artificial. They yielded to reality rather than to force. They had supposed all along that the advantages won in 1919 and subsequently—the restrictions on Germany and the alliances with East European states—were assets which they could supinely enjoy, not gains which they must fiercely defend. They did not lift a finger to assert the system of Versailles after the occupation of the Ruhr in 1923. They abandoned reparations; they acquiesced in the re-armament of Germany; they allowed the German re-occupation of the Rhineland; they did nothing to protect the independence of Austria. They kept up their alliances in Eastern Europe only from the belief that these would bring them aid if ever they were themselves attacked by Germany. They abandoned their ally, Czechoslovakia, the moment she threatened to bring them risk instead of security. Munich was the logical culmination of French policy, not its reversal. The French recognised that they had lost their predominance in Eastern Europe, and knew that it could not be restored. This is far from saying that they feared for themselves. On the contrary, they accepted the British thesis, preached ever since Locarno, that they were in less danger of war if they withdrew behind the Rhine. They had preferred safety to grandeur—an ignoble policy perhaps, but not a dangerous one. Even in 1938, though they feared air bombardment, they did not fear defeat if war were thrust upon them. Gamelin was always emphatic that the democratic powers would win; and the politicians believed him. But what would be the point of war? This was the argument which had prevented French action since 1923, and which prevented it now. Germany, even if defeated, would still be there, great, powerful, determined on redress. War might stop the clock. It could not put it back; and afterwards events would move forward to the same end. The French were therefore willing to surrender everything except their own security, and they did not believe that they had surrendered this at Munich. They had a firm and, as it turned out a well-founded, faith that the Maginot line was impregnable—so much so that they regarded the Siegfried line, less correctly, as impregnable also. They assumed that a stalemate had been established in Western Europe. They could not impede the advance of German power in Eastern Europe; equally Germany could not invade France. The French

were humiliated by Munich, not—as they supposed—endangered.
The British position was more complicated. Morality did not
enter French calculations, or entered only to be discarded. The
French recognised that it was their duty to assist Czechoslovakia;
they rejected this duty as either too dangerous or too difficult.
Léon Blum expressed French feeling best when he welcomed
the agreement of Munich with a mixture of shame and relief.
With the British, on the other hand, morality counted for a great
deal. The British statesmen used practical arguments: the
danger from air attack; the backwardness of their re-armament;
the impossibility, even if adequately armed, of helping Czechoslovakia. But these arguments were used to reinforce morality,
not to silence it. British policy over Czechoslovakia originated in
the belief that Germany had a moral right to the Sudeten
German territory, on grounds of national principle; and it drew
the further corollary that this victory for self-determination
would provide a stabler, more permanent peace in Europe. The
British government were not driven to acknowledge the dismemberment of Czechoslovakia solely from fear of war. They
deliberately set out to impose this cession of territory on the
Czechs before the threat of war raised its head. The settlement
at Munich was a triumph for British policy, which had worked
precisely to this end; not a triumph for Hitler, who had started
with no such clear intention. Nor was it merely a triumph for
selfish or cynical British statesmen, indifferent to the fate of far-
off peoples or calculating that Hitler might be launched into war
against Soviet Russia. It was a triumph for all that was best and
most enlightened in British life; a triumph for those who had
preached equal justice between peoples; a triumph for those who
had courageously denounced the harshness and short-sightedness
of Versailles. Brailsford, the leading Socialist authority on foreign
affairs, wrote in 1920 of the peace settlement: "The worst offence
was the subjection of over three million Germans to Czech rule".[1]
This was the offence redressed at Munich. Idealists could claim
that British policy had been tardy and hesitant. In 1938 it atoned
for these failings. With skill and persistence, Chamberlain brought
first the French, and then the Czechs, to follow the moral line.
    There was a case against ceding Sudeten territory to Germany—
the case that economic and geographic ties are more important

[1] Brailsford, *After the Peace* (1920), 47.

than those of nationality. This had been the case against breaking up the Habsburg Monarchy; the Czechs who had taken the lead in breaking up the Monarchy could not use this argument, nor could their advocates in Western Europe. The dispute had to be transferred from the field of morality to that of practical considerations—to what is disapprovingly called *realpolitik*. The most outspoken opponents of Munich, such as Winston Churchill, asserted quite simply that Germany was becoming too powerful in Europe and that she must be stopped by the threat of a great coalition or, if necessary, by force of arms. Self-determination— the principle to which Czechoslovakia owed her existence—was dismissed as a sham. The only moral argument used was that the frontiers of existing states were sacred and that each state could behave as it liked within its own borders. This was the argument of legitimacy; the argument of Metternich and the Congress of Vienna. If accepted, it would have forbidden not only the break-up of the Habsburg Monarchy, but even the winning of independence by the British colonies in America. It was a strange argument for the British Left to use in 1938; and it sat uneasily upon them—hence the hesitations and ineffectiveness of their criticism. Duff Cooper, First Lord of the Admiralty, had no such doubts when he resigned in protest against the Munich settlement. As became an admiring biographer of Talleyrand, he was concerned with the Balance of Power and British honour, not with self-determination or the injustices of Versailles. For him, Czechoslovakia had no more been the real issue in 1938 than Belgium had been in 1914. This argument destroyed the moral validity of the British position in the first World war, but it had an appeal for the Conservative majority in the House of Commons. Chamberlain had to answer it in its own terms of power. He could not stress the unwillingness of the French to fight, which had been the really decisive weakness on the Western side. Therefore he had to make out that Great Britain herself was in no position to fight Germany.

Chamberlain was caught by his own argument. If Great Britain had been too weak to fight, then the government must speed rearmament; and this involved doubt in Hitler's good faith, whether avowed or not. In this way, Chamberlain did more than anyone else to destroy the case for his own policy. Moreover, one suspicion breeds another. It is doubtful whether Hitler ever took Chamberlain's sincerity seriously before Munich; it is certain that he did not do so a few days afterwards. What was meant as appeasement had turned into capitulation, on Chamberlain's own showing. Hitler drew the lesson that threats were his most potent weapon. The temptation to boast of Munich as a triumph of force was too great to be resisted. Hitler no longer expected to make gains by parading his grievances against Versailles; he expected to make them by playing on British and French fears. Thus he confirmed the suspicions of those who attacked Munich as a craven surrender. International morality was at a discount. Paradoxically, Benes was the true victor of Munich in the long run. For, while Czechoslovakia lost territory and later her independence also, Hitler lost the moral advantage which had hitherto made him irresistible. Munich became an emotive word, a symbol of shame, about which men can still not speak dispassionately. What was done at Munich mattered less than the way in which it was done; and what was said about it afterwards on both sides counted for still more.

There had been two empty chairs at Munich, or rather chairs were not provided for two Great Powers, though each had claims to an invitation. President Roosevelt, at the height of the crisis, urged a meeting in some neutral capital. He did not indicate whether an American representative would attend; and in any case "the Government of the United States . . . . will assume no obligations in the conduct of the present negotiations". Roosevelt applauded Chamberlain on the news of the Munich conference: "Good man". Afterwards, when appeasement turned sour, the Americans rejoiced that they had not been at Munich. They could condemn the British and French for doing what they themselves would have done in their place. Lack of American support had helped towards making the "democratic" powers give way. Yet Americans drew from Munich the moral that they should support these feeble powers still less. Roosevelt, entangled in troubles over domestic policy, had no mind to add to his difficulties by provoking controversy over foreign affairs. Europe could go on its way without America.

The Russians had been more precise in their plan for a conference. They had wanted a meeting of the "peace-loving Powers" to co-ordinate resistance against the aggressor. They, too, could assume an attitude of moral superiority. Parading their own loyalty to treaty obligations, they laid all the blame on French weakness. One Soviet diplomatist said on 30 September: "We nearly put our foot on a rotten plank. Now we are going elsewhere." Potyomkin, the assistant commissar, made the meaning of this clear when he said to Coulondre: "My poor friend, what have you done? For us I see no other way out than a fourth partition of Poland." The Russians professed to have no fears for their own security. Litvinov told Coulondre: "Hitler will be able to attack Great Britain or the U.S.S.R. He will choose the first solution, ... and to carry this enterprise through successfully he will prefer to reach an understanding with the U.S.S.R.".[1] Inwardly the Russians were less confident. No approach came from Hitler; instead the claim that he had saved Europe from Bolshevism. Ingenious observers expected Hitler's next move to be into the Ukraine—a move expected by Western statesmen with some pleasure, by Soviet statesmen with dread. The Soviet rulers would have liked to isolate themselves from Europe; but they were by no means sure that Europe would isolate itself from them. Hence, after a short period of recrimination, they had to renew the call for a Popular Front and for collective security against aggression. It is hard to believe that they expected this policy to succeed.

Everyone talked of Hitler's next move in one direction or another. The man who talked, and apparently thought, of it least was Hitler himself. The precise timetable attributed to him by many writers—Munich in September 1938, Prague in March 1939, Danzig in September rests on no contemporary evidence. After his dazzling success at Munich, Hitler returned to the Berghof, where he spent his time drawing dream-plans for the rebuilding of Linz, the Austrian town where he went to school. Occasionally he grumbled at being denied a war against Czechoslovakia. But men must be judged by what they do, not by what they say afterwards. Once more he waited for events to provide him with future success. The military leaders sought a directive for their next activities. Hitler replied on 21 October: "The Wehrmacht must at all times be prepared for the following: (i) securing the frontiers of the German Reich and protection against surprise air attacks. (ii) Liquidation of the remainder of the Czech state". These were measures of precaution, not plans for aggression. The

[1] Coulondre, *De Staline à Hitler*, 165, 169, 171.

continuation of the directive makes this clear: "It must be possible to smash the remainder of the Czech state, should it pursue an anti-German policy".[1] On 17 December the Wehrmacht was told: "Outwardly it must be quite clear that it is only a peaceful action and not a warlike undertaking".[2] These directives have often been quoted as proof that Hitler was never sincere in accepting the Munich settlement. The truth is rather that Hitler doubted whether the settlement would work. Though often regarded as politically ignorant, he understood better than other European statesmen the problem of Bohemia; and believed, without sinister intention, that independent Czechoslovakia could not survive, when deprived of her natural frontiers and with Czech prestige broken. This was not a wish for Czechoslovakia's destruction. It was a belief held also by Masaryk and Benes, when they created Czechoslovakia in 1918; it was the principle on which Czechoslovak independence had rested from first to last.

If Czechoslovakia fell to pieces, what should take its place? At Godesberg, during the Czech crisis, Hitler had favoured a lavish distribution of Czechoslovak territory to Hungary and Poland, as a reward for their taking the initiative. Afterwards he changed his mind. Both countries had held back until the crisis was almost over; both obviously still hoped to play with both sides. He told a Hungarian representative on 14 October: "I am not annoyed with Hungary, but she has missed the bus".[3] A subservient Czechoslovakia now seemed preferable to him. Hitler was a rational, though no doubt a wicked, statesman. His object was the steady extension of German power, not theatrical displays of glory. For this purpose, satellites were more useful than the direct annexation of territory; and he accumulated satellites with great patience. They were a different version of his favourite method by which others did his work for him. Immediately after Munich, the German representatives on the International Commission applied the rules, fabricated by themselves, so ruthlessly in favour of the Sudetens that Czechoslovakia

[1] Directive by Hitler, 21 Oct. 1938. *German Foreign Policy*, series D. iv. No. 81.

[2] Directive by Keitel, 17 Dec. 1938. *Ibid*. No. 152.

[3] Hitler, conversation with Darányi, 14 Oct. 1938. *German Foreign Policy*, series D. iv. No. 62.

actually lost more territory than she would have done under the
demands made at Godesberg. It was another story when Ribbentrop and Ciano met at Vienna to settle the new frontier between
Hungary and Czechoslovakia. Ciano had the characteristically
subtle and futile idea of building up Hungary as a barrier against
Germany. Ribbentrop saw through this policy at once, and
backed the Slovak case so strongly that Ciano complained: "You
are now using in favour of Czechoslovakia all the arguments you
used against her in September". The Slovaks were a new element
in Hitler's calculations: free both from the Czech devotion to
democracy, and from the Hungarian illusions of greatness. "He
regretted that he had not known earlier of the Slovak struggle
for independence."[1] It is often held that Hitler favoured Slovakia
as a route for invading the Ukraine. Geography really made this
as impracticable as the reverse idea that Soviet Russia could
threaten Germany through Czechoslovakia. Hitler backed
Slovakia for her own sake—a steady, reliable satellite, as she
proved to be throughout the second World war.

If Hitler really aspired to reach the Ukraine, he must go
through Poland; in the autumn of 1938, this seemed by no means
a political fantasy. Poland, though still nominally allied to
France, had stretched the Non-Aggression Pact far in Germany's
interest. Thanks largely to her, the Franco-Soviet Pact had never
become a reality. During the Czech crisis, her attitude ruled out
any possibility of Soviet aid to Czechoslovakia; and, at the end
of this crisis, the Polish ultimatum to Czechoslovakia demanding
the return of Tešin finally decided Benes, according to his own
account, to abandon any idea of resisting the Munich settlement.
Poland had been so far a more useful jackal to Germany in the
East than Italy had been in the Mediterranean. There seemed no
reason why either should give up this role. There was a stumbling
block in each case: Italy had some 300,000 Germans in South
Tyrol, Poland about a million and a half Germans in Silesia and
the corridor. But these obstacles could be overcome. Hitler was
ready to forget Germans under alien rule, in exchange for political
co-operation or subservience. He did this with Italy—indeed
agreed to remove the Germans from South Tyrol—even though,
as an Austrian, he felt their cause deeply.

[1] Conversation between Hitler and Tuka, 12 Feb. 1939. *German Foreign
Policy*, series D. iv. No. 168.

He felt less deeply about the Germans in Poland; and he probably felt more friendly towards the Poles than he ever did towards the Italians. The obstacle here was German feeling, not Hitler's. The losses of territory to Poland were, for most Germans, the indelible grievance against Versailles. Hitler undertook a daring operation over this grievance when he planned co-operation with Poland. But there was a way out. The actual Germans under Polish rule might be forgotten—or withdrawn; what could not be forgiven was the "Polish corridor" which divided East Prussia from the Reich. Here, too, there was a possible compromise. Germany might be satisfied with a corridor across the corridor—a complicated idea for which there were however many precedents in German history. German feeling could be appeased by the recovery of Danzig. This seemed easy. Danzig was not part of Poland. It was a Free City, with its own autonomous administration under a High Commissioner, appointed by the League of Nations. The Poles themselves, in their false pride as a Great Power, had taken the lead in challenging the League's authority. Surely, therefore, they would not object if Germany took the League's place. Moreover, the problem had changed since 1919. Then the port of Danzig had been essential to Poland. Now, with the creation of Gdynia by the Poles, Danzig needed Poland more than the Poles needed Danzig. It should then be easy to arrange for the safeguarding of Poland's economic interests, and yet to recover Danzig for the Reich. The stumbling-block would be removed; Germany and Poland could act together in the Ukraine.

On 24 October Ribbentrop first aired these proposals to Lipski, the Polish ambassador. If Danzig and the corridor were settled, there could then be "a joint policy towards Russia on the basis of the Anti-Comintern Pact".[1] Hitler was even franker when Beck, the Polish foreign minister, visited him in January 1939: "The divisions which Poland stationed on the Russian frontier saved Germany just so much military expenditure". Of course, he added, "Danzig is German, will always remain German, and will sooner or later become part of Germany". If the question of Danzig were settled, he would be ready to guarantee the Corridor

[1] This according to Lipski's account. Ribbentrop merely recorded: "Poland would accede to the Anti-Comintern Pact", but it came to the same thing. *German Foreign Policy*, series D. v. No. 81.

to Poland.[1] Hitler may have been cheating the Poles over Danzig all along—demanding its return as the preliminary to their destruction. But Polish ambitions in the Ukraine were of long standing; Danzig seemed a triviality in comparison. Beck "made no secret of the fact that Poland had aspirations directed towards the Soviet Ukraine", when Ribbentrop visited Warsaw on 1 February.[2]

Nevertheless, the Poles did not respond to Hitler's offer. Blindly confident in their own strength and contemptuous of Czech softness, they were determined not to yield an inch; this, they believed, was the only safe method of doing business with Hitler. Moreover—a point which Hitler never understood—though they would not co-operate with Soviet Russia against Germany, they were almost equally resolved not to co-operate with Germany against Soviet Russia. They regarded themselves as an independent Great Power; and forgot that they had gained their independence in 1918 only because both Russia and Germany had been defeated. Now they had to choose between Germany and Russia. They chose neither. Only Danzig prevented co-operation between Germany and Poland. For this reason, Hitler wanted to get it out of the way. For precisely the same reason, Beck kept it in the way. It did not cross his mind that this might cause a fatal breach.

The faint cloud of estrangement between Poland and Germany was not perceived in Western Europe. On the contrary, a joint campaign in the Ukraine was believed to be imminent. Chamberlain enquired anxiously in Paris whether the Franco-Soviet Pact would operate "if Russia were to ask France for assistance on the grounds that a separatist movement in Ukraine was provoked by Germany".[3] Chamberlain clearly wanted to have nothing to do with Eastern Europe. Halifax, coached by the foreign office, was less precise. He wrote to Phipps on 1 November: "It is one thing to allow German expansion in Central Europe, which to my mind is a normal and natural thing, but we must be able to resist German expansion in Western Europe or else our whole position

[1] Conversation between Hitler and Beck, 5 Jan. 1939. *German Foreign Policy*, series D. v. No. 119.
[2] Minute by Ribbentrop, 1 Feb. 1939. *Ibid.* No. 126.
[3] Anglo-French meeting, 24 Nov. 1938. *British Foreign Policy*, third series, iii. No. 325.

is undermined". A balance against Germany was still needed. "Poland can presumably only fall more and more into the German orbit. Soviet Russia . . . can scarcely become the ally of Germany so long as Hitler lives". Therefore, "subject only to the consideration that I should hope France would protect herself—and us—from being entangled by Russia in war with Germany, I should hesitate to advise the French Government to denounce the Franco-Soviet pact as the future is still far too uncertain!"[1] In plain English: Russia should fight for British interests, but Great Britain and France should not fight for hers.

Nothing was done, however, to secure Soviet friendship. The British were more concerned to get out of such commitments in Central Europe as they already had. The guarantee, casually promised to Czechoslovakia, now weighed heavily upon them. It was an obvious absurdity to guarantee a helpless state which it had been impossible to defend when fully armed. The British implored the French to release them from their promise. On 24 November British and French ministers met at Paris. Chamberlain urged that the guarantee should be collective only; "a guarantee given by His Majesty's Government alone was not worth very much. . . . He had never conceived of a situation in which Great Britain might have to carry out her obligations alone". Halifax thought a joint guarantee "did not seem to be out of conformity with the letter of the Anglo-French declaration". Even Bonnet bridled: "it was hardly in conformity with the spirit". Since the French would not yield, it was decided to ask the Czechs to get the British out of their difficulty.[2] If Czechoslovakia were satisfied with a collective guarantee, the British conscience would be satisfied also. When the Czechs failed to respond, Halifax lost patience:

> His Majesty's Government are not prepared to consider a guarantee which might oblige them, alone or with France, to come to the assistance of Czechoslovakia in circumstances in which effective help could not be rendered. This would be the case if either Germany or Italy were the aggressor and the other declined to fulfil the guarantee.[3]

[1] Halifax to Phipps, 1 Nov. 1938. *British Foreign Policy*, third series. iii. No. 285.

[2] Anglo-French meeting, 24 Nov. 1938. *Ibid.* No. 325.

[3] Halifax to Newton, 8 Dec. 1938. *Ibid.* No. 408.

There the matter rested: the British were stuck with a guarantee which they were determined not to honour.

During the winter of 1938-39 the British were doubtful enough of the position in Western Europe, quite apart from their impossible commitments farther east. Chamberlain's special pride, the Anglo-German declaration of friendship, soon lost its glitter. Hitler aimed to "split" British opinion. He supposed that increased armaments would stir up opposition among the pro-Germans; and he denounced the British "warmongers"— Churchill, Eden, and Duff Cooper—in the belief that this would lead to an explosion against them. It had the reverse effect. Conservative members of the House of Commons were impatient at Churchill's solemn warnings; they were angry when Duff Cooper resigned. But they resented Hitler's interference in their affairs. They believed in mutual non-interference. Hitler could do what he liked in Eastern Europe; he could demolish Czechoslovakia or invade the Ukraine. But he must leave British politicians alone. Conservatives had often argued that criticism of Hitler from outside merely strengthened his hold on Germany. Now Hitler was giving the "warmongers" in Great Britain a popularity which they could not win for themselves. British statesmen were bewildered at Hitler's behaviour. They were rearming in order to increase their own security; and this would make it easier for them to accept the advance of German power in Eastern Europe. Yet Hitler, instead of applauding their policy, undermined its foundations and went out of his way to justify its critics. Still, his attacks did not shake the determination of British leaders that Germany must be appeased one way or another. Territorial and nationalist concessions had failed to mollify Hitler. Therefore the British swung back to a sort of crude Marxism. They began to argue once more that only prosperity would make Hitler pacific. A stream of trade delegations appeared in Germany with offers of economic co-operation— with the additional attraction on the British side that these schemes would enlist German assistance against American competition. Every visit from a well-meaning business man or representative of the Board of Trade increased Hitler's belief in British weakness. He was not to know that they had merely been reading Left-wing writers on the economic causes of war.

The British had further worries. Before Munich they had been the pacemakers in appeasement, the French dragging protestingly along behind. After Munich it was the other way round. Bonnet was jealous of Chamberlain's private pact with Hitler, and aspired to outdo it. Ribbentrop believed that a Franco-German declaration of friendship would further shake British resolution to interfere in Europe. On 6 December he visited Paris; and a declaration of this sort was signed. In itself it amounted to little: mutual goodwill and recognition of frontiers; readiness to confer together if international difficulties should arise in the future. It was perhaps a score for the French that Hitler, in this roundabout way, renounced Alsace-Lorraine; and future Munichs might have their attraction. Rumour went further. According to this, Ribbentrop agreed not to press the German claim for colonies; and Bonnet, in return, renounced all French interest in Eastern Europe. Probably their discussion was less precise and less sinister. No doubt Bonnet failed to show a burning devotion to the Franco-Soviet Pact. But what was said about France's alliance with Poland? Later, Ribbentrop claimed that Bonnet had virtually repudiated it. Bonnet denied the claim. The truth seems to be that Poland was not mentioned. In December 1938 she seemed to raise no difficulty for Franco-German relations. Both men assumed that Poland was a loyal German satellite and that Danzig would be quietly settled without a European crisis. This assumption was, after all, held by the Poles themselves. It is not surprising that Ribbentrop and Bonnet shared it.

The Franco-German declaration made the British anxious. They had urged France to cut down her commitments in Eastern Europe; they did not want her to abdicate altogether as a Great Power. It was an awkward dilemma. If Germany were free to pursue her aims in Eastern Europe without French interference, she might become so strong that the security of France would be "under imminent menace". If, on the other hand, the French government decided not to leave Germany with freedom of action in Eastern Europe, Great Britain might be drawn into war in order to support France.[1] The British fell back on their old resource of trying to employ Mussolini as a moderating influence on Hitler. The Anglo-Italian Agreement of 16 April was "brought into force", although the Italians had not fulfilled its pre-

[1] Sargent to Phipps, 22 Dec. 1938. *British Foreign Policy*, third series. iii. No. 885, footnote.

condition of withdrawing their forces from Spain. Halifax wrote: "Although we do not expect to detach Italy from the Axis, we believe the Agreement will increase Mussolini's power of manoeuvre and so make him less dependent on Hitler and therefore freer to resume the classic Italian role of balancing between Germany and the Western Powers".[1] In other words, by paying blackmail to Mussolini we will encourage him to demand more. Mussolini duly obliged. He launched a campaign for French territory. Italy resounded with demands for Corsica, Savoy, and Nice. The French did not fear Italy, however much they might fear Hitler. They responded fiercely to Mussolini's challenge. The British had merely offended the French without conciliating Mussolini. In January 1939, Chamberlain and Halifax went to Rome. They came empty-handed. Mussolini expected concessions at the expense of France. Instead he got a high-minded plea from Chamberlain for some assurance that Hitler was not going to war. Mussolini "thrust out his chin", and retaliated with an attack on the British press. The visit to Rome, which was designed as the culmination of Chamberlain's policy, marked instead the end of the Italian illusion. More, though the British did not know this, it pushed Mussolini further on to the German side. Immediately after the visit, he told the Germans that he was ready to conclude a formal alliance. Hitler however decided to teach him a lesson and kept him waiting.

The British had now talked themselves into a condition of extreme anxiety, and had increased it by their efforts at precaution. Halifax and the foreign office believed that Hitler was "considering an attack on the Western Powers".[2] They anticipated an attack on Holland, and resolved to treat this as a *"casus belli"*. Switzerland, too, was supposed to be endangered; or there might be a surprise air-attack on England. These were nightmares without substance. There is not the smallest fragment of evidence that Hitler ever considered such plans even in the most remote way. Nevile Henderson was more accurate when he wrote on 18 February: "My definite impression is that Herr Hitler does not contemplate any adventures at the moment".[3]

[1] Halifax to Phipps, 1 Nov. 1938. *British Foreign Policy*, third series. iii. No. 285.
[2] Halifax to Lindsay, 24 Jan. 1939. *Ibid*. No. 5.
[3] Henderson to Halifax, 18 Feb. 1939. *Ibid*. No. 118.

Why should he have done so? Eastern Europe was falling into his lap. Hungary, Rumania, Yugoslavia, were competing for his favour. France had abandoned Eastern Europe. Soviet Russia was estranged from the Western Powers. Poland remained on friendly terms with Germany, despite the exasperating failure to find a solution of the Danzig question. The only cloud came from Czechoslovakia. Not that she could pursue a foreign policy independent of or hostile to Germany. But, as both Benes and Hitler had foreseen, it was impossible to hold the state together, once Czech prestige and power were shaken. Few people appreciated this in the West; and the admirers of Czechoslovakia kept quiet about it. In Western eyes, Czechoslovakia was a happy, democratic state, wantonly dismembered by Hitler. In fact, it was a state of nationalities, created by Czech initiative and maintained by Czech authority. Once this was broken, disintegration followed, just as the collapse of the Habsburg Monarchy followed defeat in the first World war.

The Slovaks, in particular, had never been accepted as equal partners. Few of them were willing to disappear into the artificial Czechoslovak amalgam. The demand for Slovak autonomy provided a grumbling under-current throughout the twenty years of Czechoslovak history; after Munich, it came to the surface. Hitler patronised the Slovak autonomists in order to spite Hungary, to whom Slovakia had originally belonged. The movement was not created by him; he merely took advantage of it, as he had done of the German Austrians and the Sudeten Germans. He would have been satisfied with Slovak autonomy within a subservient Czechoslovak state. The Slovaks were not. Freed from their old awe of Prague, they grew turbulent. By the end of February 1939, Czecho-Slovakia (hyphenated since the previous October) was crumbling. The Prague government might have little independence left; they still felt strong enough to discipline the Slovaks—indeed had to do so if Czecho Slovakia were to survive. On 9 March the autonomous Slovak government were dismissed; Czech troops prepared to move in. Once again Hitler was taken by surprise. This new crisis came on him unawares. He could not allow the Czechs to restore their damaged prestige. On the other hand, if he insisted on Czech forces keeping out of Slovakia the Hungarians might well move in, as they had planned to do in the previous September. Now Hitler had

turned against the Hungarians; and since the Czech army could
no longer enter Slovakia to deter them, he had to do it himself.
Germany hastily recognised Slovak independence, and there-
with brought Czecho-Slovakia to an end. What was to happen to
the Czech remnant? There was no one to guide it. Benes had
resigned and left the country immediately after Munich. Hacha,
his successor, was an elderly lawyer of no political experience.
Bewildered, helpless, he could only turn to the great German
dictator. Like Schuschnigg before him, he asked to be received
by Hitler; and his request was granted. In Berlin he was received with the honours due to a head of state; and then
instructed to sign away the independence of his country. Any
fragment of reluctance was silenced by the threat that, otherwise, Prague would immediately be bombed. This was the most
casual of Hitler's many improvisations. As he confessed later,[1]
the German airfields were shrouded in fog, and no aeroplanes
could have left the ground. Hacha hardly needed inducement.
He signed as required; and harboured so little resentment that
he served as a faithful German subordinate until the end of the
war. On 15 March Bohemia became a German protectorate.
German troops occupied the country. Hitler spent the night of
15 March in Prague—his only recorded visit. All the world saw
in this the culmination of a long-planned campaign. In fact, it
was the unforeseen by-product of developments in Slovakia; and
Hitler was acting against the Hungarians rather than against the
Czechs. Nor was there anything sinister or premeditated in the
protectorate over Bohemia. Hitler, the supposed revolutionary,
was simply reverting in the most conservative way to the pattern
of previous centuries. Bohemia had always been part of the Holy
Roman Empire; it had been part of the German Confederation
between 1815 and 1866; then it had been linked to German
Austria until 1918. Independence, not subordination, was the
novelty in Czech history. Of course Hitler's protectorate brought
tyranny to Bohemia—secret police, the S.S., the concentration
camps; but no more than in Germany itself. It was this which
roused public opinion in Great Britain. Hitler's domestic
behaviour, not his foreign policy, was the real crime which
ultimately brought him—and Germany—to the ground. It did
not seem so at the time. Hitler took the decisive step in his career

[1] *Hitler's Table Talk*, 204.

when he occupied Prague. He did it without design; it brought
him slight advantage. He acted only when events had already
destroyed the settlement of Munich. But everyone outside
Germany, and especially the other makers of that settlement,
believed that he had deliberately destroyed it himself.

Even Mussolini was disgruntled. He complained to Ciano on
15 March: "every time Hitler occupies a country he sends me a
message". He dreamt of creating an anti-German front, based on
Hungary and Yugoslavia. By the evening, he had recovered his
temper: "we cannot change our policy now. After all, we are not
political whores"; and he once more paraded his loyalty to the
Axis. The French took the new blow without complaint. They
had surrendered the previous September; there was nothing they
could do now. Bonnet said complacently: "the renewed rift
between Czechs and Slovaks only shows that we nearly went to
war last autumn to boost up a State that was not 'viable' ".[1]
There was a firmer response in Great Britain. Until 15 March
English people still tried to believe that Munich was a triumph
of morality, not a surrender to force. Despite the alarms of the
foreign office, leading ministers held that all was well. On 10
March Sir Samuel Hoare told his constituents that a Golden Age
was approaching: rearmament was over; now co-operation
between the great European Powers "would raise living standards
to heights we had never before been able to attempt". Nor did
the occupation of Prague at first shake official optimism. Halifax
told the French ambassador: "the one compensating advantage
that I saw was that it had brought to a natural end the somewhat
embarrassing commitment of a guarantee, in which we and the
French had been involved".[2] In the House of Commons, Chamberlain speculated that the end of Czechoslovakia "may or may
not have been inevitable"; and Sir John Simon explained that
it was impossible to fulfil a guarantee for a state which had
ceased to exist.

There followed an underground explosion of public opinion
such as the historian cannot trace in precise terms. The occupation of Prague did not represent anything new in Hitler's policy
or behaviour. President Hacha had succumbed more easily and

---

[1] Phipps to Halifax, 14 March 1939. *British Foreign Policy*, third series,
iv. No. 234.
[2] Halifax to Phipps, 15 March 1939. *Ibid.* No. 280.

more willingly than either Schuschnigg or Benes. Yet British opinion was stirred as it had not been by the absorption of Austria or the capitulation at Munich. Hitler was supposed to have overstepped the bounds. His word could never be trusted again. Perhaps the exaggerated expectations after Munich produced this reaction. Men had assumed, against all the evidence, that "Peace for our time" meant that there would be no more changes in Europe. Perhaps there was a belief, again unfounded, that British armaments were now more adequate. Again, Conservatives were troubled by the "embarrassing" matter of the guarantee, which they had supposed really meant something. In a way impossible to define, those who had given warnings against Hitler were now listened to, where they had been ignored before. The prophets of woe operated from the most varied premises. Some, like Churchill and the anti-German members of the foreign office, regarded Hitler as merely the latest spokesman for Prussian militarism. Others attributed to him new and more grandiose plans which they claimed to have discovered by reading *Mein Kampf* in the original (Hitler forbade its publication in English). Others again, particularly on the Left, described National Socialism in Marxist terms as "the last stage of aggressive Imperialism", and believed that Hitler must pursue an aggressive course in order to please the German capitalists. Dislike of anti-semitism was the motive for many; friendship for the Czechs or Poles influenced a few. Some wanted to "liberate" Germany, others to defeat her. The remedies, too, were various: collective security, economic sanctions, increased British armaments. The differences were not important. All the prophets had said that Hitler would never rest content: he would march from one conquest to another, and could be stopped only by force or the threat of force. Like water dropping on a stone, their voices suddenly broke through the crust of incredulity. They seemed to have been proved right; and the "appeasers" wrong. The change was not final or decisive. There was still a hope of conciliating Hitler under the determination to resist him, just as previously there had been an inclination to resist under the top layer of appeasement. But henceforth the appeasers were on the defensive, easily distracted from their work and hardly surprised at their own failure.

   This change of opinion had its effect on Chamberlain—another process which the historian cannot pin down. Perhaps the

Government Whips reported disillusionment on the back-benches. Perhaps Halifax once more heard the call of conscience in the watches of the night. Perhaps there was nothing so clear-cut, merely a succession of doubts and resentments which shook Chamberlain's previous confidence. Somehow, somewhere, it was brought home to him that he must respond more forcefully to Hitler's occupation of Prague. On 17 March Nevile Henderson was recalled from Berlin, ostensibly for consultation, really in protest. The same evening Chamberlain spoke in Birmingham, and asked: "Is this the last attack upon a small state, or is it to be followed by others? Is this, in fact, a step in the direction of an attempt to dominate the world by force?" He still justified the settlement of Munich. No one "could possibly have saved Czechoslovakia from invasion and destruction"; even after a victorious war, "never could we have reconstructed Czecho-slovakia as she was framed by the Treaty of Versailles". He was still "not prepared to engage this country by new unspecified commitments operating under conditions which cannot now be foreseen". But Chamberlain also responded to the call which had come from the Whips, from Halifax's conscience, or from his own. He would not sacrifice for peace "the liberties that we have enjoyed for hundreds of years"; and "any attempt to dominate the world by force was one which the Democracies must resist". The warning remained hypothetical. The challenge to world domination still seemed to Chamberlain "incredible". However, the warning was made.

Here was the turning-point in British policy. It was not meant as such. Chamberlain saw it as a change of emphasis, not a change of direction. Previously the British government often warned Hitler in private, while pursuing appeasement in public. Now they warned him publicly and went on with appeasement in private —sometimes publicly as well. The British acknowledged the German authorities in Bohemia; the Bank of England handed over to them £6,000,000 in Czech gold. Hoare thus defined the attitude of the British government in retrospect: "The lesson of Prague was not that further efforts for peace were futile, but rather that, without greater force behind them, negotiations and agreements with Hitler were of no permanent value".[1] A general settlement with Hitler remained the British object; and they put

[1] Templewood, *Nine Troubled Years*, 377.

obstacles in his way so that he would incline more readily to agreement. The British ministers did not fear defeat in war, though they naturally dreaded war for its own sake. They supposed that the defensive position of Great Britain and France was absolutely secure; they further supposed that, if Great Britain and France went to war with Germany, they would win; they even supposed that Hitler also recognised this. What they feared, with some justification, was that Hitler would count on their standing aside. They therefore took steps to demonstrate that they might not do so. Compulsory military service of a limited kind was introduced at the end of April; guarantees were distributed to supposedly threatened states. These steps were not practical, effective preparations for a general war; they were warnings, designed to avoid such a war. Many people complained that the steps were half-hearted. This was deliberate. The door remained open for negotiations; Hitler was always being pressed to enter. The British government strove to keep a balance. As warnings increased, so did inducements also. Hitler must be "deterred"; he must not be "provoked".

Such was the ideal pattern which British policy tried to follow. In practice, the British were more pushed along by events and less in control of them than they liked to think or than they made out later. Immediately after the German occupation of Prague, they expected, without any evidence, German moves elsewhere. The French thought Hitler might at once back Italian claims in North Africa; the British that he might launch a surprise attack on their fleet. Their ears were tuned for new alarms. One duly came. On 16 March, Tilea, the Rumanian minister in London, appeared at the foreign office with the news that his country was in imminent danger. On the following day he came again, more urgently: German troops might enter Rumania at any moment. The alarm was false. It was firmly denied by the Rumanian government and by the British minister at Bucharest. Rumania was indeed being forced within Germany's economic orbit—but by the pressure of planned foreign trade, not by the threat of German divisions. Countering the bilateralism of Schacht's invention with political guarantees was like hunting big game with a pack of fox-hounds—elegant, but ineffective. Perhaps Tilea was playing for a British loan when he raised the alarm. Perhaps he shared the British misunderstanding. At any rate,

British ministers swallowed the alarm; and dismissed its denial. Something must be done at once as a demonstration against further German advance. On 19 March Chamberlain himself drafted a declaration of collective security which the French, Soviet, and Polish governments were invited to sign. They would undertake "immediately to consult together as to what steps should be taken to offer joint resistance to any action which constitutes a threat to the political independence of any European State". Despite the vague and confused phraseology, the proposal was in fact geared to the supposed threat to Rumania— hence the choice of suggested signatories.

The French agreed at once. They were already committed to consult Great Britain on almost everything. Further consultation would not harm them; on the contrary, it would alleviate the burden of their alliance with Rumania, which was still in theoretical existence. The Russians agreed also: here was the collective security which they had always advocated. But they were determined not to be manoeuvred into resisting Germany by themselves. The "peace front" must be solid before they joined it. They therefore added a condition: France and Poland must sign first. France was no obstacle. Beck, however, was presented with a veto; and he used it. He still intended to balance between Russia and Germany; the proposed declaration would commit him to the Russian side. He was, however, prepared to sign a straight declaration with Great Britain. This, he thought, would strengthen his hand over Danzig without provoking German wrath. He took care not to tell the British that negotiations with Germany had reached deadlock. On the contrary, he implied that the question of Danzig would soon be settled. Once more, the British took alarm. They feared that Poland might draw closer to Germany, as had happened in 1938. The participation of Poland in "a peace front" seemed to them vital. She alone could make the threat of a second front a reality. As Bonnet put it, with Halifax's agreement, on 21 March:

It was absolutely essential to get Poland in, Russian help would only be effective if Poland were collaborating. If Poland collaborated, Russia could give very great assistance; if not, Russia could give much less.[1]

[1] Conversation between Halifax and Bonnet, 21 March 1939. *British Foreign Policy*, third series, iv. No. 458.

The British had a poor opinion of the Red Army. They exaggerated, without inquiry, the fighting strength of the Poles— "that great virile nation", in the words of Chamberlain. No doubt they were also relieved not to be associated with Bolshevik Russia; and to have hit on a substitute. Chamberlain wrote on 26 March: "I must confess to the most profound distrust of Russia. I have no belief whatever in her ability to maintain an effective offensive, even if she wanted to. And I distrust her motives, which seem to me to have little connection with our ideas of liberty, and to be concerned only with getting everyone else by the ears".[1] But simple geography was the determining factor. Poland was next door to Germany; Russia was not.

The British hardly reflected that, by choosing Poland, they might lose Russia. Halifax, with his gift for seeing both sides, had some inkling of it. He said on 22 March: "it would be unfortunate if we were now so to act as to give the Soviet Government the idea that we were pushing her to one side".[2] No steps were taken to remove this impression. None was thought necessary. The British were unshakably convinced that Soviet Russia and Nazi Germany were irreconcilable enemies. Hence there was no need to pay a price for Soviet friendship. Moscow would respond gratefully at a casual British nod. And if it did not, nothing was lost. "Benevolent neutrality" by Soviet Russia would be as useful as her participation in war— better indeed, since it would not alarm Poland and Rumania.[3] The "peace front" would be stronger, more stable, more respectable, if Soviet Russia stayed outside. At any rate, she could be invited to join, only if the others—and especially Poland—agreed.

Meanwhile, another alarm followed, which seemed to show that Germany was ceaselessly on the march. This alarm was at Memel. Memel lay at the extreme north-east corner of East Prussia. Though predominantly German in population like Danzig, it had been acquired, in a somewhat irregular way, by Lithuania after the first World war. The inhabitants wished to return to Germany. Hitherto Hitler had restrained them— perhaps designing to use Lithuania as an associate against

---

[1] Feiling, *Chamberlain*, 408.
[2] Anglo-French conversation, 22 March 1939. *British Foreign Policy*, third series. iv. No. 484.
[3] Halifax to Kennard, 27 March 1939. *Ibid.* No. 538.

Poland, more probably casting her as an object of compensation for Poland in case of a German-Polish alliance. The German occupation of Prague flung the people of Memel into ungovernable excitement; there was no longer any holding them. On 22 March the Lithuanian foreign minister came to Berlin, where he agreed to the immediate surrender of Memel. On 23 March the annexation went through; and Hitler, just back from Prague, visited his new acquisition. He went by sea, one of his few recorded sea voyages. He is said to have been seasick; and this perhaps gave him a practical cause of resentment against the Polish corridor. The annexation of Memel seemed to involve a deliberate German plan, long matured. No such plan can be found in the records. The question of Memel appears to have exploded of itself. In any case, the purpose of the annexation, if it had one, was to prepare a deal with Poland: Memel might conceivably be a substitute for Danzig. There was also no doubt an element of warning: what had happened at Memel could happen at Danzig also. But these consequences were not seriously considered; and Memel played no part in subsequent German-Polish relations.

At the time, the annexation gave an added urgency to British policy. The immediate creation of a "peace-front" seemed vital to the British; and here everything turned on Poland. If she could be won, the "peace front" would be solid; if she stayed out, it would hardly exist. The British did not suppose that Poland herself was in imminent danger from Germany. On the contrary, they feared that she might choose the German side, particularly with Memel in the market. The Poles, too, felt in no danger. They still proposed to follow, in regard to Germany, an independent, but parallel, course, as they had done during the Munich crisis. They were however disgruntled that Hitler had established Slovakia without consulting them—and without affording them any gains. They determined to assert their equality. On 21 March Lipski called on Ribbentrop and protested against the German behaviour over Slovakia—it "could only be regarded as a blow against Poland". Ribbentrop was in a weak position; and he knew it. To protect himself, he paraded grievances in his turn. Polish newspapers, he complained, were behaving badly: "a gradual stiffening in German-Polish relations was becoming apparent". Danzig must return to the Reich—this would rivet Poland to the German side. Then there could be a German guarantee for the Corridor, a non-aggression treaty for 25 years, and "a common policy" in the Ukraine.[1] Lipski was sent off to place this offer before Beck. Co-operation with Poland was still the German aim; Danzig merely the security for it. Hitler himself thought this. On 25 March he issued a directive:

> The Fuhrer *does not* wish to solve the Danzig question by force. He does not wish to drive Poland into the arms of Britain by this.

> A possible military occupation of Danzig could be contemplated *only* if L[ipski] gave an indication that the Polish Government could not justify voluntary cession of Danzig to their own people and that a *fait accompli* would make a solution easier to them.[2]

Hitler's objective was alliance with Poland, not her destruction. Danzig was a tiresome preliminary to be got out of the way. As before, Beck kept it in the way. So long as Danzig stood between Poland and Germany, he could evade the embarrassing offer of a German alliance, and so, as he thought, preserve Polish independence.

Beck's calculations worked, though not precisely as he intended. On 26 March Lipski returned to Berlin. He brought with him a firm refusal to yield over Danzig, though not a refusal to negotiate. Until this moment everything had gone on in secret, with no public hint of German-Polish estrangement. Now it blazed into the open. Beck, to show his resolve, called up Polish reservists. Hitler, to ease things along as he supposed, allowed the German press to write, for the first time, about the German minority in Poland. There were rumours of German troop-movements towards the Polish frontier, just as there had been similar rumours of German movements against Czechoslovakia on 21 May 1938. These new rumours were equally without foundation. They seem to have been started by the Poles. They were however aided on their way by some German generals who claimed to be opponents of Hitler. These generals "warned" the British government. With what object? So that Great Britain

---

[1] Memorandum by Ribbentrop, 21 March 1939. *German Foreign Policy*, series D. vi. No. 61.

[2] Directive by the Führer, 25 March 1939. *Ibid.* No. 99.

would deter Hitler by threatening him with war? Or so that she
would cheat him of his war by making the Poles yield over
Danzig? Perhaps it was a combination of the two, with an
inclination towards the second. At any rate, these generals
briefed the correspondent of the *News Chronicle* who was just
being expelled from Germany; and on 29 March he, in turn,
sounded the alarm at the foreign office. He found willing listeners.
After the occupation of Prague and the supposed threat to
Rumania, the British were ready to believe anything. They did
not give a thought to Danzig. They supposed that Poland herself
was in imminent danger, and likely to succumb. No alarm, it is
true, came from the British ambassador in Berlin. But the
foreign office had been misled by him on previous occasions, or so
it thought; now it preferred the reports of journalists. Immediate
action seemed necessary if Polish nerve were to be strengthened
and the "peace front" saved.

On 30 March Chamberlain drafted with his own hand an
assurance to the Polish government:

> If . . . . any action were taken which clearly threatened their
> independence, and which the Polish Government accordingly
> felt obliged to resist with their national forces, His Majesty's
> Government and the French Government would at once lend
> them all the support in their power.

That afternoon Beck was discussing with the British ambassador
how to implement his proposal of a week earlier for a general
declaration, when a telegram from London was brought in. The
ambassador read out Chamberlain's assurance. Beck accepted it
"between two flicks of the ash off his cigarette". Two flicks; and
British grenadiers would die for Danzig. Two flicks; and the
illusory great Poland, created in 1919, signed her death-warrant.
The assurance was unconditional: the Poles alone were to judge
whether it should be called upon. The British could no longer
press for concessions over Danzig; equally they could no longer
urge Poland to co-operate with Soviet Russia. Germany and
Russia were regarded in the West as two dangerous Powers,
dictatorial in their governments, ruthless in their methods. Yet
from this moment peace rested on the assumption that Hitler
and Stalin would be more sensible and cautious than Chamberlain
had been—that Hitler would continue to accept conditions at

Danzig which most Englishmen had long regarded as intolerable, and that Stalin would be ready to co-operate on terms of manifest inequality. These assumptions were not likely to be fulfilled.

There was another assumption in British policy: the assumption that France would trail along uncomplainingly wherever the British chose to lead her. The assurance of 30 March was actually communicated to Beck, in the name of France as well as of Great Britain, before the French had been consulted. They had no choice but to consent, though remarking sourly that, in their opinion, Poland was in no immediate danger. They had reason to be sulky. The British had no practical means with which to fulfil their assurance; it was a declaration of words only. Translated into practical terms, it could only be a British promise that the French would not go back on their alliance with Poland, as they had done on that with Czechoslovakia. Yet the French had solid information which made them doubt the fighting value of the Polish army; and they had little moral obligation to Poland, after the part which she had played against Czechoslovakia. The two flicks of Beck's ash decided this question also. In September 1989 France would fight for the shadow of her former greatness when she had sacrificed the substance at Munich the year before.

The British were no sooner committed than they realised the flaws in what they had done: no condition that the Poles would be reasonable over Danzig; no Polish promise of support for Rumania; no prospect that Poland would co-operate with Soviet Russia. They determined to remedy these flaws when Beck came to London in the first days of April. Their hopes were disappointed. Beck had stood up to Hitler without flinching; he was not likely to be moved by gentle promptings from Chamberlain and Halifax. With his usual "great power" arrogance, he was prepared to turn the one-sided British guarantee into a pact of mutual assistance—"the only basis that any self-respecting country would accept". Otherwise he was steadily obstinate. He "had not noticed any signs of dangerous military action on the part of Germany"; "no negotiations were proceeding" over Danzig; "the German Government had never contested Polish rights in Danzig, and had recently confirmed them"; "if he were to go by what the Germans themselves said, he would say that the gravest question was the colonial question". Thus, he as good as implied that Poland was conferring a favour on Great Britain by agreeing to an alliance. But the alliance, he insisted, must be exclusive between the two; the "peace front" and collective security vanished from the scene. Extending the agreement to Rumania would be very dangerous. This would drive Hungary into the arms of Germany; and "in case of a conflict between Poland and Germany, the help that Poland could expect from Rumania would be rather negligible". Beck was even firmer against any association with Soviet Russia. "There were two things which it was impossible for Poland to do, namely, to make her policy dependent upon either Berlin or upon Moscow. . . . Any pact of mutual assistance between Poland and Soviet Russia would bring an immediate hostile reaction from Berlin and would probably accelerate the outbreak of a conflict." The British could negotiate with Soviet Russia if they liked; they could even undertake obligations towards her. "These obligations would in no way extend the obligations undertaken by Poland".[1]

Chamberlain and Halifax accepted this virtuoso performance with hardly a protest. Beck's statements received none of the sceptical criticism which had earlier been given to Daladier's. There was no attempt to question Polish strength or to urge the merits of conciliation. The false alarm of 80 March had hurried the British government into guaranteeing Poland. Now Beck could dictate his terms, and took full advantage of it. Poland did not join a "peace front". There was no promise of Polish support for Rumania; and there was virtually a Polish veto on closer relations with Soviet Russia. The British were given no opening to mediate over Danzig. The Anglo-Polish alliance was to be an isolated affair, with no associates except France and no general relevance. Beck did not believe that Poland was menaced by Germany; he simply wanted to strengthen his bargaining position over Danzig. The British cared nothing for Danzig; or, if they did, sympathised with the German case. They had intended only some vague and generous gesture to moderate the speed of Germany's advance. The one small loophole left to them was that the Anglo-Polish alliance remained provisional—the "formal agreement" still to be settled, the wish expressed that others, including Soviet Russia, should be brought in. But the loophole

[1] British conversations with Beck, 4–6 April 1989. *British Foreign Policy*, third series. v. No. 1, 2 and 10.

had no real existence; Beck could keep it closed at will. The British government were trapped not so much by their guarantee to Poland, as by their previous relations with Czechoslovakia. With her they had imposed concession; towards her they had failed to honour their guarantee. They could not go back on their word again, if they were to keep any respect in the world or with their own people. The chance of success in war was probably less; the German case stronger over Danzig than it had been over the Sudeten Germans. None of this mattered. The British government were committed to resistance. Beck reaped where Benes had sown.

CHAPTER TEN

The War of Nerves

THE Anglo-Polish alliance was a revolutionary event in international affairs. The British had entered into their first peacetime commitment to a continental Power only three years before, when they made their alliance with France. Then they had stressed that it must be unique, and strictly limited to a defensive purpose in Western Europe. Now they plunged into alliance with a country far in Eastern Europe, and one which, until almost the day before, had been judged not worth the bones of a British grenadier. The policy of the other Powers revolved round this startling new fact. The Germans planned to dissolve the Anglo-Polish alliance; the Russians to exploit it. The French and Italians both dreaded its implications for themselves and sought, in vain, a way of escape. Europe hummed with diplomatic activity; and London was its centre. British policy had, without design, made Danzig the decisive question for 1939, just as, with more deliberation, it presented the Sudeten Germans as the decisive question in 1938. But with this difference. The Sudeten German question was asked of the Czechs and the French. It was they who were pressed to make concessions, or to face the risk of war. In 1939 the British were themselves at question, faced with the choice between resistance or conciliation. British ministers preferred the second course. They were still the men of peace who had rejoiced at the settlement of Munich. They still hated the prospect of war; still hoped to find a way out by means of negotiation. Moreover, with mounting Japanese pressure in the Far East, they had increasing desire to turn their backs on Europe. Besides, in taking a stand over Danzig they were on peculiarly weak ground. Danzig was the most justified of German grievances: a city of exclusively German population which manifestly wished to return to the Reich and which Hitler himself restrained only with difficulty. The solution, too, seemed

215

peculiarly easy. Halifax never wearied of suggesting that Danzig should return to German sovereignty, with safeguards for Polish trade.

Hitler wanted this also. The destruction of Poland had been no part of his original project. On the contrary, he had wished to solve the question of Danzig so that Germany and Poland could remain on good terms. Was Polish obstinacy then the only thing which stood between Europe and a peaceful outcome? By no means. Previously Danzig might have been settled without implying any upheaval in international relations. Now it had become the symbol of Polish independence; and, with the Anglo-Polish alliance, of British independence as well. Hitler no longer wished merely to fulfil German national aspirations or to satisfy the inhabitants of Danzig. He aimed to show that he had imposed his will on the British and on the Poles. They, on their side, had to deny him this demonstration. All parties aimed at a settlement by negotiation, but only after victory in a war of nerves. There is, of course, an alternative explanation. Some, or all, of the parties may have been driving deliberately for war. There can hardly be any who believe this of Poland; few, even in Germany, who now believe that the British were planning the "encirclement" of Germany in order to impose again the "slavery" of Versailles. Many however believe that Hitler was a modern Attila, loving destruction for its own sake and therefore bent on war without thought of policy. There is no arguing with such dogmas. Hitler was an extraordinary man; and they may well be true. But his policy is capable of rational explanation; and it is on these that history is built. The escape into irrationality is no doubt easier. The blame for war can be put on Hitler's Nihilism instead of on the faults and failures of European statesmen— faults and failures which their public shared. Human blunders, however, usually do more to shape history than human wickedness. At any rate, this is a rival dogma which is worth developing, if only as an academic exercise. Of course Hitler's nature and habits played their part. It was easy for him to threaten, and hard for him to conciliate. This is far from saying that he foresaw, or deliberately projected, the European dominance which he seemed to have achieved by 1942. All statesmen aim to win. The size of the winnings often surprises them.

Rational causes have been found for a deliberate German drive to war in 1939. One is economic; another dogma, this time of crudely Marxist kind. Industrial recovery, it is suggested, was presenting Germany with a crisis of over-production. Faced with the tariff walls of other Powers, she had to conquer new markets or burst at the seams. There is little evidence for this dogma. Germany's problem was credit inflation, not over-production, as Schacht had warned when he resigned in 1938. There was too much government paper and not enough productive power to absorb it. Production was being flogged on, not choking with its own excess. When war came, Germany's conquests—far from providing markets—were greedily exploited for the war-machine. Every satellite country except Hungary had a large credit-balance in Berlin at the end of the war—the Germans, that is, had taken much and exported little. Even so, German armament production was cut back in 1940 and again in 1941; the strain was too great. Hence the economic argument ran against war, not in its favour. Or, at best, the argument was self-consuming. Germany needed the prizes of war, solely in order to make war more successfully.

German armaments in themselves provide a second possible reason why Germany should drive to war. Germany had established a lead in armaments over the other Powers; and this lead would gradually waste away. Hitler himself used this argument, but only in the summer of 1939 when already committed to war; and it was not much more serious than his other argument that he wanted to get the war over in order to devote himself to artistic creation. Previously he had asserted, with more truth, that German preponderance would be at its greatest. between 1943 and 1945; and, like all such figures, these really meant "this year, next year, sometime, . . ." The German generals best qualified to judge, argued steadily against war in 1939 on technical grounds; and the better qualified, the firmer their opposition. Hitler did not deny their case; he rejected it as irrelevant. He was intending to succeed without war, or at any rate only with a war so nominal as hardly to be distinguished from diplomacy. He was not projecting a major war; hence it did not matter that Germany was not equipped for one. Hitler deliberately ruled out the "rearmament in depth" which was pressed on him by his technical advisers. He was not interested in preparing for a long war against the Great Powers. He chose instead "rearmament in width"—a frontline army without reserves, adequate only for a quick strike. Under Hitler's direction, Germany was equipped to win the war of nerves—the only war he understood and liked; she was not equipped to conquer Europe. Great Britain and France were already secure from a strictly defensive point of view. As the years passed, they would become more so. But Germany's advantage for the immediate blow would remain. Nothing would be lost by the passage of time; and diplomatically much might be gained. In considering German armament we escape from the mystic regions of Hitler's psychology and find an answer in the realm of fact. The answer is clear. The state of German armament in 1939 gives the decisive proof that Hitler was not contemplating general war, and probably not intending war at all.

A deeper reason remains why Germany might have sought war in 1939. The world balance was moving against Germany not so much on the immediate plane of armaments as in reserves of economic strength. Germany was a greater Power economically than either Great Britain or France—slightly greater than both put together. Great Britain still ranked as a Great Power; France was almost over the edge into second-class status. This balance would tip steadily in Germany's favour. The picture was different when the rest of the world was considered. The United States had greater economic resources than the three European Great Powers combined; and her lead increased with the years. It would have made sense if Hitler had planned to unite Europe against the "American danger". He did not do so. For some obscure reason—perhaps the wilful ignorance of a land-bound Austrian—he never took the United States seriously, either in economics or politics. He supposed that, like the Western Powers, they were rotted by democracy; and Roosevelt's moral exhortations increased his contempt. It seemed inconceivable to him that these exhortations could ever be translated into material force; and he had no idea that he was bringing a formidable enemy down upon Germany when he declared war against the United States in December 1941.

The economic advance of Soviet Russia, on the other hand, obsessed Hitler. It was indeed startling. During the ten years between 1929 and 1939, while the manufacturing production of Germany increased by 27 per cent. and that of Great Britain by

17 per cent., Soviet Russia's increased by 400 per cent.; and the process was only beginning. By 1938 Soviet Russia was the second industrial Power in the world, ranking only after the United States. She had still far to go: her population was still impoverished, her resources were hardly tapped. But Germany had not much time if she were to escape being overshadowed, and still less if she hoped to seize the Soviet Ukraine. Here again, it would have made sense for Hitler to plan a great war against Soviet Russia. But, though he often talked of such a war, he did not plan it. German armaments were not designed for such a war. Hitler's rearmament in width was only intended to reinforce a diplomatic war of nerves. Even the rearmament in depth which the German generals wanted would only have equipped Germany for a long-drawn-out war of exhaustion on the Western front such as was fought during the first World war. The Germans had to improvise furiously when they went to war against Soviet Russia in June 1941; and they failed to achieve a quick decisive victory there largely because they had altogether neglected to prepare transport for a war of this nature. In the end, it is hard to tell whether Hitler took the project of war against Soviet Russia seriously; or whether it was an attractive illusion with which he hoped to mesmerise Western statesmen. If he took it seriously, this makes the actual war of 1939—not a war against Soviet Russia, but a war against the Western Powers, with Germany and Soviet Russia halfway towards an alliance—more inexplicable than ever. Or rather the old, simple explanation reasserts itself. The war of 1939, far from being premeditated, was a mistake, the result on both sides of diplomatic blunders.

Hitler contributed little to the course of diplomacy between April and August 1939. As on previous occasions, he was content to prepare and to wait, confident that the obstacles would somehow disintegrate before him. The example of the Czech crisis was always in his mind. There he had been faced with a strong Czech army and an apparently firm alliance between France and Czechoslovakia. In the end the French gave way, and the Czechs also. It would be the same over Poland. He said of the Western statesmen: "Our opponents are poor creatures [little worms]. I saw them at Munich". He no longer troubled himself about the French. He knew that they would go wherever the British led them, though acting as a brake on the road to war. This time the

British would have to decide more directly; and he expected them
to decide for concession. Did he also expect the Poles to give way
without war? This is harder to answer. On 3 April the armed
forces were told to be ready to attack Poland at any time after
1 September, together with an assurance that this would happen
only if Poland were isolated—an assurance which Hitler repeated
in rather wilder form on 23 May. But these preparations were
necessary whether Hitler planned to get his way by war or by
threats. They tell us nothing of his real intentions; and probably
he had not settled them himself. The war of nerves was enough to
be going on with. Here Hitler laid down his challenge clearly. On
28 April he repudiated both the non-aggression Pact with Poland
of 1934 and the Anglo-German Naval Agreement of 1935. On the
same day he addressed the Reichstag. He recited his offers to
Poland, and denounced Polish provocation: the Germans wished
to settle the question of Danzig by free negotiation, the Poles
answered by relying on force. He was ready to make a new agreement, but only if the Poles changed their attitude—that is, if
they gave way over Danzig and abandoned their alliance with
Great Britain. He spoke of the British in very different terms:
praised the British Empire as "an inestimable factor of value for
the whole of human economic and cultural life"; rejected the idea
of destroying it as "nothing but the effluence of human wanton
destructiveness"; and looked forward warmly to a new agreement
when the British had come to their senses. Here, too, the price
was the same: concession over Danzig and abandonment of the
alliance with Poland. Having thus stated his terms, Hitler withdrew into silence. He was beyond the reach of ambassadors,
Ribbentrop almost as much so. There were no further diplomatic
exchanges with Poland before the outbreak of war, and none
directly with Great Britain until the middle of August.

Decision therefore rested with the British; or rather it was
dictated to them by the Anglo-Polish alliance. They could not
escape from this even if they would. Not only were they the
prisoners of their own public opinion. They recognised that, by
retreating from it, they would merely return to the difficulties
which they were in before. They were ready, even eager, to give
way over Danzig; but only on condition that Hitler then settled
down to peace. He would be satisfied only if he received Danzig
without conditions. In any case, the Poles refused to yield an

inch. The British discovered belatedly that Beck had been "rather less than frank" in regard to Danzig: he had given them the impression that there was no immediate problem, when in fact Hitler was already pressing his demands. They used this as an excuse to ask that Beck should keep them better informed in future; and added a reminder that the guarantee would come into operation only "if the Polish Government decided to offer resistance in a case where Polish independence was 'clearly' threatened".[1] Here was a cautious hint that Great Britain was not committed to maintaining the *status quo* at Danzig. Beck was unrepentant: "no *casus belli* would arise in connexion with the Danzig question unless the Germans took forcible measures there"[2]—not a cheerful outlook from the British point of view. Neither party in fact dared discuss Danzig openly for fear of a quarrel; they therefore discussed nothing, each hoping to get his way at the decisive moment. The formal alliance, foreshadowed in April, was not concluded until 25 August.

In other less direct ways, the British did their best to hold the Poles back. In the staff talks held between the two countries, the British revealed nothing; but then they had nothing to reveal. Obviously the Poles did not count on direct military aid; all the more reason for them to seek financial assistance. Here the British were peculiarly obstinate. The Poles asked for a loan of £60 million in cash. The British first replied that they had no cash and could only offer credits; then they insisted that the credits must be spent in Great Britain; finally, having reduced the figure to £8 million, they explained that, as British armament factories were fully employed, the credit could not be used in any case. No credit had passed by the time war broke out; no British bomb or rifle went to Poland. It is unlikely that the Poles were mollified by Halifax's explanation: "In the event of war, one of the strongest weapons in the hand of Great Britain must be that of economic staying power, which accordingly it was essential not to impair".[3] This strange behaviour expressed the dual nature of British policy. The British were as much concerned to moderate the Poles as to restrain Hitler. Their hope was un-

[1] Halifax to Kennard, 8 May 1939. *British Foreign Policy*, third series. v. No. 346.

[2] Kennard to Halifax, 4 May 1939. *Ibid.* No. 355.

[3] Halifax to Kennard. 1 June 1939. *Ibid.* No. 692.

availing. Beck was not Benes. To his mind, a single step on the road of concession would inevitably lead to Munich; therefore no step was taken. Lord Runciman had no chance to pack his bags for another continental excursion in 1939.

The British hankered after another expedient which had proved useful in the previous year. They still hoped that Mussolini might be called in at some time as a restraining influence on Hitler. This line, too, was as good as dead. The momentary annoyance when Hitler occupied Prague was Mussolini's last splutter of indignation. He now played his own act of aggression by transforming the Italian protectorate over Albania into open annexation. This led to great diplomatic activity—the British guaranteeing Greece and, for no particular reason, Rumania; negotiating an alliance with Turkey which was fated never to operate. Such moves, though swelling the volume of foreign office papers, had little relevance to the great question of Germany. Italy, like France, was now on the side-lines; the fate of both countries determined by the actions of their greater partners. The French flung themselves into repudiating Italian claims in North Africa. Here was an opponent of their own size whom they were ready to defy. Mussolini, on his side, finally made the jump into formal alliance with Germany. The "Pact of Steel" was signed on 22 May, committing the two countries to wage war in common. No doubt Mussolini hoped that the Pact would give him some say in German counsels. Once pledged to support Germany in war, he hoped to be able to determine when the war should take place; and he tried to insist that Italy could be ready for war only in 1942 or 1943. The Germans attached less weight to the Pact. They took it up almost by accident, as a consolation prize for failing to secure a Triple Alliance with Japan.

The Far East presents a factor which is still difficult to assess in the diplomacy of 1939. Clearly there were links between the situation in Europe and that in the Far East. But what were they? The Japanese were at war with China; they were also encroaching on foreign interests there, and especially on the British settlements. Obviously the British would have liked to finish with Europe in order to defend their position in China; but it is hard to discover how far this influenced the practical course of their policy. On the other side, the Germans wanted to increase

British difficulties in the Far East; and the Japanese wished to increase them in Europe. There was a tug-of-war between the two "aggressor" Powers which the Japanese won. The Germans tried to turn the Anti-Comintern Pact into an alliance against all comers. The Japanese would only agree to co-operate against Russia. No doubt they hoped to extract concessions from the British without a war; perhaps they were deterred by the thought of the American navy. Most of all, they doubted whether a general alliance would be followed by war in Europe; rather there would be a new Munich at the expense of Poland, and the Japanese would be left alone against the British. The negotiations between Germany and Japan ran away to nothing. The Japanese squeezed concessions out of the British, who steadily gave way. Conflict in the Far East was postponed; and this made conflict in Europe more likely.

There was a further obstacle to co-operation between Germany and Japan, though neither side brought it into the open. The Japanese wanted support against Soviet Russia. The Germans, once the standard-bearers of anti-Communism, were now swinging in the opposite direction. From the moment that Poland became the immediate target of German hostility, Soviet Russia was automatically transformed for Germany into a possible neutral, or perhaps even an ally. Nor were the Russians important only for Germany: every European Power had to reckon with them. This was an epoch-making event. The year 1939 saw the outbreak of the second World war. In longer perspective it may appear even more significant that it saw the return of Soviet Russia as a Great Power, for the first time since 1917. Soviet Russia after the Bolshevik revolution had often presented a "problem"; international Communism had been a political danger, at any rate potentially. But Soviet Russia had not counted as a Great Power. When Litvinov made proposals at the League of Nations, it was with the air of a spokesman from another planet. The Western Powers had never seriously contemplated co-operation with Soviet Russia, despite the Franco-Soviet Pact. Neither they nor the Germans expected Soviet intervention during the Czech crisis of 1938. Soviet Russia seemed infinitely remote. This was in large part due to the cleavage in political outlook and to the long tradition, on both sides, of virtual non-recognition. It had also a practical basis. Soviet

Russia was truly cut off from Europe so long as the *cordon
sanitaire* existed. If she acted at all, it must be from outside,
much like Japan or the United States. This changed once Poland
was called in question. Europe had arrived on Russia's doorstep.
Whether she liked it or not, she had become again a European
Power.

What part would Russia play now that she had returned to
Europe, or Europe had returned to her? All the Powers asked
this great question. The British asked it; so did the French, the
Poles, and the Germans. The Russians asked it persistently of
themselves. It was impossible at the outset to foresee the answer,
or even to formulate alternatives. Most political questions have
long antecedents. Statesmen can draw on their previous experience and can go further along lines already laid down. Here
there were few precedents, and such as there were led in the
wrong direction—back to the time of Russian isolation and withdrawal. These misleading precedents had some influence. The
British could not shake off the habit of treating Soviet Russia as
a power of little importance; the Russians were still tempted to
assume that they could turn their backs on Europe at will. The
Germans had an advantage here. They had a precedent of a sort
in the shape of Rapallo and the subsequent Soviet-German
friendship. But times had changed. At Rapallo two defeated and
apprehensive Powers agreed not to be played off against each
other. This provided little guidance for relations between what
were now the two greatest Powers on the European continent.
Once more Hitler was content to wait until events supplied a
policy for him. Anti-Communism was damped down in Germany,
its place taken by anti-semitism. Hints were dropped that the
Germans would like to increase their trade with Soviet Russia or
even to improve political relations. No attempt was made on the
German side to work out what form this improvement might
take; and the Russians were still more reticent. The initiative
remained elsewhere.

The French, at the other end of the scale, were clear what they
wanted: there should be a straight military alliance between
Soviet Russia and the Western Powers. The French had no faith
in appeasing Hitler; and therefore equally little fear that alliance
with the Soviets might provoke him. They believed that Hitler
would be deterred only by an overwhelming show of force; and

the Soviet alliance would help to provide it. If the show failed and it came to war, the Russian threat would again divide the German forces, as it had done in 1914; and if the German attack were on Russia, the French would remain secure behind the Maginot line. The French had no thought for Polish objections; rather these made them the more eager. French obligation towards Poland was at its lowest ebb. The defection of Poland had destroyed any possibility of an eastern front during the Czech crisis; and the French were now ready to repay Polish ingratitude in kind. Gamelin had a poor opinion of the Polish army, and inclined, though with much hesitation, to rate the Soviet army higher. If therefore Poland used the excuse of a Franco-Soviet alliance to repudiate her own alliance with France, so much the better from the French point of view. They would have discarded a liability and acquired an asset. On 10 April Bonnet told the Soviet ambassador that they should settle the terms of military co-operation between themselves, and added: "We should then have to decide the attitude to take in case either Rumania or Poland refused this aid".[1] This was a simple, but an impossible, solution. The French might disregard their alliance with Poland; they could not disregard that with Great Britain, on which their entire position in the world depended. The Anglo-Polish alliance was a catastrophe for France. Since the British had no force of their own for a continental war, the alliance was in effect a British guarantee that France would not fail the Poles as she had failed the Czechs. Yet this was exactly what the French wished to do. Once their road of escape was barred, the only hope for them was to drag the British into alliance with Soviet Russia also.

The promptings did not come only from France. The need for a Soviet alliance was obvious to every competent British observer, immediately the guarantee was given to Poland. Churchill made the point in the House of Commons on 3 April:

> To stop here with a guarantee to Poland would be to halt in No-man's Land under fire of both trench lines and without the shelter of either. . . . Having begun to create a Grand Alliance against aggression, we cannot afford to fail. We shall be in mortal danger if we fail. . . . The worst folly, which no one

[1] Bonnet, *Fin d'une Europe*, 178.

proposes we should commit, would be to chill and drive away any natural co-operation which Soviet Russia in her own deep interests feels it necessary to afford.[1]

Lloyd George spoke even more strongly:

If we are going in without the help of Russia we are walking into a trap. It is the only country whose arms can get there. . . . If Russia has not been brought into this matter because of certain feelings the Poles have that they do not want the Russians there, it is for us to declare the conditions, and unless the Poles are prepared to accept the only conditions with which we can successfully help them, the responsibility must be theirs.[2]

These arguments came repeatedly from the Opposition benches. The conflicting groups in the Labour party especially could re-unite on the principle of alliance with Soviet Russia—some on practical military grounds, others from Socialist principle. The practical argument was indeed almost irresistible. It lay on the map for all to see; and Chamberlain's critics now first caught the public ear effectively. Previously they had seemed to be preaching an ideological war against Hitler; now Chamberlain seemed to be practising ideological aloofness towards the Soviet Union. This criticism by the Opposition undoubtedly pushed Chamberlain towards negotiation with Moscow; but at the same time it increased his reluctance. The British government would be discredited either way, whatever the outcome. If the negotiations failed, they would be blamed; if they succeeded, Churchill, Lloyd George, and the Labour party would be vindicated. Chamberlain was a good hater, at any rate in domestic politics; and when he peered across the distance towards the Kremlin, he saw there faces which reminded him of the Opposition front bench.

There were other considerations which made the British government hesitate. With the narrow moralism of a reformed drunkard, men who had not scrupled to desert Benes now felt themselves. bound to observe Beck's every whim. The British were guaranteeing the rights of small nations. How then could they override Polish objections to being involved with Soviet Russia? Halifax emphasised this in the House of Lords: "Our

---

[1] *Hansard*, fifth series, 345, 2500–2.
[2] *Ibid.*, 345, 2507–10.

policy is founded on the principle that the rights of smaller States shall not be set aside by the stronger, that force shall not be the deciding factor in the relations between peoples, and that negotiations should not be overshadowed or overborne by constraint".[1] The British government were not thinking, as their critics were, in terms of an inevitable war. They were not even aspiring to "deter" Hitler by an overwhelming show of strength. They were seeking to make a moral demonstration; and the moral effect of alliance with Soviet Russia would be lost if it were accompanied by protests from the smaller states. The moral effect might even count to Hitler's credit. The accusation of "encirclement" would be justified. "It would be said that—abandoning any further attempt to remain impartial—we were deliberately aligning for war between rival groups of Powers". Italy, Spain, Japan would be offended; "nor must it be forgotten that the Vatican regard Moscow even to a greater extent than Berlin as Anti-Christ".[2]

The British government were striving to preserve the peace of Europe, not to win a war. Their policy was determined by morality, not by strategical calculations. Even their morality was blinkered. They recognised the force of German grievances against the settlement of Versailles. Yet it never occurred to them that Soviet Russia might feel little eagerness to maintain in Eastern Europe a *status quo* which stemmed essentially from the two humiliating treaties of Brest-Litovsk and Riga. Russian reluctance to support a peace front irritated them; but any Russian readiness to go to war against Germany alarmed them more. What they wanted was that Russian assistance should be turned on and off at will like a tap; and they, or maybe the Poles, should alone be entitled to turn it. Halifax explained their attitude to Gafencu, the Rumanian foreign minister: "It was desirable not to estrange Russia, but always to keep her in play".[3] Soviet statesmen at the time suspected the British of planning to involve Russia in war with Germany, while remaining neutral themselves; and the accusation has been repeated by Soviet historians. This is to misunderstand the British outlook.

[1] 19 April 1939, *Hansard*, fifth series, 112, 697–8.
[2] Foreign Office memorandum, 22 May 1939. *British Foreign Policy*, third series. v. No. 576.
[3] Halifax conversation with Gafencu, 26 April 1939. *Ibid*. No. 280.

The British did not want war at all: neither on their own part against Germany, nor on hers against Russia. The outcome of general war in Europe must be disastrous from the British point of view. For either Germany or Russia would win; and whichever happened, Great Britain's position as a Great Power would be diminished, if not destroyed. There was a singular appropriateness in the Anglo-Polish alliance. Both countries were profiteers from the extraordinary circumstances in which the first World war ended, with both Germany and Russia defeated. Poland owed to these circumstances her illusory independence; Great Britain owed to them a greatness and authority which, if not quite as illusory, could be maintained with little effort. Both countries wanted the world to stand still as it had been created in 1919. Poland refused to go with either Germany or Soviet Russia. The British refused to contemplate a decisive victory for either. A Bolshevik conquest of eastern Europe was repugnant to most Englishmen. So far Soviet suspicions were justified. But it also seemed remote. The British expected the Germans to win in the event of war against Russia alone; and this, though perhaps less repugnant to them, was even more alarming. A Germany which dominated Europe from the Rhine to the Urals would, in the British view, at once turn against the British and French empires. Hence, when the Soviet rulers accused the British of planning a Soviet-German war, they flattered themselves in two ways. First, the British were too little perturbed by the "red peril" to desire its destruction in war; second, they were convinced that the Germans would win too easily and too dangerously.

There was one fear about Soviet Russia which truly moved British statesmen when they considered possible developments: the fear that she might stay out while the other European Powers tore each other to pieces. "It was essential, if there must be a war, to try to involve the Soviet Union in it, otherwise at the end of the war the Soviet Union, with her army intact and England and Germany in ruins, would dominate Europe".[1] Here, in another version, was the policy of the tap to be turned on or off at (British) will. But suppose the Soviet rulers declined this accommodating role? The British were warned again and again,

[1] Foreign Office memorandum, 22 May 1989. *British Foreign Policy*, third series. v. No. 576.

that Soviet Russia and Germany might reach some agreement; or, at the very least, that Soviet Russia might sit back while the rest of Europe ran into trouble. They were warned by Seeds, their ambassador in Moscow; they were warned by Daladier; they were even warned indirectly by Goering, who disliked the prospective pro-Soviet line of German policy. Chamberlain, Halifax, and the foreign office remained incorrigible. The warnings were dismissed time and again as "inherently improbable".[1] Did the British not see that, with the Anglo-Polish alliance, they were already pledged to fight in defence of Soviet Russia's frontiers? How then could they suppose that Soviet aid was anything other than an uncovenanted benefit? It is impossible to discover a rational answer to these questions. If British diplomacy seriously aspired to alliance with Soviet Russia in 1939, then the negotiations towards this end were the most incompetent transactions since Lord North lost the American colonies. Perhaps incompetence is the simple explanation. The British were overwhelmed by the difficulties of their position—devising policy for a World Power, which wanted to turn its back on Europe and yet had to take the lead in European affairs. They distributed guarantees in eastern Europe, and aspired to build up military alliances. Yet what they wanted in Europe was peace and peaceful revision at the expense of the states which they had guaranteed. They distrusted both Hitler and Stalin; yet strove for peace with the one and for alliance with the other. It is not surprising that they failed in both aims.

The confusion was heightened by personal differences of outlook. Chamberlain never wanted association with Soviet Russia except on impossible terms. He was dragged along by Halifax, who—himself sceptical—was dragged along by the Foreign Office. Even the permanent officials distrusted Hitler more than they trusted Stalin; and, while quick to see the dangers in alliance with Soviet Russia, rarely saw its advantages. Little would have been attempted had it not been for the constant pressure in the House of Commons and from public opinion; and ministers yielded to this pressure not so much because they thought it was right as because they could devise no alternative. But public opinion was not all one way. The demand for a Soviet

[1] Foreign Office minute on Henderson to Halifax, 8 May 1989. *British Foreign Policy*, third series. v. No. 413.

alliance was vocal; the hostility to Soviet Russia, though less vocal, was perhaps stronger—particularly among Conservative back-benchers. There was widespread relief at the final failure— indeed it removed a psychological obstacle to war. The logical consequence of British policy, if such a thing can be imagined, was Soviet neutrality, though the British were highly indignant when this consequence duly worked out.

Had the Soviet rulers on their side a logical aim clearly envisaged from the outset? No one knows the answer except maybe the forgotten exile Molotov; and he is unlikely to reveal it. We have no scrap of evidence for the internal workings of Soviet policy. We do not know what Soviet ambassadors reported to Moscow or whether the Soviet government read their reports. We do not know what Soviet statesmen said to each other or what they were told by their technical advisers. Where evidence is lacking, historians can only make conjectures from outward appearance—or from their own prejudices. Soviet historians (who seem to be as ill-informed as we are) assume the righteous-ness of their own government and the wickedness of others. In their version, Soviet Russia strove whole-heartedly for a peace front; Great Britain and France designed to lure her into isolated war against Germany; and Stalin escaped from this danger by a stroke of genius at the last moment. Western his-torians, loyally fighting the cold war, see things the other way round. According to their more extreme version, the Soviet government was bent on a deal with Germany all along; and negotiated with Great Britain and France only in order to provoke a German offer. Alternatively, Soviet Russia was negotiating with both sides, watching the bids mount up until she closed with the more satisfactory. In one view, the Soviet rulers were deliberately seeking to provoke war in Europe; in another, they were determined, at any rate, to keep out of war themselves. Though there may be some truth in these views, they have a common defect. They attribute to the Soviet leaders a foreknowledge of later events; and, however wicked these states-men might be, it is doubtful whether the Devil shared his prerogative with them to this extent. For instance, the Soviet government are held to have known from the start that Hitler would go to war on 1 September, and to have timed their tactics with this in mind. Perhaps Hitler knew this; the Soviet statesmen

did not. On this, as on other subjects, historians would do well to
bear in mind the wise saying of Maitland's: "It is very hard to
remember that events now long in the past were once in the
future".

Some of the designs, ascribed to Soviet leaders, break down
on close examination. They are generally held, for example, to
have spun out the negotiations with the Western Powers so as to
provoke a high offer from Hitler at the decisive moment. The
diplomatic exchange shows that the delays came from the West
and that the Soviet government answered with almost breath-
taking speed. The British made their first tentative suggestion
on 15 April; the Soviet counter-proposal came two days later, on
17 April. The British took three weeks before designing an
answer on 9 May; the Soviet delay was then five days. The
British then took thirteen days; the Soviet again took five. Once
more the British took thirteen days; the Soviet government
answered within twenty-four hours. Thereafter the pace quick-
ened. The British tried again in five days' time; the Soviet answer
came within twenty-four hours. The British next needed nine
days; the Soviet two. Five more days for the British; one day
for the Russians. Eight days on the British side; Soviet answer
on the same day. British delay of six days; Soviet answer the
same day. With that the exchange virtually ended. If dates mean
anything, the British were spinning things out, the Russians were
anxious to conclude. There is other evidence that the British
treated the negotiations in a casual way, more to placate public
opinion than to achieve anything. Anthony Eden offered to go
to Moscow on a special mission; Chamberlain turned down his
offer. A member of the foreign office who was sent to Moscow
for some obscure purpose (certainly not to conclude an alliance)
wrote home light-heartedly on 21 June: "I daresay we shall
arrive at something in the end. When I say 'in the end' I recall
a remark of Naggiar's [the French ambassador] this afternoon
that he will probably have reached the age limit and gone into
retirement before I get away from Moscow".[1] Would the official
have written in this irresponsible way if he and his superiors had
really regarded the Soviet alliance as making all the difference
between peace and war?

[1] Strang to Sargent, 21 June 1939. *British Foreign Policy*, third series.
vi. No. 122.

There is another curious puzzle connected with these negotiations. They were conducted with a lack of secrecy remarkable even at a time when old-style secret diplomacy had everywhere broken down. All the more or less official negotiations before the second World war were a matter of public knowledge; strange and unlikely envoys had to be used when real secrecy was desired. Still the details did not usually leak out at once. In the Anglo-Soviet negotiations, however, they often reached the press before they reached the other party; and when they did not reach the press they reached the Germans. Leakages of this sort are almost impossible to trace accurately; and it is rash to deduce too much from them. It appears, for what this is worth, that the Soviet government was the source from which the press derived its information, much to the annoyance of the British side. Soviet offers were always published at once; British proposals only when they had been communicated in Moscow. On the other hand, the German foreign ministry received its information from "a reliable source", sometimes before this reached the press and often before it was known in Moscow. This reliable source must therefore have been someone in the British foreign office, either acting on instructions or betraying secrets to the Germans on his own initiative. Some conclusions may be cautiously extracted from these facts. The Soviet government cannot have been concerned to inform or influence their own people; Soviet public opinion could be manoeuvred at a nod. The revelations were aimed then at British public opinion, presumably with the intention of forcing the hand of the British government. This would imply that the Soviet government genuinely wanted the alliance. They may have been playing a more elaborate political game, hoping to provoke in Great Britain a political upheaval which would bring the Left to power. But even this must have been desired in order to secure alliance. The "reliable source" in London, on the other hand, must have been seeking to alarm the Germans and so to provoke an Anglo-German compromise, if he had a political intention at all. Of course there may be cruder explanations. The Russians may merely have been anxious to demonstrate their own rectitude, as they have often done on later occasions; and the London informant may merely have been acting for motives of personal profit. The most we can safely say is that the faults were not all on one side.

Speculation is more rewarding if we forget about the outcome and try to reconstruct the Soviet picture of the world. Without doubt, the Soviet statesmen regarded all foreign Powers with intense suspicion, and were ready to be unscrupulous in their turn. They appreciated, half-consciously, that they were engaged in serious diplomacy for the first time. Foreign policy had been left to second-rank Communists—first Chicherin, then Litvinov (neither of them members of the Politburo)—ever since Trotsky ceased to be Foreign Commissar early in 1918. On 3 May 1989 Molotov took over from Litvinov. This is sometimes treated as a decision in favour of Germany; it is more likely to have been merely a recognition that foreign affairs mattered. Molotov was second only to Stalin in the Soviet Union. He approached foreign affairs not only with suspicion, but with that pedantic care for verbal accuracy which distinguished the Bolsheviks in their internal wranglings. There can be no doubt however that he took them seriously. Nor can there be much doubt as to the prime motive of Soviet policy. It was a desire to be left alone. The Soviets were conscious of their own weakness; they feared a hostile coalition of the capitalist states; and they were anxious to press on with their economic expansion. They agreed with the British government in wanting peace. They differed as to how peace could be preserved. They did not believe that Hitler could be made pacific by concessions; they held that he could be deterred only by a firm show of united opposition.

There were other grounds of divergence. Though, unlike Hitler, they had no burning desire to overthrow the *status quo*, they had neither affection nor enthusiasm for it; and the invitation to act in its favour first brought home to them how much they disliked it. They were reluctant to act at all; but, if they acted—particularly if they went to war—it would not be to preserve the treaty settlements of Brest-Litovsk and Riga. They would return to world affairs only as a Great Power, the equal of Great Britain and paramount in Eastern Europe. The two sides differed further in their estimate of the other's strength. The British supposed that Soviet Russia would be decisively beaten in the event of war with Germany. They were therefore almost as anxious to prevent a war between Germany and Soviet Russia as to avoid a war between Germany and themselves. The Russians assumed that Great Britain and France could maintain their

defensive positions and that a war in the West would therefore
mutually exhaust all combatants. Hence, failing general peace,
they could gamble on war, as the British could not. The British
would have to resist Hitler if they failed to conciliate him; the
Russians could choose between peace and war—or so they
imagined. The Soviet freedom of choice existed also in a more
formal way. The British were already committed to resistance by
their alliance with Poland. The Russians had to be won over, and
they were not likely to be won by the casual treatment which they
received from London—to say nothing of the obstinacy with
which the Poles refused to contemplate Soviet assistance. A
recital of these differences makes the negotiations appear doomed
in advance. Yet probably neither side appreciated this at the
beginning, nor perhaps even till nearly the end. The Russians
supposed that the Western Powers were desperate for help, as
indeed they should have been. The British counted confidently
on ideological estrangement between Fascism and Communism,
and imagined that the Soviet government would be flattered at
any nod of recognition.

The pattern of divergence was set at the start. The Soviet
government had proposed a conference of the peaceful Powers
immediately after the German occupation of Prague. The British
rejected this as "premature"—a favourite word of theirs.
Instead they distributed guarantees to the supposedly threatened
states. They would have been content with this, if left to themselves. But they were not left to themselves. They were harassed
in the House of Commons. They were even more alarmed at the
news that the French government were seeking with Soviet
Russia a pact of mutual assistance. This was the French counter
to the way in which the British had behaved over the guarantee
to Poland. The British were in danger of being rushed into
alliance with Soviet Russia just as the French had been hustled,
much against their will, into underwriting Poland's independence. Hence the British had to take the lead if they were to ward
off this danger; and their negotiations with Soviet Russia were, in
large part, designed to prevent the straight alliance which the
French wanted. On 15 April the British government grudgingly
approached Moscow: they asked for a declaration that, if any of
Russia's neighbours were attacked, "the assistance of the Soviet
Government would be available, if desired, and would be

afforded in such manner as would be found most convenient". Here, in slightly different words, was the same one-sided principle as had appeared in the Czechoslovak-Soviet pact and which had stultified Soviet policy in 1938. Then the Soviets could act only if France acted first; now they were to act only if Poland or Rumania or some Baltic state condescended to invite them. In 1938 the Soviets had perhaps welcomed the excuse to do nothing; six months later their attitude was different.[1] As the *cordon sanitaire* crumbled, they felt themselves in the front line. They were not concerned to sustain Poland or to provide some moral display against Hitler. They wished to secure precise and rigid military backing from the Western Powers in case Hitler attacked Russia—either through Poland or more directly.

On 17 April Litvinov produced his counter-proposal: there should be a pact of mutual assistance between England, France, and the Soviet Union for a period of five or ten years; and, what was more, the pact should provide for "all manner of assistance, including that of a military nature, to Eastern European States situated between Baltic and Black Seas and bordering on the U.S.S.R., in case of aggression against these States".[2] It was bad enough, in British eyes, that the Soviet government was proposing to assist Poland without previous invitation; the proposal to assist the Baltic states was even worse. The British believed that the Russians were merely trying to smuggle in an "Imperialist" ambition; and the accusation has often been repeated since. Yet the Soviet anxiety in regard to these states was genuine. The Russians feared a German attack on Leningrad; and, with Germany's naval superiority in the Baltic, this was a plausible venture. They therefore wished to strengthen their military position on land by controlling the Baltic states; and, knowing well that these states would probably prefer Germany to Russia if pressed to the wall, wished also to stipulate that Soviet "assistance" should be provided without invitation. This disregard for the independence of small states was no doubt unscrupulous, but—given that Soviet Russia was taking a line

[1] It is rather hard that the "cold war" historians who condemn the Soviet Union for observing this restriction in 1938, condemn her with equal vehemence for rejecting any similar restriction in 1939.

[2] Seeds to Halifax, 18 April 1939. *British Foreign Policy*, third series. v. No. 201.

hostile to Germany—sprang from real fears. Great Britain had guaranteed Poland and Rumania; therefore, if she kept her promise, she would have to go to war if Germany attacked Soviet Russia across either of these countries. There was no British commitment towards the Baltic States; here was the loophole for a German attack on Soviet Russia, while the Western Powers remained neutral. British rejection of the Soviet proposal convinced the Soviet rulers that their suspicions were well-founded. They were right. The British had a genuine respect for the independence of small states. Indeed they carried this respect so far in regard to Belgium that it led them and the French to strategic disaster in May 1940. Nevertheless the main motive in their opposition was reluctance to leave the decision between peace and war in Soviet hands. The Poles could have this decision; the Baltic states could have it; the Soviet government —never. "His Majesty's Government might be drawn into a war not for the preservation of a minor European state but for the support of the Soviet Union against Germany. On this issue opinion in this country . . . might be divided".[1] This is exactly what the Russians feared. The more the British defended the independence of the Baltic states, the more the Russians pressed against it; and the more the Russians pressed, the stronger British suspicion became. No agreement was ever reached on this question; and it was the point on which the negotiations technically broke down. Not so much that it was important in itself, but it represented the fundamental difference between the two sides. The British wanted a pact which would defend others and so deter Hitler without war. The Russians wanted an alliance which would defend themselves.

The British beat about for a fortnight after receiving Litvinov's reply. They enquired of Poland and Rumania what agreement these two countries would allow them to make with Soviet Russia. They were told that they could make what agreement they liked so long as it did not involve Poland or Rumania. The British also tried to invoke French diplomatic ingenuity. Bonnet, however, let them down. "In the heat of conversation" he revealed to the Soviet ambassador that France favoured a pact of mutual assistance. Still, the British held on

[1] Foreign Office memorandum, 22 May 1989. *British Foreign Policy*, third series. v. No. 576.

with persistence worthy of a better cause. On 8 May they proposed that, in view of the British guarantees to Poland and Rumania, "the Soviet Government would undertake that in the event of Great Britain and France being involved in hostilities in fulfilment of these obligations the assistance of the Soviet Government would be immediately available, if desired, and would be afforded in such manner and on such terms as might be agreed". Here was still the conception of a tap to be turned on, "if desired", by the British, but not under Soviet control. The reception of this proposal was Molotov's first appearance as foreign Commissar—not an occasion to inspire mutual trust. The atmosphere was changed, though Molotov professed that Soviet policy was not. There was none of Litvinov's good-humoured comment—no grins or light-hearted asides at the mention of "Beck" and other Poles. Instead there was "relentless questioning"; the British ambassador had "a most trying time". On 14 May Molotov formally rejected the British proposal, and demanded "reciprocity": there must be a pact of mutual assistance, a guarantee of all east European countries whether desired or not, and "the conclusion of a concrete agreement as to forms and extent of assistance".

This time the British government nearly gave up in despair— or on principle. It is not clear why they decided to try again. They were of course still being criticised in the House of Commons. Lloyd George said on 19 May: "For months we have been staring this powerful gift horse in the mouth. . . . Why do we not make up our mind, and make it up without any loss of time, that we should come to the same terms with Russia as we do with France".[1] Such arguments, though cogent, carried little weight with Chamberlain or the Conservative back-benchers. Rather the reverse. The resentment against Germany, which had followed the occupation of Prague, was working off; the older hostility to Soviet Russia was recovering its force, particularly when the Soviet rulers failed to be impressed by a condescending British request for their help. Soviet "obstinacy" eclipsed Hitler's aggressiveness. On the other hand, the problems were still there. French grievances and complaints were probably the decisive factor in pushing the British forward. The French were saddled with responsibility towards Poland, yet prevented by British

[1] *Hansard*, fifth series, 347, 1815–19.

scruples from enlisting Soviet might. To make matters worse from the French point of view, the Poles were persistently trying to extend and to modernise the obligations of the alliance. They aimed to get from the French the precise commitment over Danzig which the British had so far evaded; and they also asked, plausibly enough, that the long-standing alliance should at last be reinforced with a military convention. Daladier and Bonnet held out over the first point; even more than the British they thought it perfectly reasonable that Danzig should return to German sovereignty. They ostensibly gave way over the second. Daladier instructed Gamelin to negotiate a military convention which was duly completed on 19 May. This convention was fraudulent. It was to become operative only when a political agreement was reached; and this hung fire. The hypothetical French promises were themselves defective. Gamelin agreed that the "bulk" of the French forces would take the offensive if Germany attacked Poland. The Poles took "the bulk" to mean the entire French army—in other words the promise of a French offensive; Gamelin, or so he says, only meant to commit those forces which happened to be in the Maginot line at the time—a mere frontier operation.

It is strange that the Poles were so easily satisfied. But, being full of illusions about themselves, they were easily deluded by others; or maybe they never expected that a full-scale conflict would come—they remained confident, to the last, that they would win the war of nerves. Bonnet was delighted with his evasive action; Daladier, as usual, ashamed and irritated at what he had done. Just at this moment Halifax arrived in Paris on his way to Geneva. He found Daladier exasperated with the Poles and ready to bolt. Daladier wanted a straight pact of mutual assistance with Soviet Russia. When Halifax objected that Great Britain and France would then be committed to war even if Germany attacked Russia with Polish or Rumanian connivance or acquiescence, Daladier replied: "in such a case France would be involved by Franco-Soviet Pact and if this was so it would surely be impossible for us [Great Britain] to stand aside".[1] This was not a cheerful prospect from the British point of view. The last thing they wanted was to make a third in a revived Franco-

[1] Halifax to Cadogan, 21 May 1939. *British Foreign Policy*, third series. v. No. 576.

Russian alliance. The only way out was to accept a pact of mutual assistance on principle, but then to impose limits on its application. The British Cabinet agreed to this course on 24 May.

Negotiations with Moscow now changed their character. Previously the British had negotiated alone, the French waiting impatiently in the wings. Henceforth each step was agreed first with the French, at the price of interminable delay; despite this, the French seconded Soviet objections whenever they were raised. The British were pushed from one concession to another. They swallowed almost every piece of Soviet phraseology, each time with manifest reluctance. On the essential point they would not be moved. They rejected any definition of "indirect aggression" which allowed Soviet Russia, and not the threatened state, to decide that it had taken place: the Baltic states were not to be assisted against their will. Ostensibly this was a defence of the independence of small states. The real difference lay deeper: the British would co-operate with Soviet Russia only if Poland were attacked and agreed to accept Soviet assistance; otherwise the Russians would have to fight alone. The clumsy, obstinate negotiations lasted two months—from 27 May to 23 July. The deadlock remained unbroken. Then Molotov turned its flank by suggesting that they should proceed to military talks and hope that the question of "indirect aggression" would settle itself. The French jumped at this. They had always been ready to accept the Soviet's political terms if they could get firm military co-operation in exchange. The British once more gave way under protest. But they did not yield over the essential question. Indeed, with military talks in progress, "we feel that we can afford to take a somewhat stiffer line in regard to the one point to which we have always attached capital importance".[1] This stiffer line proved unnecessary. The political negotiations were suspended and never seriously resumed. The draft treaty, so laboriously concocted, was fated never to be signed. The British and French military missions were leisurely collected; then, with equal leisure, proceeded to Leningrad by sea. It was held that they could not cross Germany by train; and a strange chance arranged that no aeroplanes were available. The British behaved as though they had all the time in the world. By the time the

[1] Halifax to Seeds, 28 July 1939. *British Foreign Policy*, third series. vi. No. 474.

military missions reached Moscow the final crisis was upon them.

Was there ever any sense or reality in these interminable negotiations? It is tempting to think not. Certainly their course enormously increased mutual suspicion. By the end of July the Russians were undoubtedly convinced that the British and French were trying to lure them into war with Germany while remaining neutral themselves. Oddly enough, the British, on their side, did not anticipate a deal between Moscow and Berlin. They continued to assume that the ideological barrier was too great to be overcome: even if the Soviet rulers were no longer sincere Communists, Hitler, it was thought, would never weaken in his anti-Communism. Halifax telegraphed to Moscow on 28 July: "There is no danger now of an imminent breakdown during the next critical weeks". Was this blindness excusable? Should the British have been as suspicious of Russian dealings with Germany, as the Russians were of theirs? For that matter, were the Russian suspicions justified? No questions are more overlaid by controversy or more confused by hindsight. When the German records were published, evidence appeared that both Great Britain and Soviet Russia had kept in touch with Germany; and jubilant shouts went up on both sides that the mutual charges of dishonesty were well founded. Yet the evidence hardly sustains the elaborate structures which have been built upon it. The initiatives, such as they were, came from the Germans. British and Soviet representatives did little more than listen critically to what was put before them. Admittedly neither party warned the other that it was being invited to desert the common cause; and perhaps its own behaviour removed any ground for complaint. All the same, their talks with Germany were reinsurance, not the main theme of their diplomacy.

This stands out clearly on the Soviet side. There seems always to have been a "pro-German" element in Soviet counsels—men who had formerly organised the flourishing Russo-German trade, dogmatic Marxists who disliked association with the "entente criminals", Russians of the old school who thought only of Asia and who wished to turn their backs on Europe. These men were receptive of hints about better Russo-German relations, and ready to drop such hints themselves. It is unlikely that they waited for directives from the Kremlin; and their casual remarks tell little about Soviet policy. Events perhaps reveal more. The

Far East was a factor which must have weighed heavily with the Russians, though strangely enough it was never mentioned during the negotiations with Great Britain and France. This was not some hypothetical problem for the future: the Far East was ablaze even now. In the summer of 1989 Soviet and Japanese forces clashed on the frontier between Manchukuo and Outer Mongolia. This grew into a full-scale war, until the Japanese were defeated at Nomunhan in August, suffering some 18,000 casualties. It cannot have been agreeable to the Soviet government when the British, with their eyes turned on Europe, tamely swallowed humiliation from the Japanese at Tientsin; and it must have been welcome news to them, if they knew it, that negotiations between Germany and Japan were hanging fire. Soviet Russia sought security in Europe, not conquests; and it is surprising that she did not seek it earlier by a deal with Germany. The explanation lies on the surface: the Soviet statesmen feared German power and distrusted Hitler. Alliance with the Western Powers seemed the safer course, so long as it brought increased security for Soviet Russia and not merely increased obligation to support an unwilling Poland. Lacking direct evidence to the contrary—indeed lacking any such evidence on Soviet policy— we may safely guess that the Soviet government turned to Germany only when this alliance proved impossible.

This was the view even of those Germans who advocated better relations with Soviet Russia. They, too, were men of an old school—supposed heirs of Bismarck, generals and diplomatists who had worked the system of Rapallo. They recognised that they could only wait for a favourable opening. Besides, they had to walk warily on their own side. Hitler had virtually broken with Soviet Russia in 1934; and thereafter no one dared openly to question his anti-Comintern stand. Instead the "pro-Russians" tried to display the attractions of Soviet trade. This had revived somewhat in the period of Soviet disillusionment with the West which followed Munich. It languished again after the occupation of Prague. Soviet and German trade experts still wanted to co-operate and still met occasionally. No doubt each attributed the initiative to the other so as not to arouse the wrath of their respective masters. The first serious move came only at the end of May, and beyond question from the German side. Schulenburg, the ambassador at Moscow, and Weizsäcker, the secretary of state, both hankered after the old Rapallo line; both wanted to make a large "political offer". On 26 May the German foreign ministry defined the terms: Germany would mediate between Russia and Japan; and she would "pay the utmost regard to Russian interests" in regard to Poland.[1] But the draft was immediately cancelled, perhaps on instructions from Hitler himself: any approach "might be met with a peal of Tartar laughter".

A long silence followed. On 29 June Schulenburg tried an approach on his own; he got nothing from Molotov except an assurance that Soviet Russia wanted good relations with all countries, including Germany, and was then told by Ribbentrop that enough had been said. Trade talks between the two countries were, however, resumed; and towards the end of July Ribbentrop used the excuse of these talks to raise political topics as well. On 2 August he told the Soviet chargé d'affaires: "there was no problem from the Baltic to the Black Sea which could not be solved between the two of us".[2] The following day Schulenburg found Molotov "unusually open", and ready for economic co-operation. Politically Molotov was as stubborn as ever: Germany, he complained, was encouraging Japan; a peaceful solution of the Polish question depended on Germany; "proofs of a changed attitude were still lacking". Schulenburg summed up:

> My general impression is that the Soviet Government are at present determined to conclude an agreement with Britain and France if they fulfil all Soviet wishes. . . . It will require considerable effort on our part to cause a reversal in the Soviet Government's course.[3]

No outsider was a better judge than Schulenburg of Soviet policy; and on 4 August he still thought it set on alliance with the Western Powers. Of course Hitler may have arranged everything already on a private line with Stalin, which has escaped detection. But, if evidence means anything, the reconciliation between Soviet Russia and Germany, far from being planned over a long term, was very much an improvisation on the Soviet side, and almost as much so on the German.

[1] Weizsäcker to Schulenburg, draft, 26 May 1939. *German Foreign Policy*, series D. vi. No. 441.

[2] Ribbentrop to Schulenburg, 3 Aug. 1939. *Ibid.* No. 760.

[3] Schulenburg to Ribbentrop, 4 Aug. 1939. *Ibid.* No. 766.

British "appeasement", too, was mainly improvised, though with this difference: a peaceful settlement with Hitler, at the price of considerable concessions, was always the avowed aim of British policy. But the British statesmen waited to pursue this aim until they had improved their bargaining position either by securing alliance with Soviet Russia or by persuading the Poles to compromise over Danzig. Neither had been achieved by the end of July; therefore Chamberlain and Halifax made no move except to generalise about their policy in public speeches. Hitler also waited in the expectation that the British hopes in regard to Russia and Poland would not be fulfilled; then he, too, would be able to bargain on more favourable terms. There were virtually no official Anglo-German diplomatic dealings between the end of March and the middle of August. Henderson never saw Ribbentrop, let alone Hitler; and his few conversations with Weizsäcker went no further. For Weizsäcker dared not pass them on. Ribbentrop provided an almost impassable obstacle. As ambassador in London before he became foreign minister, he had set out with high boasts of achieving Anglo-German reconciliation. He had failed; and was now determined that where he had failed no one else should succeed. Dirksen, his successor, received no instructions; and his reports were ignored, when not actually condemned. Ribbentrop never wearied of telling Hitler that the British would yield only to threats, not to conciliation; and it suited Hitler to believe him.

These ideas were not universally favoured in high Nazi circles. Goering, though a blustering bully, wanted to avoid war if this were at all possible. He had had enough glory in the first World war; he was now living the glamorous life of a late Roman emperor; he liked to act as the mouthpiece of the German generals, themselves fearful of war; and maybe, as the supposed director of German economics, he grasped that Germany was not prepared to face a general war. The German approaches to both Soviet Russia and Great Britain came from economic experts—striking proof that the second World war did not have economic causes. Goering's first approaches to the British came through Swedish business-men, whom he had got to know during his exile in Sweden; and English business-men eagerly responded. These intermediaries were drawn into deep waters—exaggerating the readiness to compromise on each side, as often happens when amateurs try their hands at diplomacy. Still, the grudging responses from Halifax defined the British position clearly enough: there would be little difficulty in meeting the German wishes once Hitler showed his readiness for peace thereafter. This was much what Halifax had said long before in November 1937; and it defined the basic conflict between the two sides. Both had a plausible case. The British could argue that there was no point in making concessions to Hitler—indeed much danger—when he merely stepped up his threats after each bargain. Hitler could reply, with equal justice, that he had received the "reasonable" concessions of which Halifax had spoken only when he began to threaten; and the cases of Austria, Czechoslovakia, and Danzig were there to prove it. "Peaceful revision", to which both sides theoretically aspired, was a contradiction in terms. Revision was put forward as the way of avoiding war; yet it could be achieved only by methods which brought war nearer.

The unofficial Swedish mediators had little to show for their efforts, though one of them, Dahlerus, held on to play a big part in the final crisis. Wohltat, one of Goering's principal economic agents, got negotiations on to a more practical level. Wohltat was an important figure who had secured German economic control over the Balkan states. He was always ready to talk of Germany's need for raw materials and her shortage of capital; and this talk exactly suited the outlook of many Englishmen who accepted the current doctrine concerning the economic causes of war. Wohltat was in London between 18 and 21 July, when he saw Sir Horace Wilson, and Hudson, secretary of the department of overseas trade. Both Englishmen stressed the rewards awaiting Germany if she would drop her aggressive attitude and strike a bargain with Great Britain. Hudson dangled before Wohltat the prospect of a vast British loan—a thousand million pounds according to one report—to tide Germany over the difficulties of disarmament. He added: "Danzig in a Europe mobilised was one thing, and Danzig in a Europe disarmed and committed to economic collaboration was another".[1] Wilson produced a memorandum on 10 Downing Street note-paper, which, not surprisingly, has disappeared from the British records. This proposed an Anglo-German treaty of non-aggression and non-interference; a dis-

[1] Conversation between Hudson and Wohltat, 20 July 1939. *British Foreign Policy*, third series. vi. No. 370.

armament agreement; and co-operation in foreign trade. A pact of this kind "would enable Britain to rid herself of her commitments *vis-à-vis* Poland".[1] Wilson is said to have been ignorant in regard to foreign affairs. No one has ever accused him of disloyalty to his political superiors; and it is inconceivable that these proposals were made without Chamberlain's knowledge or approval. Nor is this surprising. The proposals represented the programme of Anglo-German collaboration which Chamberlain had always hoped for. But even Wilson made it clear that there was a condition which must be fulfilled first: the questions at issue between Germany and Poland must be settled by peaceful negotiation.

The British government can be forgiven for continuing to emphasise the rewards which Germany would gain by following a conciliatory policy. Their real fault lay elsewhere: in their failure to make clear their own resolution if Hitler followed the opposite course. Speeches by Chamberlain and Halifax carried little weight; Hitler had heard similar remarks in the previous year, and knew what they then amounted to. Nor was he impressed by the prolonged negotiations with Soviet Russia. The immediate signing of an alliance might have shaken him; three months of haggling merely increased his self-confidence. Nevile Henderson remained in Berlin; and it is difficult to believe that his hostility towards the Poles was expressed only in private letters home. Wiser counsels were not lacking. Early in July Count von Schwerin, of the German war ministry, was in England. He spoke frankly. "Hitler took no account of words, only of deeds". The British should stage a naval demonstration in the Baltic; they should take Churchill into the Cabinet; they should send the Air Striking Force to France.[2] This advice was disregarded. Men cannot change their nature, however much they change their words. The British statesmen were trying to strike a balance between firmness and conciliation; and, being what they were, inevitably struck the wrong one.

The conversations between Wohltat and Wilson gave a fair

---

[1] Conversations between Wohltat and Wilson, 24 July; record by Dirksen, 21 July 1939. *German Foreign Policy*, series D. vi. No. 716. *Dirksen Papers*, No. 18.

[2] Conversations between Schwerin and Marshall-Cornwall and Jebb, 7 and 8 July 1939. *British Foreign Policy*, third series vi. No. 269 and 277.

picture of Chamberlain's outlook, but they had no serious impact in Germany. Goering may have been impressed by them. Ribbentrop merely rebuked Dirksen for allowing them to take place; and it is unlikely that Hitler heard of them at all. The conversation between Hudson and Wohltat, though less important, created more stir. It was leaked to the press, apparently from the British side.[1] The purpose of the leak remains unknown. Perhaps it was mere talkativeness on Hudson's part; perhaps it was a deliberate attempt to wreck the negotiations with Soviet Russia—and there were many on the government side who wished to do so. The disclosure led to questions in the House of Commons; and Chamberlain, in answering them, made his own determination to resist Germany even less convincing than it was already. At the time the Soviet government ignored the story; later they blew it up as a convenient excuse for their own dealings with Hitler. The historian does not need to linger over these mutual accusations. The British and the Russians had both listened sympathetically to German approaches; and, up to the end of July, the British had listened the more sympathetically of the two. Yet their negotiations for alliance were not wrecked by German temptations. They were wrecked by failure to agree. Both sides wanted agreement, but not the same agreement. The British wanted a moral demonstration which would enable them to reach a settlement with Hitler on more favourable terms. The Russians wanted a precise military alliance for mutual assistance, which would either deter Hitler or secure his defeat. The British feared for Poland; the Russians feared for themselves. A German invasion of Russia, not any mere shifting of the European balance in Germany's favour, was their nightmare. They sought allies; and they were offered only the loss of such freedom of action as they still possessed.

Would even the conclusion of some Anglo-Soviet agreement have made all that difference? Alliances are worth while when they put into words a real community of interests; otherwise they lead only to confusion and disaster, as the French alliances did. It was inconceivable, in the circumstances of 1939, that the British should commit themselves, irretrievably and decisively,

[1] Dirksen said that the leakage did not come from Wohltat or the German embassy. Minute by Sargent, 24 July 1939. *British Foreign Policy*, third series. vi. No. 426.

in favour of Soviet Russia as against Germany; and equally inconceivable that the Russians should commit themselves to defence of the *status quo*. Ultimately Great Britain and Soviet Russia became allies, but not from policy or conviction; Hitler simply forced alliance upon them. By 1941 Hitler had lost his old gift of patience; he rushed at a second aim before achieving his first. In 1939 he was still master in the art of waiting. Lesser Germans might surrender to anxiety and put out feelers in Moscow or London. Hitler remained silent. The Anglo-Soviet negotiations were not thwarted by German offers; they were thwarted by the lack of offers. The negotiations had been started as an elaborate move in the war of nerves; they were meant to shake Hitler's determination. Instead, they strengthened it. Hitler gambled that the negotiations would fail; and once more he gambled right. He relied not on knowledge or rational information, but, as always, on his sixth sense; and it did not fail him. The war of nerves was his speciality; and, when August 1939 came, he seemed to have won another victory in this war. It is pointless to speculate whether an Anglo-Soviet alliance would have prevented the second World war. But failure to achieve this alliance did much to cause it.

CHAPTER ELEVEN

War for Danzig

THE crisis of August 1939 which led to the second World war was, ostensibly at any rate, a dispute over Danzig. This dispute was formulated in the last days of March, when Germany made demands concerning Danzig and the Corridor, and the Poles rejected them. From that moment everyone expected Danzig to be the next great topic of international conflict. Yet, in strange contrast to earlier crises, there were no negotiations over Danzig, no attempts to discover a solution; not even attempts to screw up the tension. This paradoxical calm was partly caused by the local situation at Danzig. Here both Germany and Poland had an impregnable position so long as they did not move; a step by either would start the avalanche. Hence there could be none of the manoeuvres and bargaining which had marked the Czecho- slovak crisis. The Sudeten Nazis, like the Austrians before them, built up the tension gradually without guidance from Hitler. In Danzig the tension was already complete; and Hitler, so far as he did anything, held the local Nazis back. They had already won Danzig internally; the Senate of the Free City was firmly under control. But Hitler could not take advantage of this situation. If the Danzig Nazis openly defied the treaty-settlement by voting for incorporation into Germany, the Poles would be free to intervene with the approval of their Western allies; and this intervention would be effective. For Danzig was cut off from East Prussia, the only neighbouring German territory, by the unbridged Vistula; while the Poles controlled three railways and seven roads leading into it. There could be no half-hearted German aid to Danzig, only a full-blown war; and Hitler would be ready for such a war only when his military preparations matured at the end of August.

Until then Danzig lay at Poland's mercy. But the Poles, too, could not turn this position to their advantage. Though they had alliances with Great Britain and France, they had failed to secure any firm promise of support over Danzig itself; indeed they knew that both their allies sympathised with the German case. They could retain the favour of their allies only by hanging back and waiting for the "clear threat" to Polish independence. It had to appear that action was forced on them; and in Danzig it never was. Under similar circumstances, Hitler's previous antagonists, Schuschnigg and Benes, had sought desperately for a way of escape, endlessly devising compromises which might avert the threatened crisis. The Poles faced the approaching crisis imperturbably, confident that Hitler would be exposed as an aggressor and that the justified grievances of Danzig would then be forgotten. They would not respond to Nazi provocation; but equally they ignored the pleas for concession which came to them from the West.

On the larger field of grand policy also, both Hitler and the Poles held rigid positions in the war of nerves. After 26 March Hitler did not again formulate demands concerning Danzig until the day before war broke out. This was not surprising; it was his usual method. So he had waited for offers from Schuschnigg over Austria; so he had waited for offers from Benes, from Chamberlain, finally from the conference at Munich over Czechoslovakia. Then he did not wait in vain. Did he appreciate that this time no offer would come from the Poles? It seems so from the record. On 8 April he issued instructions that preparations for an attack on Poland "must be made in such a way that the operation can be carried out at any time as from 1 September 1939".[1] But a further directive a week later explained that these preparations were purely precautionary, "should Poland change her policy . . . and adopt a threatening attitude towards Germany".[2] On 23 May, however, he spoke with less reserve to a gathering of generals: "There will be war. Our task is to isolate Poland. . . . It must not come to a simultaneous showdown with the West".[3] This sounds clear enough. But Hitler's real plans are not so easily detected. He had talked just as bravely about war against Czechoslovakia in 1938; yet then, almost certainly, he was

[1] Directive by Keitel, 3 April 1939. *German Foreign Policy*, series D. vi. No. 149.

[2] Directive by Hitler, 11 April 1939. *Ibid.* No. 185.

[3] Minutes of conference, 23 May 1939. *Ibid.* No. 433.

playing for victory in the war of nerves. Now, too, preparations
had to be made for war whether he were planning to win by war
or diplomacy. When Hitler talked to his generals, he talked for
effect, not to reveal the workings of his mind. He knew that the
generals disliked and distrusted him; he knew that some of them
had planned to overthrow him in September 1938; probably he
knew that they were constantly sounding the alarm at the
British and French embassies. He wanted to impress the generals
and, at the same time, to frighten them. Hence on 23 May he
talked not only of war against Poland, which he may have
seriously intended; but even of a great war against the Western
Powers, which was undoubtedly not part of his plan. Hitler's
calculation worked: no sooner was the conference of 23 May
ended than the generals, from Goering downwards, were imploring
the Western Powers to bring Poland to reason while there was
still time.

Hitler's later behaviour suggests that he had not made up his
mind as decisively as he indicated on 23 May. To the very last
minute he was battering away for the Polish offer which never
came. Maybe he did not expect the Polish nerve to break of
itself; but he expected the Western Powers to do the breaking
for him, as they had done predominantly with Benes in 1938. He
did not foresee exactly how the nerve of the Western Powers
would crumble or precisely what effect this would have on the
Poles. Nor was it of much moment to him whether the Poles then
gave way without war or were left to be destroyed in isolation;
the result would be much the same either way. On the larger
point—the crumbling of Western nerve—he never doubted.
There are also indications that, as the summer wore on, he began
to foresee how this would come about. A collapse of the Anglo-
Franco-Soviet negotiations would, he thought, do the trick.
Hitler's confidence that these negotiations would fail is an
extraordinary feature even in this extraordinary story. How
could he be so sure? Why did he make little effort to approach
Russia and assert that the Russians would come over to his side
of themselves? Had he secret means of information, never to be
traced by historians—some agent in Whitehall or at the Kremlin,
perhaps a direct line to Stalin himself? Was it profound social
analysis—a realisation that *bourgeois* statesmen and Communists
would not find terms of mutual understanding? Maybe; we have

no means of knowing. Probably it was simply the gambler's invariable conviction that his hunch must be right—otherwise, after all, he would not play. A casual phrase reveals more of Hitler's policy than all the grandiloquent talk to generals. On 29 August, Goering, anxious for a compromise, said: "It is time to stop this *va banque*". Hitler replied: "It is the only call I ever make".[1]

It was Hitler's misfortune (and not his alone) to encounter in the Poles political gamblers of the same school. *Va banque* was not merely the only call they made; it was the only call they could possibly make if they were to maintain their illusory position as an independent Great Power. Sober statesmen would have surrendered at discretion when they contemplated the dangers threatening Poland and the inadequacy of her means. Germany, powerful and aggressive, was on one side; Soviet Russia, potentially hostile on the other; and in the distance, two unwilling allies, eager to compromise with Hitler and geographically unable to give effective aid. The Poles had to depend on such resources as they possessed themselves; and had not even developed these efficiently. Less than half the men of military age had received military training; fewer still could hope for equipment. Czechoslovakia, the year before, with not much more than a third of Poland's population, had a larger trained manpower; and the Czechs were armed with modern weapons into the bargain. Of these the Poles had virtually none: some 250 first-line aeroplanes of antiquated type, one tank battalion also not up to date. Under such circumstances what could the Poles do except dismiss Hitler's threats as bluff? It was obvious that any move by them must involve concession; therefore they made none. After all, standing still is the best policy for anyone who favours the *status quo*, perhaps the only one. Poland's Western allies were of course an additional reason for her diplomatic immobility; it was obvious that Great Britain and France would give way over Danzig, if the Poles once opened the door to negotiation. Therefore they kept it closed. "Munich" cast a long shadow. Hitler waited for it to happen again; Beck took warning from the fate of Benes.

Germany and Poland held rigid positions. The three Western Powers—Italy, as well as Great Britain and France—shrank

[1] Weizsäcker, *Erinnerungen*, 258.

from raising the question of Danzig for the opposite reason: because their positions were so soft. All three were convinced that Danzig was not worth a war; all three were agreed that it should return to Germany, with safeguards for Polish trade. But all three recognised that Poland would not give way without a fight and that Hitler would not postpone Danzig until a more peaceful moment. Italy was committed to Germany by the Pact of Steel, Great Britain and France were committed to Poland. None of the three wanted to fight over Danzig; neither of the two principals would yield. The only course therefore was to ignore the question of Danzig and to hope that the others would ignore it also. The three Western Powers did their best to wish Danzig out of existence:

> *As I was going up the stair,*
> *I met a man who wasn't there.*
> *He wasn't there again today.*
> *I do so wish he'd go away.*

This was the spirit of European diplomacy in the summer of 1939. Danzig was not there; and if all the Powers wished hard enough it would go away.

When August arrived, it became clear that Danzig had not gone away. The local Nazis stepped up their provocations to the Poles; the Poles responded with challenging firmness. Reports of German troop movements grew stronger; and this time the rumours were well founded. Hitler, it was expected, would act soon. But how? and, still more important, when? This was the vital question in both the Czech and Polish crises. On each occasion the Western Powers assumed that Hitler would explode the crisis in public, at the Nazi party rally in Nuremberg. On each occasion this assumption was mistaken; but in the Czech crisis the Western Powers erred on the right side, in the Polish crisis on the wrong one. In 1938 the party rally was held on 12 September; Hitler's military plans were set only for 1 October, and therefore "appeasement" had an unexpected fortnight in which to operate. In 1939 the party rally was fixed for the first week in September; this time Hitler had decided to achieve success beforehand. At the "Rally of Peace", he would announce victory, not prepare for it. No one could have guessed that the

German military plans were timed for 1 September. The date—like 1 October in the previous year—was not chosen on any rational ground, meteorological or other, despite assertions to the contrary by most later writers; it was arrived at, as such dates usually are, by sticking a pin in the calendar. The margin for negotiation was narrow in any case; the diplomatic plans of the Western Powers misfired partly because the margin was about a week narrower than they thought.

At the beginning of August, the Western Powers were still marking time, in the hope that their undefined relations with the Soviet Union would deter Hitler. Others were less confident. A procession of visitors to Berchtesgaden tried to gauge Hitler's intentions. Perhaps the probings first made him decide what these were. The Hungarians led the field. On 24 July Teleki, the Hungarian prime minister, wrote two letters to Hitler. In one he promised "that in the event of a general conflict Hungary will make her policy conform to the policy of the Axis"; but in the other, "Hungary could not, on moral grounds, be in a position to take armed action against Poland".[1] On 8 August Csáky, the Hungarian foreign minister, received at Berchtesgaden a ruthless answer. Hitler did not want Hungarian assistance. But "Poland presents no military problem to us. . . . It is to be hoped that Poland will still see reason at the last minute. . . . Otherwise not only the Polish army but also the Polish state will be destroyed. . . . France and Britain will not be able to prevent us from doing this". Csáky stammered, apologised, and withdrew Teleki's letters, "as unfortunately, they had apparently been misunderstood".[2]

Three days later it was the turn of Burckhardt, the League High Commissioner at Danzig. Hitler was again bellicose: "I shall strike like lightning with the full force of a mechanised army, of which the Poles have no conception". But he also showed signs of conciliation: "if the Poles leave Danzig absolutely calm . . . then I can wait". He made it clear what he would wait for. He would still be content with the terms which he demanded on 26 March—"unfortunately that is definitely ruled out by the Poles". Then, more generally, "I want nothing from the West . . .

[1] Memorandum by Weizsäcker, 24 July 1939. *German Foreign Policy*, series D. vi. No. 712.

[2] Memorandum by Erdmannsdorff, 8 Aug. 1939. *Ibid.* No. 784.

But I must have a free hand in the East. . . . I want to live in peace with England and to conclude a definitive pact; to guarantee all the English possessions in the world and to collaborate".[1] With both Csáky and Burckhardt, Hitler was clearly talking for effect—bellicose at one moment, conciliatory at the next. It was exactly the tactic of the previous year. Why not now? If his talk of peace was play-acting, so also was his talk of war. Which would become real depended on events, not on any resolution taken by Hitler beforehand.

On 12 August a more important visitor appeared: Ciano, the Italian foreign minister. The Italians had been full of fight so long as war seemed a long way off; they grew anxious when reports accumulated that war was approaching. Italy was exhausted by her prolonged intervention in Spain—perhaps the only significant effect of the Spanish civil war. Her reserves of gold and raw materials were run down; her rearmament with modern weapons had hardly begun. She could be ready for war only in 1942; and even this was an imaginary date which merely meant "in some distant future". On 7 July Mussolini said to the British ambassador: "Tell Chamberlain that if England fought on the Polish side over Danzig, Italy would fight on that of Germany".[2] A fortnight later he swung round, and asked for a meeting with Hitler on the Brenner. He proposed to insist that war must be avoided, and that Hitler could get all he wanted at an international conference. The Germans first waved the meeting away; then said that one should be held solely to discuss the coming attack on Poland. Maybe Mussolini distrusted his ability to stand up to Hitler; at any rate he decided to send Ciano instead. Mussolini's instructions were clear: "we must avoid a conflict with Poland, since it will be impossible to localise it, and a general war would be disastrous for everybody".[3] Ciano spoke up firmly when he met Hitler on 12 August, but his remarks were swept aside. Hitler announced that he proposed to attack Poland unless he got complete satisfaction by the end of August; "he was absolutely certain that the Western democracies . . . would shrink from a general war"; the whole operation would be

[1] Minute by Makins, 14 Aug. 1939. *British Foreign Policy*, third series. vi. No. 659.
[2] Loraine to Halifax, 7 July 1939. *Ibid.* No. 261.
[3] *Ciano's Diary 1939–1943*, p. 123.

over by 15 October. This was more precise than any previous statement by Hitler; yet doubt remains. He knew that anything he said to the Italians would be passed on to the Western Powers; and he was concerned to shake their nerve, not to reveal his real plans to Mussolini.

An odd little episode showed what these plans were. While Ciano was talking to Hitler, "the Führer was handed a telegram from Moscow". Ciano was told what was in it: "the Russians agreed to a German political negotiator being sent to Moscow". According to Ciano, "the Russians asked for the sending to Moscow of a German plenipotentiary who would negotiate a pact of friendship".[1] No such telegram has been found in the German archives; and none can ever have existed. For the Russians agreed to the sending of a German negotiator only on 19 August, not on 12 August.[2] Of course Stalin may have communicated his decision to Hitler, by some hidden means, a week before he made it. But this is a fantastic hypothesis, for which all evidence is lacking. It is far more probable that the telegram was a fabrication, designed to impress Ciano and to quieten his doubts. Yet, though a fabrication, it was not without foundation. This foundation was Hitler's "hunch"—his conviction that what he wanted to happen would happen. His second sight had never failed him so far. This time he was staking everything on it, certain in advance that the Anglo-Franco-Soviet negotiations would break down and that then the Western Powers would collapse also.

On 12 August the Anglo-Franco-Soviet negotiations had not broken down. They were actually being resumed. The British and

[1] Conversation between Hitler and Ciano, 12 Aug. 1939. *German Foreign Policy*, series D. vii. No. 43; *I documenti diplomatici italiani*, eighth series. xiii. No. 4.

[2] It is now universally admitted that there was no telegram from Moscow on 12 August. But it is often suggested that agreement to the visit of a German negotiator was given by the agency of Astakov, the Soviet chargé d'affaires in Berlin. This also is untrue. Astakov merely said that "the Soviets were interested in a discussion of individual questions". He did not mention a pact of friendship; and "he left the matter open as to who was expected in Moscow to conduct the conversations, whether the Ambassador or someone else". *German Foreign Policy*, series D. vii. No. 50. Astakov was probably acting on his own initiative, as he had often done before. In any case, there is no evidence that the information was passed on to Hitler.

French military missions had at last arrived in Moscow. The French had been told by Daladier to get a military convention as quickly as possible. The British, on the other hand, were instructed to "go very slowly" until a political agreement was reached (though discussions for this had been suspended on 27 July until a military convention was made): "agreement on the many points raised may take months to achieve".[1] The British government, in fact, were not interested in solid military co-operation with Soviet Russia; they merely wanted to chalk a Red bogey on the wall, in the hope that this would keep Hitler quiet. But, when the talks started, the British spokesmen soon found themselves being bustled by the French and by Voroshilov, the Soviet leader, into serious discussion. British and French plans for war were described in detail; the resources of the two countries somewhat generously catalogued. On 14 August the Soviet turn came. Voroshilov then asked. "Can the Red Army move across North Poland . . . and across Galicia in order to make contact with the enemy? Will Soviet troops be allowed to cross Rumanian territory".[2] It was the decisive question. The British and French could not answer. The talks ran to a standstill; on 17 August they were adjourned, never to be seriously resumed.

Why did the Russians ask this question so ruthlessly and so abruptly? Was it merely to have an excuse for negotiating with Hitler? Perhaps. But the question was a real one which had to be asked—and answered. Poland and Rumania had presented insuperable obstacles against any Soviet action in 1938. These obstacles had to be overcome if Soviet Russia were to act now as an equal partner; and only the Western Powers could overcome them. The question raised the old dispute of principle in a new form. The Western Powers wanted the Soviet Union as a convenient auxiliary; the Russians were determined to be recognised as principals. There was also a difference of strategical outlook which has been less noticed. Great Britain and France still thought in terms of the Western front during the first World war. They therefore exaggerated the strength of defensive positions. The military mission had been told: if Germany

---

[1] Instructions to the British Military Mission, Aug. 1939. *British Foreign Policy*, third series. vi. Appendix v.

[2] Minutes of meeting, 14 Aug. 1939. *Ibid.* vii. Appendix ii.

attacked in the West, even through Holland and Belgium, "sooner or later, this front would be stabilised". In the East, Poland and Rumania would slow down a German advance; with Russian supplies they might stop it altogether.[1] In any case the Red Army would have plenty of time to build up lines of defence after the war had started. Then everyone would remain securely entrenched until Germany collapsed under pressure of a blockade. Holding these views, the Western Powers could see in the Russian demand to advance through Poland only a political manoeuvre; the Russians, they thought, wished to humiliate Poland or perhaps even to destroy her political independence.

No one can tell whether the Russians had such designs. But it is clear that they had different strategical conceptions which were enough in themselves to explain their demands. The Russians started from their experiences in the civil wars and wars of intervention, not from the preceding World war. Here cavalry offensives had everywhere carried the day. Moreover, as Communists, they automatically favoured a strategical doctrine more dynamic and revolutionary than that held in the decadent capitalist West. The Russians held that cavalry offensives, now in mechanised form, were irresistible, or rather they could be resisted only by similar offensives at some other part of the front. It was their intention, in case of war, to fling armoured columns into Germany, regardless of German attacks elsewhere. This remained their intention even in 1941; and they were prevented from putting it into operation only by the fact that Hitler attacked them before they were ready. Their doctrine was, in fact, mistaken, though not more so than that of the Western Powers; and in 1941 Hitler's surprise attack saved them from a disaster which might have been beyond remedy. These later experiences are irrelevant to the diplomacy of 1989. Then the Russians asked to go through Poland because they believed, however mistakenly, that this was the only way to win a war. Political aims may have existed as well; but they were subordinate to genuine military needs.

The British and French governments did not appreciate these Soviet calculations; but they realised that the unwelcome question would have to be answered, now that it had been asked.

---

[1] Instructions to Military Mission, Aug. 1939. *British Foreign Policy*, third series. vi. Appendix v, para. 83.

Both turned, though without much hope, to Warsaw. The British still used political arguments: "agreement with the Soviet Union would be calculated to deter Hitler from war". If negotiations broke down, "Russia might either share the spoils with Germany . . . or constitute the chief menace when the war was over".[1] Beck gave an equally political answer: agreement to the passage of Russian troops across Poland, far from deterring Hitler, "would lead to an immediate declaration of war on the part of Germany".[2] Both political arguments made sense; both were irrelevant to the military situation. The French thought in more practical terms. They were only concerned to get the Red Army involved in conflict with Hitler, and did not mind if this were done at the expense of Poland. Left to themselves they would gladly have jettisoned Poland if they could have won Soviet co-operation in exchange. London forbade any such threat; therefore the French had still to attempt persuasion. Bonnet thought he saw a way out. The Russians insisted on an agreement for military collaboration with the Poles before war started; the Poles would accept Soviet aid only when the war had begun. Hence Bonnet argued that a moment had arrived which still seemed like peace to the Russians but like war to the Poles. The manoeuvre failed. Beck was obdurate: "It is a new partition of Poland that we are being asked to sign". On 21 August the French lost patience. They decided to ignore the Polish refusal and to go ahead, hoping to commit the Poles willy-nilly. Doumenc, the head of the military mission in Moscow, was instructed to give "an affirmative answer in principle" to the Russian question; and he was to "negotiate and sign whatever arrangement might best serve the common interest, subject to the final approval of the French Government". The British refused to be associated with this move, though they did not protest against it.

In any case, the chance of a Soviet alliance, if it ever existed, had now been lost. On 14 August, a few hours after Voroshilov had raised his fateful question, Ribbentrop drafted a telegram to Schulenburg, his ambassador in Moscow: "There exist no real conflicts of interests between Germany and Russia. . . . There is

[1] Halifax to Kennard, 17 Aug., 20 Aug. 1939. *British Foreign Policy*, third series. vii. No. 38, 39, 91.
[2] Kennard to Halifax, 18 Aug. 1939. *Ibid.* No. 52.

no question between the Baltic Sea and the Black Sea which cannot be settled to the complete satisfaction of both parties". Ribbentrop was prepared to come to Moscow, there "to lay the foundations for a final settlement of German-Russian relations".[1] This message was the first real move in German-Soviet relations. Until then they had been stagnant; the discussions between subordinates, of which so much was to be made later by Western writers, were no more than soundings, inspired by regrets for the vanished intimacy of Rapallo. Now Hitler was at last taking the initiative. Why did he do so at this precise moment? Was it supreme political skill, a second sight which told him that the military talks would reach deadlock two days after they started? Was the coincidence of Voroshilov's question and Ribbentrop's approach arranged secretly between Stalin and Hitler in advance? Did some unknown agent in the Kremlin tell Hitler that the right moment had arrived? Or was the coincidence pure chance? Hitler had first blurted out his plan of breaking Anglo-French nerve by an agreement with Soviet Russia when he boasted untruly to Ciano of an invitation from Moscow on 12 August, and so stilled Italian fears. Perhaps Hitler only devised this strategy consciously at the moment of boasting. After all, he was always the man of daring improvisations; he made lightning decisions, and then presented them as the result of long-term policy. Ribbentrop remained at Berchtesgaden until 13 August. He returned to Berlin on 14 August. This was therefore the first day when the message to Moscow could have been sent. Probably chance is the correct answer; but this is one of the problems which we shall never be able to solve.

Schulenburg delivered Ribbentrop's message on 15 August. Molotov refused to be hurried. Though he received the message "with greatest interest", he thought negotiations would take some time. He asked: "How were the German Government disposed towards the idea of a non-aggression pact with the Soviet Union?"[2] The answer came back within less than twenty-four hours: Germany offered not only a non-aggression pact, but a joint guarantee of the Baltic States and mediation between

---

[1] Ribbentrop to Schulenburg, 14 Aug. 1939. *German Foreign Policy*, series D. vii. No. 56.

[2] Schulenburg to Ribbentrop, 16 Aug. 1939. *Ibid*. No. 70.

Soviet Russia and Japan. The essential thing was the visit by Ribbentrop.[1] The Russians still kept the way open on both sides. On 17 August Voroshilov told the British and French military missions that there was no point in a further meeting until they could answer his question about Poland; however, after some prodding, he agreed to meet again on 21 August. At almost exactly the same time Molotov told Schulenburg that the improvement in Soviet-German relations would be a long business. First there must be a commercial agreement; next a pact of non-aggression. Then perhaps they could think about a visit from Ribbentrop; but the Soviet government "preferred to do practical work without fuss".[2]

On 18 August Ribbentrop knocked harder than ever at the Soviet door. Relations must be clarified at once "so as not to be taken by surprise by the outbreak of a German-Polish conflict".[3] Once more Molotov hesitated. Ribbentrop's visit "could not be fixed even approximately". Within half an hour, Schulenburg was called back to the Kremlin; Ribbentrop, he was told, could come a week later.[4] There is no means of knowing what brought this sudden decision. Schulenburg thought that Stalin had intervened personally; but this was a guess, like all others made later. The Soviet invitation was not soon enough for Hitler; he wanted Ribbentrop to be received at once. This may have been simply the impatience which always followed his prolonged hesitations. Perhaps there is a deeper explanation. 26 August would be soon enough if Hitler merely aimed to clear the way for an attack on Poland on 1 September. It was not soon enough to give him time for two operations: first breaking the nerve of the Western Powers by an agreement with Soviet Russia; then breaking the nerve of the Poles with the assistance of the Western Powers. Hence Hitler's urgency strongly suggests that he was aiming at another "Munich", not at war.

At any rate, Hitler now acted without a diplomatic intermediary. On 20 August he sent a personal message to Stalin, agreeing to all the Soviet demands and asking that Ribbentrop

[1] Ribbentrop to Schulenburg, 16 Aug. 1939. *German Foreign Policy*, series D. vii. No. 75.

[2] Schulenburg to Ribbentrop, 18 Aug. 1939. *Ibid.* No. 105.

[3] Ribbentrop to Schulenburg, 18 Aug. 1939. *Ibid.* No. 113.

[4] Schulenburg to Ribbentrop, 19 Aug. 1939. *Ibid.* No. 132.

should be received at once.[1] The message was a milestone in world history; it marked the moment when Soviet Russia returned to Europe as a Great Power. No European statesman had ever addressed Stalin directly before. Western leaders had treated him as though he were a remote, and ineffectual, Bey of Bokhara. Now Hitler recognised him as the ruler of a great state. Stalin is supposed to have been immune to personal feelings; Hitler's approach must have flattered him all the same. The moment of decision had arrived. On 20 August the commercial treaty between Soviet Russia and Germany was settled; the first Soviet condition had been fulfilled. On the morning of 21 August Voroshilov met the two military missions. They had nothing to report; and the meeting adjourned *sine die*. At 5 p.m. Stalin agreed that Ribbentrop could come to Moscow at once—on 23 August. The news was announced that same night in Berlin, and on the following day in Moscow. The French still tried to save something. On 22 August Doumenc saw Voroshilov on his own. On Daladier's instructions, he offered to agree to the Soviet demand without waiting for a reply from the Poles. Voroshilov rejected the offer: "we do not want Poland to boast that she has refused our aid—which we have no intention of forcing her to accept".[2] The Anglo-Franco-Soviet negotiations were at an end. On the following day, 23 August, the French finally wheedled out of the Poles a grudging formula. The French might say to the Russians: "We have acquired the certainty that in the event of common action against a German aggression collaboration between Poland and the U.S.S.R. is not excluded (or: is possible)".[3] The formula was never placed before the Russians. In any case it was fraudulent. Beck agreed to it only when he knew that Ribbentrop was in Moscow and that there was no danger of Soviet aid to Poland. Nor did this dismay him. He still believed that an independent Poland had more chance of reaching agreement with Hitler. Soviet Russia, he thought, was withdrawing from Europe; and that was good news for the Poles. "It is now Ribbentrop's turn," he said complacently, "to experience Soviet bad faith".[4]

[1] Ribbentrop to Schulenburg, 20 Aug. 1939. *German Foreign Policy*, series D. vii. No. 142.

[2] Conversation between Voroshilov and Doumenc, 22 Aug. 1939. *British Foreign Policy*, third series. vii. Appendix ii. No. 10.

[3] Kennard to Halifax, 23 Aug. 1939. *Ibid.* No. 176.

[4] Noël, *L'agression allemande*, 424.

Ribbentrop did not think so. He came to Moscow to reach agreement; and he succeeded immediately. The public Pact, signed on 23 August, provided for mutual non-aggression. A secret protocol excluded Germany from the Baltic states and from the eastern parts of Poland—the territory east of the Curzon line which was inhabited by Ukrainians and White Russians. This was, after all, what the Russians had sought to obtain from the Western Powers. The Nazi-Soviet pact was only another way of doing it: not so good a way, but better than none. The settlement of Brest-Litovsk was at last undone, with the consent of Germany, instead of with the backing of the Western Powers. It was no doubt disgraceful that Soviet Russia should make any agreement with the leading Fascist state; but this reproach came ill from the statesmen who went to Munich and who were then sustained in their own countries by great majorities. The Russians, in fact, did only what the Western statesmen had hoped to do; and Western bitterness was the bitterness of disappointment, mixed with anger that professions of Communism were no more sincere than their own professions of democracy. The pact contained none of the fulsome expressions of friendship which Chamberlain had put into the Anglo-German declaration on the day after the Munich conference. Indeed Stalin rejected any such expressions: "the Soviet Government could not suddenly present to the public German-Soviet assurances of friendship after they had been covered with buckets of filth by the Nazi Government for six years".

The pact was neither an alliance nor an agreement for the partition of Poland. Munich had been a true alliance for partition: the British and French dictated partition to the Czechs. The Soviet government undertook no such action against the Poles. They merely promised to remain neutral, which is what the Poles had always asked them to do and which Western policy implied also. More than this, the agreement was in the last resort anti-German: it limited the German advance eastwards in case of war, as Winston Churchill emphasised in a speech at Manchester immediately after the end of the Polish campaign. In August the Russians were not thinking in terms of war. They assumed, like Hitler, that the Western Powers would not fight without a Soviet alliance. Poland would be compelled to yield; and, with the Polish obstacle out of the way, defensive alliance with the West might then be achieved on more equal terms. Alternatively, if the Poles remained defiant, they would fight alone; and in that case they would be driven to accept Soviet assistance after all. These calculations were falsified by the actual outcome: a war in which both Poland and the Western Powers took part. Even this was a success for the Soviet leaders: it warded off what they had most dreaded—a united capitalist attack on Soviet Russia. But it was not the intention of Soviet policy; the events of 1 September and 3 September could not be foreseen on 23 August. Both Hitler and Stalin imagined that they had prevented war, not brought it on. Hitler thought that he would score another Munich over Poland; Stalin that he had at any rate escaped an unequal war in the present, and perhaps even avoided it altogether.

However one spins the crystal and tries to look into the future from the point of view of 23 August 1939, it is difficult to see what other course Soviet Russia could have followed. The Soviet apprehensions of a European alliance against Russia were exaggerated, though not groundless. But, quite apart from this—given the Polish refusal of Soviet aid, given too the British policy of drawing out negotiations in Moscow without seriously striving for a conclusion—neutrality, with or without a formal pact, was the most that Soviet diplomacy could attain; and limitation of German gains in Poland and the Baltic was the inducement which made a formal pact attractive. The policy was right according to the textbooks of diplomacy. It contained all the same a grave blunder: by concluding a written agreement, the Soviet statesmen, like Western statesmen before them, slipped into the delusion that Hitler would keep his word. Stalin obviously had doubts. At the moment of parting with Ribbentrop he said: "The Soviet Government take the new Pact very seriously. He could guarantee on his word of honour that the Soviet Union would not betray its partner". There was a clear implication: "Do thou likewise". All the same Stalin obviously thought that the pact had value, not only as an immediate manoeuvre, but over a long period. This is curious, but not unusual. Men, themselves without scruple, often complain when they are cheated by others.

At any rate the bomb had exploded. Hitler was radiant, confident that he had pulled off the decisive stroke. On 22 August he entertained his leading generals to the wildest of his speeches: "Close your hearts to pity. Act brutally". This rigmarole was not a serious directive for action—no formal record was kept. Hitler was glorying in his own skill. Tucked away in the speech was a hard core: "Now the probability is great that the West will not intervene".[1] As well, Hitler was talking for effect. A report of the speech reached the British embassy almost at once;[2] whether intentionally or not, the so-called German "resistance" did Hitler's work for him. On 23 August Hitler took a further step. He fixed the attack on Poland for 4.40 a.m. on 26 August. This, too, was play-acting to impress the generals and, through them, the Western Powers. The German time-table could operate only from 1 September. Before then an attack on Poland was possible only if she had already surrendered. But technical considerations no longer seemed to matter: the Nazi-Soviet pact was assumed to have cleared the way for a diplomatic collapse on the part of the Western Powers.

The French almost came up to Hitler's expectations—or down to them. Bonnet had always been eager to desert the Poles. He resented the way in which they had behaved during the Czech crisis; he accepted the German case over Danzig; he had no faith in the Polish army. The Russians, Bonnet argued, claimed that they could not fight against Germany without a common frontier; a German conquest of Poland would provide one, and the Franco-Soviet Pact could then be revived to real effect. On 28 August, when Ribbentrop's journey to Moscow became known, Bonnet asked Daladier to summon the Committee of National Defence. There he hinted at his policy: "Should we blindly apply our alliance with Poland? Would it be better, on the contrary, to push Warsaw into a compromise? We could thus gain time to complete our equipment, increase our military strength, and improve our diplomatic position, so as to be able to resist Germany more effectively if she turned against France later". But Bonnet was no fighter, even for peace. He left the decision to others. The generals would not confess France's military weakness, for which they were responsible; perhaps they did not even

[1] Memorandum of speech by Hitler, 22 Aug. 1939. *German Foreign Policy*, series D. vii. No. 192 and 193.
[2] Ogilvie-Forbes to Kirkpatrick, 25 Aug. 1939. *British Foreign Policy*, third series. vii. No. 314.

appreciate it. Gamelin declared that the French army was "ready" (whatever that might mean); he further said that Poland would hold out until the spring and that by then the Western front would be impregnable.[1] No one raised the question whether it was possible actually to aid the Poles. Obviously those present all assumed that the French army would merely man the Maginot line, despite Gamelin's promise to the Poles of an offensive. There was no discussion of policy, no proposal to warn the Poles of their danger. The Poles were left free to resist Hitler or to compromise with him, just as they chose. Even more remarkable, there was no approach to the British, no Anglo-French meeting of ministers such as had marked the Czech crisis. The British, too, were left free to resist Hitler or to compromise, without any information as to French wishes or French strength. Yet the British decision would commit France. The French would either abdicate finally in eastern Europe or would carry, almost alone, the burden of a great European war, entirely according to which London preferred. There was silence towards the British, silence towards the Poles, almost silence towards the Germans. Daladier sent a letter of warning to Hitler. Otherwise French statesmen did nothing throughout the week which determined, for many years, the fate of France.

This was a strange passivity, but no stranger than the French policy during previous years. The French did not know which way to turn. They would not deliberately abandon the settlement of 1919; and yet sensed that they were incapable of maintaining it. They had behaved like this over German rearmament. They refused to allow it, yet could find no way of preventing it. It was the same over Austria: "No" was repeated until the Anschluss happened. Czechoslovakia would have seen the same story again, had it not been for British prompting. Then the British urged surrender, and the French acquiesced. Now no word came from the British; and Daladier, the most representative of French politicians, relapsed into sullen resistance. The French cared no more for Danzig than they had done for the German-speaking territories of Czechoslovakia; but they would not themselves destroy what they once had made. They wanted to make an end one way or the other. "Il faut en finir" was the universal French mood in 1989. They had no idea what the end

[1] Bonnet, *Fin d'une Europe*, 308-4.

would be. Hardly any Frenchmen foresaw military defeat;
victory over Germany seemed equally remote. There is some
slight evidence that the French secret service exaggerated the
opposition inside Germany. But there was no rational calculation
behind the decision of 23 August. The French were at a loss what
to do; they therefore decided to let things happen.

Decision thus rested exclusively with the British government.
Their policy, too, seemed in ruins; the Anglo-Soviet alliance was
gone beyond recall. This was a basic misunderstanding of the
British position—indeed a misunderstanding which did as much
as anything else to cause the second World war. Alliance with
Soviet Russia was the policy of the Opposition—the policy of
Labour, of Winston Churchill, and of Lloyd George. It was they
who insisted that resistance to Hitler was possible only if Soviet
Russia were on the Allied side. The government did not share
this view. They never attached practical value to the Soviet
alliance; and they drifted into negotiations unwillingly, driven
on by agitation in Parliament and in the country. They were
relieved when negotiations broke down; delighted to be able to
say, "we told you so", to their critics; and freed from an embarrassment. The Conservative back-benchers went further.
Many of them had favoured Hitler as a bulwark against Bolshevism; now he became, in their eyes, a traitor to the cause of
Western civilisation. At the same time as the Conservatives
swung against Hitler, Labour turned, with almost equal bitterness, against Stalin; resolved to show that they, at any rate, were
sincere in their anti-Fascism, even if it meant supporting
Chamberlain. On any rational calculation, the Nazi-Soviet Pact
ought to have discouraged the British people. Lloyd George was
almost alone in making this calculation. Otherwise the Pact
produced a resolution such as the British had not shown for
twenty years. On 22 August, to universal applause, the Cabinet
determined to stand by their obligation to Poland.

There was no discussion how this obligation could be fulfilled;
indeed there was no way of fulfilling it. Military advisers were not
called in except to consider the civil defences of London. The
British government still thought in terms of policy, not of action.
Their policy remained unchanged: on the one hand, firm warnings
to Hitler that he would face general war if he attacked Poland;
on the other, equally steady assurances that he would receive con-

cessions if he acted peacefully. They were resolved on this policy.
Hence they did not consult the French whether war were prac-
ticable, nor enquire of the Poles what concessions could be made.
Indeed they were determined on concessions over the Poles'
heads, if Hitler were reasonable. The British government still
agreed with Hitler in regard to Danzig. But even now the
question of Danzig was not formally raised. Hitler waited for
offers which could be screwed up; the British waited for claims
which could be scaled down. Whichever made the first move
would lose; hence neither made it. The British government found
a middle way: they would warn Hitler against war and, at the
same time, hint at the rewards which peace would bring him.
Their original intention had been to send a special emissary—not
Chamberlain this time, but perhaps General Ironside. In the
hurry consequent on the Nazi-Soviet pact, this was impossible.
The message had to be delivered by the ambassador, Nevile
Henderson, who flew to Berchtesgaden on 23 August.

It was an unfortunate choice. Henderson no doubt tried to
speak firmly, but his heart was not in it. With consistency
worthy of a better cause, he remained convinced that the Poles
were in the wrong. He wanted them to be forced to give way, as
the Czechs had been forced to give way the year before. A few
days previously he wrote to a friend in the Foreign Office:
"History will judge the Press generally to have been the principal
cause of the war. . . . Of all Germans, believe it or not, Hitler is
the most moderate so far as Danzig and the Corridor are concerned. . . . We could not say Boo to Benes last year till we were
on the abyss of war. And we can't say Boo to Beck now".[1] He
certainly failed to say Boo to Hitler. Though he loyally delivered
the British message, he still paraded British conciliation. He told
Hitler, quite truly: "the proof of Chamberlain's friendship was to
be found in the fact that he had refused to have Churchill in the
Cabinet"; and he said further that the hostile attitude in Great
Britain was the work of Jews and enemies of the Nazis, which was
exactly what Hitler thought himself.[2] Faced with such a half-
hearted opponent, Hitler bullied and stormed. When Henderson

[1] Henderson to Strang, 16 Aug. 1939. *British Foreign Policy*, third series.
vii. No. 37.

[2] Memorandum by Loesch, 24 Aug. 1939. *German Foreign Policy*, series
D. vii. No. 200.

left the room, Hitler slapped his thigh and said: "Chamberlain will not survive that conversation; his Cabinet will fall to-night".[1] Henderson responded as Hitler intended. Immediately on his return to Berlin, he wrote to Halifax: "I have held from the beginning that the Poles were utterly foolish and unwise"; and again: "I personally no longer see any hope of avoiding war unless the Polish Ambassador is instructed to apply today or at the latest tomorrow for personal interview with Hitler".[2]

In England, however, events did not come up to Hitler's expectation. Quite the reverse. Parliament met on 24 August, and unanimously applauded what it supposed to be the government's firm stand. Hitler began to have doubts: evidently more was needed to extract from the British government the concessions on which he still counted. On 24 August Hitler flew to Berlin. On his instructions, Goering called in the Swede Dahlerus, and sent him off to London with an unofficial appeal for British mediation. This was an ingenious trap: if the British refused, Hitler could claim that he had never made a move; if they yielded, they would be compelled to put pressure on Poland. The same evening Hitler held a meeting with Goering, Ribbentrop, and the principal generals. Should they go on with the attack on Poland, now due to begin within thirty-six hours? Hitler declared that he would make a further attempt to detach the Western Powers from their Polish allies. The attempt took the form of a "last offer", communicated to Henderson shortly after noon on 25 August. Germany, Hitler declared, was determined "to abolish the Macedonian conditions on her eastern frontier". The problems of Danzig and the Corridor must be solved—though he still did not say how. Once these problems were out of the way, Germany would make "a large, comprehensive offer"; she would guarantee the British Empire, accept an agreed limitation of armaments, and renew the assurance that her frontier in the west was final.[3] Henderson was impressed, as usual. Hitler, he reported, spoke "with great earnestness and apparent sincerity".[4] Later writers have all dismissed Hitler's offer as fraudulent; and

[1] Weizsäcker, *Erinnerungen*, 252.

[2] Henderson to Halifax, 24 Aug. 1939. *British Foreign Policy*, third series. vii. No. 257 and 241.

[3] Henderson to Halifax, 25 Aug. 1939. *Ibid*. No. 283.

[4] Henderson to Halifax, 25 Aug. 1939. *Ibid*. No. 284.

so in a sense it was. The immediate object was to isolate Poland. Yet the offer also represented Hitler's permanent policy: though he wanted a free hand to destroy conditions in the east which enlightened Western opinion had also pronounced intolerable, he had no ambitions directed against Great Britain and France.

But what could Hitler hope to achieve by this offer in the circumstances of the moment? Henderson promised to fly to London on the morning of 26 August; and by then the attack on Poland presumably would have begun. Was Hitler merely talking for the record—to clear himself in the eyes of posterity or even of his own conscience? Or had he forgotten his time-table, unable to realise that orders, once given, will be ultimately carried out? The latter seems the more likely explanation. Throughout the afternoon of 25 August, Hitler raged round the Chancellery, uncertain what to do. At 3 p.m. he ordered that the attack on Poland should be carried out. Three hours later Attolico, the Italian ambassador, arrived with a message from Mussolini: though Italy stood by Germany unconditionally, she could not "intervene militarily", unless Germany at once supplied all her needs in war material; and these, when the list came, were—in Ciano's words—"enough to kill a bull if a bull could read". Mussolini had acted the strong man till the last moment; now, with war apparently imminent, he ran away. Immediately after this blow came another. Ribbentrop reported that the formal alliance between Great Britain and Poland had just been signed in London. Hitler summoned Keitel, his chief-of-staff: "Stop everything at once, fetch Brauchitsch [the commander-in-chief] immediately. I need time for negotiations". The new orders went out shortly after 7 p.m. The premature offensive was as precipitately cancelled.

Here was another mysterious episode. Why did Hitler pull back at the last moment? Did he lose his nerve? Did the two events of Mussolini's neutrality and the Anglo-Polish alliance really take him by surprise? He himself, with the normal propensity of statesmen to put the blame on others, at once complained that it was all the fault of Mussolini: news of the Italian decision not to fight had stiffened the British just when they were on the point of surrender. This was nonsense. The British did not know of Mussolini's decision when they signed the alliance with Poland, though they could make a good guess at it. Nor was the alliance timed for its effect at that particular moment. Its conclusion had been held up during the negotiations with Soviet Russia; once these failed, there was no reason for further postponement, and the British signed it as soon as formalities could be completed. They were unaware that Hitler had fixed on 25 August as the day of crisis. They were thinking in terms of the first week in September; just as Hitler had long thought in terms of 1 September. Probably this is the explanation of his apparent hesitation on 25 August. Advancing the offensive to that date was a "try-on", an extra call rather like his exaggerated obstinacy at Godesberg the previous year. Quite apart from the diplomatic events of 25 August, there were good military reasons for reverting to the original date. On 25 August the Western frontier of Germany was still virtually undefended. Perhaps thereafter Hitler faced the fact that some sort of war with the Western Powers was in the offing. But it is more likely that he spoke the truth to Keitel: he needed time for negotiation.

The British, too, were intent on negotiation. The signing of the Anglo-Polish alliance was a preliminary to this, not a firm decision for war. There is clear evidence that the British did not take the alliance all that seriously. Their draft had been designed to fit in with an Anglo-Soviet alliance, now vanished. In the hugger-mugger which followed the Nazi-Soviet pact, clauses from a Polish draft were included as well; and one of these contained the pledge which the British had hitherto evaded—a full extension of the alliance to cover Danzig. Yet almost at the moment of signing the alliance, a member of the foreign office drafted "possible counter-proposals to Herr Hitler" which postulated that Danzig should have "the right to determine its political allegiance", subject to the recognition of Poland's economic rights;[1] and Halifax himself told the Polish ambassador that "the Polish Government would make a great mistake if they sought to adopt a position in which discussion of peaceful modifications of the status of Danzig was ruled out".[2] Thus the British government and Hitler were close to agreement on how

[1] Memorandum by Makins, 25 Aug. 1939. *British Foreign Policy*, third series. vii. No. 807.
[2] Halifax to Kennard, 25 Aug. 1939. *Ibid.* No. 809.

the crisis should end; and the Poles were out of step. The problem however was not how negotiations should end, but how they should begin; and for this no solution was found.

Preliminaries for a negotiation proceeded furiously between 26 August and 29 August: the British hinting at what they would offer, Hitler at what he would demand. Both sides hesitated to go over the brink into actual negotiations. There was further confusion in that these soundings were conducted on two levels. Nevile Henderson acted as official intermediary; Dahlerus shuttled between Berlin and London even more assiduously. He flew to London on 25 August and back to Berlin on 26 August; to London and back on 27 August; and the same again on 80 August. In Berlin he saw Goering and sometimes Hitler; in London he was received with every precaution of secrecy, and saw Chamberlain and Halifax. The British might insist that their remarks to Dahlerus were "off the record"; Hitler was bound to feel all the same that a second Munich was being prepared for him. He may have been genuinely taken aback by the signature of the Anglo-Polish alliance; this effect was lost as Henderson and Dahlerus multiplied their exertions. Yet at the same time the British, listening to Dahlerus, imagined that their position was improving. A member of the foreign office commented on the activities of Dahlerus: "This shows that the German Government are wobbling. . . . Whilst we may and should be conciliatory in form, we should be absolutely firm in substance. . . . The latest indications are that we have an unexpectedly strong hand". This minute bears the further comment: "Seen by S. of S. who says he quite agrees with it".[1] With extreme ingenuity Halifax even believed that a second Munich would discredit Hitler, not the British government. He wrote: "When we speak of Munich we must remember the change that has supervened since then in the attitude and strength of this country, and in many other directions—Italy—and let us hope Japan—etc. And if Hitler is led to accept a moderate solution now, it is perhaps not altogether wishful thinking to believe that his position will suffer a certain diminution within Germany".[2]

[1] Minute to Kirkpatrick, 27 Aug. 1989. *British Foreign Policy*, third series. vii. No. 897.
[2] Minute by Halifax on Henderson to Halifax, 29 Aug. 1989. *Ibid.* No. 455.

Thus the two sides circled round each other like wrestlers seeking advantage before the clinch. The British offered to arrange direct negotiations between Germany and Poland if Hitler would promise to behave peacefully; Hitler replied that there would be no war if he got his way over Danzig. Later writers have argued that Hitler's reply was dishonest; that he was concerned to isolate Poland, not to avoid war. This may well be true. But the offer by the British government was dishonest also: there was no chance of extracting concessions from the Poles once the danger of war was removed, and the British knew it. In the previous year Benes had appealed for British support. They had implied that he might secure it if he were conciliatory enough; and he had swallowed the bait. Now the British were already committed—their hands tied not so much by their formal alliance with Poland, as by the resolution of British public opinion. They could not dictate concessions to the Poles; they could not allow Hitler to dictate them. Yet there would be no concessions unless someone did the dictating. On 28 August Sir Horace Wilson, acting on Chamberlain's behalf, saw Kennedy, the American ambassador. After the conversation, Kennedy telephoned the State Department: "The British wanted one thing of us and one thing only, namely that we put pressure on the Poles. They felt that they could not, given their obligations, do anything of this sort but that we could".[1] President Roosevelt rejected this idea out of hand. Chamberlain—again according to Kennedy—then lost all hope: "He says the futility of it all is the thing that is frightful; after all, they cannot save the Poles; they can merely carry on a war of revenge that will mean the destruction of all Europe".[2]

The deadlock lasted until 29 August. Then it was broken by Hitler. He was in the weaker position, though the British did not know it. There was not much time left before 1 September for him to pull off diplomatic success. At 7.15 p.m. he made to Henderson a formal offer and a formal demand: he would negotiate directly with Poland if a Polish plenipotentiary arrived in Berlin the following day. This was a retreat from the

[1] *Moffat Papers 1919–43* (1956), 253. Cordell Hull supplies Wilson's name. *Memoirs*, i. 662.

[2] Kennedy to Hull, 28 Aug. 1989. *Foreign Relations of the United States*, 1989. Vol. I. General.

position Hitler had rigorously asserted since 26 March—that he would never again deal directly with the Poles. Though Henderson complained that the demand was perilously near an ultimatum, he was eager to accept it; it constituted in his opinion the "sole chance of preventing war". Henderson pressed the demand on his own government; he urged the French government to advise an immediate visit by Beck; he was most insistent of all with the Polish ambassador Lipski.[1] Lipski took no notice—apparently he did not even report Hitler's demand to Warsaw. The French government responded as clearly in the opposite direction—they told Beck to go to Berlin at once. But the decision rested with the British government. Here was the proposal which they had always wanted and which they had repeatedly hinted at to Hitler: direct negotiations between Poland and Germany. Hitler had now done his part; but they could not do theirs. They had the gravest doubt whether the Poles would thus present themselves in Berlin at Hitler's behest. Kennedy reported Chamberlain's feeling to Washington: "Frankly he is more worried about getting the Poles to be reasonable than the Germans".[2] The British gnawed over the problem throughout 30 August. Finally they hit on a sort of solution. They passed Hitler's demand on to Warsaw at 12.25 a.m. on 31 August—that is to say, twenty-five minutes after the German ultimatum, if such it were, had expired. The British had been correct in their apprehension of Polish obstinacy. Beck, when informed of Hitler's demand, at once replied: "if invited to Berlin he would of course not go, as he had no intention of being treated like President Hacha".[3] Thus the British, by acting too late, could still claim that they had offered something which they knew they could not deliver: a Polish plenipotentiary in Berlin.

Hitler had not anticipated this. He had expected that negotiations would start; and he then intended them to break down on Polish obstinacy. On his instructions detailed demands were at last prepared. These were principally the immediate return of

[1] Henderson to Halifax, 29 Aug., 30 Aug. 1939. *British Foreign Policy*, third series. vii. No. 493, 510.

[2] Kennedy to Hull, 30 Aug. 1939. *Foreign Relations of the United States*, 1939. Vol. I. General.

[3] Kennard to Halifax, 31 Aug. 1939. *British Foreign Policy*, third series. vii. No. 575.

Danzig, and a plebiscite in the Corridor[1]—the very terms which the British and French governments had themselves long favoured. But, failing a Polish plenipotentiary, the Germans had difficulty in making their terms known. At midnight on 30 August Henderson brought to Ribbentrop the news that a Polish plenipotentiary was not coming that day. Ribbentrop had only the rough draft of the proposed German terms, scribbled over with Hitler's emendations. It was not in a condition to be shown to Henderson; and Ribbentrop had instructions from Hitler not to do so. He therefore read the terms over slowly. Later a myth grew up that he had "gabbled" them, deliberately cheating Henderson with terms that were only for show. In fact Henderson got the gist clearly, and was impressed. Taken at their face value, he thought, they were "not unreasonable". On his return to the British embassy, he summoned Lipski at 2 a.m., and urged him to seek an interview with Ribbentrop at once. Lipski took no notice, and went back to bed.

The Germans were now anxious that their terms had not gone properly on record with Henderson. They once more employed Dahlerus as an allegedly unofficial emissary. Goering, claiming to be acting in defiance of Hitler, showed the terms to Dahlerus, who in turn telephoned them to the British embassy about 4 a.m. Since Goering knew that all telephone conversations were monitored by at least three government agencies (one of them his own), his defiance of Hitler was of course a fiction. The next morning Goering abandoned it. Dahlerus was given a copy of the German terms, and took it round to the British embassy. Henderson again summoned Lipski, who refused to come. Dahlerus and Ogilvie-Forbes, the British counsellor of embassy, were dispatched to see Lipski. He remained unmoved. He refused to look at the German terms. When Dahlerus was out of the room, Lipski protested against introducing this intermediary, and said: "he would stake his reputation that German morale was breaking and that the present régime would soon crack. . . . This German offer was a trap. It was also a sign of weakness on the part of the Germans".[2] In a further effort to break through the

[1] Schmidt, circular dispatch, 30 Aug. 1939. *German Foreign Policy*, series D. vii. No. 458.

[2] Henderson to Halifax, 31 Aug. 1939. *British Foreign Policy*, third series. vii. No. 597.

crust of obstinacy, Dahlerus telephoned to Horace Wilson in London. The German terms, he said, were "extremely liberal"; it was " 'obvious to us' [Dahlerus? Goering? Henderson?] that the Poles were obstructing the possibilities of a negotiation". Wilson realised that the Germans were listening-in; he told Dahlerus to shut up and put down the receiver.[1]

The precaution came too late. Every move of the last few hours had been as public as if it had been announced in the newspapers. The telephone calls between Henderson and Lipski, and between Dahlerus and Henderson, the comings and goings between the British and Polish embassies—all these were known to the Germans. They were undoubtedly known to Hitler. What conclusion could he possibly draw? Only the conclusion that he had succeeded in driving a wedge between Poland and her Western allies. This was true in regard to the French government. It was true in regard to Henderson. He wrote late on 31 August: "On German offer war would be completely unjustifiable. . . . Polish Government should announce tomorrow, in the light of German proposals which have now been made public, their intention to send a Plenipotentiary to discuss in general terms these proposals".[2] Hitler was not to know that Henderson no longer carried the weight in London which he had carried the year before. But even the British government were losing patience with the Poles. Late on the night of 31 August Halifax telegraphed to Warsaw: "I do not see why the Polish Government should feel difficulty about authorising Polish Ambassador to accept a document from the German Government".[3] Given another twenty-four hours, and the breach would be wide open. But Hitler had not got the twenty-four hours. He was the prisoner of his own time-table. With his generals watching sceptically, he could not again call off the attack of Poland unless he had something solid to show; and this was still denied him by the Poles. The breach between Poland and her allies gave him a chance. He had to gamble on it.

At 12.40 p.m. on 31 August Hitler decided that the attack should proceed. At 1 p.m. Lipski telephoned, asking for an inter-

---

[1] Minute by Cadogan, 31 Aug. 1939. *British Foreign Policy*, third series. vii. No. 589.
[2] Henderson to Halifax, 1 Sept. 1939. *Ibid*. No. 631.
[3] Halifax to Kennard, 1 Sept. 1939. *Ibid*. No. 632.

view with Ribbentrop. The Germans, who had intercepted his instructions, knew that he had been told not to enter into "any concrete negotiations". At 3 p.m. Weizsäcker telephoned Lipski to ask whether he was coming as a plenipotentiary. Lipski replied: "No, in his capacity as an ambassador". This was enough for Hitler. The Poles, it seemed, were remaining obstinate; he could go forward to the gamble of isolating them in war. At 4 p.m. the orders for war were confirmed. At 6.30 p.m. Lipski at last saw Ribbentrop. Lipski said that his government were "favourably considering" the British proposal for direct Polish-German negotiations. Ribbentrop asked whether he was a plenipotentiary. Lipski again answered No. Ribbentrop did not communicate the German terms; if he had tried to do so, Lipski would have refused to receive them. Thus ended the only direct contact between Germany and Poland since 26 March. The Poles had kept their nerve unbroken to the last moment. At 4.45 a.m. on the following morning the German attack on Poland began. At 6 a.m. German aeroplanes bombed Warsaw.

Here was a clear *casus foederis* for both Great Britain and France. Their ally had been wantonly attacked; it only remained for them to declare war on the aggressor. Nothing of the kind happened. Both governments addressed a pained remonstrance to Hitler, warning him that they would have to go to war unless he desisted. Meanwhile they waited for something to turn up; and something did. On 31 August Mussolini, carefully following the precedent of the previous year, proposed a European conference: it should meet on 5 September and should survey all causes of European conflict, with the precondition that Danzig should return to Germany in advance. The two Western governments were favourable to the proposal when it first reached them. But Mussolini had got his timing wrong. In 1938 he had three days in which to avert war; in 1939 less than twenty-four hours, and this was not enough. By 1 September, when the Western governments replied to Mussolini, they had to postulate that fighting must first stop in Poland. Nor was this all. While Bonnet was enthusiastic for Mussolini's proposal, in Great Britain public opinion took charge. The House of Commons was restive when Chamberlain explained that Germany had merely been "warned"; it expected something more solid next day. Halifax, swinging as usual with the national mood, insisted that the conference could be held only if Germany withdrew from all Polish territory. The Italians knew that it was hopeless to place such a demand before Hitler; they dropped the conference without further effort.

Yet both the British and French governments, the French especially, went on believing in a conference which had vanished before it was born. Hitler had initially replied to Mussolini that, if invited to a conference, he would give his answer at mid-day on 3 September. Therefore Bonnet, and Chamberlain with him, strove desperately to postpone a declaration of war until after that time, even though the Italians no longer intended to invite Hitler or anyone else. Bonnet conjured up the excuse that the French military wanted the delay in order to carry through mobilisation, undisturbed by German air attack (which, they knew, would not occur anyway—the German air force was fully employed in Poland). Chamberlain conjured up no excuse except that the French wanted delay and that it was always difficult to work with allies. In the evening of 2 September he was still entertaining the House of Commons with hypothetical negotiations: "If the German Government should agree to withdraw their forces then His Majesty's Government would be willing to regard the position as being the same as it was before the German forces crossed the Polish frontier. That is to say, the way would be open to discussion between the German and Polish Governments on the matters at issue". This was too much even for loyal Conservatives. Leo Amery called to Arthur Greenwood, acting leader of the Opposition: "Speak for England", a task of which Chamberlain was incapable. Ministers, led by Simon, warned Chamberlain that the government would fall unless it sent an ultimatum to Hitler before the House met again. Chamberlain gave way. The objections of the French were overruled. The British ultimatum was delivered to the Germans at 9 a.m. on 3 September. It expired at 11 a.m., and a state of war followed. When Bonnet learnt that the British were going to war in any case, his overriding anxiety was to catch up with them. The time of the French ultimatum was advanced, despite the supposed objections of the General Staff: it was delivered at noon on 3 September and expired at 5 p.m. In this curious way the French who had preached resistance to Germany for twenty years appeared to be dragged into war by the British who had for twenty years preached conciliation. Both countries went to war for that part of the peace settlement which they had long regarded as least defensible. Hitler may have projected a great war all along; yet it seems from the record that he became involved in war through launching on 29 August a diplomatic manoeuvre which he ought to have launched on 28 August.

Such were the origins of the second World war, or rather of the war between the three Western Powers over the settlement of Versailles; a war which had been implicit since the moment when the first war ended. Men will long debate whether this renewed war could have been averted by greater firmness or by greater conciliation; and no answer will be found to these hypothetical speculations. Maybe either would have succeeded, if consistently followed; the mixture of the two, practised by the British government, was the most likely to fail. These questions now seem infinitely remote. Though Hitler blundered in supposing that the two Western Powers would not go to war at all, his expectation that they would not go to war seriously turned out to be correct. Great Britain and France did nothing to help the Poles, and little to help themselves. The European struggle which began in 1918 when the German armistice delegates presented themselves before Foch in the railway-carriage at Rethondes, ended in 1940 when the French armistice delegates presented themselves before Hitler in the same carriage. There was a "new order" in Europe; it was dominated by Germany.

The British people resolved to defy Hitler, though they lacked the strength to undo his work. He himself came to their aid. His success depended on the isolation of Europe from the rest of the world. He gratuitously destroyed the source of this success. In 1941 he attacked Soviet Russia and declared war on the United States, two World Powers who asked only to be left alone. In this way a real World War began. We still live in its shadow. The war which broke out in 1939 has become a matter of historical curiosity.

Bibliography

This list, like my book, is selective for the earlier years covered and becomes more detailed towards the end. It includes only books which I have found useful at one time or another.

Sources—I. Official Publications

A selection of papers which were made public at the time appears each year in *Documents on International Affairs* (1928 and subsequent years). The volume for 1939 was not published until after the war; and it contains selections also from the documents published later.

Documents on German Foreign Policy 1918-1945 (1948 *et seq.*), with numerous American, British, and French editors in chief. This contains the records of the German foreign ministry which fell into Allied hands at the end of the war. Some records were destroyed. In any case, the records published tell us more about the professionals of the foreign ministry than about Hitler, who was not given to revealing himself on paper. The editors are somewhat chary in reproducing telegrams. Hence the volumes give a perhaps misleading impression of considered policy rather than of puzzled men doing things in a hurry. The publication is incomplete, and may never be completed. I have used:

Series C, Volumes I-III, which cover 30 January 1933 to 31 March 1935.
Series D, Volumes I-VII, which cover September 1937, with a few earlier papers, to 3 September 1939.

Documents and Materials relating to the Eve of the Second World War. Volume I: November 1937-1938 (1947). Volume II: Dirksen Papers 1938-1939 (1948). These contain German records which fell into Soviet hands. The first volume has now been superseded by the larger publication listed above. The second volume has a few documents which have otherwise disappeared.

Documents on British Foreign Policy 1919-1939 (1946 *et seq.*), edited by Rohan Butler and Sir E. L. Woodward; the place of the latter has lately been taken by J. P. T. Bury. These documents are taken almost exclusively from the official archives of the foreign office; the minutes of foreign secretaries and officials are rarely printed. Three series are in course of publication; only the third is complete. I have used:

First Series, Volume I-IX. 1 July 1919 to 1920.

Second Series, Volumes I-VIII. 23 May 1929 to 1934.

Third Series, Volumes I-IX. 9 March 1938 to 3 September 1939.

I documenti diplomatici italiani (1952). These will ultimately cover the record of Italian diplomacy from the founding of the Kingdom of Italy in 1861 to the fall of Mussolini in 1943. It is appearing in nine series. For the period covered by this book I have used:

Sixth Series, edited by R. Mosca, Volume I. 4 November 1918 to 17 January 1919.

Seventh Series, edited by R. Moscati, Volumes I-III, 11 October 1922 to 14 May 1925.

Eighth Series, edited by M. Toscano, Volumes XII-XIII, 23 May to 3 September 1939.

New Documents on the History of Munich (1958). This contains Czech and a few Soviet documents on 1938. Otherwise, for Soviet Russia, there are only the public papers selected by Jane Degras in *Soviet Documents on foreign policy*, 3 volumes (1953 *et seq.*).

Papers relating to the Foreign Relations of the United States. These papers appear annually with two supplements for the period 1931-1939. This early publication, together with the almost unrestricted access allowed to historians by the State Department, makes nonsense of the plea made by all other governments that secrecy must be preserved until some fifty years have elapsed.

II. Private Papers and Memoirs

Germany. G. Stresemann: *Diaries, Letters, and Papers,* 3 volumes. (1935-1940). This selection exaggerates the "Western" orientation of Stresemann's policy. J. Curtius: *Sechs Jahre Minister der deutschen Republik* (1947).

For the Nazi period: Hitler did not explain himself. Ribbentrop wrote defensive *Memoirs* (1954) when in prison. Papen provides an ingenious version in *Memoirs* (1952). E. von Weizsäcker, permanent head of the foreign ministry in the last years, has written an exculpatory account in *Erinnerungen* (1950). H. von Dirksen is moderately apologetic in *Moskau-Tokio-London* (1949). E. Kordt, *Nicht aus den Akten* (1950), has been superseded by the documents. P. Schmidt, *Statist auf diplomatischer Bühne* (1949), contains anecdotes by Hitler's interpreter. *The Last Attempt* by B. Dahlerus (1947) is an important source for his unofficial mediation between the British and German governments.

France. G. Suarez: *Briand, sa vie, son oeuvre*, Volumes V and VI (1940-1941), contains a certain amount about his foreign policy. *Jadis 1914-1936* by E. Herriot (1953) is too slight to be useful. *Entre deux Guerres*, 3 volumes, by J. Paul-Boncour (1945-1947), on the other hand, is almost too substantial. P. E. Flandin, *Politique francaise*, 1919-40 (1947), is useful only for the crisis over the reoccupation of the Rhineland in 1936. G. Bonnet, *Defense de la paix*. Vol. I: *De Washington au Quai d'Orsay* (1946). Vol. II: *Fin d'une Europe* (1948), is a source of immense value, in the absence of an official publication. Bonnet has been much criticised for evasiveness and inaccuracy; but his memoirs are above the usual standard of those by foreign ministers. Gamelin, *Servir*, Volume II (1947), is also of great value for policy as seen by the chief of the general staff. Three French ambassadors wrote memoirs: A. François-Poncet, *Souvenirs d'une ambassade a Berlin* (1946); R. Coulondre, *De Staline à Hitler* (1950); L. Noël, *L'agression allemande contre la Pologne* (1946).

Great Britain. Lloyd George, *The Truth about the Peace Treaties*, 2 volumes (1938), contains a great deal of material on the immediate post-war years. C. Petrie, *Austen Chamberlain*, 2 volumes (1934-1940), has a few letters. D'Abernon, *An Ambassador of Peace*, 3 volumes (1929-1931), is important for the period of Locarno. There is nothing on MacDonald, and nothing of value on Baldwin. K. Feiling, *Neville Chamberlain* (1946), gives a few letters and quotations from Chamberlain's diary. S. Hoare, *Nine Troubled Years* (1954), is of value, though it is more a defence than a record. The contributions by Lord Halifax and Lord Simon are best passed over in silence. N. Henderson, *Failure of a Mission* (1940), is an honest book which deserved a better reception than it received. I failed to derive anything useful from the writings of Vansittart, Strang, and Kirkpatrick. W. S. Churchill, *The Second World War*, Volume I: *The Gathering Storm* (1948), is the record of a critic, with occasional bits of solid information. Tom Jones, *A Diary with Letters 1931-50* (1954), gives the best picture of the "appeasers". *The History of the Times*, Volume IV (1952), is also important for this subject.

Italy. There is nothing by Mussolini. The most important source is Ciano: *Diary 1937-1938* (1952), and *Diary 1939-1943* (1947). *Ciano's Diplomatic Papers* (1948) will be superseded in time by the official publication. Aloisi, leader of the Italian delegation at Geneva, published a *Journal* (25 July 1932 to 14 June 1936) (1957). This indicates that the professional diplomatists, as against Mussolini, wanted a negotiated settlement of the Abyssinian question. Raffaele Guariglia, *Ricordi* (1950), does not reveal much, though it is useful for its account of Franco-Italian relations in the Mediterranean. M. Magistrati, *L'Italia a Berlino 1937-39* (1956), supplements Attolico's account in the official records.

Poland. Beck wrote a defence of his policy, while interned in Rumania: *Dernier rapport* (1951). The *Journal 1933-39* of Szembek (1952) gives a picture of the Polish foreign office.

Rumania: G. Gafencu, *Last Days of Europe* (1948) describes his visit to the principal capitals in April 1939, and uses documents which he derived from Bonnet.

Soviet Russia: Nothing.

United States: A great deal on Far Eastern affairs. Not much on Europe. The most substantial are Cordell Hull, *Memoirs*, 2 volumes (1948). W. Dodd, ambassador to Hitler, published a *Diary* (1945). Joseph E. Davies, *Mission to Moscow* (1941), contains little in the way of papers; but it is unusual in that the author is favourable to the Soviet Government.

Secondary Works.

General Accounts.

W. N. Medlicott: *British Foreign Policy since Versailles* (1940).
E. H. Carr, *International Relations between the Two World Wars* (1947).
A. M. Gathorne-Hardy, *Short History of International Affairs 1920-1939* (1950).
W. P. Potyomkin, edited: *Histoire de la diplomatie*, Volume 3. Useful only as giving a Soviet view.
M. Baumont: *La faillite de la paix*, 2 volumes (1951).
P. Renouvin: *Histoire des relations internationales.* Volume VII: *Les crises du XXe siècle. I. de 1914 à 1929* (1957). Volume VIII: *Les crises du XXe siècle. II. de 1929 à 1945* (1958).
F. P. Walters: *History of the League of Nations*, 2 volumes (1951).
Various aspects of the German problem are discussed in:
E. H. Carr: *The Twenty Years' Crisis* (1938), a brilliant argument in favour of appeasement.
L. Schwarzschild: *World in Trance* (1943), an equally brilliant argument in favour of firmness.
W. M. Jordan: *Great Britain, France and the German Problem 1919-1939* (1943).
R. B. McCallum: *Public Opinion and the Last Peace* (1944).
Etienne Mantoux: *The Carthaginian Peace* (1946), a demolition of the views, propagated by Keynes, concerning reparations and the peace settlement.
H. W. Gatzke: *Stresemann and the Rearmament of Germany* (1948).

Soviet-German relations have come in for more than their deserved share of attention:

E. H. Carr: *German-Soviet Relations between the Two World Wars* (1952), the best short account.
L. Kochan: *Russia and the Weimar Republic* (1954).
G. Hilger and A. G. Meyer: *The Incompatible Allies. A memoir-history of the German-Soviet Relations 1918-1941* (1953).
G. Freund: *Unholy Alliance* (1957), a strangely moralist version.

On Soviet policy generally there is only:

M. Beloff: *Foreign Policy of Soviet Russia 1929-1941*, 2 volumes (1947-1949). Inevitably, it is for the most part conjecture.

The books on international relations immediately preceding the outbreak of the second World war were mostly written before the large official collections began to appear. The principal ones are:

Alan Bullock: *Hitler* (1952), a good chapter on Hitler's foreign policy.

E. Wiskemann: *The Rome-Berlin Axis* (1949).

J. W. Wheeler-Bennett: *Munich, Prologue to Tragedy* (1948).

J. W. Wheeler-Bennett: *The Nemesis of Power* (1953), this includes some account of the abortive military resistance to Hitler.

M. Toscano: *Le origini del Patto d'Acciaio* (1948).

W. L. Langer and S. E. Gleason: *The Challenge to Isolation* (1952), the early chapters cover European pre-war diplomacy with the expected anti-Soviet slant.

L. B. Namier: *Diplomatic Prelude* (1948). *Europe in Decay* (1950). *In the Nazi Era* (1952), two volumes of supplementary essays.

W. Hofer: *War Premeditated* (1954), an analysis of the last ten days of peace.

The *Survey of International Affairs* (published annually since 1925) gives a contemporary version of international relations. The first volume for 1938 was the last to be published in this way. The series was then suspended. When it was resumed after the war, the volumes took on a more historical character. Volume II for 1938, by R. G. D. Laffan (1951), deals with the crisis over Czechoslovakia. Volume III covers the next six months to Hitler's occupation of Prague (1953). The *World in March 1939* (1952) has general essays of unequal value, the best of them being an examination of Comparative Strength of the Great Powers by H. C. Hillman. *The Eve of War 1939* (1958) describes the diplomacy of the last six months in a detailed, and somewhat confusing, way.

Index

A

Abyssinia: Italian ambitions regarding, 87; in League of Nations, 88–90; attacked by Italy, 91; crisis over, 41, 64, 92–95; conquered by Italy, 95; effects of crisis over, 96–97, 107, 120; Eden and, 126, 144; U.S.A. and, 128.

Adowa, battle of (1896), 87.

Albania: fails to operate sanctions, 91; annexed by Italy, 222.

Alexander, king of Yugoslavia: assassinated, 84.

Alsace-Lorraine: French ambitions for, 19, 40, 42; recovered by France, 26; German renunciation of, 54, 55; not claimed by Hitler, 70.

Amery, Leo, British statesman, 277.

Andrássy, Hungarian statesman, 146.

Angell, Norman, 46.

Anglo-French alliance (1936): 113, 215.

Anglo-German declaration (1938), 186, 198, 262; naval treaty (1935), made, 87, denounced by Hitler, 220.

Anglo-Italian agreement (gentleman's), 126; (16 April 1938), 162, 199, 200.

Anglo-Polish alliance: preliminary agreement made, 212–16; effects of, 220, 221; catastrophic for France, 225; appropriate, 228; formal alliance concluded, 269–70.

Anti-Comintern Pact, 111, 195, 223.

Armistice (11 November 1918): reasons for, 21, 22; terms of, 23.

Astakov, Soviet diplomatist, 255n.

Attlee, C. R., British statesman; Hitler not better than, 112.

Attolico, Italian diplomatist: gives German terms to Mussolini, 184; presents Italian demands to Hitler, 269.

Austria: forbidden to join Germany, 26; proposal for economic union of, with Germany, 62; Hitler's view of, 68; putsch of 1934 in, 81–84; influences Mussolini's Abyssinian policy, 88; fails to operate sanctions, 91; gentleman's agreement of, with Germany (1936), 109–10; German grievance regarding, 135; Halifax willing to yield, 186; restrained by Hitler, 138; crisis over, provoked by

Schuschnigg, 139–41; agreement regarding (12 Feb. 1938); 143; plebiscite proposed in, 146–48; united with Germany, 131, 149–50.

Austria-Hungary: publication of documents of, 14; goes to war (1914), 19; ceases to exist, 21, 24.

Axis (Rome-Berlin): 111, 126, 145, 162, 203.

B

Badoglio, Italian general: conquers Abyssinia, 95.

Baldwin, Stanley, British statesman; correct re German rearmament, 75; becomes prime minister, 90; outwits Labour party, 93; and Hoare-Laval plan, 94–95; and German reoccupation of Rhineland, 98–100; Hitler not better than, 112; says bomber will always get through, 116; against ministry of supply, 118; leaves office, 126–27; Neville Chamberlain's low opinion of, 134.

Balfour, A. J., British statesman: on Poland, 37; on Locarno, 55.

Baltic states: Soviet demand concerning, 235; British refusal to assist against their will, 239; German offers concerning, 259, 262.

Barthou, Louis, French statesman: becomes foreign minister, 76; assassinated, 84.

Baumont, Maurice, 9, 288.

Beck, Joseph, Polish foreign minister, makes non-aggression pact with Germany, 80–81; visits Hitler (Jan. 1939), 195; aspires towards Ukraine, 196; vetoes "peace front", 207; remains firm over Danzig, 210; accepts British guarantee, 210; visits London (April 1939), 212–14; less than frank, 221; not Benes, 222; British defer to, 226; Litvinov and, 237; remains unyielding, 251; refuses to accept Soviet aid, 258; agrees to belated formula concerning Soviet aid, 261; British cannot say Boo to, 267; refuses to go to Berlin, 273; book by, 282.

Belfort, 85.

Benes, Edward, president of Czechoslovakia: and Soviet purges, 112; diplomatic plans of, 153; does not rely on Soviet Russia, 154; Halifax impatient with, 159; negotiates with Sudetens, 161; "pig-headed", 167; and Runciman mission, 168-69; and Soviet aid, 177; accepts Anglo-French proposals, 178-79; Chamberlain's message to, 184; appeals to Soviet government, 185; influence of Polish demands on, 194; resigns, 202; Hitler shares view of, 193, 201; Beck contrasted with, 214, 222, 226, 272.

Berchtesgaden: Hitler's way of life at, 72; Halifax at, 137-38, 150; Papen at (Feb. 1938), 142; Schuschnigg at, 142, 146; Neville Chamberlain at, 174-75; Csáky and Burckhardt at, 254; Ciano at, 255; Nevile Henderson at, 267.

Berlin: Hitler summons generals to (March 1938), 146; Hacha at, 202; Beck refuses to go to, 273.

Bethmann Hollweg, German chancellor; dismayed by outbreak of war, 103.

Birmingham, speech by Neville Chamberlain at, 205.

Bismarck, Otto, German chancellor, 8, 23, 35; 130, 241; Stresemann compared with, 51.

Björkö, treaty of, 8.

Bloch, Camille, 8.

Blomberg, German general, at "Hossbach" meeting, 131-34; marries a prostitute, 141.

Blum, Léon, French statesman: Hitler better than, 112; promotes non-intervention in Spain, 107, 122, 123; ceases to be prime minister, 157; on Munich, 189.

Boer war, 7.

Bonnet, Georges, French foreign minister; renounces Austria, 137; policy of, 157, 159; visits London (April 1938), 160-61; and Litvinov, 164; disapproves of Czechoslovak mobilisation, 165; does not seek Soviet support, 172; advocates surrender, 173; visits London (18-19 Sept. 1938), 175-77; sends ultimatum to Czechs, 178-79; in London (25 Sept.), 181; doubts statement by Halifax, 182; against war, 183; and guarantee to Czechoslovakia, 197; entertains Ribbentrop, 199; on German occupation of Prague, 203; needs Poland, 207; wishes to desert Poland, 225;

seeks Soviet alliance, 237; on Danzig, 238; on Soviet aid, 258; wishes to abandon Poland, 264; wishes to accept Mussolini's offer of a conference, 276; delays declaration of war, 277; memoirs by, 281.

Brailsford, H. N., on situation in 1914, 40; on Germans in Czechoslovakia, 189.

Brandenburg, Erich, 8.

Brauchitsch, German general, 269.

Brenner, Hitler recognises, 146; Mussolini wishes to meet Hitler on, 254.

Brest-Litovsk, treaty of, 19; its effects, 20, 21; Hitler's view of, 70; Soviet resentment against, 227, 233; effects of, undone, 262.

Briand, Aristide, French statesman: on proposed British alliance, 81; and Lloyd George, 48; negotiates treaty of Locarno, 53-55; achievement of, 57-59; biography of, 281.

Bright, John, British statesman, 136.

Brüning, Heinrich, German chancellor, and economic depression, 62; leaves office, 67.

Brussels, conference at (1937), 127-28; Chamberlain fears repetition of, 144.

Bülow, Bernard, German diplomatist, on treaty of Rapallo, 79.

Bullock, Alan, 69, 284.

Burckhardt, Carl, League Commissioner at Danzig, visits Berchtesgaden, 253.

C

Caligula, Roman emperor: horse of, made a consul, 118.

Carlsbad, programme, announced by Henlein, 161.

Cavour, Camille, Italian statesman, 140.

Chamberlain, Austen, British foreign secretary, negotiates treaty of Locarno, 53; on Polish corridor, 54; at League of Nations, 55; and Mussolini, 57, 126; sympathises with France, 65; not appointed minister of supply, 118; biography of, 281.

Chamberlain, Neville, British prime minister, introduces lowest arms-estimates, 61; controls Eden, 97; thinks sanctions the midsummer of madness, 107; Hitler not better than, 112; no Keynesian, 118; becomes prime minister, 126; overshadows Eden, 127; initiates appeasement, 134-36; welcomes Italian approach, 144; forces Eden to resign, 145; on Austria, 147; character of, 157; thinks it impossible to help Czechoslovakia, 160; announces Runciman mission, 168; at Berchtesgaden, 173–75; gives guarantee of Czechoslovakia, 176; at Godesberg, 179–80; sends Horace Wilson to Hitler, 182; speaks in House of Commons, 183; at Munich conference, 184–86; defends Munich agreement, 189–91; anxious concerning Franco-Soviet pact, 196; seeks to evade fulfilling guarantee to Czechoslovakia, 197; visits Rome, 200; on German occupation of Prague, 203–04; speaks at Birmingham, 205; drafts declaration of collective security, 207; on Soviet Russia, 208; drafts guarantee to Poland, 211; outwitted by Beck, 212–13; and Soviet alliance, 226, 229; refuses to send Eden to Moscow, 231; loses interest in Soviet alliance, 237; makes no move towards Hitler, 243; negotiates with Germans through Horace Wilson, 245; sees Dahlerus, 271; despairs, 272; more worried about the Poles than about the Germans, 273; warns Germany; criticised in House of Commons, 277; biography of, 281.

Chaplin, Charles, depicts Hitler in *The Great Dictator*, 69.

Chautemps, French statesman, 137.

Chiang Kai Shek, Chinese statesman, 123.

Chicherin, Soviet foreign commissar, 233.

Chilston, British diplomatist, 158.

China: and Manchurian crisis, 62–64; Hitler and, 111; attacked by Japan, 127, 163.

Churchill, Winston, British statesman: as writer, 7; blames Hitler for war, 11; praises Mussolini, 57; wrong on German rearmament, 75; evades Abyssinian question, 92; solitary figure, 97; not appointed minister of supply, 118; and Spanish civil war, 125; against appeasement, 135; deceived by Henlein, 162; urges strong stand, 182; Halifax recommends appointment of, 186; on Germany, 190; denounced by Hitler, 198; on Hitler, 204; advocates Soviet alliance, 225, 266; welcomes Soviet advance into Poland, 262; Schwerin recommends appointment of, 245; book by, 282.

Ciano, Italian foreign minister, warns Mussolini, 139; resents German success, 144; meets Ribbentrop at Vienna, 194; Mussolini complains to, 203; at Berchtesgaden, 254–55; on Italian demands, 269; diaries of, 282.

Clemenceau, French statesman, on Anglo-American guarantee, 31, 35, 50; on succession states, 37.

Concordat, German, with Papacy, 111.

Constantinople, Russian claim to, 11, 37, 40.

Cooper, Duff, British statesman: resigns, 190, 198.

Corfu: League action over, 96.

Corsica, Italian claim to, 105, 200.

Coulondre, French diplomatist, urges staff-talks with Soviet Russia, 164; and Soviet policy, 192; book by, 281.

Csáky, Hungarian foreign minister; at Berchtesgaden, 253.

Curtius, German foreign minister, 62; book by, 281.

Czechoslovakia: Germans in (1919), 26; German treaty of arbitration with, 54; French alliance with, 37, 38, 59, 154; and League of Nations, 96; and Rhineland, 100; problem of, 103, 109; Franco neutral regarding, 124; Hitler on, 132; Neville Chamberlain on, 135; Halifax on, 137; assurances to, 148; crisis over, 151–53, 154; pressure on, 161; and Soviet Russia, 163–64; mobilisation in (May 1938), 165; no collapse of, 172; accepts Anglo-French ultimatum, 179; mobilises (Sept.), 180; excluded from Munich conference, 184; partitioned, 185; abandoned, 188; guarantee of, 189, 197; disintegrates, 201; ceases to exist, 202; results of crisis over, 192–93, 214, 210.

D

Dahlerus, Swedish business-man, used as Anglo-German intermediary, 244, 268; communicates German demands, 274–75; book by, 281.

Daladier, French prime minister: on German rearmament, 75; appoints Bonnet, 157; outlook of, 158; in London (April 1938), 160; appeals to Neville Chamberlain, 173–74; in London (18 Sept.), 175–77; approves ultimatum to Czechoslovakia, 178; in London (25 Sept.), 181; at Munich conference, 184–85; Beck does better than, 213; warns Hitler,

229, 265; on Danzig, 238; and military conversations with Soviet Russia, 256; calls committee of national defence, 264.

Danzig, Free City of: created 26, 47–48; divides Germany and Poland, 80, 82; Neville Chamberlain on, 135; Halifax on, 137; possible compromise over, 195, 197; Beck on, 207; Ribbentrop on, 209; Hitler on, 210–11; no Polish yielding over, 212–16; Hitler's claim to, 220; Beck obstinate over, 221; no French promise over, 238; British attitude concerning, 243–44; situation at, 248, 252; French attitude to, 265; British promise concerning, 270.

Davies, Joe, American diplomatist: favourable opinion of Stalin, 113; book by, 283.

Dawes Plan: 32, 43, 53, 57.

Delbos, French foreign minister, 107.

Delcassé, French foreign minister, 107.

Denmark, 101.

Depression, Great, 61.

Dirksen, German diplomatist, 243, 246; book by, 281.

Disarmament, German: 27, 42, 47; control commission of, ended, 57. — conference, 64, 65, 67; Hitler and, 72–77; ends, 77, 83.

Dollfuss, Austrian chancellor: destroys republic, 82; murdered, 83, 109.

Doumenc, French general, in Moscow, 258, 261.

E

Eden, Anthony, British foreign secretary: in Rome, 90, 92; becomes foreign secretary, 95; and non-intervention, 107; hostile to Italy, 126–27; opposed by Neville Chamberlain, 134, 136; dispute with Neville Chamberlain, 144; resigns, 145; Halifax recommends appointment of, 186; denounced by Hitler, 198; offers to go to Moscow, 231.

Egypt, 40, 41.

Esthonia: annexed by Soviet Russia, 19.

F

Far East: 40, 41; influence of, on Soviet policy, 78, 111, 127, 163, 241; influence of, on British policy, 215, 223.

Fay, S. B., 8.

Finland, 96.

Flandin, French prime minister: at

Stresa, 85; and German reoccupation of Rhineland, 97–100; book by, 281.

Four Power Pact, 77–78.

France: documents concerning policy of, 14; and Russia, 20; and armistice, 22; policy of, after first World war, 24, 27, 35, 36; and reparations, 43–45; and MacDonald, 52–53; and Locarno, 56, 58; defensive strategy of, 59; Arthur Henderson and, 65; defeated by Germany (1940), 54, 69, 115; and disarmament conference, 73–76; and Four Power Pact, 77; and Soviet alliance, 79; and Stresa front, 85; and German reoccupation of Rhineland, 97–101; and Anti-Comintern Pact, 111; and Belgium, 114; delayed rearmament of, 117; and Spanish civil war, 122; Hitler expects civil war in, 132; and annexation of Austria, 147; and Czechoslovakia, 151–53, 155, 173; ultimatum of, to Czechoslovakia, 173; and Munich, 187–89; not afraid of Italy, 200; and Poland, 212; becomes second-class power, 218; wants Soviet alliance, 224, 238; military convention of, with Poland, 238; military mission of, to Moscow, 239; and Nazi-Soviet pact, 265; declares war on Germany, 277; no help to Poland, 278.

Franco, Spanish dictator, 124, 125.

Franco-German declaration (Dec. 1938), 199.

Franco-Soviet Pact, made, 88; ratified, 97, 111, 113; nullified by Poland, 194; Neville Chamberlain on, 196; Halifax on, 197; ineffective, 223; Daladier threatens to invoke, 238.

Franz Ferdinand, Austrian archduke: assassinated, 19, 140.

Fritsch, German general: at "Hossbach" meeting, 131–34; dismissed, 141.

G

Gafencu, Rumanian foreign minister, 227: book by, 282.

Gamelin, French general: and German reoccupation of Rhineland, 98–100; on Czechoslovakia, 156; and Soviet aid, 180; on prospect of success in 1938, 181–82, 188; has low opinion of Polish army, 225; makes military convention with Poland, 238; says French army is ready, 265; loses war, 114; book by, 281.

Gdynia, 195.

Geneva, centre of Europe, 21; disliked by Mussolini, 77; Hoare at, 91; disliked by British admirals, 93; Spanish pictures at, 90; — Protocol, 52, 55.

Genoa, conference at, 49.

George VI, king of England: wishes to appoint Halifax prime minister, 137.

George, David Lloyd, British prime minister: and generals, 7; policy of, towards Germany, 25; and Danzig, 26; and French alliance, 31; and reparations, 43, 45; and Genoa conference, 48–50; leaves office, 50; emulated at Stresa, 85; and Benes, 169; advocates Soviet alliance, 226, 237; and Nazi-Soviet Pact, 266; book by, 281.

Germany: problem of, 10, 11, 40; aims of, in first World war, 19; defeat of, 20; and armistice, 22; existence of, recognised, 22–24; and treaty of Versailles, 28–30; and reparations, 46–49; and colonies, 48; and occupation of Ruhr, 50; and Locarno, 54, 58; great depression in, 62; rearmament of, 75, 217–19; naval agreement of, with Great Britain, 87–91; and sanctions, 91; reoccupies Rhineland, 97, 101; economic system of, 104–06; and Spanish civil war, 123; becomes predominant European power, 187, 190; troop movements in, 210; attacks Poland, 276; publication of documents concerning, 14, 15, 279.

Gibraltar: not threatened by Franco, 124.

Godesberg, meeting at, 179–80, 193, 194, 270.

Goering, Hermann, German statesman: at "Hossbach" meeting, 131–34; witness at Blomberg's wedding, 141; reassures Czechs, 147–48; warns British government, 229; wants peace, 243; negotiates through Wohltat, 244–46; negotiates through Dahlerus, 250, 268, 271; tries to moderate Hitler, 251; passes on German terms, 274.

Gooch, G. P., 8.

Gottwald, Czechoslovak statesman: consulted by Benes, 177.

Grandi, Italian diplomatist: assists at overthrow of Eden, 144–45.

Great Britain: favours armistice, 22; and disarmament, 33; and German recovery, 84; only World Power in

Europe, 41; and reparations, 43–46; leaves gold standard, 46; and Locarno, 52–54; and Manchurian crisis, 62–64; and Disarmament conference, 62–64; exaggerates Italian strength, 84; naval agreement of, with Germany, 87; and Abyssinian crisis, 88–90; navy of, cannot fight Italy, 92–93; general election in, 94; and German reoccupation of Rhineland, 98–99; gives guarantee to France, 113; rearmament in, 115–119; and Spanish civil war, 124–26; and Far East, 127; and United States, 128; and annexation of Austria, 147; and Czechoslovakia, 155, 159, 167; guarantee of, to Czechoslovakia, 176–77; and Munich agreement, 189–191; fear of French weakness, 199; and German occupation of Prague, 203–06; gives guarantee to Poland, 211, 214–15; Hitler's offer to, 218; and Soviet Russia, 226–31, 233, 237, 239; military mission of, to Moscow, 239, 256–58; offers to Germany of, 243; and Nazi-Soviet pact, 266; Hitler's last offer to, 268; declares war on Germany, 277; continues war against Germany, 278; publication of documents concerning, 8, 15, 280.

Greece, British guarantee of, 222.

Greenwood, Arthur, British statesman, speaks for England, 277.

Grey, Edward, British foreign secretary, 8; critics of, 11; Locarno in spirit of, 53; would not have gone to Munich, 107.

Guadalajara, battle of the, 186.

H

Hacha, president of Czechoslovakia, surrenders Czechoslovakia to Hitler, 202–03, 273.

Haile Selassie, emperor of Abyssinia, 88, 95.

Halifax, British foreign secretary: visits Berchtesgaden, 136–37; becomes foreign secretary, 145; and Austria, 147; policy of, 155–59; against war, 160; on Czechoslovak mobilisation, 165; complains of French policy, 167; sends Runciman to Czechoslovakia, 168; and chances of war, 172, 175; opposes Chamberlain's policy, 180; drafts statement of British policy, 180; and Maisky, 184; after Munich, 186; and Ukraine,

196; on guarantee to Czechoslovakia, 197; on German occupation of Prague, 203; conscience stirred, 205; on Poland, 207–08; thwarted by Beck, 212–13; accepts German case at Danzig, 216; on British economic strength, 221; and Soviet Russia, 224, 227, 229; in Paris, 238; does not fear breakdown of Soviet negotiations, 240; makes offer to Germany, 243–44; wants change at Danzig, 270; sees Dahlerus, 271; wishes to agree with Germany, 275; insists on German withdrawal from Poland, 277; book by, 282.

Hassell, German diplomatist: dismissed, 141.

Henderson, Arthur, British foreign secretary, presides over Disarmament conference, 65–66.

Henderson, Nevile, British diplomatist: and annexation of Austria, 147; on Czechoslovakia, 158; offers concessions to Germany, 162; denies German mobilisation, 165; on Benes, 167; on war, 175; believes Hitler has no plans, 200; called to London, 205; does not meet Ribbentrop, 243; half-hearted in support of Poland, 267; visits Hitler, 268; goes to London, 269; negotiates with Hitler, 271; wishes to agree with Germany, 273; sees Ribbentrop, 274; urges acceptance of German terms, 275; book by, 282.

Henlein, Sudeten leader: receives instructions from Hitler, 153; makes Carlsbad demands, 161; in London, 162.

Herriot, French statesman; and MacDonald, 52; and Hoare-Laval plan, 95; book by, 281.

Hesse, prince of: takes message to Mussolini, 146, 148.

Himmler, German statesman: produces false evidence against Fritsch, 141.

Hitler, Adolf, German dictator: dead, 7; carries sole blame for second World war, 11–12; becomes chancellor, 17, 68; policy of, 68–72; and Disarmament conference, 72–74, 76; and Four Power pact, 77; and Soviet Russia, 78–79; makes Non-Aggression pact with Poland, 80–81; succeeds Hindenburg as president, 81; and Austria (1934), 83–85; restores conscription, 85; and sanctions, 91, 97; reoccupies Rhineland, 100; on *Lebensraum*, 105–06; and

Spanish civil war, 107–08; and Austria (1936), 110; and Japan, 111–12; economic achievement of, 119; and Franco, 121, 124; at "Hossbach" meeting, 181–84; meets Halifax, 137–38; negotiates with Schuschnigg, 140–43; addresses Reichstag, 143–44; annexes Austria, 145–50; and Czechoslovakia, 152–55; Halifax on, 159; Neville Chamberlain on, 160; "hit on head", 165–66; at Nuremberg, 171; receives Neville Chamberlain at Berchtesgaden, 174; at Godesberg, 179; receives Horace Wilson, 182; at Munich conference, 183–86; has no plans after Munich, 192; and Poland, 194; receives Beck, 195; on Danzig, 196; and Slovaks, 201; receives Hacha, 202; British views of, 204; at Memel, 209; expected to be sensible, 214; restrains Germans in Danzig, 215–16; armament policy of, 217–19; intentions of, 220; and Soviet Russia, 233, 241–42; intentions of, 249–50; calls *va banque*, 251; visitors to, at Berchtesgaden, 253; approaches Soviet Russia, 255, 259; sends letter to Stalin, 260; radiant, 264; Henderson fails to say Boo to, 267; makes last offer to Great Britain, 268; cancels attack on Poland, 269; asks for Polish Plenipotentiary, 272; orders attack on Poland, 275.

Hoare, Samuel, British foreign secretary: at League of Nations, 91, 93; and Hoare-Laval plan, 94–97; on golden age, 203; on British policy in 1939, 205; book by, 282.

Hodza, Czechoslovak prime minister: asks for Anglo-French ultimatum, 178–79.

Hoover, president of United States: proposes moratorium, 43.

Hore-Belisha, British statesman; apprehensive concerning unfortified Belgian frontier, 114.

Hossbach, German officer, keeps record at "Hossbach" meeting, 181–84.

Hudson, Robert, British statesman: makes offer to Germany, 244, 246.

Hungary: Germans in, 26; supports revisionism, 40; Hitler and, 80; does not operate sanctions, 91; Mussolini and, 110; hostile to Czechoslovakia, 151; fails to act against Czechoslovakia, 171, 183, 193; Ribbentrop does not support claims of, 194; Hitler does not support, 201–02; Mussolini supports,

208; will not support Hitler against Poland, 253; in second World war, 217.

I

India, 185.
Inskip, Thomas, British statesman: becomes minister for the co-ordination of supply, 118.
Ireland, 135.
Ironside, British general: projected visit of, to Hitler, 267.
Istria, 18.
Italy: in first World war, 18: exhausted, 24; grievances of, 82; and Yugoslavia, 40; and Locarno, 53–54; in League of Nations, 56; and Four Power pact, 77; and Austria, 84–85; and Abyssinia, 87–95; poverty of, 105; and Spanish civil war, 123, 125, 162, 254; and Danzig, 252; keeps out of war, 269; publication of documents concerning, 14, 280.
Izvolski, Russian foreign minister, 8.

J

Japan: and United States, 12; and Manchuria, 62–64; Soviet fears concerning, 78; and Anti-Comintern pact, 111; makes war on China, 127, 163; policy of, in 1989, 222–24; would be offended by Anglo-Soviet alliance, 227; clashes with Soviet forces, 241.

K

Keitel, German general, 166, 269, 270.
Kennedy, American diplomatist: Horace Wilson appeals to, 272; on Neville Chamberlain, 273.
Keynes, J. M., British economist, 25, 44, 45, 48, 118, 283.
Kirkpatrick, British diplomatist: offers British support to Hitler, 162; book by, 282.

L

Labour party, British: and German colonies, 48; sympathises with Germany, 53; and Manchurian crisis, 63; and disarmament, 64, 76; and League of Nations, 80; and Abyssinian crisis, 93; and "have-not" Powers, 111; and British rearmament, 117, 119; and Spanish civil war, 122–24; opposed to Hitler, 186; favours Soviet alliance, 225; and Nazi-Soviet pact, 266; wants Halifax as prime minister, 177.

Latvia: annexed by Soviet Russia, 19.
Lausanne, conference at, 44.
Laval, French foreign minister, 84; and Italy, 85; visits Rome, 88; regrets Stresa front, 91; accepts Hoare-Laval plan, 94; leaves office, 97.
Law, Bonar, British statesman, 50.
League of Nations: supervises Danzig, 26; British and French views of, 39; Germany joins, 55; and Manchurian crisis, 62–64; Germany leaves, 76; Soviet Russia joins, 78; and Abyssinian crisis, 87–91; influence of, destroyed, 95–96, 102–03; and Rhineland, 98; Soviet Russia in, 111; China appeals to, 127; Neville Chamberlain and, 134; Benes and, 153; Litvinov at, 164.
League of Nations Union, 93.
Lebensraum, 105–06, 131.
Lebrun, president of France: approves ultimatum to Czechoslovakia, 178.
Leeper, British diplomatist: drafts statement of British policy, 182.
Lenin, Soviet statesman; on Russian revolution, 60; on causes of war, 104; would not have made Nazi-Soviet pact, 107.
Leopold, Austrian Nazi: recalled by Hitler, 144.
Linz: Hitler values above Berlin, 109; Hitler at, 149; Hitler makes plans for, 192.
Lipski, Polish diplomatist: meets Ribbentrop, 195; complains to Ribbentrop, 209; returns to Berlin, 210; Henderson urges, to negotiate with Germans, 273–74; last meeting of, with Ribbentrop, 275–76.
Lithuania: loses Memel to Germany, 209-10; annexed by Soviet Russia, 19.
Litvinov, Soviet foreign commissar: visits Washington, 67; on German reoccupation of Rhineland, 100; at League of Nations, 111; and Bonnet, 164, 172; Halifax consults, 180; after Munich, 192; negotiates with British, 235-36; leaves office, 233, 237.
Locarno, treaty of: made, 54–58; significance of, 65, 77; Hitler confirms, 86; and German reoccupation of Rhineland, 99–102, 106, 108; British substitute for, 113, 188.
London: destruction of, feared, 116; Bonnet and Daladier in (April 1938), 160; Henlein in, 162; Bonnet and Daladier in (18 Sept.), 175; (25 Sept.),

181; Beck in, 212; air defence of,
266; visits to, of Dahlerus, 271.
—, naval conference of, 58, 65.
Lytton commission, 63.

M

MacDonald, Ramsay, British prime
minister: takes office, 51; and
Germany, 52; leaves office, 53;
favours appeasement, 58; makes
National government, 63, 66; speaks
through Baldwin, 76; and Four
Power pact, 77; at Stresa, 85;
and Abyssinia, 89; leaves office, 90;
and Mussolini, 126.
Madrid: resists Franco, 121.
Maginot line, 59, 98–101, 114, 188, 225.
Maisky, Soviet diplomatist: and Hali-
fax, 125, 184.
Maitland, F. W., quoted, 231.
Manchukuo, 241.
Manchuria, crisis over, 41, 62–64, 89,
90, 96.
Mantoux, Étienne, 44, 283.
Marseilles: assassination of King
Alexander and Barthou at, 84.
Marx, Karl: on causes of war, 104.
Masaryk, president of Czechoslovakia,
154, 193.
Matteoti, Italian statesman: murdered
by Fascists, 56.
Mein Kampf: when written, 69; and
Italy, 82; and Versailles, 108; not
translated into English, 204.
Memel: annexed by Germany, 207–08.
Metternich, Austrian chancellor: days
of, 130; and non-intervention, 122;
Schuschnigg shares outlook of, 139;
Benes imitates, 153; echoes of, after
Munich, 190.
Miklas, president of Austria: refuses
to appoint Seyss-Inquart, 148.
Milner, British statesman, favours
Brest-Litovsk, 70.
Molotov, Soviet foreign commissar:
remains silent, 230; becomes foreign
commissar, 233; rejects British proposal, 237; proposes military conversations, 239; and Germany 242;
negotiates with Schulenberg, 259–60.
Morley, John, British statesman, 77.
Morocco, 40, 88.
Mosley, Oswald, 112.
Munich: geopolitician in, 70; Nazi
rising in, 152; conference at, 187–91;
significance of agreement at, 13,
107, 152, 183, 204–05, 215, 219,
222–23, 249; Hitler wants another,
260, 262, 263; Halifax wants an-
her, 271.

Mussolini, Italian dictator: dead, 7;
silent, 16; corrupting influence of,
56; and German disarmament, 73;
expects war in 1943, 74; encourages
Dollfuss, 82; meets Hitler at Venice,
83; and Abyssinia, 84–87; and
Eden, 90, and Laval, 91; British
fears of, 92–93; accepts Hoare-
Laval plan, 94; conquers Abyssinia,
95; glorifies war, 103; remains non-
belligerent, 105; and Austria (1936),
110; and Axis, 111, 120; and
Spanish civil war, 121; does not
support Austria, 139–40; condemns
plebiscite in Austria, 146; acquiesces
in annexation of Austria, 147–48;
shrinks from war, 171; appeals to
Hitler, 183; at Munich conference,
184–85; blackmails British, 199–200;
indignant at German occupation of
Prague, 203; British appeal to, 220;
refuses to go to war, 254, 269;
proposes conference over Poland,
276.

N

Naggiar, French diplomatist, quoted
by Strang, 231.
Namier, L. B., 9, 11, 284.
Napoleon III, and Italy, 140.
Nazi-Soviet Pact: 13, 107; signature of,
262.
Nelson, British admiral, has craven
successors, 93.
Neurath, German foreign minister: on
Rapallo, 79; at "Hossbach" meet-
ing, 131–34; dismissed, 141; tem-
porarily recalled, 147.
Newton, British diplomatist: reports
talk with Benes, 154; condemns
Czechs, 158; on Sudeten claims, 161.
Nice, Italian claim to, 105, 200.
Noël, French diplomatist: advocates
desertion of Czechoslovakia, 159;
book by, 281.
Nomunhan, conflict at, 241.
Non-Aggression Pact (Poland-Ger-
many): made 80, 81; effects of, 109,
151, 194; denounced by Hitler, 220.
North, British prime minister: Chamberlain's government more incompetent than, 229.
Nuremberg: Nazi party-meeting at
(1938), 167; (1939), 252; trial of
war-criminals at, 13, 15, 151, 133–34.
Nyon: conference at, 127.

O

Ogilvie-Forbes, British diplomatist:
visits Lipski, 274.

P

Pact of Steel, 222, 252.
Papen, German statesman: demands equality of arms for Germany, 62; and disarmament conference, 67; puts Hitler in power, 68, 71; as ambassador to Austria, 109; and Schuschnigg, 140; dismissed, 141; visits Hitler, 142; memoirs by, 281.
Paris: Baldwin and Simon at, 75; Hoare at, 94; Papen at, 137; Chamberlain and Halifax at, 197; Ribbentrop at, 199; Halifax at, 238.
—, treaty of, 74.
Pasich, Serbian prime minister, 192.
Passchendaele, battle of, 8.
Paul-Boncour, French foreign minister: advocates strong line, 156; leaves office, 157; book by, 281.
Peace Ballot, 89.
Pershing, American general, opposes armistice, 21.
Persia, 37, 40.
Phipps, Eric, British diplomatist: and Paul-Boncour, 156; stresses French weakness, 158; and Bonnet, 165, 178; reports French against war, 181, 183; and Halifax, 196.
Pilsudski, Polish dictator: makes non-aggression pact, 80.
Poincaré, Raymond, French statesman, 8; critics of, 11; and Genoa conference, 49; and occupation of Ruhr, 80.
Pokrovsky, 8.
Poland: change of frontiers after second World war, 18; established, 26; and France, 26; Germany cannot fight, 42; frontier with Germany, 42, 47, 51, 54; arbitration treaty with Germany, 54; alliance with France, 59; Treviranus starts agitation against, 62; and Four Power pact, 79; non-aggression pact of, with Germany, 79-81; opposes eastern Locarno, 84; and German reoccupation of Rhineland, 99-100; Hitler counts on neutrality of, 132; demands Tesin, 179; threatened by Soviet Russia, 180; Hitler approaches, 194; challenges League of Nations at Danzig, 195; balances between Germany and Soviet Russia, 196; Bonnet, Ribbentrop, and, 199; British alarm over, 207; British guarantee to, 211; French doubts concerning, 212; Hitler does not wish to destroy, 216, 220; British try to restrain, 221, 234; and Soviet Russia, 235-36; and Danzig, 248-49;

preparations of, for war, 251; expected to be able to stop Hitler, 256-57; German attack on, planned; 264; attacked by Germany, 276.
Potsdam, conference at, 131.
Potyomkin, Soviet diplomatist, 192.
Prague: Strang in, 166; no collapse in, 172; saved by Benes, 185; German occupation of, 192, 202-03; effects of German occupation of, 205, 211, 222, 234, 237, 241.
Pribram, A. F., 8.

R

Raeder, German admiral: at "Hossback" meeting, 181-84.
Rapallo, treaty of: made, 49; renewed, 55; dissolved, 78; German regrets for, 79, 241; gives no guidance, 241.
Remarque, author of *All Quiet on the Western Front*, 59.
Renouvin, P., 8; book by, 283.
Reparations; peace negotiations and, 24; connexion of, with Rhineland, 27; United States and, 32; disputes over, 42-49, 57; ended, 67.
Rhineland: Allied occupation of, 24, 27, 45; demilitarised, 53-55, 59, 61; allied troops leave, 57; reoccupied by Germany, 97-101; effects of German occupation of, 102, 109, 113-14; 120, 126, 131, 158, 188.
Ribbentrop, German foreign minister: makes Anti-Comintern pact, 111; and Eden, 137; becomes foreign minister, 141; in London, 147; meets Ciano at Vienna, 194; visits Warsaw, 196; visits Paris, 199; Lipski complains to, 209; elusive, 220; and Soviet Russia, 242; and Great Britain, 243; rebukes Dirksen, 246; wishes to visit Moscow, 258-60; invited to Moscow, 261; negotiates with Stalin, 263; reads German terms to Nevile Henderson, 274; meets Lipski, 276; memoirs by, 281.
Riga, treaty of: disliked by Soviet Russia, 227, 233.
Rome: Laval in, 88; Eden in, 90; Hitler in, 162; Chamberlain and Halifax in, 200.
Roosevelt, F. D., president of United States: dead, 7; and second World war, 12; becomes president, 66-67; isolationist policy of, 61, 128; and New Deal, 70; Eden and, 144; will not support Czechs, 172; applauds Neville Chamberlain, 191; Hitler has low opinion of, 218; refuses to bring pressure on Poland, 272.

Ruhr, occupation of, by the French, 29, 43, 50, 55, 59, 73; Hitler writes *Mein Kampf* during, 69; cannot be repeated, 55, 188.

Rumania: Germans in, 26; Czechoslovakia and, 151, 154; supposed German threat to, 206, 207, 211; Beck refuses to co-operate with, 212–13; British guarantee to, 232, 236.

Runciman, British statesman: mission of, to Prague, 168–70; report of, 175, 177; no continental excursion of, in 1939, 222.

S

Saar: plebiscite in, 80.

St. Jean de Maurienne, agreement of, 8.

Sarajevo, assassination at, 140.

Sarraut, French prime minister: and German reoccupation of Rhineland, 98.

Savoy, Italian claim to, 105, 200.

Schacht, German statesman: on colonies, 48; economic achievement of, 75, 105, 118; opposes Hitler over rearmament, 133–34, 141, 142, 217; resigns, 119.

Schmitt, B., 8.

Schulenburg, German diplomatist: and Soviet aid to Spain, 123; favours approach to Soviet Russia, 241–42; proposes visit by Ribbentrop, 258–60.

Schwerin, German general: advocates strong British line, 245.

Seeds, William, British diplomatist: warns of Nazi-Soviet pact, 229.

Seipel, Austrian Chancellor: on anti-semitism, 70–71.

Seyss-Inquart, Austrian statesman: imposed by Hitler, 148; and German annexation of Austria, 147–49.

Shanghai: British in, 62, 127.

Siegfried line: few German preparations in, 156, 167, 188.

Silesia, 42.

Simon, John, British statesman: becomes foreign secretary, 66; finds Hitler terrifying, 72; in Paris, 75; and Four Power pact, 77; at Stresa, 85; and Abyssinia, 89; leaves office, 90; as elder statesman, 97; cross-examines Daladier, 181; explains away guarantee to Czechoslovakia, 203; book by, 282.

Singapore, 68.

Sleswig: northern ceded to Denmark, 26.

Slovakia: Hungarian demand for, 179; claims of, backed by Ribbentrop, 194; becomes independent, 201–02; Polish grievance over, 209.

Smuts, South African statesman: favours Brest-Litovsk, 70.

Soviet Russia: defeated in first World war, 20–21; excluded from Europe, 37; and Rapallo, 49, 55–57; no danger, 58; recognised by United States, 67; effect of Four Power Pact on, 78; Barthou and, 84; Laval and, 85; Hitler intends to attack, 103; effect of Anti-Comintern pact on, 111; purges in, 112; and Spanish civil war, 121, 123, 125, 129–30; alliance of, with Czechoslovakia, 154; proposes conference, 160; ready to support Czechoslovakia, 163–64; policy of, during Czech crisis, 172, 177, 180, 185; effect of Munich agreement on, 191–92; supports collective guarantee, 207; British opinion of, 212–13; economic position in, 218–19; British negotiations with, 223–230; British offers rejected by, 235; and Baltic states, 236; makes approach to Germany, 240–41; military outlook of, 256–58; makes Nazi-Soviet pact, 263; expelled from League of Nations, 96; Hitler attacks, 278; few documents concerning, 14–15, 280, 282.

Spain: would be offended by British alliance with Soviet Russia, 227.

Spanish civil war: League of Nations and, 96; Hitler and Mussolini and, 106; outbreak of, 120; non-intervention in, 122–28; Eden and, 145; Benes learns from, 154; Soviet aid in, reduced, 163; continues, 186–87; Italy exhausted by, 254.

Stalin, Soviet dictator: dead, 7; silent, 16; supports national defence in France, 85; makes purges, 112; and Spanish civil war, 123; and Czechoslovakia, 164; expected to be sensible, 211–12; distrusted by British, 229; Soviet view of, 230; Hitler's assessment of, 242, 250, 255; Hitler writes to, 260–61; rejects fine phrases, 262; makes Nazi-Soviet pact, 107, 263; British Labour against, 266.

Strang, William, British diplomatist: in Prague and Berlin, 166; book by, 282.

Stresa, meeting of British, French, and Italian statesmen at, 85, 87; — front broken, 87–91, 97, 108.

Stresemann, German foreign minister: and occupation of Ruhr, 51; and Locarno, 53–54; at League of Nations, 55, 57–58; compared with Hitler, 69; book on, 280.

Sudeten Germans: problem of, 151–58, 155; Benes negotiates with, 159–61; offered all they demand, 169; abortive revolt by, 171; Chamberlain offers, to Hitler, 174–75; claims acknowledged, 184; get more territory than they deserve, 194, 214, 215, 248.

Switzerland, British fear German attack on, 200.

Syria, 41.

T

Teheran, conference at, 8.

Teleki, Hungarian prime minister, writes to Hitler, 253.

Tesin, Polish claim to: 151, 174, 183, 185, 194.

Thimme, F., 8.

Tientsin: British weakness at, 241.

Tilea, Rumanian diplomatist: appeals for British aid, 206.

Times, The: sympathetic to Germany, 76; and corridor for camels, 94.

Tout, T. F., 9.

Treviranus, German statesman: claims Danzig, 62.

Trevor-Roper, H. R., 69.

Trotsky, Soviet statesman, 107, 233.

Tukhachevsky, Soviet general: shot, 112.

Turkey: in first World war, 19; British alliance with, 222.

Tyrol: threat of, to Italy, 82; French troops promised for, 85; renounced by Hitler, 80, 194.

U

Ukraine: Soviet fears for, 78; Hitler and, 106; supposedly threatened, 192; Poland, Germany and, 194–96, 210, 219.

United Nations, 96.

United States of America: enters first World war, 20; and war debts, 27; rejects guarantee to France, 81; and Europe, 82; and Far East, 41; and reparations, 43–44; Depression in, 51; and Manchuria, 63; isolationist, 66; recognises Soviet Russia, 67; would not support action against Germany, 73; and sanctions, 91; and Far Eastern war, 127–29; Eden and, 144; useless, 158; not represented at Munich conference, 191; economic position of, 218; Hitler attacks, 278.

V

Vansittart, British diplomatist: and League of Nations, 92; drafts Hoare-Laval plan, 94; seeks alliance with Italy, 126; regarded as cynical, 135; chooses Nevile Henderson, 158n; thinks Henlein sincere, 162; book by, 282.

Vatican: regards Moscow as Anti-Christ, 227.

Venice: Hitler and Mussolini meet at, 88.

Versailles, treaty of, 15; accepted by Germany, 23; terms of, 23–28; Clemenceau and, 35; reparations, provisions of, 47–49; German co-operation necessary for working of, 50–51; disarmament clauses of, repudiated by Hitler, 86; provisions of, concerning Rhineland, 100–02; destroyed, 87, 108; Hitler regarded as product of, 136; settlement of, criticised, 189, 195.

Vienna: Nazi putsch in, 83; Hitler and, 109; Ribbentrop and Ciano meet at, 194; congress of, 190.

Voroshilov, Soviet general: and aid to Czechoslovakia, 164; asks whether Poland will accept Soviet aid, 256, 258, 260–61.

W

War debts, 27.

Warsaw: Soviet defeat before, 40.

Washington: Litvinov at, 67; naval treaty of, 58, 68.

Waterloo, battle of, 42.

Wegerer, o.

Weizsäcker, German diplomatist, favours approach to Soviet Russia, 241, 243; and Lipski, 276.

West German government, 81.

Wheeler-Bennett, J. W., 9; book by, 284.

William II, German emperor, 8, not tried as war criminal, 42.

Wilson, Horace, British civil servant: advises Neville Chamberlain on foreign policy, 136; accompanies Neville Chamberlain to Berchtesgaden, 174; sent to Berlin, 174; makes offer to Wohltat, 244–45; appeals to Kennedy, 272; and Dahlerus, 275.

Wilson, Woodrow, president of United States; policy of, 8; critics of, 11; Fourteen Points of, 22; and treaty of Versailles, 28; resisted by Senate, 81; 66.

Wiskemann, E., 9, 69; book by, 284.

Wohltat, German civil servant; in London, 244–45.

World war, first: study of, 7-11, 14, 16; contrasted with second, 2, 18; causes of, 19; ends at Locarno, 54; profound causes of, 103; economic causes of, 104; Italy in, 105; military lesson of, 115; power discredited by, 135; Benes during, 153.

World war, second: now remote, 7; study of, 9-13; compared with first, 18; causes of, 103; British defeat Italy in, 92; France defeated in, 115; Spanish policy during, 124; end of, 131; real, begins only in 1941, 278.

Y

Yalta, conference at, 8.

Young plan, 82, 43, 57.

Yugoslavia: and Italy, 40; and Czechoslovakia, 154; and Hitler, 201; Mussolini and, 203.